Que Tarantino's *Inglourious Basterds*

Quentin Tarantino's *Inglourious Basterds*

A Manipulation of Metacinema

Edited by
Robert von Dassanowsky

continuum

Continuum International Publishing Group
A Bloomsbury Company
80 Maiden Lane, New York, NY 10038
50 Bedford Square, London, WC1B 3DP

www.continuumbooks.com

Library of Congress Cataloging-in-Publication Data
Quentin Tarantino's Inglourious basterds : a manipulation of metacinema / edited
by Robert von Dassanowsky.
p. cm.
Includes bibliographical references and index.
ISBN 978-1-4411-3821-7 (hardcover : alk. paper) – ISBN 1-4411-3821-8
(hardcover : alk. paper) – ISBN 978-1-4411-3869-9 (pbk. : alk. paper) – ISBN
1-4411-3869-2 (pbk. : alk. paper) 1. Inglourious basterds (Motion picture) I.
Dassanowsky, Robert. II. Title: Inglourious basterds. III. Title: Inglorious bastards.
PN1997.I5145Q84 2012
791.43'72–dc23
2011051721

ISBN: HB: 978-1-4411-3821-7
PB: 978-1-4411-3869-9

Typeset by Fakenham Prepress Solutions, Fakenham, Norfolk NR21 8NN
Printed and bound in the United States of America

CONTENTS

Introduction

Locating Mr. Tarantino or, who's afraid of metacinema?

"We're not interested in photographing the reality. We're interested in photographing the photograph of the reality," was Stanley Kubrick's definition of his essential POV.[1] This formula is certainly also recognizable in the cinema of Quentin Tarantino, and even if the methods of Kubrick and Tarantino may diverge to the point of extreme opposites (Kubrick being more interested in content and its ambiguity rather than style or meta-commentary) the philosophy of distancing relates them. Both construct a cinema with the "aesthetics of contingency."[2] Kubrick's postmodern fissures in late high modernism demonstrate a "conditional rather than a dialectical" worldview.[3] But something else haunts his oeuvre as well, the idea that our contemporary Western civilization has not truly developed as it might have from the promises of the eighteenth-century Enlightenment: a Louis XVI-style bedroom as sum cosmic total; Nabokov's nymphet as bullet-ridden Romantic court portrait; M.A.D. rationalism as blueprint for our acceptance of the apocalypse and how to love it; Beethoven with snake. Suggesting René Magritte's 1929 painting on perception and reality, *The Treachery of Images* ("Ceci n'est pas une pipe"), Kubrick's clocks do not hint at time, they are merely mechanisms without utility, purposeless machines. Base human desires and needs short-circuit the prowess above the neck. The existentialist choice exists until it too soon collides with those of others just around the corner; just as hubris breaks out. And the fear of being discovered a failure, a fraud, or an outsider begins to blossom.

Tarantino, so nourished by the exploitations of the art, offers what might be understood as Dadaist reflection of the pessimistic irony that pervades Kubrick's elegant symbolist murals. While Tarantino's filmmaking at this stage is not intentionally meant as counter-Kubrick, or counter-cinema in the sense of his idol Jean-Luc Godard's complete rupture of dominant film, it is a counter to the aesthetic materialism of cinematic snobbery that surrounds most of his models and even to the specific intentions of exploitation. Kubrick's characters are knowingly or unknowingly enacting the Jungian "duality of man" while Tarantino is the fantasist doubling as Greek chorus. Embracing the extremes of human deed and emotion, and distressing such visions further by distancing it as nightmarish fun house, Tarantino is in this respect, truly an artistic grandson of his beloved French New Wavers, who always paid tribute to Hollywood as they cooked its concepts.

What returns Tarantino's metafilmic mash-ups to the Kubrickian is the instinctive comprehension of the failure of the grand narrative as Jean-François Lyotard would call it. Both look to the mirage of the "real," the minor and major catastrophes it would lead to, and go from there. It is the irrational belief in the ideal of rational thought that provides the faulty security of Kubrick's characters, while their actual chaos is always expected by Tarantino's. There is no need for organic beauty or terror; the borrowed is already pre-tested and will do just fine for Tarantino. His talky set pieces are chained together into station-dramas resembling a medieval religious pageant or Brechtian play. He offers re-produced (re-directed?) baroque visual pleasure vacillating between destabilized tributes to classic cinema (in the way Warhol's sloppy color transfer comments on the fake perfection of Marilyn Monroe as icon) and Grand Guignol mated with underground cinema's obliteration of the values of mass bourgeois culture. Tarantino's admiration for Godard has thus a very specific influence in *Inglourious Basterds*. Like his hero's demolition of linear narrative along with the reputations of both the establishment and the counter-culture in a melodrama/ musical/horror/romance/crime-film/soft-core porn/western/ apocalyptic assemblage in *Week-end* (1967), Tarantino certainly gives spectators quotations of the traditional cinematic elements they have come to expect and desire, and sutures them in such a way that they cheat the uncritical audience–screen relationship. But unlike Godard, Tarantino does not need to so observably deconstruct to make the revolutionary point. Instead he reconstructs, overcodes, and subverts signifiers to shock and create the illusion of melodrama.

Tarantino's particular rage, which is the platform for all his films, may not be unique but it is extraordinarily focused and engaging. It is not the broody anger at the manipulation of the masses which Kubrick combats with his characters' painful, transforming awakenings, nor is it like the pessimism of Polanski the Holocaust survivor, who finds a pinhole of hope incongruously puncturing a smothered landscape. It is not Michael Haneke's nagging moral and ethical irritations embedded in the faux entertainment films that confront the audience with their "Stockholm syndrome" of accepting uncritical cinematic norms.[4] Haneke might even be seen as the direct opposite of Tarantino, attacking the desire for the hyper-violence of slasher films, horror-porn and apocalyptic epics. Yet Tarantino's commonality with them is extraordinary female sympathy. Kubrick's films are scantly populated by women, but all his narratives are propelled by the search for the objectified "Woman." Polanski mourns his mother and his wife, and finds the feminine outside of caustic male-dominated social structures to be an ambiguous corrective. Haneke sees the woman as the automatic victim of "rape culture" in fascistic control structures and exploitive globalization. Tarantino, however, does not simply underscore a masculinity that lynches the female, he experiences it. His films are couched in powerful impulses of empathy and revenge that may well be influenced by such second-wave feminist exploitation films as *I Spit on Your Grave* a.k.a. *The Day of the Woman* (1978) and *Ms. 45* (1981) watched long ago in a video store, but Antigone and a handful of female rebels and martyrs imagined by other gender/role-conscious men are here as well: Aeschylus' Clytemnestra, Shakespeare's Desdemona and Ophelia, Goethe's Iphigenia, Ibsen's Nora, Klimt's Judith, Puccini's Tosca, Sargent's Madame X, Hugo's Fantine, Kleist's Marquise of O, Schnitzler's Fräulein Else, Dreyer's Joan of Arc, Cain's Mildred Pierce, Sembène's Black Girl. Beyond the visual bloodletting, Tarantino's responses to female abuse have such intuitive power in that they are not quasi-feminist gestures, but a clear identification of the director with the pathos of the victim, and with the victim herself.

The cryptic-heroic female and female despair appear in most of his films, and his father figures and children enforce this. In *Pulp Fiction*, the boy who loses himself in television is given an artifact of a mythic non-father, and comes to echo his mother's emotional destitution. It leads him into a hopeless life of defining himself as a commodity through male violence. There is the sexually abusive monster-father, a brutal grotesque of all sitcom dads, whose attentions on his daughter has made her one of the *Natural Born Killers*; and the bride of the *Kill Bill* saga, whose unborn child is killed by its father when she is assaulted and left to die. Reductive to the point of abstraction, female fury pitted against the murderous intentions of the male auto-maniac in *Death Proof* functions like an étude for the grander works. The Tarantinian theme of female maltreatment and resulting male consequences returns as the shadow plot in the wargrounded/Holocaust-shadowed *Inglourious Basterds*. Shosanna finds her power to avenge the obliteration she suffers at the hand of Nazism. As an outsider to both the male-dominated and racist culture, she partners with a man who can certainly empathize, an Afro-Frenchman. One might consider that the entire disaster of Operation Kino is linked to Bridget von Hammersmark's relationship with the new father in the La Louisiane pub. His drunken approaches result in her autograph for his infant son that ultimately seals her fate. But her original celebration of his fatherhood takes on a dire note when she tells him not to fire at the Basterds for the sake of living for his new son. Yet she is the one who icily kills him—not in response to his nationalist anger regarding her treason, but to his invective against her as woman. Von Hammersmark acts out Tarantino's bête noir: better Max grows up without a father than with this paragon of self-indulgent abusiveness.

The women in *Inglourious Basterds* are annihilated by and for their connection with male authority. Colonel Landa, the man who calls all other men "Hermann," an indication of his alpha-male superiority and their interchangeable accessibility, uncovers the misogynistic side of fairy tales, in particular the Cinderella myth, as the Nazi prince links shoe to woman and strangles her to death for daring to be his equal. Goebbels' translator/mistress Francesca Mondino, already appearing half-devoured by the tiger head she is wearing as a hat, is contextualized by Shosanna, whose "pop-out" extranarrative is of Goebbels mounting her like the beast couture she wears. His fate will also be hers. There is the innocent French pub girl at La Louisiane caught in the crossfire along with the muscular young woman who originally vows to protect her from the men, but has already victimized herself as a member of the Nazi *Bund Deutscher Mädel* (female version of the Hitler Youth). Even Shosanna, who certainly comprehends the propaganda power of cinema, is ultimately killed by a man she regrets shooting because she is momentarily manipulated by his portrayal on the screen.

Inglourious Basterds offers Tarantino's most trenchant portrayals of the female struggle for agency because it is allohistorically grounded in a battle of male superiority and touches on the symbolism of national father figures (Hitler, Churchill), male bonding, homosocial behavior and thuggery (the Basterds; Landa), male superiority-as-racist ideology (the Nazis), and images of a father's failed dominance (LaPadite) and the daughter's (Shosanna) re-vision of gender role domination. Problematic male role playing and the specter of fatherhood haunt the film: "What about his [Tarantino's] father?" asks Benjamin Secher who produced a telling interview with the director in 2010:

> "Now he's an actor only because he has my last name. But he was never part of my life. I didn't know him. I've never met him." Once more he laughs that humorless laugh ... "I've been alone most of my life, I was an only child, raised by a single mother, so I am very comfortable with my own company." And most revealingly Tarantino admits: "All my movies are achingly personal," he insists. "People who really know me can see that in my work. In a film, I may be talking about a bomb in a theatre, but that's not what I'm really talking about." As he says this he laughs an evasive, slightly goading laugh. So, what is he really talking about? "Well, it's not my job to tell you," he says. "My job is to hide it."[5]

Even more than Polanski, rather than show the betrayed boy, Tarantino focuses on the female figure as the bearer of truth in his films.

It ultimately became more important for Joseph Goebbels to win the war cinematically with his 1944 Agfacolor Prussia-beats-Napoleon war epic, *Kolberg* (he would have detested the black-and-white mock-Soviet/Italian neorealism of the so-called imitation Nazi film, *Stolz der Nation*), than to actually understand why Hitler had lost it. Tarantino's *Inglourious Basterds* uses this particular obsession to present an allohistorical fantasy that is structured by the wry reduction of history-as-visual coding. Leni Riefenstahl, who stars in *The White Hell of Pitz Palu* (among other mountain films), directed *Triumph of the Will*, which may not have started Nazism, but certainly became a font of its iconic self-imagery. She thus symbolically shaped Nazism with a film, and for Tarantino, the regime could therefore be ended with one as well. The old money imperialists—the British—are represented by Churchill brooding at a piano in an empty ballroom. The frame hides everything other than the feet of mythic monarchs in large paintings hanging in the blacked-out space and a small antique globe (why would it be either large or new for the sons of the British Empire?) which reveals a handy liquor service. The nouveau-riche warlord Hitler attempts to insert himself significantly into history with a giant painting of a romantically caped likeness, and sits in front of a monumental map of a Europe labeled in gold German script. This recycled Hollywood kitsch fantasy (it seems to be a copy of one used in the 1962 B-Movie *Hitler*) comments on the performance qualities of Nazism. While Tarantino's many references to actor George Sanders as the sole model for the British characterizations in his films may indeed have had some influence on them, these statements are perhaps intentionally misleading.[6] The elegant, knowledgeable, slightly foppish Lt. Hicox so resembles a young Sean Connery here, that the mention of the OSS and Churchill's role in "Operation Kino" provides an embryonic suggestion of James Bond and M. At the same time, it feeds off Mike Myers' attempts to be the Peter Sellers of the 1990s (and doesn't quite suppress his *Austin Powers* "Dr. Evil" body language in his role as General Ed Fenech). It is also a prismatic parody of *Dr. Strangelove* and the many other military cabals in Kubrick where plans of serious men go astray. The focus on eating and drinking in *Inglourious Basterds* also recalls Kubrick, but Tarantino makes a point of how and what his characters consume, particularly those that chew with their mouths open or speak when they eat. Based on Landa's questionable table manners, the odd turns of history have greatly helped his social standing.

It is the Nazi collaboration of two countries that actually represents Tarantino's war: France (occupied Paris, mention of Vichy, French film, Shosanna and Marcel) and the shadow of an annexed Austria (Landa, the exile "Basterd" Wicki, and Hitler). Both nations have approached their involvement as "victims" of the Third Reich in very different ways. While France has managed to allow the myth of its victory alongside the Allies to displace its Occupation and Vichy period, Austria's post-war attempt to step out of history failed and it has, since the late 1980s, come to face its unique role as both victim and perpetrator. The Austrian Hans Landa changes loyalties and self-definitions with a swiftness that defies credibility. Is this a reflection of the identity tribulations that have beset Austria since the collapse of the Danube Monarchy in 1918 and its reinvention as a nation in 1945? Von Hammersmark's belief that the Basterds' infiltration of the film premiere as Italian filmmakers will likely succeed because "Germans have a bad ear for Italian," is yet another miscommunication of identity and purpose: her logic does not apply to Landa, the polyglot Austrian hidden by his deep German Reich cover which he then easily abandons for future American identity. The German characters in the film, however, seem as vaguely sketched as the British. Heinrich Himmler, the head of the SS and Gestapo is missing from this collection of Hitler's "Inner Circle." Given his direct representation of the Holocaust, perhaps he was best left outside parody and therefore does not exist in this allohistorical universe. The Italians only appear in reference or absurd characterizations by the Basterds (which recall the Marx Brothers or even the Three Stooges); the Soviets, whose massive war dead and genocidal leader would surely crack the smooth contours of Tarantino's tightly focused fantasy, are not even mentioned. Despite its daring reinventions, Tarantino's film articulates its limits by its omissions.

By now it is certainly a relatively undisputed fact that Tarantino's *Inglourious Basterds* is not about a specific war but about the making of the war film and its discourse in society and history:

Tarantino's script takes up the challenge of an explanation and as he veers into scatology, he gives the finger to the false norm of noble death in all such war clichés. But Tarantino is interested less in making an anti-war gesture than in doing a send-up of a movie cliché. Similarly, this is not an anti-violence film. It is a send up of movie violence.[7]

His is not the only brazen attempt to skewer cinema's reception of history in American film. John Schlesinger's underappreciated 1975 treatment of Nathanael West's vitriolic novel *The Day of the Locust* is useful in attempting to locate Tarantino's metafilmic antecedents. Presenting the forgotten bit-players of Golden Age Hollywood and their dreams of stardom turned bitter, Schlesinger's abuse-or-die social-Darwinism is a statement on the impossible promises of cinema, even for those who know it is an illusion. Famed screenwriter Ben Hecht once commented that movies "have slipped into the American mind more misinformation in one evening than the Dark Ages could muster in a decade" and *Locust* is relentless in showing the banal (re-)inventions that pass for historical fact, experience or wisdom. Schlesinger's late-1930s Hollywood becomes a dark fun-house mirror of European fascism, which recreates history to serve the purpose of creating a dependency of the masses. It fosters elitism that encourages emulation, demands devotion and suggests progress, but never truly gives of itself. Schlesinger's painstakingly detailed recreation of a star-studded premiere at Hollywood's Chinese Theater is as factually wrong as the "historical" films being made in *Locust*'s narrative. The catastrophic riot it sparks is one of fury at the illusion. Movie stars and studio heads are attacked, the mob tramples spectators to death, and the city is looted, smashed, immolated. The fire appears to burn the projected film and screen the audience is watching.

Tarantino makes no reference to Schlesinger's *The Day of the Locust*, but its influence, even unconsciously, is evident. The film was a flop at the box office and critics (in a Hollywood that could still remember the era) were uncomfortable, even angry at the destruction of the Hollywood mythos. Time and cinema have moved on and Tarantino's desire to skewer the WWII film genre (in *Locust* the creation of the fictional historical epic "Waterloo" attacks an irresponsible Hollywood approach) still provides a reductive play between good and evil that Schlesinger's late-depression allegory rejected.[8] Tarantino is no less critical of the process of making film, but far more so in the crucial manipulations that frame spectatorship. Schlesinger's film attempts to exist in both the "real" and the cinematically created world, with an allohistorical falseness that is seemingly unimportant to the central drama until the finale. Tarantino's film instead vacillates wildly between its fine historical detailing and its intentionally flawed, even laughably wrong information. German character names like Fredrick and Bridget are so unlikely that the German-speaking actors have difficulty pronouncing them. Tarantino's Hitler offers a very convincing vocal impersonation, but has intentionally striking brown eyes instead of blue. Accurate uniforms have inaccurate decorations and while there is a fine knowledge of German cinema and beautifully imitative UFA film posters, we watch an impossibly wrong "Nazi" film. The repeatedly mentioned origin of the Austrian Jewish member of the Basterds as "Munich" (which certainly Landa would know is in Germany even after the Anschluss of Austria) is as calculated as the traces of recutting which play with continuity. This is particularly evident in the scenes where Shosanna entertains the Nazi brass and checks on the film projector at the premiere of "Stolz der Nation" ("Nation's Pride" or "Pride of the Nation" which would more likely have been "Pride of the *Reich*" given the expansionist/racist ideology). Tarantino's film is about language accuracy, but it is the high level of authentic (mis-)communication that covers these factual errors as if to say we never really watch a film closely enough, we are not critical enough, we desire to look at what we want but do not see.

Beyond the almost endless international film homage games one can play with the pastiche that is *Inglourious Basterds*, the work is most strongly linked to the Spaghetti Western, the Italian *giallo* film, Hollywood war action films and B-movies. Generalities aside, there is an anarchic nihilism that is clearly informed by a few specific narratives. In addition to the obvious use of the cinema theater immolation scene from *Gremlins* (1984), there are fascinating correspondences with two WWII war films that have been generally been neglected by film criticism. The first is a near surrealist approach to the Hollywood battle picture with a counter-culture sensibility that has Vietnam appearing at its edges. Set during the Battle of the Bulge, *Castle Keep* (1969) is based on the novel by William Eastlake, directed by Sydney Pollack and stars Burt Lancaster as a cynical eye-patch wearing major leading his own troop of "Basterds." Ultimately they destroy the symbolic culture of Old Europe (a castle filled with art and literary treasures belonging to the Count of Maldorais and his beautiful young wife) in attempting to "save" it from the Nazis. They succeed in rescuing only an American future: one G.I. considers the money to be made by exporting an abandoned Volkswagen floating in the castle

moat; another finds hope in replacing culture and the destruction
of war with evangelism; still another occupies the bakery and the
baker's wife when the baker fails to return from the war. The only
"Europeans" that survive in the town are the inhabitants of the
bordello.

The other possible model is the semi-dramatic (often unevenly
self-parodic) all-star war/adventure film *Escape to Athena* directed
by George Pan Cosmatos in 1979. The film is set on a Greek
island turned Nazi POW camp in 1944, where a far less complex
and non-lethal version of Colonel Landa, a Major Hecht (also
said to be an Austrian—a crooked pre-war Viennese antiques
dealer rather than a "Jew Hunter") has put his charges to work
excavating Greek antiquities. He ultimately switches sides to save
himself and the art he has pilfered. A sadistic Nazi occupation
commandant imprisons the townspeople while a resistance group
utilizes the opportunity of a show by two captured USO artists to
assault the Germans. One of these performers is Charlie, played
by Elliott Gould, revisiting the anti-war wisecracker he perfected
in *M.A.S.H.* a decade earlier, this time in a self-spoofing Jewish
characterization. It gives his incarceration by the Nazis an unstable,
even menacing quality in this metafilmic narrative (among other
scattered references and anachronisms, William Holden appears
in cameo in his character from Billy Wilder's *Stalag 17*). Charlie's
bloody spree gunning down Nazi occupation soldiers as he careens
through the maze of a Greek town on a motorcycle and later in
confronting them to destroy a secret missile base suggests both
an earlier "Jewish revenge fantasy" and also the concept of the
"muscle Jew."[9] Charlie noticeably becomes a physical threat
that belies the literary/cinematic stereotype of the passive Jewish
character.

Tarantino campaigned heavily to direct the reboot of the James
Bond franchise with the serious version of Ian Fleming's first
007 novel, *Casino Royale*, the only source material that escaped
the grasp of the makers of the Bond series. It appeared instead
in 1967 as an epic, psychedelic send-up of Bond and his world.
Tarantino condemned the spoof in the press, promising to make
a better version, but his neo-1960s concept of Bond obviously
did not appeal.[10] There was a rumor that he would work on
another spy film remake, or on an original spy film, but instead it
would be *Inglourious Basterds*. The influence of what Tarantino

protested too much is apparent. His casting of Mike Myers who all but remade the 1967 film in his first *Austin Powers*, and the Bond-ish recruitment of Lt. Hicox (played by Michael Fassbender) for "Operation Kino" has already been noted. The reproduction of Ursula Andress' knowingly sexual grasp of the ball knob of a slot machine arm in the 1967 film by Shosanna with the projector lever (the only difference in design between the two is the color of the knob) at the "Nation's Pride" premiere indicates the sexual subtext of the literal grasp for control in both films. Moreover, the slapstick endgame chaos in the 1967 *Casino Royale*, which not only parodies the Bond film finales but also the Western film brawl, and ends with the explosion of the venue, seems to be darkly echoed in *Inglourious Basterds*. The good characters ascend to heaven while the single evil one is blown into hell. Yet even dancing on the edge of the volcano in dealing with the Cold War and elevating absurdity to an aesthetic, there was a need to convey celestial justice.[11]

The true influence of Tarantino's film on American cinema has yet to be seen. Certainly *Captain America: The First Avenger* (2011), seems to have taken inspiration in its new film incarnation from *Inglourious Basterds* to some extent (a fictional "1943" NY World's Fair; characters that suggest a politically revisionist Einstein and Howard Hughes; the Nazi development of a super weapon beyond the atomic bomb) to allow it a more multivalent bite than provided by its comic book origins. While the title hero is clearly an American version of the fantasy "Aryan" superman, it is "Hail *Hydra*" rather than Hitler here. The evil adversary is Red Skull, a rogue German scientist who has rejected Hitler as a weak leader. Swastikas are replaced by his hydras and most intriguingly, the Himmler-like character (recall Himmler is missing in *Basterds*) who commands Red Skull to end his bizarre master race experiments is promptly evaporated by the power he has harnessed from an ancient Nordic tesseract. In underscoring the power of cinema to still manipulate a media savvy audience to the point of applauding the images of a theater filled with burning spectators (albeit Nazis), has Tarantino's allohistorical experiment opened the doors for blockbuster Hollywood films in which historical revisionism becomes acceptable pseudo-nostalgia in response to the possibly daunting conditions of an American national identity in flux?

This collection, a multidisciplinary analysis of Tarantino's provocative manipulation of metafilm in *Inglourious Basterds*, seeks to explore and contextualize the work through cinematic, socio-political, historical, gender role, psychological, philosophical, and pop-cultural approaches. The film generated an unusual amount of critical blog chatter at its unveiling, so it is only apt that this book should begin with one of the most intriguing examples of such flash analysis. Reproduced here in print is the web-essay from October 2009 by Srikanth Srinivasan, whose Bangalore-based blog, *The Seventh Art* was selected as one of the 43 top film criticism sites by *Film Comment* in 2010. Imke Meyer sets up the examinations of breaking the Hitler fiction taboo with discussions of recent visual art, Baudrillard, and New Austrian Film. In exploring *Inglourious Basterds* as a liberation of imagination and a volley aimed at politically correct cinema, Meyer posits how Hollywood's image of the Nazis and the Holocaust has remained a lucrative box office staple but also a prisoner of the kind of totalizing cinema that is hardly differentiated from propaganda films. Chris Fujiwara examines the patterns and rhythms of Tarantino's camera and finds the excessive information a principal of the narration. Fujiwara compares the "unmotivated" shots in Tarantino's film to traditionalist "motivated" lenses and finds a semiotic play with language that is also mirrored in the constant reflections and doublings of the narrative. Lisa Coulthard reveals the sonic structure of the film in Tarantino's use of eclectic music cues from popular sources and several cinematic compositions, particularly those from Ennio Morricone. She finds that the director's choices do not only articulate Spaghetti Western influence and intertext as critics have pointed out, but is also a progressive attempt to break dominant Hollywood scoring patterns by using music as a distancing commentary.

In a discourse analysis that ranges from an identity-suggesting prop found in G. W. Pabst's *Pandora's Box* (1929) through the Frankfurt School and New German Cinema to Oshima and Pasolini, Justin Vicari examines how Tarantino's film attempts to reinvent the idea of anti-fascism by denying simplification of ambiguous meaning with images that "refuse to doubt their own purpose as single-minded conveyors of meaning." Does then *Inglourious Basterds* represent successful allohistory, or does it defy the term's essential theory? Michael D. Richardson's investigation of this and the reversal of victims and perpetrators in Tarantino's film reveal perhaps far less "liberation" of narrative possibilities than touted by the film's enthusiasts. Instead, Richardson finds correspondences with Nazi film aesthetics and considers the work as a not-so-subtle reaction to post-9/11 angst.

Gender role destabilization, homosocial linkages, and the questionable agency of woman in particular is a strong subtext in Tarantino's oeuvre and Heidi Schlipphacke's neofeminist reading takes on *Inglourious Basterds* from the aspect of both the postmodern pastiche and the female revenge narrative. She finds that Tarantino's Shosanna defies simple characterization as a female vengeance figure and considers her a wholly new element in his "orgy of citationality." More than any other reductive categorization of *Inglourious Basterds*, the concept of the film as a "Jewish revenge fantasy" has been both celebrated and highly criticized by Jewish critics and scholars. Would Jews behave like Nazis? Eric Kligerman finds Tarantino's film shares its complex deconstructions of cinema art and audience engagement with Marcel Ophüls' provocative 1969 documentary of Nazism in France, *The Sorrow and the Pity*. Calling *Inglourious Basterds*' approach to history a form of "Talmudic hermeneutics," Kligerman finds Tarantino linkage of the Holocaust to French racism and the film's emergence during the release of information on Abu Ghraib vital to a deeper comprehension of the work.

In exploring Tarantino's cinephilic fantasy of film intervening directly into history, Sharon Willis details how the director reworks the citationality of Jean-Luc Godard into a game for its own sake while he attempts to manipulate the spectator reception to a new "cinematic primitivity." Willis considers how Tarantino attempts to intervene in *film history* by referencing Henri-Georges Clouzot, Carl Theodor Dreyer, and overwriting Nazi cinema by shooting *Basterds* at the former UFA studios in Berlin. Willis underscores that Tarantino's film exists in what Siegfried Kracauer considers a no-man's land that is "neither past nor present." Oliver Speck responds to and amplifies the idea of such a vacuum by examining Tarantino's narrative through the philosophy of Giorgio Agamben's *homo sacer*. Agamben finds this concept of exception and non-status from archaic Roman law to be at the core of modern politics. Speck reads *Inglourious Basterds*' "hunting the hunters" as the chronicle of a *homo sacer* declaring himself sovereign and reducing the "other" to his bare life. Moreover, on the topic of identity, Speck compares the intellectual and moral differences of the German and American characters and evaluates Tarantino's status as *auteur* vis-à-vis the director's influential filmmakers. Alexander Ornella, who assesses the moral imprint of the film, also finds significance in the paradox of ambiguous time and place in the rewriting of "history." In evoking the Babylonian creation myth in which violence can bring forth the range of existential possibilities, Ornella posits that our contemporary Western culture is totally embedded in stories of violence and that Tarantino's film and other media explorations of this nature provide a needed experimental frame for understanding social behavior.

The value of counterfactuals in the understanding of sociocultural self-reflection is taken on by William Brown's examination of concepts from the realm of physics in which "alternative" outcomes of particle measurements may be regarded as equally "real." Brown considers cinema to be our popular generator of alternate universes and views *Inglourious Basterds* not as an expression of the "history" of WWII but as a "a monstrous monstration of a possible world, which touches us and has an effect/affect on our world." Collecting the variant international reviews of the film and distilling how the shock of Tarantino's provocative play with history, culture and cinematic structure found supporters and detractors, Todd Herzog explores how and why *Inglourious Basterds* has become a cult film on cult films. Spawning fanfiction websites and the phenomenon of adult slash narratives that sexualize character interaction, Herzog analyzes how these alternate narratives echo or reinvent Tarantino's creations, altering the film's "history" and its finalities in order to continue the saga of its characters. Herzog posits that Tarantino's unexpected collision with the way German intellectuals look at a "history that will not go away" has resulted in liberation from the strictures in the telling and imagining of that history.

For their generous encouragement, support and most useful advice in the presentation of these contributions to the study of the director and this unique film, I thank Brandon Fibbs, Daniel Magilow, Ed Sikov, Oliver Speck, Fernando Feliu-Moggi, Thomas Ballhausen, Teresa Meadows Sohlich, K. J. Donnelly, Ken Marchand, Eileen Wimshurst for her copy-editing expertise, and especially Katie Gallof and the staff at Continuum.

Robert von Dassanowsky

Notes

1 "Stanley Kubrick Filmmaking Techniques," *Film Directors.co*. http://
filmdirectors.co/stanley-kubrick-filmmaking-techniques/ (accessed
October 25, 2011).

2 See Thomas Allen Nelson, *Kubrick: Inside a Film Artist's Maze*
(Bloomington and Indianapolis, Indiana University Press, 2000),
1–19.

3 Nelson, 13.

4 On this topic see Catherine Wheatley, *Michael Haneke's Cinema:
The Ethic of the Image* (Oxford and New York: Berghahn, 2009),
41.

5 Quentin Tarantino," All my movies are achingly personal,"
interview by Benjamin Secher, http://www.telegraph.co.uk/culture/
film/7165045/Quentin-Tarantino-interview-All-my-movies-are-
achingly-personal.html (accessed October 25, 2011).

6 Ella Taylor, "Quentin Tarantino: The *Inglourious Basterds*
Interview." http://www.villagevoice.com/2009-08-18/film/quentin-
tarantino-the-inglourious-basterds-interview/2/ (accessed February 2,
2011).

7 Alan A. Stone, "*Pulp Fiction*" April/May 1995 issue of *Boston
Review*. http://bostonreview.net/ (accessed October 23, 2011).

8 See Robert von Dassanowsky, "'You Wouldn't Even Believe What
Your Eyes Can See': Cinema's Messianism and Fascist Reflection
in John Schlesinger's *The Day of the Locust*," *Senses of Cinema*
39 (2006), http://www.sensesofcinema.com/2006/feature-articles/
day_locust/ (accessed October 1, 2011).

9 On the topic of the concept of a "muscle Jew" as symbol of the
development of the Zionist "body" in opposition to the stereotype
of the weak, intellectual Jew, see Todd Samuel Presner, *Muscular
Judaism: The Jewish Body and the Politics of Regeneration* (London
and New York: Routledge, 2007).

10 See "Tarantino's Lost Projects: *Casino Royale*," *Movie Geeks* August
18, 2009, http://wearemoviegeeks.com/2009/08/tarantinos-lost-
projects-casino-royale/ (accessed October 1, 2011).

11 See Robert von Dassanowsky, "*Casino Royale* at 33: The
Postmodern Epic in Spite of Itself." *Bright Lights Film Journal*
28 (2000), http://www.brightlightsfilm.com/28/casinoroyale1.php
(accessed October 25, 2011).

Works cited

Austin Powers: International Man of Mystery. Directed by Jay Roach. USA, 1997.

Captain America: The First Avenger. Directed by Joe Johnston. USA, 2011.

Casino Royale. Directed by John Huston, Val Guest, Ken Hughes, Joseph McGrath, Robert Parrish. UK/USA, 1967.

Castle Keep. Directed by Sydney Pollack. USA, 1969.

Dassanowsky, Robert von. "*Casino Royale* at 33: The Postmodern Epic in Spite of Itself." *Bright Lights Film Journal*, 28, 2000. http://www.brightlightsfilm.com/28/casinoroyale1.php (accessed October 25, 2011).

—"'You Wouldn't Even Believe What Your Eyes Can See': Cinema's Messianism and Fascist Reflection in John Schlesinger's *The Day of the Locust*." *Senses of Cinema*, 39, 2006. http://www.sensesofcinema.com/2006/feature-articles/day_locust/ (accessed October 1, 2011).

The Day of the Locust. Directed by John Schlesinger. USA, 1975.

Death Proof. Directed by Quentin Tarantino. USA, 2007.

Die weiße Hölle vom Piz Palü/The White Hell of Pitz Palu. Directed by G. W. Pabst and Arnold Fanck. Germany, 1929.

Dr. Strangelove: or How I Learned to Stop Worrying and Love the Bomb. Directed by Stanley Kubrick. UK, 1964.

Escape to Athena. Directed by George P. Cosmatos. UK, 1979.

Gremlins. Directed by Joe Dante. USA, 1984.

Hitler. Directed by Stuart Heisler. USA, 1962.

I Spit on Your Grave (a.k.a. *The Day of the Woman*). Directed by Meir Zarchi. USA, 1978.

Inglourious Basterds. Directed by Quentin Tarantino. USA/Germany, 2009.

Kill Bill: Vol 1. Directed by Quentin Tarantino. USA, 2003.

Kill Bill: Vol 2. Directed by Quentin Tarantino. USA, 2004.

Kolberg. Directed by Veit Harlan. Germany, 1945.

Magritte, René. *The Treachery of Images/La trahison des images* ("Ceci n'est pas une pipe"). Oil on canvas, 1929. (Los Angeles County Museum of Art). http://collectionsonline.lacma.org/mwebcgi/mweb.exe? request=record;id=34438;type=101 (accessed October 25, 2011).

M.A.S.H. Directed by Robert Altman. USA, 1970.

Ms. 45. Directed by Abel Ferrara. USA, 1981.

Natural Born Killers. Directed by Oliver Stone. USA, 1994.

Nelson, Thomas Allen. *Kubrick: Inside a Film Artist's Maze*. Bloomington and Indianapolis, Indiana University Press, 2000.

Pandora's Box/Die Büchse der Pandora. Directed by G. W. Pabst. Germany, 1929.

Paths of Glory. Directed by Stanley Kubrick. USA, 1957.

Presner, Todd Samuel. *Muscular Judaism: The Jewish Body and the Politics of Regeneration*. London and New York: Routledge, 2007.

Pulp Fiction. Directed by Quentin Tarantino. USA, 1994.

Reservoir Dogs. Directed by Quentin Tarantino. USA, 1992.

Stalag 17. Directed by Billy Wilder. USA, 1953.

"Stanley Kubrick Filmmaking Techniques." *Film Directors co.* http://filmdirectors.co/stanley-kubrick-filmmaking-techniques/ (accessed October 23, 2011).

Stone, Alan A. "*Pulp Fiction*." *Boston Review*, April/May 1995. http://bostonreview.net/ (accessed October 23, 2011).

Tarantino, Quentin. "All my movies are achingly personal." By Benjamin Secher.

"Tarantino's Lost Projects: *Casino Royale*," *Movie Geeks*, August 18, 2009. http://wearemoviegeeks.com/2009/08/tarantinos-lost-projects-casino-royale/ (accessed October 1, 2011).

Taylor, Ella. "Quentin Tarantino: The *Inglourious Basterds* Interview—Two decades after the severed ear of *Reservoir Dogs*, Quentin Tarantino serves up Hitler's head on a plate." *The Village Voice*, Tuesday, August 18, 2009. http://www.villagevoice.com/2009-08-18/film/quentin-tarantino-the-inglourious-basterds-interview/2/ (accessed February 2, 2011).

The *Telegraph*, http://www.telegraph.co.uk/culture/film/7165045/Quentin-Tarantino-interview-All-my-movies-are-achingly-personal.html (accessed October 25, 2011).

Triumph des Willens/Triumph of the Will. Directed by Leni Riefenstahl. Germany, 1935.

Week-end. Directed by Jean-Luc Godard. France/Italy, 1967.

Wheatley, Catherine. *Michael Haneke's Cinema: The Ethic of the Image*. Oxford and New York: Berghahn, 2009.

1

The grand illousion

Srikanth Srinivasan

The Seventh Art blog, October 3, 2009

If there is any filmmaker whose single film could evoke comparisons ranging from *Happy Gilmore* (1996) to *La Dolce Vita* (1960), it would have to be Quentin Tarantino. But why not? Here is a director who has made a name with his unique style that more or less marries the crassest and the classiest of film elements. It almost seems that, no matter which film you name, you can always find a connection to Tarantino's. Here he is, with his ultra-violent WWII epic *Inglourious Basterds*, released in India on the birthday of a person who has become an icon of non-violence (*Inglourious Basterds* opened in India on the 140th birth anniversary of Mohandas Gandhi).

An unimaginably large number of essays, analyses, critiques, blog posts and reviews cropped up within weeks of its release, running the gamut of opinions, which shows just how provocative this one is. The film has even raised questions about creative license. With *Inglourious Basterds*, Tarantino strays out of what many people would have until now called his comfort zone and has proven once and for all his status as a pop *auteur*. *Inglourious Basterds* may not be the film of the year, it may not even be the director's best film, but it sure is the most important film of the decade.

For the uninitiated, here is the central premise of the film: Nazi propaganda minister Joseph Goebbels (Sylvester Groth) has just produced a film titled *Nation's Pride* involving the real-life exploits of a Nazi private Frederick Zoller (Daniel Brühl), who plays himself in the movie, which is going to be screened at a cozy little theater in Paris owned by a woman called Emmanuelle a.k.a. Shosanna (Mélanie Laurent). A group of American Jewish soldiers, now called The Basterds, led by Lieutenant Aldo "The Apache" Raine (Brad Pitt), along with inputs from the Allied forces, plans to blow up the theater in order to get the leading Nazi men including Hitler (Martin Wuttke). However, to complete their mission they have to get through the cunning and powerful Colonel Hans Landa (Christoph Waltz) who is in charge of the security at the grand event and who never leaves any stone unturned to track down Jews being hunted by the Nazis. Meanwhile, Shosanna, whose family was murdered four years ago by Landa, plans her own revenge by blowing up the cinema hall using inflammable nitrate films that she has stocked through the years. Of course, as always with Tarantino, this summary is completely unimportant in comparison to what he achieves in the film.

With *Inglourious Basterds*, gone are the romantic days of Renoir when a couple of gentlemanly officers could end the war over a cup of tea. Now, deals are meant to be broken, enemies are meant to be stabbed in the back and friends are meant to be ratted on. Enemy corpses aren't supposed to be given a proper burial, but should have their scalps removed. Instead of receiving a gentle kiss on their hands, ladies have their necks wrung. Scheduled duels are substituted by under-the-table gunfights. "I respectfully disagree" makes way for a "fuck you" and "Nat-zi ain't got no humanity" replaces universal brotherhood. Everything in *Inglourious Basterds* is guerrilla-esque, everyone in the film remains true to the title of the movie. Nothing is sacrosanct, everything is to be questioned. Tarantino's army is one that lives and moves in the shadows. What you see most definitely isn't what it is. As hinted in the card game that the officers play in the tavern in the fourth chapter, the inhabitants of Tarantino's new universe wear so many masks one over the other that it almost reduces to a *Scooby Doo* adventure. One isn't supposed to believe what one sees, even if it's all written on the face.

The idea is simple. *Inglourious Basterds* is a five-set tennis match. The Jews win it 3–2. For every Nazi set, there is a Jewish set that follows. Throughout the film we see characters trying to get the upper hand and stay on top in whatever way possible. Even within individual chapters small scale power games are at work and one isn't always sure how it is all going to turn out. The final images of these chapters alternate between images of the Nazis and those of the Jewish characters—Landa kissing Shosanna goodbye, Raine carving out a swastika on a Nazi soldier, Shosanna planning the film, Landa digging out Hammersmark's shoe and Raine, again, with his masterpiece—much like a close tennis match. Each sequence, each shot and each dialogue looks and feels like a tennis rally. The director regularly places his actors on either side of the widescreen and the audience's eyeballs are made to go left and right throughout each conversation. Tarantino's editing pattern could well apply to a Wimbledon telecast, for it mixes over-the-shoulder shots and two shots effectively as if providing both the audience's and the camera's viewpoints of the "match." And of course, Tarantino's writing ensures that we get the reward for the tense stretch of time he puts us through during each conversation.

The mere skeleton of the plot would reveal that Tarantino is reversing conventions here. For once, he is allowing Jews to kill Hitler. And he keeps underlining, hinting, presaging and highlighting this reversal of roles between Jews and Nazis throughout the picture. There is some reversal or other going on within each structure and substructure of the film. Take the magnificent first chapter where Tarantino tosses samples of everything that the film will offer in the next four. As Landa sits at the table, surrounded by the farmer's family, it looks as if it is Landa who is being questioned. We are soon proven wrong and Tarantino's majestic chain of role reversals kicks off as Landa starts digging. With a Bertoluccian touch, Tarantino keeps breaking the 180-degree rule without any hesitation, allowing his camera (helmed by ace cinematographer Robert Richardson) to wander into both sides of the two-shot setup, suggesting the inversion of the hunter-prey relationship that underscores the whole conversation. Even the dialogue is marked by rhetorical clauses like "If I were in your position ... " and "If you were in my shoes ... " Or consider the way he writes the first and final chapters such that they mirror each other entirely. If Nazis kill a few Jews hiding below them during the first chapter, the Basterds will similarly gun down a hundred times that number of Nazis in the last one. If Landa lights up his pipe to create a small smoke cloud in the farm house, a whole cinema hall will be burnt down by Jews. If LaPadite (Denis Menochet) is the betrayer of Jews in the opening chapter, Landa will become the traitor among Nazis in the final chapter. Both Tarantino's camera angles and his actor choreography locate and relocate the relative positions of Jews and Nazis throughout the film in a manner that recalls the way young Bertolucci handled his *mise en scène* in *The Conformist* (1970), which too revolved around faked identities and interchangeable personas and which Tarantino seems to be alluding to in the final few minutes of his movie.

Tarantino really puts his audience in a dicey situation here. *Inglourious Basterds* has been called a revenge fantasy. But never does a character in the film mention that it is a mission of revenge. The Holocaust hasn't yet happened in the diegetic time and there are only hints of the Nazis' plans for the Jews. It is only in hindsight, with the knowledge of what happened in reality, that we are able to call the movie a revenge saga. If there is someone in the audience who is oblivious to the Holocaust, the film might just appear otherwise. Tarantino teases us with the notion that an act of revenge isn't far from the one that instigates it, but aided and justified by the passage of time—an idea that was explored in Gaspar Noé's positively disturbing *Irreversible* (2002). Tarantino lets the two worlds—the "real" reality and the film's reality—collide and one's response just depends on how much of a balance one wants to maintain between "what happened" and "what happens". We can choose to either draw the line between "what-might-have-happened" fiction and "what-couldn't-have-happened" fiction early on or wait till Tarantino draws it for us in the last chapter.

Some commentators have suggested that *Inglourious Basterds* tries to humanize the Nazis and gain sympathy for them. But, surely, it isn't entirely the film's fault that we pity the German officer when the Bear Jew (Eli Roth) walks towards him menacingly or when Nazis turn to ashes in the theater. It is simply the ways movies work. Given a narrative pattern, we generally seem to tend to support the weak, the suffering and the oppressed, thanks to our liberal tendencies. Be it aliens from sci-fi works, tribes in exotic countries or mute animals of the wild, we tend to patronize them, placing them on our moral scales. When, in *A Clockwork Orange* (1971), Alex de Large (Malcolm McDowell) is being trained at the reformatory to respond to certain impulses in a predictable fashion, Kubrick, in a way, is speaking self-reflexively. Alex is evil and there can be no justification for his actions. Even so, the director makes us accomplices to his acts, eventually making us sympathize with him. Four decades later Tarantino's film surfaces to thoroughly provoke us in a similar manner and, in the process, make us re-evaluate our own moral standing and the way we tend to judge characters—on- and off-screen. Speaking of *A Clockwork Orange*, Hans Landa drinking a glass of milk is reminiscent of and as chilling as Alex holding one at the Korova Milkbar.

Tarantino adorns the movie with a slew of sight gags, not unlike the ones we see in the *Looney Toons* cartoons. During Landa's interrogation of LaPadite, at one point, he unveils his gigantic, almost unreal, smoking pipe dwarfing that of LaPadite. In the fourth chapter, when the Gestapo officer comes from within the tavern to question the British spy about his accent, we see a huge whisky glass in front of him that's unlike anything we've seen in the scene. Even in the last scene, when Landa hands over his knife to Raine, we are shown that Raine's is the bigger one! Furthermore, during the second chapter, when we are introduced to Hitler, he is posing for a massive portrait, indicating that his image is much more formidable than the man himself, whom Tarantino is happy to caricature. In fact, all these in-jokes would have fallen flat had *Inglourious Basterds* indeed played out as straightforward drama. Thankfully, Tarantino's characters are cartoon-ish themselves, hence justifying the deformation Tarantino bestows upon them and his attempts to reduce intense and delicate power plays to petty mine-is-bigger arguments.

Tarantino doesn't just bend and blend genres here; he takes them along with the movie. His characters don't simply absorb from genres, they *are* the genres. *Inglourious Basterds* is the kind of movie that would happen if a filmmaker cast non-actor cinephiles to act in a WWII picture. Tarantino's history is not a history given to him by text books (which by itself is a questionable version), but one given to him by cinema. His characters aren't those defined by the WWII setting of the film, but ones from our age that have strayed into a WWII movie. These aren't characters evolved from within the film, but ones that have been pushed into it. What Tarantino does here is pick stereotypes from every genre of popular cinema and cook them up in his WWII broth. In Godard's *Pierrot*

Le Fou (1965), the titular madman tries to bite off more than he can chew by jumping from one genre of cinema to another and trying to pirate the film away from the director to places only he wants to be. (Early in the film, Samuel Fuller tells us that movies are all about emotions.) Continuing the tradition of Godard's influence on Tarantino, *Inglourious Basterds* too absorbs quite a bit from the French, especially *Pierrot*. In Tarantino's film, too, each character tries to hijack the movie from the genre it is supposed to be, as if protesting the director's decision of forcefully situating them out of place.

Almost every character in the film tries to own a sub-genre. With his ultra-neat conversational ethics and table manners, not to mention the tinge of narcissism, Landa is the quintessential smooth-talking secret agent. (Landa himself insists that he is a detective later on.) Aldo Raine is the leader of the men-on-a-mission type, with his I-don't-give-a-damn attitude. Shosanna thinks she is the next Beatrix Kiddo, with her all-red femme fatale act. Poor little Zoller tries to be the romantic hero despite his designation in the film. Bridget von Hammersmark (Diane Kruger), already an actress, wants to be the deadly female spy (someone mentions Mata Hari as she talks during the tavern scene). Lt. Hicox (Michael Fassbender) is altogether from a different country's cinema, with all his ethnic and lingual idiosyncrasies intact. ("Well, if this is it, old boy, I hope you don't mind if I go out speaking the King's?") Even Herr Goebbels seems to think that he is in a B-grade sci-fi flick. ("*I have created a monster*," he says.) Much has been said about the corny celebratory ritual that Donny Donowitz performs at the end of his "innings," but that only conforms to the B-Comedy subgenre that he is in. (Apparently, Adam Sandler was to play this part—who else?) You'll either love his lines (and his bizarre nasal accent) or hate them, depending on how much you appreciate such type of comedy.

Apart from playing out their genres in the movie, the characters in *Inglourious Basterds* keep assuming different nationalities and ethnicities. Faking accents, speaking multiple languages, feigning papers and changing appearances seems to be order of the day. Characters are recognized using ethnic slurs and covers are blown with the minutest of faux pas. "I am a slave to appearances," confesses Aldo Raine as he handcuffs Landa in the final scene. Everyone in the film is. The multilingual Landa wants the Italian names to have a ring to them. The "little man" is unhappy about the unfair nickname that the Germans have given him. Hitler is convinced that the Bear Jew is a golem. Shosanna goes to the extent of performing a fully fledged ritual for this purpose. Right from the misspelled title you are told that what it looks or sounds like isn't what it is. Tarantino pulls our legs as he switches the subtitles on and off throughout the movie, giving us only the most basic of information and leaving the rest to our 'expertise'.

Tarantino's relative disregard for the content of his film and his prankster attitude towards it are characteristic of Jean-Luc Godard too. But even with all that influence, Tarantino has managed to kill his "father," with a distinct style that borrows from Godard's yet deviates starkly. The greatest asset that Tarantino seems to possess is the ability to maintain a consistent tone for the movie. Even when he marries genres as wide and fatal as melodrama and thriller, he maintains a certain kind of detachment from it that lends these sequences a tongue-in-cheek flavor which unites them under a single stylistic umbrella despite their vast disparity. Even when he cuts to cheesy in-movie documentaries (narrated by Samuel L. Jackson), again reminding us of Godard's *My Life To Live* (1962) in which the director seamlessly included a mini-documentary that lists statistics and factoids about prostitution in Paris, Tarantino maintains a strong grip on the filmmaker's attitude towards his subject, never allowing us to mistake him for inconsistency of style.

Tarantino's idea of filmmaking is akin to blowing a balloon. He blows and blows, till the onlookers cringe, and then he allows it to pop. The mantra, for him, seems to be not "if it bends it's funny, if it breaks it's not funny" but "if it bends it's funny, if it breaks it's funnier." This way, one might call him anti-Hitchcockian. Hitchcock sums up his legendary theory of suspense thus (in François Truffaut's *Hitchcock*):

There is a distinct difference between 'suspense' and 'surprise', and yet many pictures continually confuse the two. I'll explain what I mean. We are now having a very innocent little chat. Let us suppose that there is a bomb underneath this table between us. Nothing happens, and then all of a sudden, 'Boom!' There is an explosion. The public is surprised, but prior to this surprise, it has seen an absolutely ordinary scene, of no special conse-quence. Now, let us take a suspense situation. The bomb is underneath the table, and the public knows it, probably because they have seen the anarchist place it there. The public is aware that the bomb is going to explode at one o'clock and there is a clock in the décor. The public can see that it is a quarter to one. In these conditions this same innocuous conversation becomes fascinating because the public is participating in the scene. The audience is longing to warn the characters on the screen: 'You shouldn't be talking about such trivial matters. There's a bomb underneath you and it's about to explode!' In the first case we have given the public fifteen seconds of surprise at the moment of the explosion. In the second case we have provided them with fifteen minutes of suspense. The conclusion is that whenever possible the public must be informed. Except when the surprise is a twist, that is, when the unexpected ending is, in itself, the highlight of the story.

Take the case of Tarantino. The audience always knows the outcome of his set pieces; that the balloon is going to pop one way or the other. However, he doesn't inform his audience of the popping time. Instead of making us ask questions like what will happen, he makes us ask when will it happen (and here, Tarantino likes to stretch the audience's patience). Furthermore, Hitchcock preferred not to make that bomb of suspense explode, for he believed that it would make the audience uncomfortable, whereas one can bet that Tarantino will relish showing what you expect (not only will the Hitchcockian bomb explode, but limbs will fly, heads will roll and blood will flow). In fact, in *Inglourious Basterds*, not only do the Basterds' bombs explode, but the theater burns as per Shosanna's plans, Landa's "private" bomb goes off and Donowitz and Ulmer (Omar Doom) manage to machine gun down the Nazis. Talk about beating a dead horse. But, on the other hand, Tarantino also uses a lot of Hitchcockian techniques as well and he builds the film atop a series of Red Herrings and MacGuffins (one could have sworn that Landa had Shosanna when he orders milk).

But Tarantino's film, at heart, like all his other works, is about cinema. His stream of movie references and tributes continues as he recalls a number of films from the past that he seems to have grown up with. He pays homage to German cinema throughout *Inglourious Basterds* with a large number of Dutch angles that never once feel forced or out of context. In the final chapter, which begins with images recalling Fassbinder's *The Marriage of Maria Braun* (1979) complete with the 360 degree Ballhaus shot, Tarantino takes this fetish to a whole new level. The film within the film, *Nation's Pride* (actually directed by the Bear Jew), presents to us a German propaganda movie made in the style of a Soviet propaganda movie, *Battleship Potemkin* (1925) in particular, forming an unusual alliance between two countries that could have only been possible in cinema. This whole set piece works on multiple levels of reality. If Goebbels is making a fiction within the fiction based on a distorted form of reality within the fiction, Tarantino, too, is making a fantastical fiction that relies on betraying reality. Tarantino's ethical stance is a long way from that of Goebbels (which is actually the way Hollywood tells it). It's certainly less exploitative to heavily exaggerate a reality that never was than to mildly dress up a reality that was.

Early this year, Tarantino called Woody Allen's widely and undeservedly trashed *Anything Else* (2003) as one of the twenty best films made after he entered the industry (*Sky Movies* "Indie program," August, 2009). And not surprisingly, much is common between these two films despite their stylistic differences. In *Anything Else*, David Dobel (Woody Allen) tries to break out of the schlemiel image that the director had created for himself through the 1970s and the 1980s. "The issue is always fascism," he says in the film and he smashes the car windows of two thugs who bully him out of a parking space. What Woody was trying to do here was to undo history—both personal and collective—as he guides his younger self, Jerry Falk (Jason Biggs), who prefers "writing a biting satire in the quiet and safety of some delicatessen," away from what he has become. Tarantino realizes that the only way to undo history, if not in reality, is through art and that art, in many ways, does not owe anything to political and historical "reality". When Shosanna switches from one projector to another during the screening, she is, in fact, shifting the movie from one reality into another—from a history we all know to a history that could have been.

Tarantino's mission of trying to carve out a fantastical alternate reality isn't really a unique one. In *History of Cinema*, Godard keeps talking about two kinds of histories—the history that was and history that could have been—of cinema and that of the world. He argues that cinema could have indeed prevented large scale mishaps and put an end to Nazism once and for all. Tarantino realizes that this is nothing more than an elegiac fantasy and makes a joke out of it all telling us that the only way cinema could have brought about a political change was physically—by blowing itself up. And that the only way it could have ended Nazism was by putting them all into a large theater and burning it down. In a scene that echoes the final few minutes of *The Cameraman's Revenge* (1912), which was a film that reflected our tendency to believe that if it is cinema it must be true, Marcel (Jacky Ido) burns the pile of nitrate films to blow up the theater as a huge heap of bullets piles up on the screen resembling it. With that, Tarantino is happy to plainly flesh out his idea of history that could (should) have been.

His attempt, like Allen's in *Anything Else*, is to shatter the image that, especially popular cinema, has bestowed upon minorities of America through its incessant ethnic stereotyping—the suffering Jew, the benign black and the noble Native American. So in a way, the revenge, led by Aldo-Shosanna-Marcel, isn't merely a fantastical Jewish retaliation for the Holocaust, but a revenge for all the minorities and nonconformists of a cinema industry whose high-handed producers insist upon maintaining the status quo and sticking to a "final solution" (no wonder Marcel burns the movie reels). For Tarantino, who has been a popular nonconformist throughout his career in Hollywood, this is surely the sweetest revenge fantasy possible. It is his fairy tale and he is telling it the way he wants it to be. When Landa finds a single shoe in the tavern following the shootout he must have realized he is in someone's Cinderella story. The truth is that it's Tarantino's.

The Seventh Art blog, excerpt from October 11, 2009

Brandon Colvin is of the opinion that *Inglourious Basterds* is primarily a comedy (*Out 1 Film Journal*, September, 2009). I'm going to take a diametrically opposite path and say that this movie, when reduced to its human elements, stripped of all its film references and modernist facets, is a tragedy with a martyr called Shosanna at its heart. The word "tragedy" is often used loosely and seems to denote every tale that has a pathetic, miserable and depressing outcome. But, surely, tragedy does not base itself upon plain emotions. In fact, it is quite the opposite. A tale is truly tragic when two morally unquestionable and righteous forces are made to clash and a situation evolves when one of them has to let go of its stance, despite all convictions for the greater good. Tragedy is always the result of a choice that calls for a great sacrifice to go with it. As they say, it is our choices that define us. And a tragic choice defines us for life—either as a hero or as a coward ("merely human" would be the euphemism). *Sansho the Bailiff* (1954), even with its heavy pathos, is a melodrama whereas *The Dark Knight* (2008), despite its uplifting upshot, remains a tragedy. Shosanna could well have married Zoller and led a very easy life. Instead, she repudiates that path and takes up the task of liberating Jews at the cost of her own life. Tarantino, besides using Ennio Morricone's moving piece *Un Amico*, employs mythological and historical iconographies to underline the magnitude of this tragedy.

The final chapter of *Inglourious Basterds* has got to be the densest that Tarantino has ever filmed. The chapter is ambiguously titled "Revenge of the Giant Face" as if recalling some B-movie from the 1950s. But more than that, it seems to me, it tries to allude to two of the most iconic "giant faces" of women we know. The first would be that of Maria Falconetti in Carl Dreyer's *The Passion of Joan of Arc* (1928)—a film that is constructed out of hundreds of such giant faces. The tale of Joan of Arc by itself is a tragedy in which Joan sacrifices a normal life for her Faith, much like Shosanna, who goes down in flames at the end of her journey. Only Shosanna doesn't suffer alone, instead taking all of them along with her. And then there is the most dreaded giant head in Greek mythology—that of Medusa the Gorgon—a mere gaze into whose eyes is supposed to petrify one. Daniel Ogden describes this stare of Medusa's as "seemingly looking out from its own iconographical context and directly challenging the viewer." Nazi officers in the final chapter are watching a fictional film, seated safely away from real life action, without any apparent threat from the images on the screen. When Shosanna slips in her own film, with her gaze directed towards them, she essentially "looks out of the context of the movie," challenging, literally, the viewers in a manner in which modernist directors use their actors, and petrifying them by dragging them out of their passive state.

But then, our ideas about these two iconic characters are derived only through images and shadows—through paintings, through Dreyer's film and through textual accounts. As George Steiner put it, "It is not the literal past that rules us, save, possibly, in a biological sense. It is images of the past." With the passage of time, history and mythology mingle to such an extent that it becomes virtually impossible to separate them. In Chris Marker's monumental *The Owl's Legacy* (1989) Jean-Pierre Vernant describes the mythos behind this practice of image (which is a word that referred to doubles, miniatures, copies and ghosts in general in Ancient Greece, the land of tragedies) creation. He tells us that images, for Ancient Greeks, were a means of facing man's worst fears by reducing them down to caricatures. In Medusa's case, this meant that they could see her directly in the eyes (à la Perseus who used a mirror—an image creating device—to slay her) and subsequently use these images to intimidate enemies. In Vernant's own words: "So there is a way, through images and through stories of disarming the horror of death that the monstrous face expresses and which the image carries out so that what can't be seen can be depicted in many ways" (recalling Godard's quote about movies in his magnum opus *History of Cinema* 1988–1998, a film that Tarantino's picture so closely traces: "How marvelous to be able to look at what we cannot see").

In the final chapter of *Inglourious Basterds*, Tarantino absorbs these images of dead tragic characters from mythology and history, blends them with the "image" of the tragic Shosanna, who too is now dead, and, in essence, creates a mythology (Shosanna the martyr) and history (Shosanna the WWII hero) of his own. Now, this is not far from what he does with his other characters in his movies, wherein he imbibes mythos and facts from within cinematic history to create new ones for his own characters. Only that, with *Inglourious Basterds*, his canvas seems to have expanded, with his universe now transgressing boundaries defined by the history of cinema. Furthermore, Tarantino uses the images of his movie—his Medusa mask—to "look at what he cannot see" in reality. Throughout the film, he keeps attacking Hitler's "image." He depicts Hitler as a weak and paranoid individual with vermin-like attributes. When he kills him in the final shootout, it is the "image" of Hitler that he wants to kill (much like the mentality behind voodoo and effigy-burning practices), for he can't kill him in reality—exactly the same thing that Florya (Aleksei Kravchenko) does in *Come and See* (1985) when he fires at a photograph of

Hitler in an attempt to undo the images of history, if not history itself.

In *The Conformist*, Bertolucci equates fascists with Plato's prisoners of the cave, suggesting that they are blinded by fake ideologies fuelled by personal insecurities. In *The Owl's Legacy*, Marker equates the audience in the cinema hall (citing Simone Weil) to those prisoners, proposing that they are blinded by images they see on-screen and take them for reality. In *Inglourious Basterds*, Tarantino combines both these notions and presents us with Nazis watching movies in a cinema hall. These "blind" Nazis appear to be enjoying the massacre that Zoller is unleashing on-screen, assuming that this is how it all was. Zoller, on the other hand, is the only person there who knows it wasn't so and leaves the hall, breaking free from the cave. Additionally, Tarantino does not forget to free his audience from the chains of their cave. Like in Bertolucci's film, he keeps reminding us that we are watching a movie and whatever we are seeing is a mere painting on a plastic canvas (contrary to what other films on historical subjects want us to believe). In chapter two, Raine, seated at the center of an arrangement that resembles a Greek theater, tells the captured Nazi officer that "watching Danny beat the Nazis to death is the closest we ever get to going to the movies." Raine seems to know that he is just the shadow of a man placed on a simple image. And because he regularly attempts to remind us of the fakery of it all, Tarantino's violence also helps to serve the same purpose—to try to disengage us from whatever is depicted on cinema screen even when it is unmitigated and concrete. As the movie's title confesses, it's all a fraud and a very beautiful one at that.

2

Exploding cinema, exploding Hollywood: *Inglourious Basterds* and the limits of cinema

Imke Meyer

"Greetings, Jerusalem, I am deeply sorry." These are the words Hitler speaks—in Hebrew—in a video the artist Boaz Arad created in the year 2000. Arad spliced together many "very short film clips from Hitler's propaganda speeches to produce a montage in which the Führer's strung-together German syllables are transformed into a Hebrew sentence."[1] The video, entitled *Hebrew Lesson*, was on view at the Jewish Museum in New York in 2002, as part of the exhibit *Mirroring Evil: Nazi Imagery/Recent Art*. At the time, this show created quite a controversy. Many of the objects in the exhibit—such as Zbigniew Libera's infamous *LEGO Concentration Camp Set* (1996)—were considered too controversial to be shown at, of all places, the Jewish Museum. Tom Sach's *Prada Deathcamp* (1998) and Alan Schechtner's *It's the Real Thing—Self-Portrait at Buchenwald* (1993) (which shows an image of the artist holding a can of Diet Coke inserted into a famous photograph of concentration camp inmates at Buchenwald), among other objects, were considered facile and so shallow in their approach to the Holocaust as to be offensive. The opening of the exhibit was greeted with protests from Holocaust survivors, and the show received reviews that ranged from lukewarm to highly critical. Arad's video was among the few pieces in the exhibit that resonated with critics as a collage work that both rewrites history and reminds us of the seeming impossibility of leaving the past behind.[2]

In the same year in which the *Mirroring Evil* exhibit opened in New York, Robert Schindel and Lukas Stepanik released their film *Gebürtig* in Austria. The film, based on Robert Schindel's 1992 novel of the same name, is set in Vienna and centers on a group of people made up of Holocaust survivors, the children of Jewish survivors and non-Jewish resistance fighters, and the children of perpetrators. As the film opens, however, it has the distinct look of a Hollywood-style Holocaust movie: prisoners are lined up in front of the gates of a concentration camp that could be Auschwitz, and they are guarded by a Kapo.[3] It is snowing, and the prisoners are shivering in the cold. The washed-out color palette and the faint light suggest misery, as does the howling wind on the soundtrack. Nazi officers in immaculate uniforms are standing nearby, chatting and drinking coffee from metal cups. We see a semi-close-up of the face of one of the officers. His cap features a small silver skull and bones. The viewers can now identify him as a member of the SS. In response to a signal from the Kapo, the prisoners turn and begin to march. German shepherds, kept in check by the Nazi officers, start barking. One of the prisoners slips on the icy ground but is caught by the prisoner walking behind him. Seconds later, an elderly prisoner also slips, and he falls to the ground. The frame of the scene shifts slightly; the camera moves back a few feet, and the viewer can now identify the gates in front of which the prisoners are marching as indeed those of Auschwitz. The tension of the scene increases as the officer approaches the prisoner on the ground. We fully expect the SS man brutally to mistreat the prisoner. The camera focuses on the prisoner and then on the SS officer. After a few seconds of hesitation, the SS man holds out his right hand; the prisoner, looking up at the officer, grasps the hand, and he is pulled up from the ground by the officer. Non-diegetic piano music in a minor key can now be heard on the soundtrack. The prisoner fumbles with his cap, takes it off, and pulls a cigarette out of it. The SS officer leans over and gives the prisoner a light. The screen goes dark, and the credits of the film start rolling. Only later on in the movie does the viewer learn that the opening scene depicts the filming of a film within the film. Part of *Gebürtig*'s plot revolves around a Hollywood production crew that is filming a Holocaust movie in Europe, recruiting many extras the casting team determines to be "Jewish-looking" to play the prisoners. Only then do we realize that we did not watch a cinematic representation of an SS officer acting with kindness towards a prisoner, but that we rather saw a representation of two actors interacting with one another.

Boaz Arad's *Hebrew Lesson* and the opening scene of *Gebürtig* are both fantasy scenarios centering on Nazism and the Holocaust. The video of Hitler apologizing to his Jewish victims is an affront: how dare the man responsible for the murder of six million Jews apologize to his victims? Is he expecting forgiveness? At the same time, the video stages a simple wish fulfillment: Hitler realizes what he has wrought; perhaps he now sees himself for what he is, and the German language—the language in which the fate of the Jews was decided—is turned into the language adopted by those Holocaust survivors who settled in what would become Israel.[4] The opening scene of *Gebürtig* presents us with a similar fantasy: the SS officer, assumed to be brutal and barbaric, turns out to have a humane and caring side. These two scenarios may represent fantasies not primarily aimed at a Jewish audience. They also work as a form of revisionism for German and Austrian spectators: if only the Führer were still alive and could, in the name of all Germans and Austrians, apologize to the Jewish people; if only barbarism were not the only association invoked by thoughts of SS officers, the post-Nazi task of the re-constructing of German and Austrian identity might be marginally eased.

Quentin Tarantino's *Inglourious Basterds* (2009) also presents us with a fantasy scenario. Tarantino, however, constructs a fantasy very different from those of Arad and Schindel and Stepanik. *Hebrew Lesson* and *Gebürtig* focus on the perpetrators, thus affirming the omnipotence of the Nazis vis-à-vis the Jews. In other words, if the Nazis had decided to act differently, the fate of their victims might have been altered. In these fantasies, the Jews ultimately remain fixed in the powerless position of the eternal victim. Tarantino turns these scenarios on their heads. Rather than locking the Jews in a position of subservience, the director releases them to launch a powerful fight against the evil of Nazism—a fight so potent, in fact, that it ends WWII early and sends Hitler and his minions to a fiery grave.

Tarantino's film, however, does not merely dislodge positions of power that previously appeared to be discursively fixed. The film also shows that Hollywood and its culture industry apparatus bear much of the responsibility for the repeated reinscription and reaffirmation of these discursive relations. Hollywood, as Tarantino reminds us, needs the Nazis. Who better than a sadistic Nazi to represent an arch villain? Who better than the Nazis to represent evil incarnate? What better scenario than the mistreatment of innocent victims by evil Nazis to help sketch out a black-and-white moral universe? In *Inglourious Basterds* Tarantino dramatizes the insight that Hollywood cinema simply cannot do without the Nazis. Tarantino's killing of the Nazis literally explodes the cinema: Hitler, Goebbels & Co. die in a French movie theater where they had been attending the screening of Goebbels' latest film. As the cinema is engulfed in a ball of fire, it "dies" along with its most overused characterizations of evil.

The destabilization of the dichotomy between what have become archetypal embodiments of Good and Evil—namely Jewish Holocaust victims and sadistic Nazi killers—does Hollywood no favors. Nazi connections are invoked or Nazi paraphernalia are shown in many a Hollywood film not because their historic specificity supplies an essential element in the development of a given plot, but rather because they can serve as an aural or visual shorthand for Absolute Evil. Conversely, innocence, suffering, and Absolute Powerlessness can be signified most effectively via references to Holocaust victims. As Tarantino stated in his conversation with *The Atlantic*'s Jeffrey Goldberg: "Holocaust movies always have Jews as victims ... We've seen that story before. I want to see something different. Let's see Germans that are scared of Jews. Let's not have everything build up to a big misery, let's actually take the fun of action-movie cinema and apply it to this situation."[5]

Representing the empowerment of a victim that had seemed forever trapped in its historic/symbolic position must severely disrupt the economies of signification upon which Hollywood's cinematic conventions rely. Tarantino's revenge fantasy, then, releases Jews from the dead end of eternal victimhood, at the same time that it confronts Hollywood with its instrumentalization of the Holocaust for the mere purpose of "good" storytelling. Abstaining from such instrumentalization, and letting go of the Nazi figures that have signified evil so efficiently for decades, would lead to the death of one of Hollywood cinema's most basic plot conventions. It is this insight that is made visible in the cinema explosion that kills Hitler and his minions. In *Inglourious Basterds*, Shosanna, a Jewish character who, early in the film, escapes the role she was meant to play, namely that of the victim, takes charge. She sets fire to her movie theater, thereby destroying the Nazi leadership. For the viewers, the spectacle of the exploding theater also signals the indictment of a cinema that, in Hollywood, has become an institution that refuses to let go of narrative conventions that are not only built on the backs of Jewish victims, but also reaffirm a victim–perpetrator dichotomy that condemns Jews to eternal powerlessness.

With *Inglourious Basterds*, Tarantino has made the Hollywood Nazi film to end all Hollywood Nazi films. By giving us, in Christoph Waltz's memorable embodiment of (Austrian) SS officer Hans Landa, one of the most perfect and formidable movie villains ever, he exposes the dependence of his own Hollywood plot on the representation of unrepentant evil. At the same time, the director forces his audience to admit to the pleasure it gets from watching Landa dominate the screen—as well as his victims. As spectators, we are made aware that the typical Hollywood good-versus-evil formula can be realized in almost ideal fashion via the representation of Nazis and their victims. Consequently, if good had triumphed over evil in real life—if the Jews had been able to eliminate the Nazis—American cinema would have been deprived not only of a host of Jewish émigrés who fled Germany and Austria and contributed their talents to Hollywood,[6] but also of stock characters—the absolute victim, the absolute villain—on whose presence so many Hollywood films depend. If the Jews had overpowered the Nazis, Hollywood cinema would not be what it is today. That the cinematic fantasy of strong Jews victorious over the Nazis had not been realized in Hollywood until the screening of Tarantino's film more than sixty years after the war may point to Hollywood's desire to leave intact the easy power relations upon which so many of its plots depend. The absence in post-war Hollywood cinema of a plot like Tarantino's reveals a lack of desire to liberate those figures (victims of the Holocaust) that international audiences have come to expect to be powerless. In his cinematic tour de force, Tarantino radicalizes this insight: instead of disempowering Jews yet again, he turns them into Wild West-style avengers, thus both altering one of Hollywood's most "respected" and "respectful" conventions and revealing the foundations upon which this convention is built. When the Nazi villains are vanquished by Jews who refuse to play the role of the victim, the result is and must be that cinema explodes. This insight is brought about simultaneously with the help of cinema, and at its expense: the fire that engulfs the movie theater towards the conclusion of *Inglourious Basterds* is started through the deliberate ignition of a library of film stock, i.e., a representation of traditional film history itself.

This, then, is precisely the point where my reading differs from the nuanced analysis of *Inglourious Basterds* that Georg Seeßlen has presented, first in his German *Der Spiegel* magazine article and then in his book-length study. Seeßlen writes that Tarantino must sacrifice cinema so that he can kill Hitler and his minions: "Tarantino sacrifices his sanctum. When people have to be protected from evil, one even has to be willing to burn the cinema. The coming of age of Tarantinism may be contained in this radical gesture. As paradoxical as this sacrifice may be: the space of dream is sacrificed for reality, but only in a dream for which reality is sacrificed."[7] In contrast to Seeßlen, I do not believe that Tarantino is interested primarily in representing the death of Hitler and his inner circle, or in warning against evil. Rather, Tarantino seeks to show that the very cinema that believes itself to be a "good" and democratic one builds its representations of the good-versus-evil moral universe on simplistic binary structures that reproduce for

Jewish characters the role that the Nazis assigned them, namely that of the eternal victim.

Inglourious Basterds was well received in Germany, although its reception there reiterates the very dichotomy between Hollywood cinema and Nazi film that Tarantino, I argue, seeks to undo. David Kleingers' analysis can serve to illustrate this point:

> Just like the emigrants in Curtiz' *Casablanca* could, on the silver screen, raise their voices against the injustice that reigned in their homeland, with Tarantino the polyphonic and democratic Hollywood, which is aware of its global roots, triumphs over Goebbels' authoritarian national cinema. And the fact that *Inglourious Basterds* was filmed almost entirely in the Studios of Babelsberg, from which the Nazis, starting in 1933, had expelled Jewish filmmakers and the artistic tradition of Weimar cinema, makes this victory considerably sweeter.[8]

Kleingers reads Tarantino's film as a triumph of democratic Hollywood over Goebbels' cinematic propaganda machine. In my view, though, this is precisely what Tarantino's film does not want to show. To be sure, Tarantino reminds us that Hollywood cinema, at its best, borrows from and is in dialogue with other national cinemas. At the same time, however, Tarantino's film reveals that Hollywood appropriates not only untainted sources but likewise liberally utilizes Nazi iconography in order to perpetuate its established conventions. This is made especially obvious in a scene in which Shosanna Dreyfus, the Jewish woman who had escaped Colonel Landa's murder of her family at the outset of the film and who now, under an assumed name, runs a cinema in Paris, is shown changing the lettering on her theater's marquee to announce a new film. Shosanna is forced by the German occupiers to screen German films during "German Night." The last movie that was shown is Arnold Fanck and G. W. Pabst's 1929 silent mountain film *Die weiße Hölle vom Piz Palü*/*The White Hell of Pitz Palu*. The film stars Leni Riefenstahl, and the lettering above the cinema lists her name along with that of G. W. Pabst. Literally inscribed into the frame of Tarantino's Hollywood film, then, are both a "good" ancestor—revered Weimar Republic director G. W. Pabst—and an "evil" one—Weimar Republic actress and later Nazi film director Leni Riefenstahl. *Inglourious Basterds* sets up a visual confrontation between the names Riefenstahl and Pabst. At the same time, we are reminded that Pabst and Riefenstahl were collaborators on pre-Nazi film projects.[9] Tarantino signals that Hollywood learned from both Pabst and Riefenstahl; however, the assumed absolute opposition between the two directors is as constructed as Riefenstahl's infamous shots of a heroic *Führer* in her Nazi propaganda film *Triumph des Willens/Triumph of the Will* (1935)[10]—and as artificial as Hollywood's black-and-white moral universe.

When the 'heroic" German soldier Frederick Zoller strikes up a conversation with Shosanna outside the theater, she claims that the French, contrary to the Germans, as she implies, respect film directors. However, the name of Arnold Fanck, the other German director of the *Pitz Palu* film, is clearly missing on the marquee.[11] The omission of Fanck's name belies the claim of Shosanna, who is, of course, both the character with whom the audience empathizes, and the figure that the audience is led to trust. The shadow cast on Shosanna's nature here is admittedly a very small one, but it is just significant enough to make us see that Hollywood's ceaseless construction of black-and-white moral universes not only takes away shades of gray but rather leads to the production of half-truths and inaccuracies. The inclusion of Fanck's name on the marquee would have disturbed the binary opposition between Riefenstahl and Pabst that Tarantino's film at once sets up and deconstructs. Tarantino shows us that Hollywood has no qualms about altering the historical record if it suits its storytelling needs. *Inglourious Basterds*, as a film that both partakes of and critiques Hollywood conventions, seems suspended here between the utilization of artificial binary oppositions for purposes of plot construction and the critique of such a device.[12]

Tarantino further underscores the fact that Hollywood and Goebbels' cinema share some narrative techniques by representing the screening of a film within the film. German Private Zoller, who is attracted to Shosanna, convinces Goebbels to hold the premiere of *Stolz der Nation* (Nation's Pride), a film in which Zoller stars as himself, at Shosanna's theater. Zoller is famous for singlehandedly having killed hundreds of Americans from a sniper position in a tower, and *Stolz der Nation* docu-dramatizes his deeds. When the film is screened for us and for the Nazis at Shosanna's theater, we see Zoller madly shooting at his enemies, improbably killing all of them and finding time, in between reloads of his machine gun, to carve a swastika into the floorboards of the tower in which he has barricaded himself. Here, the Nazi soldier, whom we are used to perceiving as evil, is cast as the hero who is fighting other evil forces. This black-and-white film within Tarantino's film was created by director/producer/actor Eli Roth (who also plays Sergeant Donny Donowitz, the "Bear Jew"), and it lets the audience see that this fictitious Nazi movie is not so different in structure from many Hollywood action films. In a simplistic black-and-white moral universe, good wins out over evil, even in situations where such a win seems most unlikely and in which the audience must suspend disbelief. The Zoller docu-drama *Stolz der Nation* reminds us that the events represented on-screen likely do not add up to a historically accurate depiction of the world. Nor do they accurately reflect the complexity of the moral choices humans have to make. What Tarantino's film indicts is both Hollywood's time-honored pretense of offering narratives that help us "understand" history, and our eagerness to believe in this pretense when we watch realist films such as Steven Spielberg's *Schindler's List* or *Saving Private Ryan*.

Indeed, *Inglourious Basterds* has on numerous occasions been compared unfavorably to films like *Schindler's List*. Manohla Dargis observes in her review of Tarantino's film in the *New York Times*:

> The film's most egregious failure—its giddy, at times gleeful embrace and narrative elevation of the seductive Nazi villain—can largely be explained as a problem of form. Landa simply has no equal in the film, no counterpart who can match him in verbal dexterity and charisma ... Cartoon Nazis are not new to the movies, and neither are fascinating fascists, as evidenced by Ralph Fiennes' Oscar-nominated turn in *Schindler's List*. Unlike those in *Schindler's List*, Mr. Tarantino's Nazis exist in an insistently fictional cinematic space where heroes and villains converge amid a welter of movie allusions. He's not making a documentary or trying to be Steven Spielberg: Mr. Tarantino is really only serious about his own films, not history.[13]

Dargis is certainly correct in observing that cartoonish Nazis have populated movie screens for decades. And it is likewise true that Tarantino's narrative elevates "the seductive Nazi villain." As Susan Sontag taught us in her seminal essay "Fascinating Fascism," there exists "a general fantasy" centered upon uniforms, and there is a particularly powerful and even erotic fantasy linked to representations of SS uniforms:

> ... [b]ecause the SS seems to be the most perfect incarnation of fascism's overt assertion of the righteousness of violence, the right to have total power over others and to treat them as absolutely inferior. It was in the SS that this assertion seemed most complete, because they acted it out in a singularly brutal and efficient manner; and because they dramatized it by linking themselves to certain aesthetic standards. The SS was designed as an elite military community that would be not only supremely violent but also supremely beautiful.[14]

Landa, as Dargis notes, has "no equal" in the film—no one can match his sadism, his elegance, his cosmopolitanism, his well-rounded education and refined manners (his *Bildung*, in a word), or his evil. This lack of an equal to Landa repeatedly confronts the spectator with his or her own problematic pleasure in seeing this SS man dominate both the screen and his victims. The spectator has no choice but to grapple with a perverse attraction to the villain. If Landa had a match in any other character in the film, we could indulge in the pleasure of watching the sadist while safely taking refuge in an equal pleasure of watching a positive role model of a stature similar to that of Landa. Tarantino's film, however, denies us such a moral cover and forces us to face up to our fascination with evil, and to the erotic charge with which we invest it.

The fact that Spielberg's *Schindler's List* is, as Dargis puts it, less "insistently fictional" than *Inglourious Basterds* does not make it the superior film treatment of the subject of Nazism. One might even argue that it is precisely the fact that *Schindler's List* purports to tell the real-life story of German industrialist Oskar Schindler that makes it problematic. History here is pressed into the two-dimensional schema of a typical Spielberg action movie with melodramatic contours built around a basic good-versus-evil formula, and the rescue of the Jewish characters that occurs in the film can be enjoyed as a triumph of the human spirit, along with the melodramatic catharsis offered by this pseudo-happy ending. Because the film claims a close link to historical reality, the spectator is never forced to admit to the pleasure she receives from watching the Nazi villain portrayed by actor Ralph Fiennes. Worse yet, the heavily fictionalized narrative of *Schindler's List* distorts the larger historical account of the Holocaust. As *The Village Voice*'s J. Hoberman memorably put it during a round table discussion of the film:

> At the end of *Close Encounters* when the hero goes back into the mother ship, it is not even that he is born again, he's reversed the process of life. That's *Schindler's List*. This is a movie about World War II in which all the Jews live. The selection is "life," the Nazi turns out to be a good guy, and human nature is revealed to be sunny and bright. It's a total reversal.[15]

One might argue, then, that the "insistently fictional" character of *Inglourious Basterds* makes it into a film more honest than many other Holocaust movies. Nowhere does Tarantino's film pretend to represent history accurately or attempt an analysis of Nazism. *Schindler's List* purports to tell a true story, but it serves up a fantasy. The difference is that Spielberg's fantasy is of the rather disturbing kind Hoberman describes. Not only does it leave the Jews in a position of complete dependence and powerlessness, but in addition, Schindler, the Nazi (normally a signifier of absolute evil), appropriates the position of the actively good man that would normally be embodied by one of the Jews. *Schindler's List* allows us complacently to believe that we are witnessing a re-enactment of history. We believe that we know "what things were really like,"[16] when in reality we indulge in the escapist fantasy that the Nazis really sometimes turned into good guys. In contrast, Tarantino's film seems a testament to the insight that the historical truth is always already out of reach and that all we can access are representations of history, rather than history itself.

Time and again, however, we are seduced into trying to get at the historical truth at the core of Nazism. As Jean Baudrillard reminds us in *The Transparency of Evil*, "there is a perverse fascination with returning to the source of the violence: a collective hallucinatory vision of the historical truth of Evil."[17] However, entry into the realm of history is foreclosed. Baudrillard argues that the filtering of our experience of the world through media is responsible for this lack of access to the past:[18]

History should have been understood while history still existed
... But we have now been transplanted elsewhere, and it is
simply too late, as the television programme *Holocaust*, and
even the film *Shoah*, clearly demonstrated ... [The events of the
past] never will be [understood] because such basic notions as
responsibility, objective causes, or the meaning of history (or the
lack thereof) have disappeared, or are in the process of disap-
pearing. The moral or social conscience is now a phenomenon
entirely governed by the media, and the therapeutic zeal applied
to its resuscitation is itself an index of how little wind it has left.
(Baudrillard, 103)

If we agree with Baudrillard's claim, then it would seem that
Inglourious Basterds is more honest than other Holocaust films,
as it does not claim to be anything other than a representation
referencing other representations, such as Hollywood film, German
film, Spaghetti Westerns, and other national film conventions and
genres. In addition, *Inglourious Basterds* also turns to its advantage
the fact that we cannot deal in anything other than representations.
It dislodges Nazis and Jews from the discursive perpetrator-victim
trap in which they have been caught for decades and frees Jews
to be represented as something other than the eternal victim.
The discursive rescue operation Tarantino's film performs may
have come just in the nick of time, for, as Baudrillard points
out, paradoxically, the more we discuss the Holocaust, the less
believable it is that it ever even occurred:

Consider how continual scrutiny of Nazism, of the gas
chambers and so on, has merely rendered them less and less
comprehensible, so that it has eventually become logical to
ask an incredible question: 'But, in the last reckoning, did all
those things really exist?' The question is perhaps an intol-
erable one, but ... what makes it possible is the media's way
of replacing any event, any idea, any history, with any other,
with the result that the more we scrutinize the facts, the more
carefully we study details with a view to identifying causes, the
greater is the tendency for them to cease to exist, and to cease
to *have existed*. Confusion over the identity of things is thus
a function of our very attempts to substantiate them, to fix
them in memory. This indifference of memory, this indifference

to history, is proportional to our efforts to achieve historical objectivity. (Baudrillard, 104)

Baudrillard feels that we are so "mesmerized by the horror of the [twentieth] century's origins that forgetting is an impossibility" for us, and so "the only way out is denial" (Baudrillard, 104). If we follow Baudrillard's logic, then it was necessary to make a film about Nazis to end all such films now rather than later, when the unreality we feel as we encounter representation after representation of the Holocaust will only have grown. And as we know, Hollywood representations of Nazism and the Holocaust frequently indulge in the pleasures of the depiction of Nazi evil while utilizing some of the same representational conventions as Nazi cinema itself.

In "Fascinating Fascism," Susan Sontag delineates her understanding of fascist aesthetics, and reminds her readers that Hollywood is not immune to the seductive properties of such representational codes:

> Fascist art glorifies surrender, it exalts mindlessness, it glamorizes death. Such art is hardly confined to works labeled as fascist or produced under fascist governments. (To cite films only: Walt Disney's *Fantasia*, Busby Berkeley's *The Gang's All Here*, and Kubrick's *2001* also strikingly exemplify certain formal structures and themes of fascist art.)[19]

The fact that Hollywood has borrowed representational and genre conventions from fascist aesthetics underscores the eminent interchangeability of victim and perpetrator positions in conventional narrative cinema. Here, again, lies one of the reasons for the "[c]onfusion over the identity of things" and for the gradual disappearance of the "responsibility" and "moral or social conscience" Baudrillard refers to. *Inglourious Basterds* illustrates this problem beautifully via its dual representation of the Frederick Zoller character: Zoller appears both as an evil Nazi occupier of France, and—in *Stolz der Nation*, the fictitious Nazi film within the film—as a good Nazi hero who vanquished evil enemies, namely members of the Allied forces. If good and evil are no longer notions that have inherent meaning but are produced purely by generic structures in which historical context merely serves as a decorative backdrop, then the crimes of the Holocaust can truly no longer be grasped as real events.

Inglourious Basterds unmasks Hollywood cinema's fraught relationship with fascist aesthetics. Moreover, Tarantino's film studiously avoids indulging in any of the trappings of these aesthetics. Instead of glorified surrenders, we are shown quivering and fearful Nazi soldiers who fly into a panic at the sight of the Jewish gang of "Basterds" who either unceremoniously kill their Nazi enemies or carve swastikas into their foreheads prior to releasing them.[20] The one seeming exception in this context is a particularly "Aryan"-looking German soldier. Instead of surrendering to the "Basterds" and giving away the location of other German troops, he prefers to die at the hands of the "Basterds." However, his death is deprived of heroic glamour through the manner in which it occurs: one of the "Basterds" known as the "Bear Jew" bludgeons the German soldier's head with a baseball bat. The "Basterds" also do not appear in "characteristic pageantry" (Sontag), marching in formation as a "mass ornament," to use Siegfried Kracauer's terminology.[21] Rather, they are a motley crew of individuals, looking somewhat disheveled in ill-fitting and often mismatched uniforms. And as Georg Seeßlen points out, instead of indulging in the staging of an overdramatized movie death for Hitler and his henchmen, Tarantino's film lets them die a most inglorious death:

> At the end of *Inglourious Basterds*, the representatives of absolute evil are more than dead. They are *kaputt*. Hitler is shot apart, burnt, and torn to pieces. And the film does not even grant him a great exit, no fade-out, no freeze frame, no last gaze into the camera, no insert and no grandiose music. Not even a real image of the process of falling apart, if one wants to be precise.[22]

While Tarantino's film abstains from glorifying death, it does indulge in the representation of the Hollywood stock character of the coldly sadistic SS officer. In contrast to some other Nazi officers in Hollywood cinema, SS Colonel Hans Landa is certainly no ideologue. To the contrary, towards the end of the film when he wants to strike a deal with Aldo Raine (Brad Pitt), the leader of the "Basterds," he has no problem offering his bureaucratic and detection skills to the Americans. Rather than a semi-educated petit-bourgeois, Landa is a polyglot *Bildungsbürger*, a well-educated member of the Austrian middle class with perfect manners and a café denizen's taste for Strudel with whipped cream.[23] Landa's evil is of the elegant sort—not of the purely cartoonish kind we see embodied in the film's Hitler, who echoes the famous parody of the *Führer* Charlie Chaplin gave us in *The Great Dictator* (1940). Colonel Landa is dressed in the SS uniform with which cinema has made us familiar and whose erotic appeal Susan Sontag analyzed, and in numerous scenes he wears the kind of black leather SS coat that has become a signifier for sadism and impending doom even in films not explicitly concerned with Nazism. The sleek representational surface of this perfect movie villain is disrupted in a few places, however. In the film's first chapter, as Colonel Landa talks to LaPadite, the French farmer who is hiding Jews underneath the floorboards of his house, Landa pulls out a ridiculously large pipe and begins to smoke it. The pipe links Landa to touristic images of Alpine coziness, rather than to the cosmopolitanism with which we otherwise associate him.[24] In addition, in the film's last chapter, Landa confronts the actress Bridget von Hammersmark with evidence of her involvement in the planning of an attempt on Hitler's life. Von Hammersmark is helping the "Basterds" with "Operation Kino," a plot designed to kill Hitler and his henchmen during the premiere of *Stolz der Nation*. When she realizes that denying her part in the plot would be useless, von Hammersmark prepares to bargain. For the first time in the film, Landa loses his composure, leaps out of his chair, jumps at von Hammersmark's throat, and brutally strangles her to death with his bare hands. It is arguable whether Landa ever recognizes in Emmanuelle Mimieux the Jewish woman Shosanna he allowed to escape earlier, or if he gives credence to the threat that she embodies. However, he reads the erudite, intelligent and aristocratic actress von Hammersmark as the one woman who has the nerve to try to trick him.[25] Whereas Landa seems to have no trouble ever keeping his cool in the company of men, here he loses his composure. Arguably, then, it is misogyny that turns Landa from an elegant, worldly sadist into a brutish monster who resorts to the most primitive type of physical violence to subdue the female who dared to stand up to him. But Landa's homosocial world goes up in flames. The fire that Shosanna sets together with her Afro-French lover wipes out the Nazis and their cinema—and, on a meta-level, rattles some of the very foundations upon which Hollywood cinema is built.

With *Inglourious Basterds*, Quentin Tarantino has made a Hollywood film about Nazis that not only takes this genre to a new level, but rather—by liberating the Jews from the position of eternal victimhood to which they had seemed to be irrevocably assigned by Hollywood—queers the genre to such an extent that the problematic structures that undergird both it and Hollywood cinema in general are exposed. It remains to be seen whether, after *Inglourious Basterds*, Hollywood can pretend that nothing happened and go back to making Holocaust movies in its accustomed mold. If mainstream Hollywood does go back to its old conventions, it is up to us—critics and audiences—to remember that telling a different kind of story is indeed possible.

Notes

1 Joanna Lindenbaum, "The Villain Speaks the Victim's Language," 121. This volume was published in conjunction with the *Mirroring Evil* exhibit that was on view at the Jewish Museum in New York in 2002.

2 Michael Kimmelman of the *New York Times* described *Hebrew Lessons* as "haunting." Michael Kimmelman, "Evil, the Nazis, and Shock Value," http://www.nytimes.com/2002/03/15/arts/art-review-evil-the-nazis-and-shock-value.html.

3 As concentration camp inmates who had been charged by their Nazi captors with supervising and disciplining their fellow inmates, "Kapos" often enjoyed privileges denied to other prisoners. The Kapo system devised by the Nazis thus served to undermine solidarity among the concentration camp inmates.

4 On this latter point, see also Lindenbaum, 122.

5 Jeffrey Goldberg, "Hollywood's Jewish Avenger," http://www.theatlantic.com/magazine/archive/2009/09/hollywood-8217-s-jewish-avenger/7619/. Goldberg further notes: "Tarantino told me he has received only positive reactions from his Jewish friends. 'The Jewish males that I've known since I've been writing the film and telling them about it, they've just been, "Man, I can't fucking wait for this fucking movie!"' he told me. 'And they tell their dads, and they're like, "I want to see that movie!"' It is not an accident that it took a

non-Jewish director to concoct this story of brutal Jewish revenge. It is difficult to imagine a Jew in Hollywood—each one more self-conscious than the next—portraying Jews as vengeance-seeking knifemen."

6   One might think here both of those who fled from Germany and Austria, and of those who did not return to Europe from stints in Hollywood after the Nazis came to power. Among the émigrés who rose to prominence in Hollywood were Billy Wilder, Otto Preminger, Michael Curtiz a.k.a. Mihály Kertész, and Douglas Sirk a.k.a. Detlev Sierck, to name but a few.

7   Georg Seeßlen, "Nazi-Jäger-Film *Inglourious Basterds:* Mr. Tarantinos Kriegserklärung," *Spiegel Online,* http://www.spiegel. de/kultur/kino/0,1518,642401,00.html. See also Georg Seeßlen, *Quentin Tarantino gegen die Nazis: Alles über "Inglourious Basterds"*, 152. These and all other translations from the German are my own.

8   David Kleingers, "Tarantinos *Inglourious Basterds*: Spiel mir das Lied vom Apfelstrudel," *Spiegel Online,* http://www.spiegel.de/ kultur/kino/0,1518,643524,00.html.

9   In this context, one might also want to remember that while the main thesis of Siegfried Kracauer's *From Caligari to Hitler: A Psychological History of the German Film* originally published in 1947, has been critiqued and amended over the decades, it has by no means lost all of its validity: Weimar cinema can be said to contain both radical critiques of, and fantasies of subjugation under, the power of an absolute authority.

10 Incidentally, Walter Ruttmann, the director of the famous Weimar montage film *Berlin: Die Sinfonie der Großstadt/Berlin: Symphony of the City* (1927), assisted Riefenstahl in the making of *Triumph of the Will.* The collaboration between Ruttmann and Riefenstahl is yet another reminder that one cannot assume a radical dichotomy of Weimar cinema and Nazi film production.

11 This omission is noted by Seeßlen in *Tarantino gegen die Nazis,* 52.

12 In this context, see also Robert von Dassanowsky, "'You Wouldn't Even Believe What Your Eyes Can See': Cinema's Messianism and Fascist Reflection in John Schlesinger's *The Day of the Locust,*" http://www.sensesofcinema.com/2006/feature-articles/day_locust/. Dassanowsky's analysis highlights the ways in which Schlesinger's film both emulates and critiques fascist aesthetics.

13 Manohla Dargis, "*Inglourious Basterds* (2009): Tarantino Avengers

in Nazi Movieland, http://movies.nytimes.com/2009/08/21/movies/21inglourious.html.

14 Susan Sontag, "Fascinating Fascism." http://www.nybooks.com/articles/archives/1975/feb/06/fascinating-fascism/.

15 "Schindler's List: Myth, Movie and Memory," 24–31.

16 "Wie es denn eigentlich gewesen ist." See Walter Benjamin's critique of historism in "Über den Begriff der Geschichte," in *Illuminationen* (Frankfurt am Main: Suhrkamp, 1977), 251–61; here: 253.

17 Jean Baudrillard, "Necrospective," in *The Transparency of Evil: Essays on Extreme Phenomena*, trans. James Benedict (London/New York: Verso, 1993), 101–13; here: 101.

18 James Young, too, asks: "How is a post-Holocaust generation of artists supposed to 'remember' events they never experienced directly?" While Young is keenly aware of our "inability to know the history of the Holocaust outside of the ways it has been passed down," he is far less cynical than Baudrillard about our ability still to access this history via testimonials and history books, and the ability of those born after to engage in remembrance of the Holocaust. See James E. Young, *At Memory's Edge: After-Images of the Holocaust in Contemporary Art and Architecture* (New Haven and London: Yale UP, 2000), 1–2.

19 Sontag, "Fascinating Fascism." In his "Nazi-Jäger" piece, Georg Seeßlen, too, points out that *"[i]n der faschistischen Ästhetik stirbt der Held, um zum ewigen Bild zu werden, zu jenem Märtyrer, der immer im Geiste mitmarschiert"* ("in fascist aesthetics, the hero dies to be turned into an eternal image, into the martyr who always marches along in spirit"), and he reminds his readers that Tarantino's film refuses to reproduce these aesthetics.

20 The Nazis' fixation on questions of the legibility of otherness (and in particular racial otherness) is well known, and it is, of course, linked to a long tradition of physiognomic thought in German intellectual history, as Richard T. Gray has detailed in his *About Face: German Physiognomic Thought from Lavater to Auschwitz* (Detroit: Wayne State University Press, 2004). The Nazis' concerns about the legibility—and fears of the potential illegibility—of otherness have been infamously dramatized in Veit Harlan's 1940 Nazi film *Jud Süß/Jew Suess*, and these concerns, of course, find one of their most harrowing expressions in the numbers tattooed onto the arms of Nazi concentration camp inmates. The fact that the Basterds mark many of their Nazi enemies by carving swastikas into their foreheads may be read as their retort to the Nazis' fears surrounding the (il)

legibility of race: by indelibly marking their enemies with swastikas, the Basterds make legible their enemies' adherence to fascist ideology.

21 Siegfried Kracauer, "The Mass Ornament," in *The Mass Ornament. Weimar Essays*, trans. and ed. Thomas Y. Levin (Cambridge, MA/ London: Harvard University Press, 1995), 75–86.

22 Seeßlen, *Tarantino gegen die Nazis*, 139.

23 On this point, see also Seeßlen, *Tarantino gegen die Nazis*, 145–46.

24 Seeßlen reads the pipe differently, namely as an attribute we associate with Sherlock Holmes. The association of Landa the "Jew Hunter" with the master detective is as apt as it is disconcerting.

25 One wonders whether, via the von Hammersmark character, Tarantino engages obliquely with films such as *Stauffenberg* (2004) and the Tom Cruise vehicle *Valkyrie* (2008). Both of these films dramatize the Stauffenberg plot, the failed 1944 attempt by mostly aristocratic Nazi officers to assassinate Hitler. To an extent, the Stauffenberg plot has allowed Germans to cling to the idea that educated, high-ranking, high-class members of the military tended not to support Hitler, and the recent German film about the events surrounding the plot is further evidence of continued interest in this reading. With von Hammersmark, Tarantino, too, gives us an aristocratic character, but he gives us a hyper-feminine but assertive woman rather than yet another version of heroic masculinity as embodied by Tom Cruise. In addition, the name "von Hammersmark" is vaguely reminiscent of the name of the director of the 2006 German film *Das Leben der Anderen/The Lives of Others*, Florian Henckel von Donnersmarck. Tarantino's film may thus also comment implicitly on the problematic rendering of GDR history found in *Das Leben der Anderen*. Whereas von Donnersmarck's film makes an implicit claim to represent German history, Tarantino's film makes it abundantly clear that we are watching fiction, a pure fantasy scenario.

Works cited

Baudrillard, Jean. "Necrospective." In *The Transparency of Evil: Essays On Extreme Phenomena*, translated by James Benedict. London/New York: Verso, 1993, 101–13

Benjamin, Walter. "Über den Begriff der Geschichte." In *Illuminationen*. Frankfurt am Main: Suhrkamp, 1977, 252–61.

Berlin: Die Sinfonie der Großstadt. Directed by Walter Ruttmann. Germany, 1927.

Casablanca. Directed by Michael Curtiz. USA, 1942.

Close Encounters of the Third Kind. Directed by Steven Spielberg. USA, 1977.

Dargis, Manohla. "*Inglourious Basterds*: Tarantino Avengers in Nazi Movieland." *New York Times*, August 21, 2009. http://movies. nytimes.com/2009/08/21/movies/21inglourious.html (accessed December 11, 2010).

Das Leben der Anderen/The Lives of Others. Directed by Florian Henckel von Donnersmarck. Germany, 2006.

Dassanowsky, Robert von. " 'You Wouldn't Even Believe What Your Eyes Can See': Cinema's Messianism and Fascist Reflection in John Schlesinger's *The Day of the Locust*." *Senses of Cinema*, 39, 2006. http://www.sensesofcinema.com/2006/feature-articles/day_locust/ (accessed September 3, 2011).

Die weiße Hölle vom Piz Palü/The White Hell of Pitz Palu. Directed by Arnold Fanck and G. W. Pabst. Germany, 1929.

Gebürtig. Directed by Robert Schindel and Lukas Stepanik. Austria, 2002.

Goldberg, Jeffrey. "Hollywood's Jewish Avenger." *The Atlantic*, September 2009. http://www.theatlantic.com/magazine/ archive/2009/09/hollywood-8217-s-jewish-avenger/7619/ (accessed December 11, 2010).

Gray, Richard T. *About Face: German Physiognomic Thought from Lavater to Auschwitz*. Detroit: Wayne State University Press, 2004.

The Great Dictator. Directed by Charles Chaplin. USA, 1940.

Hoberman, J., et al. "Schindler's List: Myth, Movie and Memory." *Village Voice*, March 29, 1994.

Inglourious Basterds. Directed by Quentin Tarantino. USA, 2009.

Jud Süß/Jew Suess. Directed by Veit Harlan. Germany, 1940.

Kimmelman, Michael. "Evil, the Nazis, and Shock Value." *New York Times*, March 15, 2002. http://www.nytimes.com/2002/03/15/arts/ art-review-evil-the-nazis-and-shock-value.html (accessed December 11, 2010).

Kleingers, David. "Tarantinos *Inglourious Basterds*: Spiel mir das Lied vom Apfelstrudel," *Spiegel Online*, August 19, 2009. http://www.spiegel.de/ kultur/kino/0,1518,643524,00.html (accessed December 10, 2010).

Kracauer, Siegfried. *From Caligari to Hitler: A Psychological History of the German Film*. Princeton: Princeton University Press, 1974.

—"The Mass Ornament." In *The Mass Ornament. Weimar Essays*, translated and edited by Thomas Y. Levin. Cambridge, MA and London: Harvard University Press, 1995, 75–86.

Lindenbaum, Joanna. "The Villain Speaks the Victim's Language."
  In *Mirroring Evil: Nazi Imagery/Recent Art*, edited by Norman L.
  Kleeblatt. New Brunswick and London: Rutgers UP, 2001, 21.
Saving Private Ryan. Directed by Steven Spielberg. USA, 1998.
Schindler's List. Directed by Steven Spielberg. USA, 1993.
Seeßlen, Georg. "Nazi-Jäger-Film *Inglourious Basterds*: Mr. Tarantinos
  Kriegserklärung," *Spiegel Online*, August 16, 2009. http://www.
  spiegel.de/kultur/kino/0,1518,642401,00.html (accessed December 11,
  2010).
—*Quentin Tarantino gegen die Nazis: Alles über "Inglourious Basterds."*
  Berlin: Bertz+Fischer, 2009.
Sontag, Susan. "Fascinating Fascism." *The New York Review of Books*,
  February 6, 1975. htttp://www.nybooks.com/articles/archives/1975/
  feb/06/fascinating-fascism/ (accessed December 10, 2010).
Stauffenberg. Directed by Jo Baier. Germany, 2004.
Triumph des Willens/Triumph of the Will. Directed by Leni Riefenstal.
  Germany, 1935.
Valkyrie. Directed by Bryan Singer. USA/Germany, 2008.
Young, James E. *At Memory's Edge: After-Images of the Holocaust in
  Contemporary Art and Architecture*. New Haven and London: Yale
  University Press, 2000.

3

"A slight duplication of efforts": redundancy and the excessive camera in *Inglourious Basterds*

Chris Fujiwara

At the end of the opening credits, a white-on-black title appears: Chapter One/Once upon a time ... /in Nazi-occupied France. It is the first of five titles that divide *Inglourious Basterds* into chapters. After the title, the first shot is a brightly lit daytime long shot of a farm, with a man whom we will shortly identify as Perrier LaPadite chopping wood. Over this shot, the film superimposes another title: 1941. The laconic specificity of 1941 denies the allusive expansiveness suggested by the chapter title, limits the free movement of time that has already begun to spread out in a leisurely manner over the film, and, to the narrative-as-legend announced by "once upon a time," counters a historical date. It is as if the film were the composite work of two editors, neither of them mindful of the other's intentions.

A parallel in Tarantino's work might be the main title of *Death Proof*, which replaces the briefly glimpsed "Quentin Tarantino's Thunder Bolt," as if it were the retitling of a carelessly assembled re-release version of a film that had already circulated under the other name. The opening titles of *Inglourious Basterds* give the cast names in several different typefaces, plus the hand-scrawled letters of the main title, suggesting that the film is a composite of different films. This will, in fact prove to be true in at least two senses. Like earlier Tarantino films, *Inglourious Basterds* interweaves several different plotlines that, for much of the film, are functionally independent of one another; moreover, the film incorporates as films-within-the-film not only *Stolz der Nation* (Nation's Pride), which was shot by a director other than Tarantino (Eli Roth, who also plays Donny in *Inglourious Basterds*), but also the film made by Shosanna and Marcel as a final message to the Nazis. Or it is as if the film had to start twice: first as a fable set in a historical place and period, second as a narrative inscribing itself more precisely in history.

Or, more simply, as if the film were obsessed with giving information, to the point of not recognizing when enough information has been given, or when the same information has been given twice in two different forms. This is a well-known problem with narrative, and with narrative cinema: when has enough information been given? Where would be that rigorous line marking off the adequate from the excessive, and how can it be recognized? But in *Inglourious Basterds*, excessive information is not merely an ordinary hazard of storytelling but a thematic preoccupation, even a principle of the narration.

Another example from Tarantino's film will indicate the scope of the question. Chapter Five (the night of the premiere of *Stolz der Nation*) begins with four progressively closer shots, linked by dissolves, showing Shosanna, in a red dress, standing at a circular window in her movie theater at night. In the fourth shot, she turns and starts to walk away, cuing a cut to an extremely close shot of her face. This shot starts a new series of shots (interrupted by a long flashback sequence showing the making, processing, and editing of Shosanna's film) in which Shosanna makes up her face, loads a revolver and puts it in her purse, and puts on a hat and veil.

The first series of four shots is remarkable because both Shosanna's figure and the camera remain static until her movement in the fourth shot puts an end to the series. The lack of movement by either the character or the camera calls attention to the redundancy that is the principle of the series. Each shot simply "says" the same thing, the same configuration of feminine body, red dress, mirror images (a redundancy within the single image), red Nazi flags (in the background through the window). Above all, the shots testify to the image as a construction, a composition: Shosanna has already become her own fixed image.

The choice of David Bowie's "Cat People (Putting Out Fire)" (from Paul Schrader's *Cat People*) to accompany the entire sequence is apt, because the lyrics underline not only Shosanna's own self-control and the slow-burning endurance of her desire for revenge ("I can stare for a thousand years/Colder than the moon"), but also the redundancy of the camerawork and editing. Bowie's phrase "putting out fire with gasoline," suggesting a drive to intensify a feeling that remains essentially unchanging, repeats the impulse of the film to come closer to an image that itself doesn't change, either in its own internal coordination or in the information it imparts to the viewer.

Deciding whether or not a given detail in a film is excessive is, however, not just a matter of information. The farmhouse sequence in *Inglourious Basterds* is entirely based on the principle of redundancy and takes place under the sign of redundancy. As Landa begins interrogating LaPadite, the farmer observes that the Germans already searched his house for Jews. "Like any enterprise," Landa replies, "when under new management, there is always a slight duplication of efforts." Duplication is indeed one of the main themes of the sequence, from almost the beginning, as Landa confirms what he says he has already heard: that LaPadite has beautiful daughters. The scene continues with the SS officer asking the farmer to verify facts that are already written in Landa's notebook. A remarkable feature of this long set-piece scene, which concludes with the SS's massacre of the Dreyfus family (whom LaPadite has been hiding under the floorboards) and the escape of Shosanna, is that even when it elicits hitherto unrecorded information, the interrogation of LaPadite appears to be completely unnecessary, since LaPadite merely agrees silently to what Landa already seems to know: that the Dreyfuses are hiding under the floorboards. The only new information he provides is the area where they are hiding, a piece of knowledge that it would seem unnecessary for Landa to go to such trouble to obtain, since to carry out the massacre he simply has his men shoot blindly through the floor with machine guns.

Visual signals indicate that the informational content of the dialogue is not the point of the scene. During the interrogation of LaPadite, the camera progressively becomes detached from the dialogue. After Landa has LaPadite clear his family from the room, the scene is shot for a while in a fairly conventional manner, with alternating medium close shots of the two men. A turning point comes when LaPadite says that he has heard that the Dreyfuses escaped to Spain. After he says this, Tarantino cuts to an extremely close shot on LaPadite's face. The shot pans down to reframe the bowl of LaPadite's pipe as he lights it with a match, pans up again to frame a tight close-up of his face as he puffs on the pipe repeatedly, getting it lit, then pans down with his hand as he drops the match into an ashtray on the table. The shot covers an unusual amount of detail for such a seemingly trivial action. Undoubtedly the director is seeking to build the suspense of a scene that might threaten to become rather boring: Tarantino uses an extreme close-up both to suggest the psychological pressure the man is under and to highlight the fact that the elaborate routine of lighting and smoking the pipe is an attempt to relieve that pressure. The shot thus tells us, for the first time in the scene, that LaPadite is lying, i.e., that there is something at stake in the scene apart from the denotational content of the dialogue and apart from the social-political portrayal of power and submission.

The effect of the shot is not limited to these functions. The shot creates a certain oddness, a sense of things not fitting, since LaPadite's procedure with his pipe is pointedly irrelevant to the dialogue and even attempts to defeat the informational function of language. Tarantino participates in this attempt by devoting a detailed close-up to the process, but in its excessiveness, the close-up seems to subject LaPadite to the requirement of giving information, delivering him again into the linguistic trap from which he seeks to escape.

After LaPadite drops the match into the ashtray, Tarantino cuts to a medium two-shot of the two men, as LaPadite lists the members of the Dreyfus family. The shot is initially static, but as LaPadite goes through the performance of recalling the name of Mrs. Dreyfus' brother, the camera begins a slow traveling movement around the table and behind Landa's back, stopping when it reaches a position almost exactly opposite from its initial one, as LaPadite attempts to recall the age of the young Dreyfus boy. The irrelevance of the circular camera movement to the informational content of the dialogue exposes the dialogue as a ritual; the camera movement is related to levels of the scene that are not articulated through the dialogue. Since Landa already knows who the members of the family are, getting LaPadite to confirm the information is a mere going-through-the-motions, of which the excessive camera movement is a correlative. Moreover, by moving from a position across the table from LaPadite to a position close to him, the camera suggests that LaPadite knows something that he is not revealing and that is not written in Landa's notes. At the same time, the camera aligns the viewer with LaPadite, going literally behind Landa's back in order to move us closer to the farmer, preparing us for the moment, shortly to come, when the film divulges to us LaPadite's secret knowledge.

Tarantino now cuts to an extreme close-up of part of Landa's notes: three typewritten names, Miriam, *Shoshanna*, and Amos.[1] Next to the name Amos, as LaPadite is heard on the soundtrack guessing at the boy's age, Landa's pen writes "9–10." This close-up too is excessive, placing exceptional weight (through the size of the shot and the unusualness of the device of the insert) on information that has already been revealed in the dialogue and that appears to be of no great importance. We might say, however, that the insert has five functions. The first two are relatively trivial: to highlight the referential, confirmatory, repetitious nature of the dialogue by placing it in direct contact with the text of which it is the double; and to heighten the suspense, again, by magnifying a seemingly unimportant detail.

The third function of the insert is also perhaps minor but not negligible: this is to show us how the name Shosanna is (mis) spelled, with an additional "h" and a double "n." The latter feature of her proper name will again be doubly inscribed in the film: a superimposed title identifying Emmanuelle Mimieux, Paris cinema proprietor, as the relocated and renamed Shosanna Dreyfus, appears over a freeze-frame showing her on a ladder as, in the process of taking down letters from the cinema marquee, she tosses a red "N" to the ground. The freezing of the frame suspends the "N" in its flight, lending it a contradictory significance. At the same time and in the same image as she is shown divesting herself of her "N," unspelling her own name, the film, by the superimposed title, establishes her identity and re-binds her to her discarded name.

The fourth function is perhaps weightier, though also more doubtful: to suggest the possible emotional stakes for Shosanna, who will be the sole survivor of the massacre that is about to occur. We are told that the other victims are her parents and her uncle, and the insert of the typewritten note (together with LaPadite's voice-off) puts a special emphasis on the fourth victim, Shosanna's much younger brother and in particular on his age. This brother is never mentioned again in the film, but the insert allows us to infer that the traumatic power of his death will be especially great.

The insert has a fifth function, which relates to what it not only represents, but introduces into the film. Landa's notebook is the archive, the legal, historical record, and as such it is the reverse of the experience of the characters as the film shows it. It is important to the film to show this reversal, in its form of a denial of the truth that the film will reveal. This is one of the conflicts of the film: between the experience as constructed and brought to light by the film (and which, in some sense, only the film can know, or which would not exist without the film) and history as recorded and maintained in a text that exists outside the film. The insert of Landa's notebook is a reference to this exterior text, which will be invoked again when, in his negotiations with Raine, Landa asks grandly, "What shall the history books read?"

To confirm that this fifth function is indeed one that the shot assigns itself, the shot that immediately follows the notebook insert directly activates the buried dimension of the scene and instances the power of film to constitute a denied reality. It starts as a close shot of LaPadite, taken from a similar angle to the camera's position at the end of the semi-circular traveling movement just before the insert. Once again unmotivated by anything in the dialogue or action, the camera slowly moves down the man's body, down his leg, and across the floorboards, revealing Miriam Dreyfus (Eva Löbau) lying with her hand pressed tightly to her mouth; in the background, other members of the family are indistinctly visible.

The movement of the camera under the floor is no doubt the most striking of Tarantino's "unmotivated" shots in the farmhouse sequence. This is because, unlike the previous unmotivated or weakly motivated, excessive-seeming shots—the close-up of LaPadite's procedure with his pipe and match, the semi-circular camera movement around the table, the insert of the notebook—this shot gives new information that is directly relevant to the narrative. On the other hand, the camera movement rather aggressively violates an unwritten law of what might be called classical film aesthetics. This law has been articulated in interviews with practitioners of classical cinema in a form pertinent to the present analysis, since the example given involves camera height. This is screenwriter and director Norman Krasna's version:

> My masters were Lubitsch and Wilder. They, maybe, sometimes, made mistakes, but their standards! Every frame, every shot had to mean something. Unless you work with someone like René Clair, you don't understand about the technique of these old-timers. When René Clair came to Hollywood, he was considered one of the world's greatest directors; they gave him a dinner and introduced him as that. If I had a scene at a table and then wanted to cut underneath to show a couple playing footsie, he wouldn't allow that. "Why did the camera go under the table?" he would ask. "The camera went there—," I'd say— "What do you mean?" "No," he'd say, "something has to fall off the table before the camera can go under the table. And I have to have a tick or something, a thread that has to be established earlier." Jesus, the standards of these people! All the finger-points, the wonderful chess game, that's what I like.[2]

Tarantino could have easily found a less obtrusive way to reveal the Dreyfuses' presence and LaPadite's complicity, a way more in keeping with the standards of Krasna's "old-timers," whose rules, after all, are not entirely disregarded even in the Hollywood of today. For example, the farmer could have noticed a boy's toy lying in an inconspicuous area of the floor. Amos having already been mentioned, and it having been established at the start of the scene that the members of LaPadite's family are all girls, the audience would understand the significance of the toy; LaPadite might have risen and crossed to it on some pretext and surreptitiously hidden it from Landa with his foot, cuing a camera movement or a cut revealing the Dreyfuses under the floorboards. But to have done this would have violated one of the laws of the film, which is that no one can hide anything from Landa. The same thing would have happened had Tarantino, even more simply, shown that the Dreyfuses were there at the beginning of the sequence. That strategy would have also removed all ambiguity from LaPadite's behavior, so that the other weakly motivated shots in the scene would have been, if not impossible, at least ineffective. If those shots work, it's because the viewer is in a position of incomplete knowledge: we do not know why we are being shown LaPadite lighting his pipe, or the notebook in close-up, or why the camera moves to the other side of the table; and our lack of knowledge is a hidden justification for these outwardly aberrant devices. Tarantino wants to bring us to share the position of LaPadite—to know that the Dreyfuses are there and to feel the psychological pressure of Landa's questioning—but he wants this to happen gradually, so that the scene retains its ambiguity (and the revelation of the Dreyfuses comes off as momentous); moreover, Tarantino wants us, for reasons that will become clearer later in this essay, also to share the point of view of Landa.

René Clair's criteria for an unusual camera placement, according to Krasna, would seem to be twofold. First, the placement has to be motivated by an event that is normally visible within the pre-existing world of the film (something falling off the table, as seen from the eye-level of people sitting at the table). Second, the placement has to be justified in terms of previously established long-term formal and narrative strategies of the film ("a thread that has to be established earlier"). Neither is true of Tarantino's camera movement, the unusualness of which is compounded by having the camera accomplish the feat of passing through the floor.

The downward movement of the camera proves indeed to be part of a "thread" in *Inglourious Basterds*, a theme of height, but since this is a thread that the movement establishes for the first time, rather than a previously established thread that the movement continues, the first-time viewer of the film is unable to recognize it as part of a thematic pattern. This pattern soon emerges. As their dialogue continues, Landa compares Germans to hawks and Jews to rats (linking the height theme to race and animality). There is a series of shots from directly overhead: two of the Dreyfuses staring up through a crack between floorboards; the SS soldiers firing their machine guns through the floor; Landa walking across the room (in a traveling shot that will be repeated in a shot of Shosanna at the *Stolz der Nation* premiere); Shosanna (seen from Landa's point of view above) escaping from her hiding place.

Amid this profusion of overhead shots, only one shot is taken from a markedly low angle: the shot of Landa as he sees Shosanna escaping. Thus, the film forces the audience to identify with the position of the "hawk" (or a godlike observer), except for the one moment when Landa the "Jew Hunter" is seen in relation to Shosanna (seen from the space that she occupies, though not from her literal point of view, since she is not looking up at him). The implications of this directorial choice are crucial. It establishes, first, the film's determining concept of the reversibility of the relationship between victim and persecutor. Second, the paired low-angle/high-angle shots of Landa and Shosanna hint that the two characters share a dual relationship that is of special importance (as I will later discuss). Third, the film acknowledges, by its emphasis on the high angle, that the place from which the maximum can be seen is the most privileged and desirable place and that, as an entertainment film, *Inglourious Basterds* is in the business of enabling the audience to occupy this place (and "business is a-boomin'," to quote Lt. Aldo Raine). That this is also, in the situation, the place of Nazis who are hunting and killing Jews may or may not be felt by the audience as uncomfortable. I would say that the narrative mechanism of the film prevents the audience from feeling much discomfort over this. The high vantage point, the point of maximum visibility, is occupied by various characters in turn, and the audience is encouraged to identify with the place itself rather than with the occupant. The moral implications of this mechanism are no doubt worth examining, but the orientation of this essay will be more formal, or structural: toward the mechanism as it functions in relation to excess and redundancy.

Later in the film, Tarantino again uses a downward camera movement to reveal information that is unknown to the public, normal view of a scene. At the premiere of *Stolz der Nation*, two of the Basterds, Donny and Omar, posing as Italian members of Bridget von Hammersmark's entourage, are seated in the middle of an orchestra row. The camera cranes down their bodies to their legs; then a round image-within-the-image pops up over the shot, showing the explosives strapped to both men's ankles. The pop-up internal image adds a further arbitrariness to a camera movement that is already (like the camera movement that first reveals the Dreyfuses hiding under the floorboards) marked by the arbitrary intervention of the director in managing narrative information.

The pop-up image belongs to a range of specialized devices that the film uses to reveal information directly to the audience, outside the circuit of the narrative world and without using the pretexts or alibis available there. The two downward camera movements just discussed belong to the outward fringe of this range, where it merges with the narrative circuit: the camera movements, even though marked as direct address since they appear to say "Now look *here*," or "But what these people don't know is ... " remain within the diegetic space (the same can be said of the elaborate crane shots that sweep from the balcony to the lobby and back during the sequence of the premiere). Other, more unequivocally authorial, devices for directly revealing information include the superimposed titles that introduce Goebbels, Göring, Bormann, and other figures, and that identify Emmanuelle Mimieux as Shosanna Dreyfus; passages of voiceover narration that explain Hugo Stiglitz's background or the flammability of nitrate film; and the flashbacks that give background information on Stiglitz, Francesca, and other characters. These flashbacks, in turn, approach the more conventional, less obtrusive use of flashback exemplified by the shot of Landa kicking a bundle of dynamite under Goebbels' seat in the movie theater: this flashback also serves the function of revealing information to the audience, but it is naturalized by being accompanied by the diegetic speech of Landa, which the image amplifies and explains.

Within the narrative regime established in the farmhouse sequence and presided over by the directorial figure of Landa, all knowledge is available and nothing can remain hidden. Because of this, the image necessarily becomes excess: an unveiling of what can never be veiled and a gratuitous exercise of cinematic power. The process by which the image becomes excess is made clear in the film-within-a-film of *Stolz der Nation*, which appears to be nothing but a series of functionally interchangeable scenes of Fredrick killing Americans. If, for the Basterds, brutality and torture are a kind of cinema ("Watching Donny beat Nazis to death is the closest we ever get to going to the movies," says Raine), the Nazi viewers of *Stolz der Nation* receive the deeds of Fredrick as a pure spectacle of serial killing, characteristically presented with emphasis on extreme contrasts of height: Fredrick, from his tower, shoots down at the advancing Americans, or causes them to fall to their deaths from another high place.

The most prominent of the excessive details in the farmhouse sequence—Landa's savoring LaPadite's milk, LaPadite lighting his pipe—have to do with oral consumption (with the mouth, the organ of speech, underlying the linguistic nature of Landa's game with the farmer). Later in the film, in the scene of Landa questioning Shosanna in the café, Landa's praise of the strudel elevates that dessert to a level of importance equal to the ostensible theme of their dialogue (the suitability of her cinema for the premiere of *Stolz der Nation*), an elevation in which Tarantino participates by devoting a series of extreme close-ups to the arrival of the crème fraîche, Shosanna's fork slicing into her strudel, and finally Landa extinguishing his cigarette in the cream atop his strudel (a shot that recalls Jessie Royce Landis putting out her cigarette in the yolk of a fried egg in Hitchcock's *To Catch a Thief*).

This close-up is another of the downward movements of the film: Landa's gesture is one of moving his hand down, putting the cigarette out (it is doubled, later, by Marcel's flicking *his* lit cigarette toward a pile of nitrate film), and, to follow it, the camera must, again (as in the farmhouse shot revealing the Dreyfuses), take up an unusual point of view, one not belonging to either character in the scene and not part of the informational content and themes of the dialogue. For all that, the strudel shots do not quite come off as direct address by the filmmaker, but, like the shot of LaPadite lighting his pipe, exist in an ambiguous zone where direct address merges into the narrative circuit: the ambiguity comes from the possibility that the details shown have a narrative function that is covert, related to the secret intentions of the characters. In this scene, unusually, Landa appears not to realize his interlocutor's secret (that Emmanuelle is Shosanna), but the emphasis on the strudel suggests that he at least suspects she *has* a secret and is playing a hidden game with her (as he did with LaPadite, over the milk). Tarantino strengthens this suggestion by having Landa announce ominously, "There was something else I wanted to ask you—" and then take a long pause, during which the camera keeps Landa's face in a taut close-up (which recalls the moment when he compels LaPadite to confess) before continuing, "but for the life of me, I can't remember what it was." As he concludes, "It must not have been important," Landa puts out his cigarette in the crème fraîche: the gesture closes (this episode of) Landa's game with a light brutality that dismisses its props (not just the strudel and the cream but also the German cigarette to which Landa has also called attention in his dialogue) and renders them unusable.

Landa here allows Shosanna to escape from him a second time. This (perhaps unconscious) second gesture of release signals, perhaps even more strongly than the first one (Landa, outside the doorway of the farmhouse, lowering his gun and shouting "Au revoir, Shoshanna"; his declining to shoot is echoed, in the café scene, by his suspension of the interrogation) an occult complicity between the two characters, which Landa's later participation in Operation Kino will certify. Landa and Shosanna can be seen as split parts of a single will to mastery, a will that we can identify with the director function.

As the dual emphasis on excess and height in *Inglourious Basterds* may perhaps suggest, one of Tarantino's concerns in the film is to make his function as director thematically explicit. One way of doing this is through the proliferation of the characters that perform an analogous function. Not only are Shosanna and Landa directors, but so is Goebbels, so is Raine (who casts the Basterds and recruits Stiglitz in a notably Hollywood-like manner, and who is also an artist with his mutilating knife), and so are Churchill and Fenech, the British general in command of Operation Kino. Bridget takes on a director's role in choosing the basement tavern as the site for her rendezvous with Hicox and the Basterds ("One could even say that Operation Kino was her brainchild," says General Fenech); there, the Gestapo major Hellstrom becomes the "director" of the game of identity in which they all take part, a game that involves the assignment of roles. Of the major characters, almost the only one who does not at some point perform the director function is Fredrick; it is as if the traditional figure of the male action hero were somehow, in Tarantino's eyes, disqualified from directing.

The drive to self-reference becomes quite visible in the last shot of the film, or more exactly, the cut from that last shot, a medium close low-angle shot (again, height is marked) of Raine and Utivich looking down admiringly at the swastika Raine has just carved into Landa's forehead, to the title card "Written and directed by

Quentin Tarantino." Raine's line—"You know something, Utivich? I think this just might be my masterpiece"—claims an authorial function for the character, equates facial mutilation with art (as Raine did in an earlier scene, in a similar low-angle two-shot as he and Donny look down at another of Raine's victims: "You know how you get to Carnegie Hall, don't you? Practice"), and also identifies the writer-director's function with the Basterds' project of terror and revenge, while also characterizing filmmaking as a serial activity and thus inscribing the entirety of *Inglourious Basterds* within repetition.

Exaggerating authorial power, the camera position glorifies Raine, placing him in the position occupied by Landa at the climax of the farmhouse scene, when he sees Shosanna through the cracks in the floorboards. Landa's exceptional sight matches Tarantino's ability to show, and both are reinscribed, at the end of the film, in Raine's skill at marking, or writing. Nor is it insignificant that the low camera position of the final shot espouses the point of view of the mutilated Landa: the shot confirms the reversibility of vision staged in the farmhouse sequence and recalls Landa's self-praise in his conversation with LaPadite: "The feature that makes me such an effective hunter of the Jews is, as opposed to most German soldiers, I can think like a Jew." In the visual terms of the film as established by Landa's racial allegory of hawks and rats, thinking like a Jew means abandoning the heights of the hawk and imaginatively occupying the low, inconspicuous place of the rat.

As director figures, Landa and Shosanna both take on a certain ambiguity that colors the way the audience views them. The point is not merely that Landa's charm makes it difficult for us to hate him, or that Shosanna's coldness toward Fredrick makes her less likeable (since, though he, too, is an ambiguous, mixed character, Fredrick is endowed by the film with enough positive attributes that we perhaps want Shosanna to respond to his courtship more generously). The more important point is that Landa's status as the one who knows, and the one for whom knowledge is all-important, makes it impossible for the viewer (who comes before this film, as before all films, in the position of one who seeks to learn) not to identify with him, whereas Shosanna's progressive transformation into pure image makes it difficult even to see her as human.

In the farmhouse scene, Landa, after getting the reluctant LaPadite to acknowledge that the French people call him "the Jew

Hunter," claims that far from being offended by the nickname, "I love my unofficial title, precisely because I've earned it." In his interview with Raine and Utivich, however, Landa appears to repudiate the name. When Raine says, "So you're the Jew Hunter," Landa snaps back: "I'm a detective. A damn good detective. Finding people is my specialty." He goes on, defensively: "So naturally I worked for the Nazis finding people. And, yes, some of them were Jews. But Jew Hunter? Just a name that stuck." By casting himself in the role of detective, Landa dissociates himself from the Nazis. The German detective, as represented notably in Weimar cinema by the character of Wenk in Fritz Lang's *Dr. Mabuse, der Spieler* (*Dr. Mabuse, The Gambler*) (1922) and Lohmann in Lang's *M* (1931) and *Das Testament des Dr. Mabuse* (*The Testament of Dr. Mabuse*) (filmed in 1932 and banned by the new German government in 1933), is a figure from a period prior to the consolidation of power by the Nazis. Moreover, the detective is an isolated individual, someone who must, in order to do his job well, stand apart from the mainstream of society and mingle with the lowest classes (as Landa does in interacting with Jews and the French people who shelter them). Such a figure is, obviously, antithetical to totalitarianism.

In his individuality and his detective function, Landa recalls Inspector Gruber, a character in Fritz Lang's 1943 anti-Nazi film *Hangmen Also Die!*, which deals with the assassination of Heydrich. (Landa's invocation of Heydrich and his "Hangman" nickname in the farmhouse scene of *Inglourious Basterds* may be a veiled allusion to Lang's film.) In a famous analysis, Jean-Louis Comolli and François Géré show that the fiction of *Hangmen Also Die!* constructs an opposition between two terms—the Nazi occupation and the Czech resistance—that inevitably come to be seen as equivalent.[3] (In *Inglourious Basterds*, too, a logic of equivalence functions. Like the Nazis, Shosanna and the Basterds are mass murderers. Moreover, both the Nazis and their opponents use cinema: the battle is one between representation and representation—"taking on the Jews at their own game," as Churchill says in the film.) Meanwhile, among all the characters in *Hangmen Also Die!*, it is Gruber, the Gestapo policeman who is charged with unraveling the conspiracy to kill Heydrich, with whom the audience identifies. Unlike the other Nazis, he is "devoid of uniform or ritual. He does not give the automatic 'Heil Hitler' salute. He makes no profession of Nazism ... If he is so concerned with the truth, it is for its own sake, and not for any political reason or from practical necessity. He considers the secret as a *challenge* which must be fully accepted."[4] Gruber's refusal to be ensnared by appearances and lies gives him "a subjective element" that is completely lacking not only in the other Nazis but also in the members of the Czech resistance: "he is not driven like the other characters by a principle which programs him from head to foot while robbing him of his own substance"[5] (139).

Landa is free of the commitment to Nazism that glows so darkly in Major Hellstrom, who is marked in other ways (by his fierce intellect and a special relation to language—in Hellstrom's case, an ear for German accents) as Landa's double. Though a racist (as he reveals when, on being told by Shosanna that Marcel is a good projectionist, he replies mildly, "One could see where that might be a good trade for them"—i.e., Negroes), Landa does not appear to be a person consumed by loathing for Jews. Rather, he seems proud of his ability to "think like a Jew" and makes a point of saying that, unlike Hitler and Goebbels, he does not think it insulting to liken Jews to rats but instead founds the comparison on the objective basis of the threatening nature of the environment in which both must try to survive. More subtly, Christoph Waltz as Landa uses vocal mannerisms that sound markedly "Jewish." An example is the very first English line he speaks: "While I'm very familiar with you and your family, I have no way of knowing if you are familiar with who *I* am." The high-pitched voice (startlingly different from the voice he has been using to speak French), the somewhat broken rhythm, and the emphasis on "I" are all reminiscent of the voice of Woody Allen. In adopting the guise of a punctilious functionary enslaved by his notebook, Landa performs, for LaPadite, a "Jewish" masquerade. Even Landa's multilingualism (he is fluent not only in German, English, and French, but also Italian, a language for which Bridget has informed us the Germans "don't have a good ear") could be taken as a sign of Jewishness (and also of Austrianness).

Landa's ambiguity, like Shosanna's, also serves as a limitation that keeps the character from merging totally with the director function. The director is not "the subject supposed to know" but the one who is capable of filling all lack, endlessly and superfluously. The narrative of *Inglourious Basterds* is a fantasmatic narrative in which everything is repeated, in a proliferation of doubles that denies absence. Private Butz, who alone escapes the ambushing of a German battalion by the Basterds, doubles Shosanna who escapes the massacre of her family (bearing with her the extra "n" of her name just as Butz bears the swastika Raine carves into his forehead); Landa's "Au revoir, Shoshanna" is heard twice; Landa is twice seen in Goebbels' box in the cinema; there are two low-angle two-shots of Raine and another Basterd looking down at mutilated Germans; Fredrick and Shosanna are both doubled by their own film images, in which they also confront each other as each other's doubles (across the splice we see Shosanna make, inserting her own film in the middle of *Stolz der Nation*). There are even two plots to kill the Nazi high command—Shosanna's and Operation Kino—and both plots are successful; thus the main narrative action of the second half of the film is a total redundancy.

The fantasy nature of Tarantino's reimagination of history is not only acknowledged, but played up by the narrative. An intensification of fantasy takes place at various levels throughout the sequence of the destruction of the cinema. Shosanna's becoming-image, a process begun in the series of shots (already discussed) of her standing in the red dress by the circular window, is completed when, after her death, she becomes the phantom of her film. Killed by Fredrick, she is reborn twice: first as a projected image on the cinema screen, then as a phantom image wavering on billows of smoke. Donny fires his machine gun repetitively into Hitler's already dead body (a moment that echoes the scene in Samuel Fuller's *The Big Red One* of an American soldier firing his rifle again and again at the body of a German officer in a concentration camp).

The fantasy of killing Hitler declares itself as such through a repetition that deprives us of the satisfaction that the fantasy would seem to be designed to produce. In being killed redundantly, Hitler changes from a living creature into a puppet (animated by the multiple bullets that cause his body to shake) and thus into a surrogate object of a revenge that has lost its true object. The denial of satisfaction is an important aspect of the whole sequence of the premiere. The *Stolz der Nation* film-within-a-film is discordant because it uses a visual style that is clearly unlike Nazi cinema and that appears indebted both to Italian neorealism (thus, to anti-fascist cinema) and to the mixture of documentary and expressionism that characterizes much of Hollywood cinema in the two decades after the end of WWII. Furthermore, Shosanna's self-made film in which she taunts the Nazis combines a stark, crudely lit facial close-up with maniacal laughter in a way that unavoidably recalls the kind of exploitation cinema from the late 1960s and the 1970s that has been a well-known inspiration to Tarantino. Her film both constructs the image of a strong female action heroine (as earlier Tarantino films have done) and de-fetishizes that image, rendering it disturbing and difficult to consume. As with the *Stolz der Nation* film, the style of Shosanna's "message to Germany" creates a rupture in *Inglourious Basterds* that the film appears not to acknowledge (since none of the characters, of course, comments on these stylistic shifts) and that it leaves, disturbingly, as an unaccounted-for element which we must deal with or repress on our own—a challenge that places the viewers of Tarantino's film in a position equivalent to that of the Nazis in the cinema. As Fredrick becomes the face of German military might (an image that disconcerts the real Fredrick and forces him to leave the theater), Shosanna becomes "the face of Jewish vengeance," dehumanized and dispassionately jubilant.

The satisfaction that is disturbed and denied in the cinema sequence is restored in the epilogue of the film. In marking Landa with the swastika, Raine performs the gesture that Shosanna cannot. It is a human vengeance, based on the potential continued suffering of the victim (who is to be shamed by the ineradicable mark of his past allegiance). Landa's becoming-victim is a sign of humanity (whereas Shosanna joins the inhuman in becoming image), something marked in the shooting script of the film by an important description of the action. Raine asks Landa: "When you get to your little place on Nantucket Island, I imagine you are going to take off that handsome-looking SS uniform of yours, ain't you?" At this point in the script, Tarantino notes: "For the first time in the movie, Colonel Landa doesn't respond."[6] In Landa's exceptional silence, he now identifies fully with the position of his previous victims (the Dreyfuses, seen hiding under the floorboards with their hands pressed over their mouths) and abandons the function of director (who, if not supposed always to know, is supposed at least to be able to respond). It is at this point that the film can turn over the director function to its "true" holder, Tarantino. For this to happen, the function must be relayed: from Landa to Raine (just as Landa hands Raine's knife to him after they cross the American lines) and from Raine to Tarantino (in the cut from the final low-angle shot to the first end credit). The redundancy of masteries in the film (the proliferation of characters who exercise mastery) is finally reassigned to a single point of origin.

But since this reassignment also means the restoration of the dominion of writing—Tarantino emerges not as a figure in the representation but as a proper name designated in a title, an effect of writing—Tarantino, too, cannot escape being reduced to one of the series of doubles that proliferate in the fantasmatic text of the film. *Inglourious Basterds* is obsessed with the proper name (cf. Werner pugnaciously Germanizing Raine's Tennessee pronunciation of "Hugo Stiglitz"), with writing (the extreme close-up insert of Landa's notebook; Landa's "when the military history of this night is written ... "), with the letter (Shosanna's "N"; the extra letters in the spelling of the title of the film, which also appear carved on the butt of Raine's rifle). The proper name is one's passport into the narrative circuit: the players of the tavern guessing game bear on their foreheads the names of well-known people or fictional characters (the two categories intermingling, as the fictional characters of *Inglourious Basterds* mingle with historical figures such as Goebbels and Churchill); since a name, like a uniform, can be discarded or changed (as Shosanna changes hers), Raine with his knife gives the Nazis "something they can't take off." The sign becomes that which betrays (as Hicox betrays to Hellstrom that he is not the German he claims to be by raising the wrong three fingers to signify the number three—the raised fingers also form a letter). The figures of the film are doubled by their names, which sometimes accompany them visually on-screen as titles. In the domain of redundant signs that circulate and mirror one another throughout the film, Tarantino's claim of authorship becomes another fantasmatic gesture, the capping item of excess, the cream on the strudel.

Notes

1   The name Shosanna is spelled "Shoshanna" in the notes, though it is given as "Shosanna" all three times it appears on-screen in title

cards (in the opening and ending credits and in a title introducing the character in her new identity as Emmanuelle). The discrepancy in Landa's notebook both suggests a certain blindness on the part of the Nazis and exemplifies the insistence of the redundant letter, or of the letter as redundancy, that runs throughout the film.

2 Patrick McGilligan, *Backstory: Interviews with Screenwriters of Hollywood's Golden Age*. Berkeley: University of California Press, 1986, 239.

3 Jean-Louis Comolli and François Géré, "Two Fictions Concerning Hate," in Stephen Jenkins, ed., *Fritz Lang: The Image and the Look*. London: BFI Publishing, 1981, 125–46.

4 Comolli and Géré, 134–5.

5 Comolli and Géré, 139.

6 Quentin Tarantino, *Inglourious Basterds* ("Last Draft, July 2, 2008"), 164. The digitized image of this unpublished script is available, presumably without authorization, from various Internet sources.

Works cited

The Big Red One. Directed by Samuel Fuller. USA, 1980.

Cat People. Directed by Paul Schrader. USA, 1982.

Comolli, Jean-Louis, and François Géré. "Two Fictions Concerning Hate." In *Fritz Lang: The Image and the Look*, edited by Stephen Jenkins. London: BFI Publishing, 1981.

Das Testament des Dr. Mabuse/The Testament of Dr. Mabuse. Directed by Fritz Lang. Germany, 1932

Dr. Mabuse, der Spieler/Dr. Mabuse, The Gambler. Directed by Fritz Lang. Germany, 1922.

Death Proof. Directed by Quentin Tarantino. USA, 2007.

Hangmen Also Die! Directed by Fritz Lang. USA, 1943.

M. Directed by Fritz Lang. Germany, 1931.

McGilligan, Patrick. *Backstory: Interviews with Screenwriters of Hollywood's Golden Age*. Berkeley: University of California Press, 1986.

Tarantino, Quentin. *Inglourious Basterds*, last draft screenplay, 2008.

To Catch a Thief. Directed by Alfred Hitchcock. USA, 1955.

4

Inglourious music: revenge, reflexivity, and Morricone as muse in *Inglourious Basterds*

Lisa Coulthard

While *Inglourious Basterds* shares its focus on revenge with many of Tarantino's other films, it distinguishes itself by the way in which this vengeance moves beyond human parameters to encompass the revenge of cinema itself. Cinema as an artistic, historical, and cultural force is central to the plot of *Inglourious Basterds*: loosely organized around the double mission Operation Kino/Revenge of the Giant Face, the narrative climax occurs in a cinema and involves an actress (Bridget von Hammersmark), a film critic (Archie), a cinema owner (Shosanna), a projectionist

(Marcel), and the Basterds (Aldo, Omar and Donnie) posing as Italian filmmakers and industry workers. Their enemies are equally cinematically defined (Friedrich Zoller the war hero and actor, Goebbels the propaganda minister and producer) and the action occurs within a cinema, with film acting as both the agent and message of revenge. This focus on the cinematic is paralleled in the film by a wider attention to performance, as each of the main characters masquerades, performs and puts on appearances. From Hans Landa's deliberate speech patterns, gestures and feigning (saying, for instance, that he has exhausted his French—a ploy that allows him to converse about the victims under the floorboards without their knowledge), to Shosanna's masquerade as Emmanuelle Mimieux (a name reference to the French-American Hollywood actress Yvette Mimieux, who appeared in *Dark of the Sun*—a film whose score is used in *Basterds*) to the Basterds' multiple performances, everyone in the film plays a role at one point or another.

This foregrounding of film history, culture and performance has led many to view the film as a celebration of the power of cinema (and condemnation of its abuses in the hands of National Socialism) or as a self-reflexive genre parody. Whether understood as a kind of American Nazi themed WWII film to end all American Nazi themed WWII films (and here the distinction between WWII action/adventure films involving Nazis and films about the Holocaust ought to be emphasized, a point missed by many critics) or as a comment on the power of cinema to survive political suffocation and control, it is clear that cinema is the topic and theme. Indeed, if we see the film as taking on cinematic history rather than history per se, the exuberantly inaccurate ending becomes both suitable and narrationally, if not historically, logical as it takes on the vengeance of cinema itself.

The interpretation of *Inglourious Basterds* as cinema's revenge is crucial to approaching the pastiched score and recognizing its uniqueness as well as its suitability. Film history is key to the impact of *Inglourious Basterds* and the compilation score of pre-existing film music is an integral element of this self-reflexive cinematic vengeance. Composed entirely of songs and scores that have appeared in other films, the music for the film alludes to German cinema of the National Socialist era, 1960s and 1970s Italian cinema and American genre film in its representation of vengeance as a narrational, historical and, most importantly, cinematic theme.

Using songs from popular culture is common in cinema today, but it is rare in American cinema to use an original score that was composed for another film. Quoting musical scores and songs from other films, Tarantino's *Inglourious Basterds* resonates with the cultural references that attend that music as well as the cinematic objects with which this music is associated. A bravura strategy, this musical quoting is also an integral thematic structuring device that renders overt the film's engagement with the past and with cinema. Ranging from German and French popular songs from the 1940s, Morricone scores, Charles Bernstein compositions for American genre cinema and 1960s motorcycle movie music, the score of *Inglourious Basterds* is clearly ingloriously eclectic. As a sassy play on conventional "glory" in war narrative, the film title multiplies the irreverence of their ingloriousness with the redundancy of "basterds". These are neither glorious bastards nor inglorious men, but a rather ignoble combination of the two, the scandalous nature of which is writ large in the inglorious spelling of the title itself. In the same way, the musical citationality is equally irreverent, blending well-known and respected composers such as Morricone with scores from the cinematic abject (Nazi era cinema, motorcycle movies, horror films, exploitation cinema and Italian cult cinema): the soundtrack evinces its own ingloriousness as it revels in a musical mix that does not respect boundaries of genre, form or taste.

And yet, despite this inglorious musical eclecticism and pastiche, the soundscape of *Inglourious Basterds* has a clear musical dominant: Ennio Morricone. As a film written with a Morricone score in mind—and Tarantino always writes with music in mind, even if the final soundtrack might make changes and variations— the soundtrack of *Inglourious Basterds* can be seen to be sonically and rhythmically shaped by Morricone's influence, even though only eight of the over twenty music cues can be identified as quotes from Morricone scores.[1] In interviews Tarantino frequently divides the film into two halves (the Spaghetti Western first half and the men-on-a-mission war movie in the second) and the Morricone music clearly informs this split as five of the eight Morricone cues occur within the film's first thirty-five minutes.[2] But the three Morricone cues in the so-called second half are narrationally, affectively and structurally so crucial that they insist upon a reconsideration of this simple division. Further, the use of music from Italian crime films, motorcycle films, Asian action cinema, Nazi light romantic comedies, and 1980s horror cinema for the film's second half indicates the film's very restricted use of conventional "man on a mission" spy music (communicated by fragments from Lalo Schifrin's score for *Kelly's Heroes* and Jacques Loussier's for *Dark of the Sun*). Despite the variation in score and the influential use of Charles Bernstein's music, the music for *Inglourious Basterds* maintains a certain sonic cohesion wrought by the structural and affective dominance of Morricone's music. With this acoustic unity, the seeming narrative split becomes less significant.

Revenge is a dish best served … with spaghetti

A composer for both film and concert, Ennio Morricone is best known by North American film scholars, critics and enthusiasts for his scoring of Sergio Leone's film Westerns starring Clint Eastwood (*A Fistful of Dollars, For a Few Dollars More* and *The Good, the Bad and the Ugly*), even though these scores represent a minuscule portion of his oeuvre. Blending multiple musical idioms, his scores are known for experimentation and distinctive resonance, timbre and instrumentation. In particular, he is best known for the prominent use of electric guitar, eccentric percussion (rifle shots, whip cracks) and the human voice as a musical instrument—all arguably devalued, inglorious forms of instrumentation. These musical distinctions work in concert with the prominent place that music holds within the films themselves. Especially in the Leone Westerns, but arguably in many of the films Morricone scored, music is eccentric, played loud and given center stage. Morricone's scores are not background, accompanying or secondary elements, but central and integral to the films in which they appear.[3]

Michel Chion notes this centrality when he argues that Morricone's scores for Leone's films surpass the musical to achieve the level of sound. That is, music becomes like a film's other components, "something concrete, solid and incarnate … that exists for itself, not just for rhetorical purposes or expressive function."[4] Arguing that Leone's films can be seen as part of a wider move away from filmic verbocentrism and toward mannerist and rhetorically self-conscious stylistic modes, Chion notes the role of Morricone's score in Leone's sonic and narrational eccentricities. More specifically, Chion argues that Leone's films are examples of "ritualized film,"[5] a temporally fluid form of filmmaking characterized by laconically ceremonial dialogue and a manipulation of time, in part through the foregrounding of sonic rhythms and musical feeling. Marked by set pieces of "temporal bravura,"[6] the ritual films of Leone and Morricone use sound and music in cross-fertilizing and imbricated ways; rather than distinct units, sound takes on musical qualities and, in turn, music uses non-traditional acoustic elements, a transfer of functions that allows music to take on narrative centrality and move to the foreground in emphatic ways.[7]

Chion's linking of Morricone and Leone with a ritualized cinema highlights the temporal manipulation and distension that are associated with the violent action of those films: time expands in the moment before action as dialogue ceases, the camera cuts to close-ups and music takes over. Most obvious in the set piece of the cinematic showdown, this sonic technique is found throughout Morricone scored Westerns. In these moments music becomes not just a cue, but a concrete presence and frozen moment of anticipation that expands and distends the temporal action. As Royal S. Brown notes, in Leone Westerns moments of action "are stretched to the breaking point," which "allows the music more room to expand."[8]

This lyrical expansion and suspension is what shapes much of Tarantino's borrowed score in *Inglourious Basterds*. With its numerous extended Morricone cues, *Basterds* has the sonic texture, rhythm and pace of a Spaghetti Western. As Brown notes regarding Morricone, there is a lack of a cue mentality in his scores: rather they work according to affect, lyricism and a cine-musical logic, as themes get repeated, varied and fractioned throughout the score.[9] Although lacking the cohesion of a sole-authored score, music in *Inglourious Basterds* nonetheless operates according to similar principles of repetition, variation and moments of cine-musical lyricism. Foregrounded and working to expand and intensify both action and affect, music in *Basterds* operates not as isolated cues but as heightened moments of intensity, moments during which music dominates to the exclusion of all else.

Time expanded: the cine-musical moment

Avoiding conventional cue structure, Morricone's music in Leone Westerns tends to anticipate or comment on the action rather than accompany it and this placement is crucial to its impact, functions and effects. Noting that he likes to predict a cue, ease the audience into a theme, Morricone stresses the importance of music in directing response. It is equally important that a cue concludes in an appropriate way, which for Morricone frequently means a gradual extinction rather than severe cut, a preference that he comments leads him "to suggest to the director to stretch the durations."[10] Reiterating this sense of the expansion of time in the moment of musical presence, Morricone's comments also remind us of the importance of the editing, duration, opening and closing of musical cues—the overall structure is what matters rather than only the musical characteristics or interaction with the image.

It is no surprise then to note that many of the key narrational and emotionally charged sequences of *Inglourious Basterds* use Morricone cues in ways that expand, delay or slow down the pace of action: the arrival of the car at the LaPadite farm, Landa's discovery of Shosanna's family, the slow motion surrender of the German officer to the Basterds and the death of Shosanna. While only two of these scenes involve actual slow motion (Shosanna's death and the officer's surrender), all of them create a sense of time expanded. This temporal distension and affective intensification are particularly prominent in the opening sequence (Chapter One), which is in many ways the most "Western" chapter in the film. After the credits—accompanied by Dmitri Tiomkin's "The Green Leaves of Summer" from *The Alamo* (performed by Nick Perito without lyrics)—the first chapter cuts to an outdoor scene reminiscent of film Westerns: a man chops a stump in his yard, a woman hangs laundry and from a distance some unknown men dressed in dark clothes slowly approach. Morricone's "The Verdict" from *The Big Gundown* slowly rises in the mix to dominate the sequence until the music fades into the car engine motor as it reaches the farmhouse. Time is expansive: the car seems to approach as slowly as a man on horseback—that iconic image seen in the distance at the beginning of innumerable Westerns. Dialogue is spoken but it is mixed only loud enough to be audible and the music is not brought down to accommodate it; this is a musical moment and when it has ended, sound effects and dialogue take the foreground for the bulk of the scene until the moment of conclusive and catastrophic action that is again scored by Morricone—this time "L'incontro Con La Figlia" from *The Return of Ringo*.

Beginning with a visual reference to *Once Upon a Time in the West* and including visual and acoustic references to *The Big Gundown*, *Death Rides a Horse* and *The Return of Ringo*, Chapter One of *Inglourious Basterds* clearly frames the action in generic terms as that of a Spaghetti Western.[11] Other than the car and the Nazi uniforms, the visual iconography places the action earlier than the 1940s—the stump, the water pump, clothing and log house are all suggestive of the period Western. Indeed, even though the car's presence undermines this impression, its presence is transformed through its drawn out advance: temporally delayed and expanded, the car's approach to the house is decelerated and has an impact similar to that of the suspense-building slow approach of horse and rider.

But it is the music that primarily imbues the scene with the atmosphere, tone and context of the film Western through the music of Morricone. Lasting well over a minute, the first Morricone cue expands and unifies the temporal duration of the opening scene, indicating danger, threat and unease. Opening with the sound of an axe chopping, the scene's sonically regular rhythm sets the tone for the car engine sounds that both prompt and conclude the musical cue. Moving from axe to car to music, the transitions are seamless and gradual and build suspense around the car itself as its sounds are tied to the unnerving minor key music that attends its approach. The first words are spoken only after the music begins and the sound effects are rarefied and selective (water splashes, some footsteps); the music takes center stage. Without words or other information, the narrative and emotional context is set. The threat is clear and our response to it is an anxiety that parallels that of Monsieur LaPadite.

The second musical cue in this visually and acoustically sophisticated opening sequence is associated with the terror of attack. In acoustic terms, the tension has built slowly in the scene through a very selective soundscape: dialogue with long pauses and slow delivery and the isolation of a few sounds at key moments (a clock ticking, the sound of pipes put to lips and smoked, a fountain pen being filled and put to paper, the pouring and drinking of milk, the creaking leather of Hans Landa's Gestapo coat). The tension is created and communicated through the pauses and empty spaces between what is said and meant. The cat and mouse (or rather "hawk and rat") dialogue is sparse, with both sides restricting speech at crucial moments. This is of course truer of Monsieur LaPadite than the chatty Landa, but even Landa's delivery is carefully plotted and timed. His shrewd delivery indicates his verbal, physical and socio-political control of the situation and his pauses contain potent threats and implied meanings. The background sounds amplify both the sense of Landa's threatening presence (the leather creaks) and the very visceral anxiety of LaPadite (the ticking clock with all of its symbolic resonance), while simultaneously placing both within the banal world of everyday farm life (pouring milk, a cow mooing, a pipe being filled and smoked).

Each sound in this sequence becomes an element of tension, information and anxiety as the listener's attention is piqued. By stripping the sounds to the essential elements, which are similarly reduced to a very few key gestures and objects, the film's opening constructs or at least invites an acoustically activated spectator. The sequence demands our listening attention and it is these aural cues that convey the anxiety and action of the scene. Marked visually by balanced composition, luminescent lighting and a warm color palette, the opening and the farmhouse scenes offer bucolic, peaceful beauty. Viewed without sound, we witness a man chopping a tree stump in a beautiful field as a young woman hangs laundry, followed by a scene in which two men sit, talk and smoke at a table. Only the historical significance of the uniforms and the death's head on the Nazi cap on the table (seemingly lit from the glow of the milk) indicate that something is awry. Watched with sound, however, the sequence is one filled with tension, threat and danger: the music along with the uncomfortable pauses, amplifi-cation of sounds and their weighty impact all communicate the expected outcome of this conversation.

This building of emotional intensity and suspense through the isolation of sounds also paves the way for the sonic trauma of the action to come. Acoustically it is a scene of total destruction: the concluding music is elevated in volume and epic in tone, which emphasizes its disturbing impact and makes clear that the stakes are important not just for Shosanna alone but rather for all victims. Apocalyptic in its sonic dissonance, the music combines with gunfire (creating Morricone-like eccentric percussion) to give the scene a gravitas and generic thematic abstraction. The music does not cut out until we know Shosanna is free. As a kind of musical coda, Landa's mocking and sing-songy "Au reeeevoir Shoshaaaannaaaaa" concludes the emotionally intense scene.

These two scenes thus set the stage for the entire film and do so with very little narratively significant dialogue. The dialogue is deceptive, indicative of the cat and mouse game that the two protagonists are playing. Landa's strategies of overblown politeness (especially exaggerated in the first part when he speaks in what is perhaps the most structurally polite of languages—French) are an interrogatory technique, one that we recognize clearly through vocal intonation, facial expression and gesture. Monsieur LaPadite's recalcitrant response is equally uninformative in verbal terms. It is the sound, music and visual composition that fleshes out the stakes and directs audience attention and engagement. Blended and interwoven with the soundscape as a whole, the music does not become a mere accompanying element but an integral, concrete part of the contour of the scene. Stemming from and returning to the car engine in the first cue and interweaving with gunfire and destruction in the second, the music merges and confuses the borders of sound effects, dialogue and music. But from these blurred transitions, the music takes over, extending, dilating and focusing the action.

Music and emotion: the affective structure of Tarantino's musical pastiche

These musical moments are crucial to understanding the impact of Tarantino's film as well as its repurposing of Morricone score. Although frequently criticized for a postmodern lack of affect, excessive pastiche and superficial characterization, Tarantino's films nonetheless focus on an intense emotional landscape of violation, victimization and revenge. Yet like Leone's Western heroes, Tarantino's characters do not discuss emotional invest-ments or affective states of mind. Rather, the music tends to speak for them: when Max first sees Jackie in *Jackie Brown*, Bloodstone's

"Natural High" expresses his love; *Kill Bill*'s Bride's hatred is manifested through the *Ironside/Fists of Death* cue; Shosanna's traumatic memory of the murder of her family is rendered by Charles Bernstein's music from the female character's ghost rape in *The Entity*. In each instance, music works to not merely cue, enhance or convey emotion, but rather becomes emotion itself. That is, it highlights emotionally charged moments of suspense that freeze, anticipate and shape the action and, in so doing, it creates an affective space where none would otherwise be. Line delivery in Tarantino is frequently terse, deadpan or comedic; actor emotion is severely restrained and dialogue does not delve into subtexts, psychology or emotional depth. The surface is all and, like the laconic verbal silence of the Spaghetti Western, music takes over as a singular emotive gesture and moment.

This emotional resonance is significant when one notes that the largest number of music cues in the film are associated with Shosanna, including the much commented upon extended David Bowie "Putting out Fire (with gasoline)." Of the twenty-three non-diegetic cues (that is, excluding the German and French background songs played very low in the bar and restaurant scenes), nine deal with Shosanna, the highest number associated with a single character and a large percentage of the overall musical time excluding opening and closing credit sequences.

This musical emphasis on Shosanna ought not to surprise insofar as music is usually discussed in affective terms as cuing, creating and inviting audience emotional engagement and Shosanna is established early on as the affective center for the film. More than Shosanna alone though, these cues point to the film's tripartite narrative structure of Landa, Shosanna and the Basterds. All but three of Shosanna's musical moments are shared with Landa (or his henchmen); the score in the Shosanna/Landa scenes is either Bernstein or Morricone and, in each instance, the music scores the scene itself, rather than being tied to any individual character or character group. Each cue is a musical representation of threat, danger or anxiety and thus each has a more general, dispersed affective impact than the clarity that one associates with character themes. The result unquestionably yokes the audience to Shosanna through an unambiguous definition of the villain. The affective and moral parameters could not be more certain.

This moral and affective certainty is key to approaching the use of Morricone in Tarantino's film. Foreground music in *Basterds* creates, shapes and cues our affective engagement, rather than complicating it or nuancing it. The Morricone cues are particularly effective insofar as these cues occur in key narrational moments: the opening and introduction of conflict (and establishment of the enemy); the act of murder and the victim's escape; the establishment of the Basterds' enemy and their acts of violent revenge; the coming together of enemy and insurgent forces (in the battlefield of the cinema); the death of the heroine/victim; the conclusion of the film. Taken together, these scenes offer the emotional contour of the film itself, moving from threat and murder to revenge, sacrifice and the neutralizing of the opening threat. In each moment we also note the signature elements that are associated with Morricone's cine-musical moments: expansion of time, pausing of action, foregrounding of music as a concrete narrative and formal element and the use of music as a stand-in for emotional context and affective feeling.

What I am arguing, then, is not merely that *Inglourious Basterds* references Spaghetti Westerns or even Morricone, but that its entire sonic composition can be seen to operate in a way that parallels a Morricone score for a Spaghetti Western. In borrowing, repurposing and adapting Morricone's music, Tarantino's *Basterds* enhances and exploits those defining elements that we associate with the scores of Leone's Westerns: the integration of voice, sound effect and music; the irreverent mixing of idioms (popular, avant-garde, classical); the use of music as a foreground, not background element; the sonic referencing of regular, rhythmic, kinetic movement frequently associated with action and adventure; the frequency of musical interludes that heighten emotion and freeze or extend narrative action. Even though the film has a composite score and thus lacks the cohesion of an original score that can repeat, vary and play with musical motifs, it nonetheless achieves a similar function in focusing on Morricone as a musical anchor. It is almost as if Morricone had indeed scored the film, as he was initially recruited to do. With Morricone leading the inglorious musical mixing of genres and styles, the film never veers far from its central vengeance motif as the final scene comes full circle and a Morricone score closes the film.

Notes

1   First reported by IGN (Italy Global Nation—www.adnkronos. com/ IGN/ News), the rumor that Ennio Morricone was slated to compose the score for Tarantino's *Inglourious Basterds* received the most press when it was revealed to no longer be true because of scheduling difficulties. See the following websites for articles regarding this:

www.slashfilm.com/ennio-morricone-to-score-tarantino's-basterds

www.variety.com/article/VR1117995914?refCatId=2525

http://theplaylist.blogspot.com/2009/01/ennio-morricone-wont-be-scoring.html

www.tarantino.info/2009/01/09/ennio-morricone-is-no-basterd

2   See http://www.npr.org/templates/story/story. php?storyId=112286584

3   Jeff Smith notes that in Leone's *The Good, the Bad and the Ugly*, it appears as if the film accompanies the music: "Instead of using Morricone's music to score the film, it seems rather Leone has 'imaged' the music." See Smith, Jeff, *The Sounds of Commerce: Marketing Popular Film Music* (New York: Columbia University Press, 1998), 152.

4   Michel Chion, *Film, A Sound Art*, trans. Claudia Gorbman (New York: Columbia University Press, 2009), 106.

5   Chion 2009, 107.

6   Chion 2009, 112.

7   As Chion notes in *Audio-Vision*, while it is true that Leone achieves ritualized effects even when Morricone's music is not present (the opening fifteen minutes of *Once Upon a Time in the West* for instance), "Morricone's music is crucial in creating the sense of temporal immobilization" in other scenes and is a large part of the overall operatic tendencies in Leone's cinema. See Chion, Michel, *Audio-Vision: Sound on Screen*, ed. and trans. Claudia Gorbman (New York: Columbia University Press, 1994), 82.

8   Royal S. Brown, *Overtones and Undertones: Reading Film Music*. (Berkeley: University of California Press, 1994), 227.

9   Brown, 228.

10 Ennio Morricone, "A Composer behind the Film Camera," trans. by Elena Boschi, *Music, Sound and the Moving Image* 1.1 (Spring 2007), 100.

11 *Kill Bill: Vol. 1* similarly frames its vengeance in Western terms through the music of Morricone, specifically the scores for *Navajo Joe* and *Death Rides a Horse*. Indeed, the fabulous *Death Rides a Horse* is the source for a number of references in *Kill Bill: Vol. 1*, including the aphoristic reference to cold revenge (that is attributed within the film to *Star Trek*'s Klingons), the red tinged close-up on the eyes for traumatic flashbacks as well as the notion that the murderer must wait for the child witness's revenge. But more than these isolated references, it is the score that indicates the indebtedness to the Spaghetti Western and to the emotional and stylistic rhythms associated with it.

Works cited

The Alamo. Directed by John Wayne. USA, 1960.

Brown, Royal S. *Overtones and Undertones: Reading Film Music*. Berkeley: University of California Press, 1994.

C'era una volta il West/Once Upon a Time in the West. Directed by Sergio Leone. Italy, 1968.

Chion, Michel. *Audio-Vision: Sound on Screen*, edited and translated by Claudia Gorbman. New York: Columbia University Press, 1994.

—*Film, A Sound Art*. Translated by Claudia Gorbman. New York: Columbia University Press, 2009.

Dark of the Sun/The Mercenaries. Directed by Jack Cardiff. UK, 1968.

Da uomo a uomo/Death Rides a Horse. Directed by Giulo Petroni. Italy, 1967.

The Entity. Directed by Sidney J. Furie. USA, 1982.

Il buono, il brutto, il cattivo/The Good, the Bad, and the Ugly. Directed by Sergio Leone. Italy, 1966.

Il ritorno di Ringo/The Return of Ringo. Directed by Duccio Tessari. Italy, 1965.

Ironside. TV series. National Broadcasting Company, USA, 1967–1975.

Jackie Brown. Directed by Quentin Tarantino. USA, 1997.

Kelly's Heroes. Directed by Brian G. Hutton. USA, 1970.

Kill Bill: Vol. 1. Directed by Quentin Tarantino. USA, 2003.

Kill Bill: Vol. 2. Directed by Quentin Tarantino. USA, 2004.

La resa dei conti/The Big Gundown. Directed by Sergio Sollima. Italy, 1966.

Morricone, Ennio, "A Composer behind the Film Camera," translated by Elena Boschi. *Music, Sound and the Moving Image*, 1.1, Spring 2007, 95–105.

Navajo Joe. Directed by Sergio Corbucci. Italy, 1966.

Per qualche dollaro in piu/For a Few Dollars More. Directed by Sergio Leone. Italy, 1965.

Per un pugno di dollari/Fistful of Dollars. Directed by Sergio Leone. Italy, 1964.

Smith, Jeff. *The Sounds of Commerce: Marketing Popular Film Music.* New York: Columbia University Press, 1998.

5

Lulu's menorah: seeing and Nazi-ing

Justin Vicari

"No one must be hungry or cold. Anyone failing to comply goes to a concentration camp." The joke from Hitler's Germany might well shine out as a maxim above all the portals of the culture industry. Max Horkheimer and Theodor W. Adorno, Dialectic of Enlightenment[1]

Life seemed to paralyze his imagination ... On the other hand his pessimistic temperament tirelessly won new lighting effects from the ceremony of death. The carefully developed artistic demagoguery had real high points, when he strode down the broad avenue between hundreds of thousands to honor the dead on the Königsplatz or on the grounds of the Nürnberg party congress with gloomy music in the background, for example. In such scenes out of a political good Friday magic—"magnificence is used to

advertise death," as Adorno said about Wagner's music—
Hitler's idea of aesthetic politics matches the concept.
Joachim Fest, *Hitler*[2]

An early scene in Pabst's *Pandora's Box* (1929) takes place in the apartment which Dr. Schon keeps for his mistress Lulu. Lulu's "father," a drifter named Schigolch, has turned up for an unannounced visit, and Lulu wishes to keep his presence a secret from Schon. As Schigolch crouches in hiding, he is briefly framed against what is clearly a menorah, on a table in the background. Lulu is revealed to be many things in this scene: spontaneous, lusty, sexy, powerful, manipulative, sneaky, mercenary—is she also, by some implication, Jewish? One does not necessarily want to see a menorah, perhaps *the* pre-eminent symbol of Judaism, in the apartment of this femme fatale, in the middle of this Weimar-era German film no less—but there it is, and if it is not a signifier, if it is not a hiding place of sympathies and antipathies, then how exactly is it to be registered?

First of all, it is not my intention to argue that *Pandora's Box* is an anti-Semitic or a fascist film. The menorah exists, of course; but many things exist in any given film, and what interests me here, what I think is most productive, is the extent to which this axiomatic fact of the medium's visual density and its relation to the real often go unnoticed. Thus, *Pandora's Box* could conceivably be called fascist, but only to the degree that nearly all films partake of a certain inevitable degree of fascist thought-in-practice, in the sense that by its strongly visual-mimetic nature, film tends to simplify complex, open-ended realities into one-dimensional, literal, closed fields of meaning. This is different from painting, for instance, where the artist's abstract vision mediates between the meaning of the real and the meaning of the image: objects entering the charged field of vision cease to be literal objects and become figurative ones. If ambiguity is one of the fundamental enemies of fascist thought—whose rhetoric promotes puffed-up, overde-termined definitions—that same ambiguity is also the enemy of cinema as well (at least mainstream, narrative cinema), in the sense that the objects in a film are always literal, identifiable. Traced backwards, one reasons that one cannot have a car in a film unless one purchases or rents an actual car, etc., on down to the smallest, most unassuming pieces of décor. This points to a consideration of fascism in its largest sense, as an imperialism of the mind: to lay one's hands on a thing and employ it, to assert one single thing as uniquely "provable" out of a whirlwind of unformed potential meanings, is already to participate in a kind of fascism, more aggressive and controlling than simply letting multiple meanings (uncomfortably) co-exist.

In most films, taking all the physical stuff in each scene for granted is a relatively simple mental operation, part of our well-trained suspension of disbelief, and something which not only does not preclude the enjoyment we take from watching films, but often occurs more or less unconsciously. Furthermore, even if we bring into consciousness an awareness of the film's stuff (its physical world), we might still appreciate the film, not so naively perhaps, but ready to accept that, of course, film is not by nature a "poor" medium, in the way Jerzy Grotowski's Marxist, radicalized theater in *Towards a Poor Theater* could be stripped of illusions. Film, even when its maker's intentions may be somewhat close to Grotowski's, is a medium in which the real and the illusion are continuously flowing back and forth into each other, charging each other with their respective powerful energies; to make the *mise-en-scène* of film "poor" is still not to account for technical accoutrements and costs such as camera, lights, film-stock. The entire inventory of the budget sheet mediates between two sets of dreams, the one which begins in the minds of the filmmakers and the one which ends inside ours, the audience's.

Is there such thing as an innocent audience? Postmodern cinema denies this possibility, even when it remains genre-friendly, in its own pop way as difficult and tense as that difficult art favored by the Frankfurt School of Max Horkheimer and Theodor W. Adorno. Negative dialectics have been explicitly and implicitly invoked to explain films that operate at the outer limits of spectator pleasure (Béla Tarr, Michael Haneke, Catherine Breillat) or which reveal and question the commodification of bodies under capitalism (Jean-Luc Godard, Rainer Werner Fassbinder, David Cronenberg, Spike Lee). The fondest hope is that there is, within the history of cinema, a kind of secret history which links to the WWII-era fight against fascism in its most basic, historically pristine form. And yet, Horkheimer and Adorno make it abundantly clear that they see film as part of the problem, by which I mean part of fascism, although in fact it can be said that they *do not see* cinema, in two senses: the first by refusing to watch and patronize movies, the second by failing to see the admittedly rare dimension in which film transcends its own production-consumption nexus to become self-contradictory art.

How to enjoy cinema on two levels, with a kind of double consciousness as it were—a consciousness that responds naively to the sensuous illusions of cinematic magic, and also thinks critically about the meanings behind those illusions? One way is for the aware critic to become a bastard (or "basterd": deliberate misspelling bridges a crucial gap between what we are and are not supposed to know): a kind of renegade or raider, making up rules in an uncharted terrain—the highbrow interpretation of an inherently middlebrow/lowbrow form.

I do not share in Horkheimer and Adorno's detestation of cinema, but I am deeply informed by their recognition that films, like all products of the culture industry, are socially conditioned and mediated, and can be, for this reason, manipulative tools for keeping people enslaved (through entertainment) to second-class status in the world. Horkheimer and Adorno read any artistic merit as deliberate camouflage for the culture industry's true agenda: "infecting everything with sameness."[3] "Films ... no longer need to present themselves as art. The truth that they are nothing but business is used as an ideology to legitimize the trash they intentionally produce. They call themselves industries, and the published figures for their directors' incomes quell any doubts about the social necessity of their finished products."[4] No one would be paid so much in a totalitarian society (advanced capitalism is totalitarian in its concentration of power and its invidious use of propaganda) who was not directly engaged as a representative of "the haves" against "the have-nots," the powerful against the powerless. "Technical rationality today is the rationality of domination. It is the compulsive character of a society alienated from itself. Automobiles, bombs, and films hold the totality together *until their leveling element demonstrates its power against the very system of injustice it served.*"[5] I interpret this last phrase (my emphasis) as acknowledging a revolutionary power latent in films; however, within a consumerist structure this potential is not to be realized: "Sharp distinctions like those between A and B films, or between short stories published in magazines in different price segments, do not so much reflect real differences as assist in the classification, organization, and identification of consumers. Something is provided for everyone so that no one can escape; differences are hammered home and propagated."[6] Even an Orson Welles, then, exists only to placate the highbrow search for "art" while revealing that this is to be a headachy exception rather than the rule; the artistic director lends his respectability to the rule of mediocre commercialism even as he finds himself a martyr to it.[7]

Since it is impossible to change or suppress desire, desire is accepted into the system for purposes of exploitation. Thus, one by one, the oppressed minorities who fought and died for justice in the 1960s and 1970s—blacks, women, gays—have been, at first grudgingly, allowed to flourish by being transformed into niche markets. Capitalist logic absorbs any positive gain toward social good and turns it into its reductive opposite: the success of a minority political agenda is quickly measured not in terms of actual powers gained but in how many specialized magazines and TV shows it can generate and support. The absorbed viewers are distracted from the fact that their own individual "freedom" remains dubious and contingent at best.

Likewise, we have known for a long time that the indie film has been wholly co-opted by the mainstream, which recognized that people with non-mainstream taste also have money, and need to have those consumer dollars harvested by the same conglomerates that produce mainstream films. Granted, these may be dollars that want to think of themselves as being less easily "bought"— however, in their odyssey to eventually fill producers' coffers, the high-minded dollar of the indie fan may start out as an act of protest and individualism, but in the end, is only herded back into the fold of sameness and control. Again, ledger sheets reduce ambiguity to mere overhead.

This might not be so dangerous, perhaps, if lack of real choice in films themselves did not prepare the citizenry for a democracy-in-name-only, where the parties advertise their differences only as a distraction from the fact that both generally serve as shills for the centralized corporate-capitalist system. Because it bluntly and literally reproduces reality, film hypnotizes its audiences into an inability to discern reality from imitation; the final decay of subjectivity occurs when workers come to mistake their day-to-day lives for a less empowered imitation of the movies, and hence stop questioning why things are the way they are. Standing up to corrupt corporate institutions is something which only Julia Roberts or Charlize Theron can do, in films that cast their spell with the inevitable, wearying power of myth, just as, in Teutonic myths, Siegfried slew the dragon and Parsifal recovered the Grail. It was these myths which eventually brought individual Germans to a position of false heroism or even anti-heroism, completely on the side of the fascist state (no matter that myths often originate in images of justice). Finally, cinema makes it possible for the corporation to pick your pocket even while removing from you any will to fight against it, by bracketing that fight within a cinematic fantasy that can be safely applauded because it has been so successfully mythologized that it can no longer be enacted.

And yet, I still believe that in the hands of its best artists cinema can also be a tool for freeing the mind, just as I would like to believe that political and socioeconomic change in the U.S. remains within the power of its citizenry to change. Much depends on the elements of reality—specific signifiers—within a film itself. In the case of *Pandora's Box*, to return to our initial example, we become particularly suspicious of Lulu's menorah for two reasons: first, we are not certain what it meant to the filmmaker; and second, we are not certain how it will be interpreted by audiences (is it an incitement?). "Giving aid and comfort to the enemy" is something which no one ever wishes to see art—or reality, for that matter—doing. But even here, obsession occludes the eye of political reason, hatreds spawn other hatreds, in an ongoing dynamic which subordinates the spontaneous act of seeing to a series of preconceived reactions, and which brings anti-fascism closer to the power-mad cast of fascism itself. Why can't our eyes be free, at least, to see ambiguity in the blunt, literal object?

Put otherwise: is there a way out of fascist control as it exemplifies itself in capitalist representation? To find the way out, we must first look for the way in, again … One of the long-standing fascinations of the Weimar era was that it became the breeding ground of Nazism, even, and perhaps especially, where it attempted to fight directly against Hitler and his political rise. The abortive 1923 putsch and Hitler's subsequent prison sentence were eventually held up by his followers as proofs of his sincerity: this is a commonplace of political history. We are close perhaps to a similar moment, in which Sarah Palin's resignation of her governorship, under shady and as yet unexplained circumstances, may be held up as proof that she is deserving of the presidency (!), since the system ostensibly "failed" her. Although they implacably remain the system wherever the system acts as such, the forces of the capitalist right have learned to mimic leftist complaints about a dehumanized and paranoid-inducing government. The political heirs of Nixon have become fluent in the same language of the appalled outsider, the betrayed "little guy," who condemned Nixon himself during Watergate. And lest this seem like a glib and hysterical comparison of Nixon or Palin with the author of the Holocaust—certainly (and fortunately) Hitler's crimes remain untouchable—the comparison is not meant to be with that aspect of Hitler that has come to stand for demonic evil incarnate, for larger-than-life allegory, even for mass murderer, although this last role begins to shade into issues of how evil intentions trickle down the pyramid of any command chain. What approving, encouraging icons are needed, looking down from the top, for the average foot-soldier in the street to eventually pull his trigger? All of this aside, what Hitler was, first and foremost, and in his plainest role, was no more or less than a right-wing, anti-Communist, pseudo-populist demagogue, the entrancer of mass followers via rhetoric of lost entitlement for the "majority."

Nazism's great tactical victory (and a strategy which even now continues to be deployed by the fringe and not-so-fringe discourse of western democracies) was its successful cultivation of enemies, whom it thrived on, using them as evidence that it was a perennial underdog on the political stage, always struggling to be taken seriously and to survive. As a sign of the bad faith which always already defined it, this propaganda technique (what we would probably call "spin" today, after our tendency to render sinister activities innocuous with breezy, "fun" language: "friendly fire," "focus group," "person of interest" and "run-up to war" are other examples) persisted long after the Nazis managed to seize total power: Hitler was never in short supply of manufactured enemies, a veritable roulette wheel changing to suit his own needs of the moment. A phony populism and hatred of intellectualism are only the most tendentious and ubiquitous guises under which larger patterns of demagoguery operate. This is the insidious nature of fascism's ability to distort, and what often makes it difficult to eradicate once it gains a voice in a national discourse. Like Proteus falling to the ground, it becomes even stronger when agitated or unsettled, and especially when attacked directly, since such attacks only serve to justify its vaunted paranoia.

So, although Lulu's menorah may well mean less than it appears to, Judaism is presumably never a wholly empty signifier in the art of the Weimar period. Returning to cinema's inevitable mimesis, every frame of Pabst's film is a kind of cryogenically preserved slice of living Nazi-era reality: it teems with intended and unintended meanings; its fate is to have been conceived as fiction but to have ended up as inadvertent, ambivalent documentary. This is the fate of all cinema, that it inevitably includes, within its roving visual frame, signifiers anchoring it to its time and place, even when it might be trying to escape precisely from such time- and place-bound identifications. Things of all natures and kinds—not only interiors but sidewalks and buildings; not only hairstyles but the very expressions on the actors' faces—elbow their way into every shot to condemn even the most original director to the status of Curator of Social History as-it-is-lived. Fritz Lang understood this, and crowded out the offices and living rooms of his U.S. films with uncanny photographs, blown up and framed: almost always photographs of people in some uniform or another. These mementos of power become quasi-religious, taking over both wartime Nazi boardrooms and the private homes of post-war U.S. policemen. Beliefs that have become objects, these are the most difficult and dogmatic beliefs to dislodge because they are infected with the same personal charisma as the portrait, the cameo, the icon. But the demands of dramaturgy almost require that everything becomes swallowed up in this dogma of props. Even the simplest kind of farm living must be depicted through objects in a production-consumption nexus: an axe, a bed sheet hanging on a laundry line. Exponentially, this danger becomes greater when the sheer mass of stuff within a film increases: thus, this bad faith of cinematic representation reaches its ultimate crisis in "the big film," that overproduced, lavish monster of verisimilitude whose first and final duty is always to the dead and dated things which constitute its *mise en scène*. Again, Grotowski wanted a poor theater, for its rawness and most of all its (political) honesty. Perhaps a certain impoverishment of cinematic *mise en scène*—that style of shooting people in nearly bare rooms, against white walls, which we find in so much of early Godard, Warhol, early Fassbinder, even some mid-1960s Bergman—truly is the most likely way of ensuring that the people, the living matter, in a film will remain most truly visible, most particular and spontaneous, and least in danger of being dragged down into the realm of the non-living. What is human simply "stands out," as opposed to being made to compete with things, or rather being made to exchange its human energy with the inanimate energy of things, the way Lulu and the menorah are roped into their dubious exchange.

But what exactly constitutes this exchange? Does the strange, perhaps accidental signifier of Lulu's menorah become a hiding place of fascism? Its placement-intention (if it even has one) is difficult to ascertain. Was it the brainchild of a sardonic Nazi set-dresser, the token of a stillborn film within the film? Was it merely a hastily selected prop? If it *was* chosen to advertise Lulu's "Jewishness," then it occupies the same subliminal space as many advertising images, in that it goes unnamed while quietly emanating meaning in the background. Like the tell-tale heart in Poe, it speaks loudest, perhaps, to an already established sense of internalized guilt. It says nothing in itself: only as much or as little as we invest in it. Yet, the more one does invest in it, the more the symmetrical menorah bifurcates Pabst's entire film. Schigolch emerges as a shadow from anti-Semitic propaganda in his wandering rootlessness if not his generic "shabbiness" and "degeneracy," And one begins to wonder about Lulu's black hair and porcelain complexion. Understanding dawns that *Pandora's Box*—like so many films, "big films" in particular, expensive films, epic films, blockbusters, lavishly produced films—is a divided text. On one hand it is an unqualified masterpiece of subversively erotic spectacle, rendering its highly sexualized heroine as fully human; on the other hand, it is a punitive, puritanical allegory, exploiting the tension between the rights of "the pure" and the rights of "the impure," with these impure elements deleted from the social combine one by one. The pleasure of the text—as it almost always does—goes both ways. And in the end, it does not need to choose a side: in its mimetic promiscuity, its closeness to untrammeled life itself, a film always stirs up a multitude of emotions which it has no intention or need of defending.

This bad faith of the accidental signifier figures not a little in Tarantino's *Inglourious Basterds* (2009), which specifically invokes Pabst.[8] By its own artistic lights there are no accidental signifiers in *Inglourious Basterds*, no doors ajar on mystery or doubt. Just as the film reduces the complex historical battles of philo-Semitism and anti-Semitism to the crush of a Jewish-wielded baseball bat against a Nazi skull, so the film's images are contrived to be concretely and inarguably anti-fascist, whether we are seeing the frightened eyes of refugees peering up from between the floorboards where a Nazi officer paces back and forth, or a German cigarette obnoxiously extinguished in a puddle of French whipped cream. I have suggested that any simplification of ambiguous meaning is always already a gateway to fascist thought; therefore, a truly anti-fascist film cannot be made with images that refuse to doubt their own purpose as single-minded conveyors of meaning. (It may be true that only a demagogue can defeat a demagogue, but the end result produces nothing but more demagoguery.) For if it is true that all films amount to helpless catalogues, advertising a dizzying array of things-in-themselves, it is also true that, by an almost alchemical process which remains vague even when it is taking place before our eyes, a great director can sometimes train our vision on actual objects which nonetheless become more, or less, or other, than their literal meanings. Robert Bresson was a great exemplar of the object that became harder to read the more plainly and directly it was filmed; Godard's inter-images of comic strips, magazine spreads and billboards offer a similar bafflement, by becoming recontextualized images of images.

The "advertising image," then, in the hands of a great artist, can overcome its devalued status as mere manipulation. Three specific examples come to mind, all involving women: the crumpled, dun-colored slacks which the criminal-lover hurls from the window of the car in Barbara Loden's *Wanda* (1970) as he instructs Wanda in how to dress; the incongruous gun which inexplicably makes its way into Marlene's suitcase as she packs to leave her mistress at the end of Fassbinder's *The Bitter Tears of Petra von Kant* (1972); finally, the cup of yogurt in the prostitute's apartment which turns out to be conflated, insanely enough, with a cup of semen in Godard's *Slow Motion* (1980). All have the jolt of making us look twice at something that would otherwise be an overly familiar, easily read signifier.

But we are not only speaking of things, the obvious objects and commodities which appear in every frame of film, but of all things (faces, figures) which pass through the allegorical mirror of art: in the greatest films a hero no longer advertises blatant, one-dimensional "heroism," or a villain "villainy" for that matter. This is the last, most ironic lesson of Lulu's menorah, which finally, in the overall context of Pabst's film, evades any significance whatsoever, since, in her very amorphousness Lulu is always already cast as everything under the sun—killer/martyr, innocent/whore, straight/queer—so her contradictory nature cannot ever be completely defined.

As much driven by unquestioning vengeance and sub-cultural identity-branding as the characters in Tarantino's other films, however, the people in *Inglourious Basterds* are not human in the same messy, contradictory, overflowing way as Lulu; needless to say, no one in this film would display a menorah who was not "supposed to" display one (i.e., a good, heroic Jew). It is *Inglourious Basterds'* overall methodology which becomes an "accidental signifier" of bad faith, because the film's feel-good anti-fascist posturing is possible only within the language of the escapist film, with its master narrative of Good Guys and Bad Guys—the equivalent of fascism's pet tendency to oversimplify and over-determine human meanings.

Fascism is dehumanizing: its goal is the systematic destruction of individual subjectivity in its followers as well as its victims. A number of important directors have explored this theme of the damaged goods of fascist subjectivity, but not until after the sexual revolution, significantly. In the war years and immediate post-war years, films about spies and Nazi-hunters had all the sexlessness of *Hardy Boys'* adventures: propaganda ensured that the heroes would sublimate any renegade sexual impulse into the overriding goal of defeating Hitler. Fritz Lang's *Man Hunt* (1941), in which the plucky girl dies to reinforce the wavering hero's commitment to overthrowing Nazism, is the textbook case of this sublimation. The implication exploded in the late 1960s, in which a distinct subgenre of films began to appear that traced the roots of societal fascism back to individual and collective crises of erotic meaning. Some of these films view Nazism as an aberration of heterosexist conformism. The centerpiece of Luchino Visconti's *The Damned* (1969) is an extended sequence in which the SA is massacred by the SS during a massive gay orgy which Saul Friedländer describes as "a furious sexual debauch, a dazzling pagan feast."[9] Much of Fassbinder's *Berlin Alexanderplatz* (1980), set during the Weimar era, is meant to show how the denial of homoerotic desire gives rise to acts of individual violence, reflective of, and reflected by, a society rushing toward the ultimate collective violence of Nazism. In Helma Sanders-Brahms' *Germany, Pale Mother* (1980), not even the most intimate personal alliance within the Third Reich can be considered innocent: a man pointedly joins the Nazi party so the woman he loves will marry him; their marriage then, becomes infected by, and dedicated to, fascist evil.

Other films, such as Liliana Cavani's *The Night Porter* (1974), Pier Paolo Pasolini's *Salo* (1975) and Bernardo Bertolucci's *1900* (1977), describe blatant links between fascism and sadomasochism. In particular, *Salo* infamously overturns many of the beloved emblems from Roberto Rossellini's resistance masterpiece, *Rome, Open City* (1945), to make Pasolini's sardonic critique of modern capitalist Italy as harsh and unpleasant as possible. The scarf, which is all that is left of love in *Rome*, turns into an unwanted token which a sobbing mother tries to wrap around her son's neck as he is being recruited by the Nazi/fascist guards. The pudgy priest who refuses to crack under torture and whose martyrdom is witnessed by the boys who love him becomes, in Pasolini, the obscene child molester in church regalia. Finally, the perverse Nazi commandant and his vampiric moll, who order the tortures and celebrate languorously in the other room, pervade *Salo*, except there they are performing the tortures themselves and are defined as the cultural winners rather than the losers. *Salo* needs to be reconsidered as a re-reading of *Rome, Open City*, bringing into focus the extremely bitter protest which Pasolini felt the need to make against the current Italian government, his accusation that the capitalist right had sold out the brave martyrdom of the wartime anti-fascist Resistance. Hence, the scene in *Salo* where everyone sits around gloomily singing war anthems about how "the best lie under the ground."

Nagisa Oshima's *In the Realm of the Senses* (1976) is also a complex examination of these links between fascism and sadomasochism. The film focuses, claustrophobically and intensely, on the obsessive sexual relationship of a man and woman in Japan in 1936; this relationship becomes increasingly violent and morbid, as the woman begins to strangle her lover to achieve more satisfying orgasms. Late in the film, Oshima shows us that the couple is trying to get away from the depressing rise of militarism and fascism in their nation; their sadomasochism is partly pressured and triggered by the fascism which surrounds them, but it is also a fanciful utopian alternative to that fascism, in that the man chooses to die not as an anonymous soldier for the state, but as a lover for the orgasm of his mistress. Oshima's final shot shows the mistress in fetal position beside the body of her lover, whose penis she has cut off and whose nude body she has decorated with calligraphy, using blood instead of ink. He is dead; she has become insane. Disturbing and doomed, this strange couple is one of the most touching in all of film, because the stakes are so high for them, as the stakes typically are in anti-fascist cinema: the individual's attempted rebellion against fascism is carried out wholly on fascism's terms. The bid for personal freedom within the incipient fascist state is doomed only to reify fascism (in the act of murder) and lead to an ultimate loss of self.[10]

These themes reoccur compellingly in Henry Bean's *The Believer* (2001), whose anti-hero, Danny Balint, is a Jew posing as a neo-Nazi skinhead. Committing acts of fascist violence (against minorities) enables him to overcome the fear which, for him, has always accompanied his Jewish identity, not only because of the Holocaust but biblical references such as the story of Abraham and Isaac. In a key turning point, Danny argues with concentration camp survivors, telling them they should have fought back. But unlike Danny, the survivors pointedly do not have a fascist mentality. In spite of what the Nazis did to them, they have not become creatures of violent revenge; one even speaks of Hitler being God's punishment to the Jews for abandoning the Torah. Danny projects himself into a repeated historical flashback, first as an SS officer impaling a Jewish infant on a bayonet, and later, as the infant's father who subsequently attacks the killer of his child. In this way, he finally comes to reconcile his Jewish identity with the feeling of being able to protect himself as a man; however, this breakthrough does little to help him overcome his basic fear, or the fascist mentality on which this fear is predicated. His final act of resistance is to commit suicide by blowing himself up inside a synagogue. It is as if the Third Reich has reached out to claim another Jewish victim, some fifty years after the fact.

In a coda to *The Believer*, meant to suggest a kind of afterlife purgatory, Danny repeatedly runs up the same flight of steps in his old Yeshiva, while his former teacher tells him: "Where do you think you're going? Don't you know? There's nothing up there." Indeed, in all of these anti-fascist films I have been describing, there is no imaginable way out of the fascist phenomenon. Like a virus in a Cronenberg film, the experience of fascism is unstoppable, fatalistic and, just as one cannot be "a little bit pregnant," all-or-nothing. Finally, one abdicates becoming one of the killers only by becoming one of those led to slaughter in some form or another. One passively goes down in order to avoid taking on the characteristics of oppression. And even in this, the anti-fascists only end up advertising that cult of death and destruction which so thoroughly imbues the Nazi imagination. The nihilism of fascism contaminates even the attempts of its discontented to oppose it, and turns their very meaning against them.

What is most profound about these films is also what is despairing and disturbing about them: there is no hero able to rise up against fascism, because there is no individual subjectivity strong enough to withstand exposure to it. Everything becomes an advertisement for that aestheticization of death which entirely consumes Nazi life. Anti-fascism becomes fascist, and nullifies its own best intentions; even when nominal fascism is defeated its values win according to a psychosocial ecology which measures everything precisely by wins and losses, survivals and decimations. A truly anti-fascist viewpoint would be one which begins somewhere beyond the division (endemic, also, to the visceral racisms and prejudices which fascism exploits) into Good Guys to be worshipped and Bad Guys to be hated. For, as revealed by the films of Oshima, Pasolini, et al., the ultimate fascist always comes from within (rather than being supremely inhuman, fascism is an expression of the sadly all-too-human), both in the mechanisms of sexual repression as well as sexual experience itself. Influence, impact, charisma—all things which obtain in sexual attraction between individuals—are also attributes of interpersonal fascism at work. *The Boys from Brazil* (1978) re-imagines the ideological war of aging Nazis and Nazi-hunters as a showdown between the Charisma of Evil and the Charisma of Good. Both mortally wounded, the Nazi concentration camp doctor Josef Mengele and his chief foe, a fictitious Nazi hunter, must fight to convince—using cheap actorly "sincerity" and breathless, extemporaneous, self-justifying rhetoric—the Hitler clone to sick his killer Dobermans on the other one. We know, objectively, that Mengele is a vicious, hypocritical liar, and his foe a righteous man; but the stage has been set for what anti-fascism has become at the turn of the millennium, and what it always incipiently was: precisely a battle of individual charismas. Sex appeal will never be absent from such a battle. Indeed, what Mengele tries to clone from Hitler's DNA in *The Boys from Brazil* is not just sadism and will to power, but that gleam in the blue eye, that likeable *ingénu* energy of a young man who says things like, "My teachers are nowhere" and "Far out" while he commands his attack dogs. And Mengele acknowledges that the success of his protégé is precisely his appeal: "You are a clever boy, are you not?" Getting the masses to submit to one's will is the same process as getting one person to submit. In the presence of fascism, everything which elicits the spontaneous reaction, "I like it—it turns me on," becomes deeply suspect. To feel, to enjoy— these are the first casualties of subjectivity.[11]

Charisma—the charisma of objects, the charisma of people—is the advertisement's stock in trade. Those passive-aggressive games of conversational chess which constitute Tarantino's dialogue (his characters browbeat each other with their "coolness," bullying and pulling rank over every little thing) make for a suspect if oddly effective method of explicating fascism's psychological stranglehold on its victims. In the opening scene of *Inglourious Basterds*, the fearsome and determined "Jew Hunter" is negotiating with a French farmer who is hiding Jewish refugees; the Jew Hunter asks leading questions, intended to frighten the farmer and break him down: "Are you aware of my existence? ... Now, are you aware of the job I have been ordered to carry out in France? ... Please tell me what you've heard ... Are you aware of the nickname the people of France have given me?" The essence of fascism is that it cuts off all hope of resisting it. This occurs at the very level of naming. A few scenes later, the leader of the Basterds will intimidate captured German prisoners in much the same way, with questions about whether they know who the Basterds are, and whether they know that the Bear Jew will kill them. To know who one's enemy is, is to already know that one is dead.[12]

Again, we see this in relation to "rep" or "bad rep" in advertising: apart from the fact that the ante has been upped because the exchange now takes place between people rather than, say, between rolls of paper towels, it is the exact same teasing, coy, bullying conversational exchange to get there. Sooner or later, the odds-on favorite, the biggest-best-most-absorbent towel will "blow away" its nearest competition; as the most highly vaunted, "secret weapon" killer will be unleashed to do whatever only he can do to the enemy of the moment. Tarantino understands that these showdowns must have a certain sameness, and must obey the logic of (loaded) choice which advertisers use; knows also that the outcome can never be random, for if the product most hyped to come out on top actually failed (in the commercial), the consumer will learn something, but money will suffer, money will be hurt. When the Bride kills dozens of martial arts fighters, working her way pyramidically up toward the kingpin Bill, money sleeps much more safely with each new level she achieves. Although tricked out as an avenger from within, a challenger to complacent criminality, she is actually nothing more than the roll of paper towels the money happens to be riding on.

In fact, such negotiated conversations like the one between the Jewish farmer and the Jew Hunter are deliberately structured in such a way that it is hardly different from any other crises of authority which occur in Tarantino dialogue: one thinks of the police interrogator trying to get Jackie Brown to confess to stealing the decoy money, and most obviously, the famous "tyranny of evil men" speech which Samuel L. Jackson's hit man delivers to his quarries in *Pulp Fiction* (1994). Tarantino's twist on the thriller genre (not a wholly new twist, but certainly one which he has made his own) is precisely that the hit man passively-aggressively intimidates and brutalizes his victims with language prior to shooting them. Responding with appropriate fear, the victims embody the intuition that to be spoken to at all by such a character, to attract his attention in the first place, is to be as good as dead; just as the French farmer automatically fears the Jew Hunter. In this sense, we can read much of Tarantino's work, retroactively through *Inglourious Basterds*, as an extended proposition that modern life is inherently totalitarian. A black woman from the ghetto lives in expectation of being harassed by cops; she and they are deemed natural antagonists; she knows no other possible reality. With less sociological specificity (Tarantino's sociology is always somewhat dubious, hitting the mark sometimes and at other times tending

only to reify hipster stereotypes and movie situations), citizens of
L.A. live in fear of being on the wrong end of a gangster's gun.
Within a supposedly free society, an entire subset of the social
order—with its own hierarchies, tastes, even special codes of
manners—exists to keep everyone in place. (Even when arguing
back and forth, the gangster characters in *Pulp Fiction* generally
defer to each other with the elaborate obsequies of those who are
extremely powerful or extremely psychopathic.) The Third Reich
leaves fewer options for survival, perhaps, than contemporary L.A.
(though Tarantino's films seem to want to refute this somewhat),
but paranoia is similarly institutionalized in both worlds: it exists
as a law of life.

To understand paranoia's intricate rules for daily social conduct
is to be, in a word, "cool" (though this word is inadequate to
express the darkest portions of the nihilist philosophy which
Tarantino dramatizes); to live in unawareness of those rules
is to become a likely victim. "Cool," in other words, means
precisely knowing one's place. The thundering rumble of bad guys'
fearsome reputations rolls out and precedes them, not only in ways
suggestive of a criminal underworld that encodes each member in
the simplest possible terms (what he is likely to do to hurt you; how
you are best off hurting him, if you can), long before the inevitable
showdown. The one who lives up to his or her reputation, the
one who has most successfully mastered life *as a constant job*, is
the winner, also the coolest one—as much as mass-manufactured
objects can be cool.

In either event, cool or un-cool, one is a kind of shaky employee
impaired by the universal condition of living under chronic fear.
Again, the Third Reich presents a referent for this condition on
a par with the gang wars and drug wars (and samurai wars) of
previous Tarantino offerings. In *Inglourious Basterds*, the hunted
Jewish refugee Shosanna whose family has been murdered by
Nazis manages to hold on to her individual subjectivity despite
all odds. The tendency toward masochism is one of fascism's first
entry points to the psyche; it is wholly absent in Shosanna. A motif
of the film is that she is pursued romantically by several Nazis,
and always recoils, unwilling to amplify their power over her by
viewing them romantically. Indeed, the shame of masochism is
something she, and the film, project onto other characters who
are French collaborators: when introduced to Goebbels and his

mistress, Shosanna has a mental image of the couple having doggy-style sex and emitting barnyard noises. As with (un-righteous) violence, obscenity is always a trademark of "the other."

Tarantino has visited this terrain before with a female character, sometimes with mixed results. Shosanna's revenge against the Nazis occupies the same territory as Beatrix Kiddo's rampage against the Deadly Viper Assassination Squad in *Kill Bill 1 and 2*, or Jackie Brown's plan to free herself from the ghetto; it is neither any more personal, nor any more inherently political (shouldn't it at least be the latter?). However, there is one difference, which suggests that Tarantino has attempted to internalize the fatalism of cinematic anti-fascists such as Oshima or Pasolini: unlike Beatrix and Jackie, Shosanna dies during her mission and implements her all-but-meaningless final revenge as a (literal) ghost in the machine, speaking, appropriately enough, from a film-within-the-film. Fascism has turned everything into a final artifice, and an advertisement—even a dead heroine's effort to destroy it.

However, this sophisticated moment of seeing even anti-fascism as a helpless projection taking place within an inscribed pattern of fascist thought and behavior is not the overriding strategy of *Inglourious Basterds*. What is more typical of the film is Tarantino's attempt to suggest a thuggish anti-fascism. To do this, he must distinguish between two kinds of violence, the violence committed by fascists and the violence committed by anti-fascists. This is a naive distinction, the mark of someone who learned about Nazism only through *Raiders of the Lost Ark* (1981), since fascist violence differs from anti-fascist violence, as one might expect, in very few ways: both are bloody and bloodthirsty, ruthless, vengeful, and (in dramaturgical terms) thrilling. One cannot even say that only the fascists make a point of preying on the weak and helpless: they do, but so do the anti-fascists as well. The only real difference is that the fascists, in playground logic, "started it"; therefore, fascists are evil and anti-fascists good. This simplistic dualism is already contaminated with fascist philosophy, specifically the idea that anything, even the most ruthless act of violence, can be justified. In this sense, we are watching a battle of uniforms rather than subjectivities, a battle of Good Guys and Bad Guys, with an obvious rooting interest, which elicits our own lust for blood in a specious and hypocritical way, even as it condemns that same lust for blood in the fascists. The language of Good Guys and Bad Guys reduces even heroes to object-status, robbing them of their individual human complexity, as in the trippy moment where Tarantino introduces the character of Hugo Stiglitz—killer of thirteen Gestapo officers—with his name spelled out in 1970's style cartoon letters.

Ultimately, the choice between subscribing to Frankfurt School pessimism or becoming a "basterd"-raider of cultural history may be a false one. The future of criticism will be to attempt a middle course between the two, although this way is perilous and requires a certain vigilance. Not only we who love film, but all of us, need to resist the idea that there is no way out of the bind created by capitalist representation, even though capitalism today (with its wholesale privatization of life and death) stands much closer to fascism than anything else on the planet. Capitalism's endless movie-show, however, already contains the moves needed to wrestle out from the chokehold of "sameness" and "domination," although we must each (literally) see our own way through.

It is axiomatic that Hitler's politics were aesthetic as opposed to moral; that the Third Reich was an enormous, frenzied show-business epic. Hitler has even been called the greatest filmmaker of the twentieth century, in that he used reality itself as raw material for his imagination of death, and thereby altered that reality on a massive scale. He re-orchestrated the German people's ways of seeing, though these turned out to be ways of *not seeing*. Joachim Fest finds it impossible to describe Hitler's usage of spectacle without making reference to filmmaking: "new lighting effects"; "the broad avenue between hundreds of thousands"; "gloomy music in the background"; "in such scenes." Nazism was a manipulation of phenomenological reality which could have perhaps only worked on people already accustomed—addicted, even—to viewing life through the reconstructed image of film. It is yet another way in which fascism remains an all-too-human syndrome. Among the multiple legacies of mistrust which Nazism has bequeathed to us and to every successive generation is this: when it comes to films, to be carried away by an epic master narrative, or by dazzling technical prowess, is already to surrender one's subjectivity to an experience which replicates the psychological effects of fascism upon the average cortex. Unless we are willing to do without aesthetic sensibility altogether, or do without suspense and even meaning, this is where the vigilance of seeing must take place; for these psychological effects of fascism take over even when a film's stated intention is meant to be anti-fascist; the appeal of instinctual emotional reactions defeats rationality nearly every time, and provides a crevice for the spirit of fascism to re-implant itself.

Notes

1   Max Horkheimer and Theodor W. Adorno, *Dialectic of Enlightenment*, ed. Gunzelin Schmid Noerr, trans. by Edmund Jephcott. (Stanford: Stanford University Press, 2002), 120.

2   Saul Friedlander, *Reflections of Nazism: An Essay on Kitsch and Death*, trans. Thomas Weyr. (New York: Harper & Row, 1984), 41–2.

3   Horkheimer and Adorno, 94.

4   Horkheimer and Adorno, 95.

5   Horkheimer and Adorno, 95.

6   Horkheimer and Adorno, 96–7.

7   Horkheimer and Adorno, 102.

8   For Tarantino's overdetermined purposes, only one Pabst is evoked: the engineer of one of Leni Riefenstahl's nationalistic Alpine-climbing vehicles, *The White Hell of Pitz Palu* (1929). In fact, there were many Pabsts: the rarefied Expressionist of *Secrets of a Soul* (1926), the purveyor of sophisticated social melodrama in *Joyless Street* (1925) and *Diary of a Lost Girl* (1929); and, the one that angered Goebbels most, the instinctual communist of *Comradeship* (1930), and *The Threepenny Opera* (1931).

9   Friedlander, 43.

10 The links between fascism and perverse sexuality have become so commonplace that even a mainstream film, Stephen Daldry's *The Reader* (2008), can lean on them without feeling the slightest need either to untangle the knotted enigma at the heart of the Nazi-sex genre or deviate from the trappings of the same. An escaped female war criminal in hiding engages in an illicit sexual affair over a period of time with a young boy, with the implicit implication that her Nazi past has triggered the need for precisely this kind of redemption-through-unlikely-romance, and also with the blatant fear that she is using the warmth and passion of sexual education to indoctrinate the future generation with sympathy for Nazis.

11 Just as "sentiment" and "enjoyment" are also turned against their bearer in the manipulative world of commercial advertising.

12 It is to reverse this power of naming that Hitler decrees that Bear Jew will no longer be called "Bear Jew."

Works cited

Ai no korîda/In the Realm of the Senses. Directed by Nagisa Oshima. Japan/France, 1976.

The Believer. Directed by Henry Bean. USA, 2001.

Berlin Alexanderplatz. Directed by Rainer Werner Fassbinder. West Germany/Italy, 1980.

The Boys from Brazil. Directed by Franklin J. Schaffner. UK/USA, 1978.

Deutschland bleiche Mutter/Germany, Pale Mother. Directed by Helma Sanders-Brahms. West Germany, 1980.

Die bitteren Tränen der Petra von Kant/The Bitter Tears of Petra von Kant. Directed by Rainer Werner Fassbinder. West Germany, 1972.

Die Büchse der Pandora /Pandora's Box. Directed by G. W. Pabst. Germany, 1929.

Fest, Joachim. *Hitler.* Boston: Mariner Books, 2002.

Friedlander, Saul. *Reflections of Nazism: An Essay on Kitsch and Death.* Translated by Thomas Weyr. New York: Harper & Row, 1984.

Grotowski, Jerzy. *Towards a Poor Theater.* London: Routledge, 2002.

Horkheimer, Max, and Theodor W. Adorno. *Dialectic of Enlightenment.* Edited by Gunzelin Schmid Noerr and translated by Edmund Jephcott. Stanford: Stanford University Press, 2002.

Il portiere di notte/The Night Porter. Directed by Liliana Cavani. Italy, 1974.

Inglourious Basterds. Directed by Quentin Tarantino. USA/Germany, 2009.

Jackie Brown. Directed by Quentin Tarantino. USA, 1997.

Kill Bill: Vol. 1. Directed by Quentin Tarantino. USA, 2003.

Kill Bill: Vol. 2. Directed by Quentin Tarantino. USA, 2004.

La caduto degli dei/Götterdämmerung a.k.a. *The Damned.* Directed by Luchino Visconti. Italy/West Germany, 1969.

Man Hunt. Directed by Fritz Lang. USA, 1941.

Novecento/1900. Directed by Bernardo Bertolucci. Italy/France/West Germany, 1976.

Pulp Fiction. Directed by Quentin Tarantino. USA, 1994.

Raiders of the Lost Ark. Directed by Steven Spielberg. USA, 1981.

Roma, città aperta/Rome, Open City. Directed by Roberto Rossellini. Italy, 1945.

Salò o le 120 giornate di Sodoma/Salò or the 120 Days of Sodom.
   Directed by Pier Paolo Pasolini. Italy/France, 1975.
Sauve qui peut (la vie)/Slow Motion a.k.a. *Every Man for Himself.*
   Directed by Jean-Luc Godard. France/Austria/West Germany/
   Switzerland, 1980.
Wanda. Directed by Barbara Loden. USA, 1970.

6

Vengeful violence: *Inglourious Basterds*, allohistory, and the inversion of victims and perpetrators

Michael D. Richardson

When Quentin Tarantino's long-planned war film premiered at Cannes, it received a nearly ten-minute-long standing ovation.[1] Following its full release, the film continued to garner a significant amount of critical and popular success worldwide, grossing over $320 million, making it Tarantino's most successful film to date.[2] For his role as the charming yet malevolent Colonel Hans Landa, Christoph Waltz won numerous awards, including an Academy Award for Best supporting actor. But the film was not without its critics, unsurprising perhaps given its irreverent treatment of the

Second World War and its fantastical alternate account of the death of Hitler. Some of the criticisms concerned Tarantino's stylistic tendencies—his love of scenes with extended conversations, his repeated citations of other films and almost obsessive "cinema scholasticism."[3] Others castigated Tarantino for his penchant for excessive and sometimes graphic violence. But the film provoked the strongest negative reaction from critics who saw it as an affront to victims of the Holocaust and a dangerous reconstruction of the Holocaust and the Nazi regime. These criticisms of the film centered around two main issues: the brutality of the protagonists, a group of Jewish G.I.s who infiltrate Germany and spread terror and carnage, and the alternate history in which Hitler is blown up along with the high command during a screening of a propaganda film. In his review of *Inglourious Basterds*, Daniel Mendelsohn castigates the film for its inversion of German perpetrators and Jewish victims, asking, "Do you really want audiences cheering for a revenge that turns Jews into carbon copies of Nazis, that makes Jews into 'sickening' perpetrators?"[4] Jonathan Rosenbaum concurred, but added that the film was "morally akin to Holocaust denial."[5]

It might strike one as unfair to apply arguments that are more at home in discussions of filmic representations of the Holocaust, where both the moral identities of Jewish characters and a film's claims to authenticity—its ability to represent the Holocaust accurately or comprehensively—are key points of debate, particularly since Tarantino's film avoids any direct reference to the Holocaust itself. Its invocation here by critics is both a tactical move—to accuse Tarantino of this sort of sacrilege elevates their moral condemnation of their critiques to the ultimate level—and a reflection that the Holocaust remains a central image in U.S. popular consciousness about the Second World War, one that even when not invoked directly, is nonetheless implied in discussions of Hitler and the Nazis, particularly when anti-Semitism is invoked. Moreover, the points of contention here—the inversion of victim and perpetrator, the use of alternate history—are not new to Tarantino's film, but represent two recurring, and linked, tropes in films about Hitler and the Nazis. The inversion of victim and perpetrator, or Ally and Nazi, is common to works which take as their subject an alternate history of the Nazi era or its aftermath, a history in which Hitler remains very much alive—at least until he can be destroyed all over again, this time with certainty and with a degree of brutality—and takes two forms. The first, dating back to Chaplin's *The Great Dictator* (1941), involves characters coded as victims mistakenly identified as perpetrators. Often done to comic effect, these instances of passing—Chaplin's Jewish Barber passing for the Dictator Adenoid Hynkel, Salomon Perel in *Europa, Europa* (1990), posing as a Hitler Youth soldier—serve to undermine Nazi claims of racial superiority by rendering Nazis themselves unable to perceive physical differences between Jews and Aryans. The second such inversion is one in which Allied soldiers masquerade as Nazis, sometimes even as Hitler, an impersonation that both undermines the Hitler myth and enables protagonists to embody Nazis, to the extent that they commit transgressive acts that would otherwise be seen as immoral.[6]

Nonetheless, the location of Tarantino's film in these two contexts does not mitigate the criticisms regarding the controversial nature of his film, as these sets of representations carry their own concerns. While the ostensible intent of those films that resurrect Hitler in order to kill him once again is an empowerment of Nazi victims and the reclamation of a possibility of closure lost with Hitler's suicide and the disappearance of his body, these works are problematic on two levels. They not only uncritically engage the audience in revenge fantasies that replicate the appeal of a violent fascist aesthetics, but the dubious righteousness of the protagonists (coded as former victims) also allows them to circumvent moral restrictions, undermining precisely those moral and ethical standards that are seen as distinguishing Nazi from victim. In situating itself within these two contexts, *Tarantino's* film, on the level of both content and form, seeks to appropriate fascist tactics, and in doing so ultimately replicates, not critiques, Nazi aesthetics.

To best understand how Tarantino's film fails to escape the object of its critique, it is important to situate the film within two larger generic contexts: alternate history narratives that focus on the death of Hitler, and war films of the late 1960s and early 1970s. While *Basterds* took a not insignificant amount of criticism for its fictionalization of the war, there is a long-established literary corpus of alternate histories (or allohistory) of the Second World War. These range from well-researched counterfactual tales in which a single moment or event tips the balance in favor of the Nazis (e.g.

Harry Turtledove's novel *In the Presence of Mine Enemies*, where the U.S. policy of continued isolationism allows the Axis to win), to more fantastic alien interventions or time travel: the almost trite motif of going back in time to kill Hitler before he comes to power. What is interesting to note here, however, is that, while Hitler's eventual death or rather his survival, followed by his death, is a key element in these stories, very few posit an alternate history in which Hitler is killed before 1944. Instead, they focus on Hitler's continued survival into the post-war period, either as part of a Nazi victory over the Allies, or as a fugitive hiding out in South America, or even the United States—or imagine a world in which Hitler has never come to power.[7]

Ironically, the few narratives that do concern Hitler suffering an untimely death, or which imagine the possibility of returning to the past to thwart his career or end his life, portray an alternate reality in which Hitler's absence has negative consequences for geopolitical history.[8] In Stephen Fry's *Making History*, a successful experiment by a young history student and the son of a Nazi doctor at Auschwitz to send a birth control pill back in time to the well used by Hitler's father, rendering him infertile, leads to a more successful Nazi state lead by a *Führer* who is even more ruthless and committed than Hitler. Even the death of Hitler relatively late in the war, such as in Douglas Niles and Michael Dobson's *Fox on the Rhine*, where Hitler is indeed killed by the 1944 conspirators, does nothing to alter history for the better. Since these works are, by their very nature, not opposed to counterfactual history, the reason for this is puzzling. Gavriel Rosenfeld offers two possible reasons for the lack of scenarios in which Hitler's early death is positive: a generally high degree of satisfaction with the post-war world that Hitler's later defeat helped to create, and a recognition that eliminating Hitler, a single individual, would do little to counter larger tendencies of nationalism and racism prevalent in post-WWI Germany.

To this I would add a third reason: Hitler's singular status in popular culture as an embodiment of pure evil. Even in the realm of fiction, Hitler looms too large as a figure to be completely deprived of his power. Killing Hitler before he becomes Hitler proper offers none of the emotional satisfaction that the death of Hitler, mass murderer, scourge of the Western world provides. It also deprives popular culture of the sort of absolute villain that transcends cultural and political shifts. The persistence of Hitler, or rather representations of Hitler and the Nazis in popular culture since the end of the Second World War, is indicative of the way in which Hitler and Nazism have come to stand in for evil itself; though such representations are ostensibly about the Nazi regime, their cultural import lay much more in their reflection of the political and cultural circumstances of their production. Thus, representations of Hitler during the cold war functioned primarily as vehicles for anti-Communist messages by collapsing Nazism into Communism under the concept of totalitarianism, decoupling Nazism from its historical referent and allowing it to function as a generalized icon of evil.[9] Films such as *He Lives: The Search for the Evil One* (1967) or *They Saved Hitler's Brain* (1968), which depict Hitler surviving in Latin America plotting his return to power, serve as justifications for the aggressive, interventionist anti-Communist foreign policy of the time. Even more contemporary films function in this way: *Hitler's Daughter* (1990), a television movie in which one of three powerful women could be Hitler's illegitimate daughter, can be read as a not-so-subtle critique of the proliferation of women in politics in the late 1980s. In times when the U.S. lacked a strong aggressor, identifying a villain as a neo-Nazi is sufficient, as this provides an easily recognizable reference for evil: the film version of *The Sum of All Fears* (2002) features a neo-Nazi terrorist who attempts to reignite U.S.–Russian tensions to the point that they destroy each other.

As the last example above demonstrates, this use of Nazism and the Second World War as an allegory for contemporary political and cultural concerns is not limited to alternate history accounts of Hitler's death, but can be seen in the evolving nature of films depicting the war. What links these two genres—alternate history accounts of Hitler's death and war films of the late 1960s and early 1970s—is their often excessive displays of violence towards Hitler and the Nazis, an excess that is clearly present in Tarantino's film. On the most general level, the film's depiction of Allied soldiers acting violently or even brutally is not problematic. If anything, this representation offers a counterbalance to long-held cultural myths of WWII as a 'clean' war, at least in terms of Allied behavior. As Charles Taylor notes in his defense of the film's moral vision, "In a real war, everyone commits atrocities, the Allied forces in the Second World War included."[10] Recent films about the Second

World War, such as *Saving Private Ryan* (1998), have focused particularly on the psychic toll that soldiers experienced during the war, the impossibility of acting virtuously in the face of carnage, the realization that war is inherently violent, brutal, and without clearly demarcated boundaries of good and evil behavior. But the problem with this defense is that it fails to recognize the ways in which this violence is presented in war films of the sort that Tarantino imitates in *Inglourious Basterds*.

There was no shortage of films produced during and immediately after the Second World War that featured heroic protagonists defeating the Nazis. While these films did not shy away from showing fatalities, they generally offered a sanitized view of the violence of war, focused significantly on subplots involving romantic encounters, and offered resolutions that neatly mapped the conflict onto pre-existing binarisms of good and evil. As time progressed, films about the Second World War began to offer slightly more complex visions of the conflict, or at least of the soldiers involved. Robert Aldrich's controversial portrayal of incompetence and corruption in the military leadership in *Attack* (1956) was considered so unflattering that the U.S. military refused to cooperate in its filming. *The Young Lions* (1958) featured a protagonist (Montgomery Clift) who faced anti-Semitism within the ranks of the U.S. military. Carl Foreman's *The Victors* (1963) eschewed battle scenes and focused on the psychic toll that the war had on Allied soldiers, whose battle weariness was mixed with cruelty and indifference. Two general threads began to emerge in this next generation of war films. First, battle scenes become more explicit and more sensational, with increasingly graphic depictions of injury and death. Second, the protagonists at the center of these films become increasingly anti-heroic and even unlikeable. No longer were soldiers cast in the mold of Audie Murphy; instead they were often troubled, prone to violence, and emotionally unstable. These anti-heroes were not without their redeeming qualities—as always, the baseline for determining their inherent goodness was their willingness to combat fascism—but their disdain for military hierarchy, for the rules of war, indeed for rules of any sort, often located them on the criminal fringe of society.

The best example of this new type of war film was Aldrich's *The Dirty Dozen* (1967). In this film, the titular dozen are military prisoners, condemned either to life in prison or death for murder, rape, and assorted violent criminal acts. Promised a pardon in exchange for participating in what is clearly a suicide mission, the dozen soldiers, under the direction of a flinty major who himself is often insubordinate and borderline criminal, eventually cohere into a crack commando unit. Much like *Attack*, *The Dirty Dozen* revolves to a great extent around the tension between opportunistic careerists in the military and soldiers coded as 'real soldiers' who are more than capable of fighting the war on their own terms. But this anti-authoritarian tendency is only an obstacle for the commandos to overcome on their way to their ultimate goal, namely the assassination of a number of German generals holed up in a chalet. The final third of the movie consists of the attack on the chalet and the soldiers' attempt to escape. In these new war films, as in *Inglourious Basterds*, there are no rules of engagement, no mercy for the unarmed or even the civilian. While the original mission in *The Dirty Dozen* is the assassination of military personnel in an effort to disrupt German forces on the eve of the D-Day invasion, by the end of the assault the generals, along with a number of female companions, have locked themselves in a cellar. As the commando unit is cut down one by one by German soldiers lurking in windows and rooftops, they dump hand grenades and gasoline into the air vents, after which Jefferson (former all-pro running back Jim Brown) sprints across the compound dropping live grenades in the vents. This taut sequence predictably focuses on Jefferson's heroic and ultimately fatal run; having successfully dropped the final grenade, he is cut down by sniper just yards from the vehicle the other soldiers are using to escape.

The film's treatment of Jefferson's death is in stark contrast to its treatment of the mass murder that his actions have caused. While the film cuts back and forth between close-ups of Jefferson's stunned and saddened comrades and his lifeless body, it only fleetingly shows the doomed Germans trying to escape, instead focusing on the explosions and the destruction of the chateau. In an odd exchange shortly before the explosion, the film acknowledges somewhat the gruesomeness of this crime: after dumping bags of the grenades down the air vents, Reisman orders the others to pour gasoline as well. Sergeant Bowren hesitates, as if to wonder if this is not too much, before complying with the request. Why it would be acceptable to kill the Germans with hand grenades but not gasoline is an interesting question. What makes this hesitation even more puzzling is that Bowren had, only moments ago, ordered another one of the soldiers to summarily execute a group of German soldiers who had surrendered, saying gruffly, "You know what you have to do." These deaths, as well, take place off-screen. It is not difficult to read this film, and particularly the destruction of the chateau, in terms of contemporary anxieties about the Vietnam War—an enemy hiding in the shadows that can only be defeated by a sort of firebombing, the indiscriminate death of civilians.

Still, what distinguishes *The Dirty Dozen* from *Inglourious Basterds* is the fate of the soldiers in the former. Of the original dozen soldiers, only one (Wladislaw) survives, along with Major Reisman and Sergeant Bowren. The others are given posthumous pardons and recognized as war heroes, but it is telling that their redemption came at the cost of their lives. Also telling is the fact that all of the soldiers (except perhaps Wladislaw, whose crime was to shoot a fleeing commanding officer) recruited for this mission had already proven themselves to be morally deficient. Immoral or even atrocious acts are left to those who have already been judged as criminal and thus in violation of existing norms of behavior: the commandos in *The Dirty Dozen*, *The Devil's Brigade* (1968), and the original *The Inglorious Bastards* (1978) are all current or former military prisoners, who continue to fight only (at least at first) to secure their freedom. These films thus sanction immoral behavior, but carefully circumscribe who actually commits such acts. The commanding officers of these troops straddle a line between military authority and insubordination, identifying in part with each group, but allied enough with establishment norms to give their command legitimacy. Tellingly, even though the actions of these soldiers are shown to be in the service of the greater good, nearly all of them fail to survive; to do so, to give such soldiers a pardon or other military honors, would undermine the moral legitimacy of the Allied cause and render the actions of other soldiers potentially suspect; thus the film's narrative provides a distance between the actions of regular soldiers and those of a prisoner brigade. This was also the case in Tarantino's ostensible inspiration, the Italian film *The Inglorious Basterds*, whose title characters were also criminals, and their heroics a necessary step in their reintegration into the military, or at least their escape from military service.

It is not insignificant that a key moment in the plot of *The Dirty Dozen* is the successful infiltration of the Nazi chateau by two of the main characters (Reisman and Wladislaw), for which they must don German uniforms and pass themselves off as German officers. While this masquerade is necessary to the mission of the commandos, it also represents a symbolic transformation of the soldiers, who, now dressed in Nazi regalia, can begin their mission of assassination without any moral qualms. The power of the uniform in WWII films is significant, both on the level of enabling protagonists to engage in actions that fall outside of the realm of soldierly behavior, and on the level of aesthetic appeal.[11] Going back to the war films of the 1940s, the frequent trope of impersonation often serves as the prelude to violence. In the 1944 film *Hitler, Dead or Alive*, in which a group of Chicago gangsters go undercover in Germany to kill Hitler in order to collect a million dollar bounty, it is only once the gangsters have donned Nazi uniforms that they begin killing. In these moments, one can see how the Nazi uniform itself seems to serve as a sort of supernatural garment, one that exercises an evil influence over whomever wears it. Even in a comedy such as Radu Mihaileanu's *Train de Vie/ Train of Life* (1998), in which an entire Jewish shtetl fakes its own deportation in order to escape to Palestine, Mordechai, the butcher who only reluctantly agrees to serve as the Kommandant, becomes increasingly authoritarian and harsh the longer he must inhabit the uniform.

There is a sort of double inversion that takes place in *Inglourious Basterds*, where the Nazi-imitating heroes are not only U.S. soldiers, but Jews as well. Yet while this gives the film its emotional power as a revenge fantasy (as opposed to merely a re-hash of earlier war films), it does not make the inversion any less problematic. In his study, *The "Jew" in Cinema*, Omer Bartov notes that, while the Jew as victim was unsurprisingly a common trope in post-Second World War cinema, there also emerged a need to create a post-war, heroic Jew, one capable of charting a path to liberty and self-assertion.[12] In language that prefigures Mendelsohn's critique of *Inglourious Basterds*, Bartov argues that making Jews out to be heroes meant inverting the characteristics of victim and perpetrator, to the extent that the heroic Jew, "eventually emerges as a figure that bears a disturbing resemblance to the persecutor himself: callous, brutal, humorless, and deadly."[13] Rather than empowering Jews and shattering the image of the weak, passive Jew, this inversion functions to confirm anti-Semitic stereotypes:

"The notion of Jewish heroism as finding expression only in a Nazi uniform is of course an extreme version of the entire discourse on Jewish degeneration, masculinity, and passivity that formed an important element of anti-Semitic, Zionist, and post-Holocaust discourse."[14] For all of the film's valorization of the Jewish "Basterds," they remain relatively faceless: we learn nothing of the backstories of the soldiers who volunteer to become part of the Basterds, with many lacking names entirely. Having a Jewish heritage replaces a criminal background as a qualification for this group. And what are we to make of the fact that they are led by a particularly non-Jewish figure—the blond-haired, blue-eyed Aldo Raine? The only Jewish soldier who is noticeably distinct from the others, Donny Donowitz (Eli Roth), is distinguished for his brutality. Known as the "Bear Jew," Donny executes captive German soldiers by beating them to death with a baseball bat.

There is a curious relationship between the two revenge narratives that comprise the film. While they ultimately converge in the climactic scene in the cinema, the protagonists remain, until the end, oblivious of the other's plot to assassinate Hitler and the High Command, to the point that the Basterds nearly spoil Shosanna's well-laid plan for revenge. It is clear, however, that we are to understand these narratives as following similar tracks, primarily since they are driven by Jewish protagonists. By linking the narratives in this way, Shosanna's deeply personal desire for retribution for the murder of her family as depicted at the beginning of the film lends an air of moral credibility and legitimates the actions of the Basterds beyond their stated project of spreading terror. Thus, while the film provides no individual histories of the soldiers, they are connected, by virtue of their Jewish heritage, to a traumatic past that functions to temper the brutality of their actions.

For defenders of the film, *Inglourious Basterds'* revisionist history and its use of sadistic violence in the name of ending the war is negated by the fact that the film makes no pretense at reality. Framing his story as he does—introducing it with the classic fairy tale formulation "Once Upon A Time" is not only an intertextual reference to Sergio Leone's *Once Upon a Time in The West* (purportedly considered for the title of the film as well), but an attempt to mark the film as mere fantasy, set in a time and place distant from the present, thus immunizing it from criticisms about its lack of authenticity or realism. Just as films that begin with an epigraph attesting to the veracity of the events about to be depicted set up a contract with viewers binding them to the film's content, however unlikely, this disavowal of authenticity in *Inglourious Basterds* establishes viewers in a relationship with the film that exonerates them from making moral judgments on the violence that they are about to see.[15] Because it makes no pretense to historical accuracy and thus realism, the film is exempted from the normal sort of moral engagement that viewers have. While viewers will, inevitably, respond on a visceral and a judgmental level as they do in almost all cases, they are inoculated against charges of sadism by presenting the events as pure fantasy. For viewers, the meaning of the violence depicted in the film has been pre-established through its choice of subject matter. Hitler and the Nazis as signifiers produce reflexive moral judgments difficult to overcome. There is no question of a need or justification to fight against such villains, nor is there a question of limitation on the means of such confrontation.

Inglourious Basterds only reinforces this calcified moral judgment by establishing the film's villain (the self-professed Jew Hunter Colonel Landa) not its heroes, in the long opening scene. Landa arrives as the farmhouse of a French villager suspected of harboring a neighboring Jewish family that has thus far eluded him. Sitting alone with the farmer, Landa delivers a speech, in which he describes, in terms familiar to anyone aware of Nazi anti-Semitic stereotypes, Jews as rats that need to be exterminated. His calm, even cheerful demeanor only serves to highlight his malevolence: even when he produces an oversized calabash pipe, this does not mitigate the sinister nature of his talk, and instead serves to prefigure the actual violence that is about to take place—the massacre of the Jewish family hiding under the floorboards.

Although the mission that drives the second half of the film is the assassination of Hitler and the high command, Hitler himself is portrayed throughout the film as precisely the sort of impotent and cartoonish figure that has defined Hitler representations going back to Chaplin's *Great Dictator*. Instead it is the figure of Colonel Landa who stands in for the seemingly all-powerful, menacing Nazi. This split is in some ways nothing new—one sees it in Chaplin's *Great Dictator* as well, where Hynkel is an absurd clown and Garbitsch (i.e., Goebbels) is a more sinister figure. Indeed, most filmic representations of Hitler and the Nazis pendulate between two extremes—Hitler as evil incarnate or inept loser.[16]

It is Landa who is responsible for much of the film's action, occupying a significant amount of screen time. He offers a striking counterpoint to his ostensible nemesis Aldo Raine. Where Landa is handsome and dapper, Raine is scarred, rumpled; Landa speaks several languages fluently and eloquently, while Raine's southern accent renders his English comical and his non-existent Italian unconvincing; Landa possesses a quick intelligence, while Raine relies more on gut instincts. Typically "Jewish" character traits, as articulated in anti-Semitic rhetoric—valuing or respecting the individual over the community and privileging intellect over feeling—describe Landa as well, particularly when he not only aids the Basterds, but actually increases the charge on the bomb that kills Hitler and his minions. Whereas Landa lacks any sort of allegiance save to himself, Shosanna, Raine and the other Basterds are not only willing to die for their cause (only Raine and Utivich actually survive), but they act out of emotional rather than intellectual reasons. This opposition between Raine and Landa extends to all of the characters in the film. As Georg Seeßlen notes, the heroes behave like barbaric murderers from B-movies, while the Nazis are represented by cultivated citizens of the world: "A German film diva is a double-agent, a charming young man is a monster and destroys as radically as possible the image of the young men who 'abuse' the Nazis; the fleeing Jewish girl is anything but a sacrificial lamb, and makes her requests in sentences like these clear: 'Either you do what we want, or this axe will land in your head.'"[17]

It is fair to say that, on a certain level, Raine himself functions as a fascist leader figure. He demands complete obedience from his soldiers, heroically represses sexual impulses (unlike other war movie heroes, Raine has no romantic interests) and as implied by his unexplained scar, has undergone a physical ordeal and survived, meaning that his vitality is high. In this regard, we can see Raine and the aesthetics of the film in general to be in line with National Socialist aesthetics as summarized by Susan Sontag in her essay "Fascinating Fascism." Sontag posits that National Socialism stands for "the ideal of life as art, the cult of beauty, the fetishism of courage, the dissolution of alienation in ecstatic feelings of community; the repudiation of the intellect; the family of man (under the parenthood of leaders)."[18] Raine's habit of

carving a swastika into the foreheads of Nazis whom he has spared
is explained as a desire to prevent them from ever shedding their
Nazi identity and presumably their guilt. Yet in Landa's case it also
functions to bring him down to Raine's level, to disfigure him as
Raine himself is disfigured.

While the film contains no shortage of scenes of death, of all of
the graphic violence in the film, including several acts repeatedly
committed by the Basterds, three stand out as particularly gruesome:
the bludgeoning to death with a baseball bat of defenseless German
soldiers, the scalping of dead Germans, and Raine's habit of carving
a swastika into the foreheads of the Nazis he has spared. The way
in which Tarantino stages these moments—they are extremely
graphic and yet highly stylized—does not challenge viewers, but
rather soothes the initial revulsion to witnessing such brutal
actions. This mixture of excessive and aestheticized violence is a
trademark of Tarantino's work: from the scene in *Reservoir Dogs*
featuring Mr. Blonde (Michael Madsen) torturing and maiming
a captive police officer to the somewhat incongruous sounds of
"Stuck in the Middle with You," to the stylized killing of dozens
of Yakuza assassins in *Kill Bill*, his films have featured set pieces
whose primary purpose is to foreground Tarantino's filmmaking
skills and knowledge of pop culture. But the violence depicted in
Tarantino's films, is, to use a formulation coined by writer Devin
McKinney, "weak." That is to say, it functions as mere formal
device, something that does not engage the viewer on any level
other than the aesthetic. "Strong" violence by contrast not only
evokes the sort of unmitigated, unsocialized emotions that Linda
Williams ascribes to the "body" genres or excessive film types, but
it also "acts on the mind by refusing it glib comfort and immediate
resolutions."[19] Such violence thus not only engages audiences on an
emotional level, but it brings this engagement to bear on rational
and ultimately moral questions, carrying consequences for both
film protagonists and viewers that go beyond the level of plot.
But in Tarantino's films, violence, no matter how graphic, always
remains superficial in that neither victim, nor victimizer is a figure
of identification for the viewer, who remains at a cool distance.[20]
In the aforementioned scene in *Reservoir Dogs*, Mr. Blonde's
motivations for mutilating the police officer are explicitly sadistic:
"I don't give a good fuck what you know, or don't know, but I'm
gonna torture you anyway, regardless. Not to get information.

It's amusing, to me, to torture a cop:" The violence serves only to entertain Mr. Blonde and by extension the audience. Even in those films where violent acts are part of the protagonist's well-motivated desire for revenge (*Kill Bill*: Vols. 1 & 2; *Death Proof*) violence is portrayed in a way that mitigates an emotional engagement with the act. By overlaying somewhat ironic pop tunes, switching to black-and-white or animated scenes, and introducing humor, Tarantino relieves the audience of its discomfort with the brutality of the images and induces an enjoyable aesthetic experience.

One should consider, however, if the gruesome, over-the-top violence in *Basterds* is intended parodically or with the same degree of irony as in his earlier works such as *Grindhouse*. Humor in *Inglourious Basterds* is of a much less self-deprecating and more sadistic variety. The quips delivered by Raine in his down-home patois shortly before or after the murder of German soldiers are intended for his own amusement and that of the audience. Moreover, in as much as one can use the term with regard to this film, the violence is much more *realistic*. Whereas *Kill Bill* featured a fight sequence in which the protagonist is literally drenched in the blood of her defeated opponents, the violent bludgeonings of defenseless German soldiers and their scalpings at the hands of the Basterds are graphic, yet restrained enough to provide them with a sense of verité.

Although it is the Basterds who are featured prominently in the film's publicity materials, the other revenge narrative, which focuses on a young French-Jewish girl Shosanna Dreyfus, whose family is massacred at the beginning of the film by Landa's men, carries equal weight in the film. Unlike the story of Raine and his commandos, Shosanna's narrative is played straight. From her frantic escape from the farmhouse basement where her family is massacred to her furtive plans at revenge, her character is given a depth and emotional backstory that the other protagonists lack. As such, both her motive for revenge and the audience's identification with her from the opening scene, enable viewers to elide the moral issues regarding her plan to immolate the Nazi brass and understand it as a just form of retribution. Shosanna is in many ways the opposite of other cinematic female Jewish survivors (i.e., *The Night Porter*, 1974) who are assumed to have survived only through sexual acquiescence or whose experiences have left them traumatized to the point of paralysis; she is single-minded in her determination to exact revenge.

Nevertheless, Shosanna's narrative, thematized as it is, suffers from the same problematic aestheticization of violence as does the narrative of the Basterds. It is with Shosanna that the self-referentiality of Tarantino's film reaches an apotheosis, as it is film itself, i.e., the pile of highly flammable nitrate film stock, that is responsible for the burning of the cinema's audience. As the crowd futilely attempts to escape the locked cinema, Shosanna's face appears on-screen through footage surreptitiously spliced into the propaganda film *Nation's Pride* to announce that she, a Jew, is responsible for their death.[21] As Raine remarks when speaking to a group of German prisoners about to be executed, "Watching Donnie beat Nazis to death is the closest we ever get to the movies." Tarantino himself puts it even more bluntly: "I like that it's the power of cinema that fights the Nazis. But not just as a metaphor, as a literal reality."[22] This execution scene indeed affords viewers a similar instance of cinematic pleasure, building tension until the moment that the "Bear Jew" makes a somewhat theatrical entrance, as if he were waiting offstage for a signal to enter from the wings.

But it is fair to ask if the film's highly stylized images of death, the linkage of "violence with the pleasures of film for film's sake" particularly in the climactic scene, afford the viewer any sense of a detachment that would allow them to critically engage with the "the sadistic-scopophilic joys of cinematic masquerade?"[23] It is highly unlikely, given Tarantino's unabashed and uncritical love of cinematic history, as well as the film's final line uttered by Raine as he contemplates the swastika he has carved into Landa's head: "This may just be my masterpiece." This privileging of cinematic truth over reality, the confidence in the power of film to provide a revisionist notion of history and to shape the public's image of the present, is itself reminiscent of the Nazi film aesthetics, which privileged cinematic fantasy over reality. As Eric Rentschler notes, Nazi film was a cinema dedicated to illusion:

> Nazi film theorists stressed the importance of kinetic images as well as galvanizing soundtracks. Music worked together with visuals to make the spectator lose touch with conceptual logic and discursive frameworks ... The ideal film would spirit people away from the real world and grant viewers access to a pleasant, compelling, and convincing alternative space.[24]

Tarantino's film, with its representation of an alternate history in which Jews were able to exact revenge on the Nazis, makes just such a case for an escape to fantasy.

Ultimately, the film fails to achieve any critical distance between itself and the actions and images that it ostensibly re-appropriates. Instead of turning the tables on the Nazis and on Nazi film, it replicates them and in doing so, legitimates that which it seeks to devalue. As I have argued, fictional portrayals of Hitler and the Nazis reveal much more about contemporary values than they do about the object of their representation. Thus, what is most disturbing about the film are the moral implications that its aestheticization of violence and death has for a contemporary reception. The film's message of justified torture and its Manichean worldview is not very far afield from other post-9/11 glorifications of sadism and brutality in the name of a greater good such as the U.S. television show *24* (2001–2010), which on a nearly weekly basis featured extended scenes of torture and brutality. None of the numerous wars and conflicts that followed the Second World War ever had the same level of moral legitimacy in the eyes of the American populace. From the Korean War through Vietnam and into the current wars in Afghanistan and Iraq, U.S. military action and by extension the country's status as a symbol of "the good guys" has been increasingly under fire. By returning to an ostensibly "pure" war and by portraying the actions of the Allies as unabashedly sadistic and brutal, Tarantino's film is indeed a "fairy tale" for a contemporary age.

Notes

1 Wigney, James, "Quentin's Glory Days." *Sunday Mail* (South Australia), August 16, 2009, 91.

2 According to the website *Box Office Mojo*, the total earnings for the film were $321,455,689, with roughly $200,000,000 coming from foreign grosses. See http://boxofficemojo.com/movies/?id=inglouriousbasterds.htm

3 See, for example, David Denby, "Americans in Paris." *The New Yorker*, August 24, 2009, 82; Peter Bradshaw, "A Nazi Piece of Work: *Inglourious Basterds*." The *Guardian*, August 21, 2009, 7.

4 Daniel Mendelsohn, "'*Inglourious Basterds*': When Jews Attack." *Newsweek*, August 18, 2009, 72.

5 See Jonathan Rosenbaum, "Recommended Reading: Daniel Mendelsohn on the New Tarantino." August 17, 2009. http://www. jonathanrosenbaum.com/?p=16514

6 For an extended discussion of the trope of impersonation in Hitler representations, see Michael D. Richardson, "'Heil Myself!' Impersonation and Identity in Comedic Representations of Hitler." In *Visualizing the Holocaust: Documents, Aesthetics, Memory*, eds. David Bathrick, Brad Prager and Michael D. Richardson. (Rochester: Camden House, 2008), 277–97.

7 For a thorough discussion of fictionalized accounts of Hitler's life (and death), see Gavriel D. Rosenfeld, *The World Hitler Never Made*. (Cambridge: Cambridge University Press, 2005).

8 See Rosenfeld, *The World Hitler Never Made*, 309–24.

9 For an extended discussion of the use of Nazism as an allegory for Cold War fears, see Joanna Lindenbaum, "The Villain Speaks the Victim's Language," ed. Tony Barta. (Westport: Praeger, 1998), 136.

10 Charles Taylor, "Violence as the Best Revenge: Fantasies of Dead Nazis." *Dissent* 57.1, (Winter 2010), 104.

11 Susan Sontag discusses the continuing fascination with Nazi uniforms, particularly in sexualized contexts. See Susan Sontag, "Fascinating Fascism [1974]," *Under the Sign of Saturn*. (New York: Farrar, Straus, Giroux, 1980), 73–105. See also Piotr Uklanski, *The Nazis* (Zurich, Berlin: Edition Patrick Frey, 1999).

12 Omer Bartov, *The "Jew" in Cinema: From The Golem to Don't Touch My Holocaust*. (Bloomington: Indiana University Press, 2005), 120.

13 Bartov, *The "Jew" in Cinema*, 121.

14 Bartov, *The "Jew" in Cinema*, 138.

15 Marco Abel, *Violent Affect: Literature, Cinema, and Critique after Representation*. (Lincoln: University of Nebraska Press, 2008), 18.

16 See Richardson, "'Heil Myself!'", 287–8.

17 Georg Seeßlen, *Quentin Tarantino gegen die Nazis: Alles über Inglourious Basterds*, 2nd revised and expanded edition. (Berlin: Bertz + Fischer, 2010), 199.

18 Sontag, "Fascinating Fascism," 96.

19 Williams uses the term "body genres" to describe those film genres that are intended to elicit physical reactions on the part of

viewers—horror, melodrama, pornography. See Devin McKinney, "Violence: The Strong and the Weak." *Film Quarterly* 46.4, (Summer 1993), 17.

20 McKinney, "Violence," 21.

21 This "Nazi" film is rife with cinematic references, both incidental and central to the point that the characters themselves are in on the joke. For a thorough list—and analysis—of the film's various cinematic references, see Ben Walters, "Debating *Inglourious Basterds*." *Film Quarterly* 63.2, (Winter 2009), 19–22.

22 "Bunch of Basterds," *Empire*, March, 2009, 30.

23 John Rieder, "Race and revenge fantasies in *Avatar*, *District 9*, and *Inglourious Basterds*." *Science Fiction Film and Television* 4.1, (2011), 54.

24 Eric Rentschler, *The Ministry of Illusion: Nazi Cinema and Its Afterlife*. (Cambridge, MA: Harvard University Press, 1996), 217.

Works cited

Abel, Marco. *Violent Affect: Literature, Cinema, and Critique after Representation*. Lincoln: University of Nebraska Press, 2008.

Attack. Directed by Robert Aldrich. USA, 1956.

Barta, Tony. "Film Nazis: The Great Escape." In *Screening the Past: Film and the Representation of History*, edited by Tony Barta. Westport: Praeger, 1998, 1–18.

Bartov, Omer. *The "Jew" in Cinema: From The Golem to Don't Touch My Holocaust*. Bloomington: Indiana University Press, 2005.

Bradshaw, Peter. "A Nazi Piece of Work: *Inglourious Basterds*." The *Guardian*, August 21, 2009.

"Bunch of Basterds." *Empire*. March, 2009, 30.

Denby, David. "Americans in Paris." *The New Yorker*, August 24, 2009.

The Devil's Brigade. Directed by Andrew V. McLaglen. USA, 1968.

The Dirty Dozen. Directed by Robert Aldrich. USA/UK, 1967.

Europa, Europa. Directed by Agnieszka Holland. Poland/Germany/France, 1990.

Fry, Stephen. *Making History*. London: Hutchinson, 1996.

The Great Dictator. Directed by Charlie Chaplin. USA, 1941.

Grindhouse: Death Proof. Directed by Quentin Tarantino. USA, 2007.

He Lives: The Search for the Evil One. Directed by Joseph Kane. USA, 1967.

Hitler, Dead or Alive. Directed by Nick Grinde. USA, 1942.

Hitler's Daughter. Directed by James A. Contner. USA, 1990.

The Inglorious Bastards/Quel maledetto treno blindato. Directed by Enzo G. Castellari. Italy, 1978.

Inglourious Basterds. Directed by Quentin Tarantino. USA/Germany, 2009.

Kill Bill: Vol 1. Directed by Quentin Tarantino. USA, 2003.

Kill Bill: Vol 2. Directed by Quentin Tarantino. USA, 2004.

McKinney, Devin. "Violence: The Strong and the Weak." *Film Quarterly*, 46.4, Summer 1993, 16–22.

Mendelsohn, Daniel. "'*Inglourious Basterds*': When Jews Attack." *Newsweek*, August 18, 2009.

The Night Porter/Il portiere di notte. Liliana Cavani. Italy, 1974.

Niles, Douglas and Michael Dobson. *Fox on the Rhine*. New York: Forge, 2000.

Once Upon a Time in The West/C'era una volta il West. Directed by Sergio Leone, Italy/USA, 1968.

Rentschler, Eric. *The Ministry of Illusion: Nazi Cinema and Its Afterlife*. Cambridge, MA: Harvard University Press, 1996.

Reservoir Dogs. Directed by Quentin Tarantino. USA, 1992.

Richardson, Michael D. "'Heil Myself!' Impersonation and Identity in Comedic Representations of Hitler." In *Visualizing the Holocaust: Documents, Aesthetics, Memory*, edited by David Bathrick, Brad Prager, and Michael D. Richardson. Rochester: Camden House, 2008, 277–97.

Rieder, John. "Race and revenge fantasies in *Avatar*, *District 9*, and *Inglourious Basterds*." *Science Fiction Film and Television*, 4.1, 2011, 41–56.

Rosenbaum, Jonathan. "Recommended Reading: Daniel Mendelsohn on the New Tarantino." http://www.jonathanrosenbaum.com/?p=16514

Rosenfeld, Gavriel D. *The World Hitler Never Made*. Cambridge: Cambridge University Press, 2005.

Saving Private Ryan. Directed by Steven Spielberg. USA, 1998.

Seeßlen, Georg. *Quentin Tarantino gegen die Nazis: Alles über Inglourious Basterds*. 2nd revised and expanded edition. Berlin: Bertz + Fischer, 2010.

Sontag, Susan. "Fascinating Fascism [1974]." In *Under the Sign of Saturn*. New York: Farrar, Straus, Giroux, 1980, 73–105.

The Sum of All Fears. Directed by Phil Alden Robinson. USA/Germany, 2002.

Taylor, Charles. "Violence as the Best Revenge: Fantasies of Dead Nazis," *Dissent*, 57.1, Winter 2010, 103–6.

They Saved Hitler's Brain. Directed by David Bradley. USA, 1968.

Train of Life/Train de Vie. Directed by Radu Mihaileanu. France/Belgium/Netherlands/Israel/Romania, 1998.

Turtledove, Harry. *In the Presence of Mine Enemies*. New York: Penguin, 2003.

Uklanski, Piotr. *The Nazis*. Zurich, Berlin: Edition Patrick Frey, 1999.

The Victors. Directed by Carl Foreman. USA, 1963.

Walters, Ben. "Debating *Inglourious Basterds*." *Film Quarterly* 63.2, Winter 2009, 19–22.

Wigney, James. "Quentin's Glory Days." *Sunday Mail* (South Australia). August 16, 2009.

The Young Lions. Directed by Edward Dmytryk. USA, 1958.

7

Inglourious Basterds and the gender of revenge

Heidi Schlipphacke

Quentin Tarantino's re-telling of the history of WWII, *Inglourious Basterds*, begins with an extreme long shot of a pristine French meadow with a simple farmhouse in the background. To the left of the farmhouse we see a small figure, and to the right of the house the farmer himself is chopping wood. The director seems to have presented us with a classic establishing shot, yet the scope is not quite broad enough to give us the overview that an establishing shot should provide. Perhaps more importantly, the camera is placed not at a height that would offer an omniscient view of the scene at hand but rather at a relatively low angle, the height of a small person with a camera, as if it were recording a child's experience. The camera is close enough to the grass to picture clearly the gentle waving of the blades in the wind. The traditional establishing shot is slightly off-kilter here; the convention is apparent, but the spectator is lured into a perspective that is more tangible and visceral, somewhat closer to the space of action than the convention dictates. The camera perspective here is one of a voyeur crouching in the grass; we can almost hear our own breath above the gentle sound of the wind. The contrast between the near-stasis of the scene in the background and the heightened presence of the foreground injects a split temporality into the film from the outset: in the background history is being (creatively) recreated, but the spectator experiences this history viscerally and in the present.

This opening shot is mirrored later in the same scene, as Shosanna Dreyfus (Mélanie Laurent), a Jewish girl hiding with her family under the farmer's floorboards, escapes while Nazi SS officers murder members of her family. The shot in which Shosanna runs toward the camera and away from the Nazis recreates the opening shot of the film: the camera records the waving blades of grass, inserting the spectator in a visceral manner into the environment of the scene. Here again, the presumed linearity of a represented history is cut through by the cinematic pause, the momentary reflection on the waving blades of grass that remind us that we are engaging with at least three temporalities: our own present, the present of each movement of the grass recorded during the filming of the scene, and the present of the story itself, as Shosanna escapes her fate. Via Shosanna's escape and the various screen memories layered within this scene and the subsequent revenge narratives, we are reminded of more than cinema's ability to complicate traditional notions of history and temporality. I also want to suggest that Tarantino's film tells us something about the non-linear nature of revenge fantasies. In particular, Shosanna's narrative highlights the lack of equivalence between even imagined revenge scenarios and the crimes that inspired the fantasies to begin with. The camera's complex relationship with the fetishized female figure highlights the temporal ruptures that undermine Tarantino's task: to re-write the most infamous narrative of the twentieth century. Via the projections and representations of Shosanna, the only Jewish figure in the film with an axe to grind based on her own experiences of persecution, Tarantino explores the impossible temporality of revenge. And when the gender of revenge is feminine, it is both mythic and self-destructive. Shosanna's success and failure in *Inglourious Basterds* ultimately point to the radical disjuncture between revenge and its source and to the impossibility of a "just" equilibrium in modern narratives.

The temporal complexity reflected in the film is already apparent in the beginning as the credits roll and as the title for Chapter One is presented on the screen. The film begins with a black screen, and the film's title and the main actors are listed in sequence with each name being represented for an equal amount of time. The list of main actors is followed, then, by the text "And Mélanie Laurent as Shosanna." Whereas none of the names of the main actors (including Brad Pitt, Christoph Waltz, and Daniel Brühl) are listed along with their characters, Mélanie Laurent must, it seems, be linked explicitly to the character she plays. What is more, her name appears on the screen slightly (about one second) longer than the other names: Mélanie Laurent and Shosanna represent an anomaly, a pause in the film. Already in the opening credits, Shosanna disrupts the flow of the narrative. Tarantino subtly nudges us to pay attention to this character (and the actress who plays her). The figure who claims "This is the face of Jewish vengeance" as the cinema holding Hitler, Goebbels, and other Nazi leaders burns down both drives the action of the film and slows it, embodying both a problem and a solution.

The enigma of Shosanna, however, does not seem to have captured the attention of critics and reviewers up to this point. Despite her use of more time in the display of credits and the almost indestructible nature of this figure whose face on the screen in the cinema filled with Nazis will, like a ghost, not disappear, reviewers have not concentrated on Shosanna in their discussions of the film. She seems, rather, to be a side note in responses to the film, not mentioned at all by Rafael Seligmann in his impassioned approval of a Jewish revenge narrative written for *Stern*.[1] In Georg Seeßlen's monograph on *Inglourious Basterds* which offers an exhaustive analysis of the motifs in the film, its historical context and interfilmic citations, the author likewise devotes little time to the representation and function of Shosanna in the film.[2] Indeed, critics seem to be at least as interested in Diane Kruger's character, the fictional German film actress, Bridget von Hammersmark, and the ways in which she cites German film history. Whereas Bridget von Hammersmark is not a problem, Shosanna Dreyfus is. Is this why she has been largely overlooked by critics and reviewers eager to solve the puzzle of Tarantino's film, de-ciphering the numerous citations from modern film history? Cultural discussions have focused largely on the film's violence, on the question of revenge fantasies and of whether those who were largely victims of Hitler could be re-imagined as righteous persecutors. But what of Shosanna, the single Jewish figure in the film who has sustained profound trauma at the hands of the Nazis and who, ultimately, is the true heroine of "Operation Kino," burning down Hitler, the cinema, and herself? Tarantino invites us to focus on this figure from the very first moment her name appears on the screen, yet the conventions of looking at the female body seem to complicate the ability of the spectator to see the anomaly embodied by Shosanna.

Screen memories

Both of the main female figures in the film are linked explicitly to the cinema. Bridget von Hammersmark is a famous German actress in the vein of Marlene Dietrich, and Shosanna owns a cinema and is herself a cinephile. Of course, almost every character in the film represents a citation of a director or character in Tarantino's film archive, but it is the female figures that are intrinsically linked to cinema in the film narrative itself. Frederick Zoller (Daniel Brühl) is an actor, too, but only due to his heroism in battle; his role in the film *Stolz der Nation* (Nation's Pride) is based entirely on his escapades in the "bird's nest" in Italy in which he purportedly shot and killed up to 300 U.S. soldiers. In Zoller's case, he is an actor because he is a warrior, and the two roles are identical. In contrast, the female leads cannot distance themselves from the cinema and from the cinematic projections of femininity with which Tarantino plays.

Shosanna, in particular, is the object of interconnecting screen memories or, as Freud calls them, *"Deckerinnerungen."* As *"Deckerinnerungen,"* literally "layered memories," screen memories offer displaced representations of wish fulfillment. At the end of the first scene of *Inglourious Basterds*, Colonel Hans Landa (Christoph Waltz), an SS officer who is searching for Jews in the French countryside, allows Shosanna, the daughter of the Jewish family hiding under the farmer's floorboards, to escape. This is the scene that cites the opening shot of the film, gently waving grass blades shot from a slightly lower angle than convention dictates, in which Shosanna runs across the field and away from the Nazis. The *mise-en-scène* and editing of this portion of the scene, in which Shosanna traverses a wide green field with yellow flowers, recall Freud's description of a childhood memory in his "Screen Memories" essay of 1899. Landa watches Shosanna run away, and we have no idea why he allows her to escape, but it is clear that Landa consciously chooses not to kill her: he points the gun at her but does not pull the trigger. Cutting between shots that track in to reveal Landa's gaze in close-up and long shots of Shosanna running away through the field, the spectator is made aware of the fact that Shosanna's escape speaks not only to our desires, but also to those of Landa (though we never get an insight into exactly of what those desires might consist). Of course, cross-cultural fantasies are also met in this scene: the German/Austrian spectator needs the trope of escape to imagine a different outcome of the war, and the American audience is invested in the Hollywood narrative of survival and, ultimately, success.

That this scene is represented as a *"Deckerinnerung"* reminiscent of the childhood memory related in Freud's "Screen Memories" offers a key to comprehension of the *mise-en-abyme* that is *Inglourious Basterds*. In the essay, a man (who is generally presumed to be Freud himself, disguised in the form of a case history of one of his patients) describes a vivid memory from his childhood in Moravia: "I see a rectangular, rather steeply sloping piece of meadow-land, green and thickly grown; in the green there are a great number of yellow flowers—evidently common dandelions. At the top of the meadow there is a cottage."[3] The scene described in Freud's essay is uncannily similar to the setting of the first scene in Tarantino's film: the "sloping" green and yellow meadow, the small farmhouse at the "top," and the young girl mentioned later by Freud's "patient." Freud's memory scene contains the green meadow with yellow flowers and a girl whose flowers Freud's former patient rips away. This memory is laid over by another memory (*"Deckerinnerung"*) of his return to his childhood home at the age of 17 when he meets a neighbor's 15-year-old daughter to whom he is sexually attracted. Layers of memory are interconnected like a palimpsest, and all memories are revealed to be screen memories insofar as memory consists of images that are called forth in the service of current concerns (in the case of Freud's patient, the memory resurfaced due to sexual desire that was unrelated to the original scene with the meadow). This notion of screen memories closely resembles the processes of borrowing and projection that characterize the interconnectedness between Hollywood and German *cultural* images. Just as Tarantino borrows from Nazi iconography in order to stage his fantasy of revenge, so too does the film itself reflect upon its appropriation of screen memories. Hence, the scene in which Shosanna gets away reflects not only the current desires (desires that do not entirely coincide) of the American and German spectator for escape and revenge, but also the ways in which cinematic images can both mask and reveal a multiplicity of displacements and desires. Indeed, the "escape scene" begins with a filmic citation of Tarantino's *Kill Bill: Volume 2* (2004), in which John Ford's *The Searchers* (1956) is likewise cited. Here, the camera is located behind "the Bride" (Uma Thurman) within a dark church, and we see "the Bride" Beatrix looking out into the light, framed by the doorway. When Beatrix walks outside, she encounters danger in the form of "Bill." Likewise, the "escape" scene in *Inglourious Basterds* is preceded by a similarly quiet moment in which Landa looks out from the dark cottage to the light framed in a doorway, and it is into this light that Shosanna runs.

It is important to remember that screen memories are traditionally coded as male, as displaced sexual desire. In Freud's text, the memory from the meadow is linked not only to the meadow but also to a moment in which the patient and his boy cousin take away flowers from the girl cousin, causing her to "run up the meadow in tears."[4] Once again, the scene described in Freud's text is uncannily mirrored in the *Inglourious Basterds* scene, as Shosanna runs crying through the field. In the Freud text, though, the girl is consoled by a peasant woman who gives her "a big piece of black bread,"[5] and the two boys run to receive some bread, too, which is described in the Freud text as "delicious." In his analysis of the screen memory of the patient, Freud emphasizes the bread as reflecting the comforts that the patient imagines he would have enjoyed had he stayed in Moravia and married his cousin. The bread, then, signifies the innocence and comforts of childhood, while the crying girl and stolen flowers reflect the patient's later sexual desires. And in the Landa/Shosanna scene, we see elements of innocence and comfort and of sexual desire. When Landa looks with some delight and fascination at Shosanna, that look reflects a multi-layered temporality: Landa's delight in watching the girl run away is clearly a "*Deckerinnerung*" of its own, as his wistful smile suggests memory and desire. One of the most jarring moments in

Chapter One is Landa's fixation on the "delicious" milk produced by Monsieur LaPadite's cows. The farmer's lovely daughter fetches a glass of milk for Landa at his request (in lieu of wine), and he emphatically expresses his pleasure in drinking the milk, even asking later for another glass. Hence, the brutal scene in which Landa hunts and kills Shosanna's family while letting her go also contains Landa's fetishization of the simplicity and comfort of a glass of pure white milk, a reminder of the pleasures of childhood. In his next encounter with Shosanna at a Paris restaurant, Landa once again reveals this fetish, forbidding her to taste of her "*Apfelstrudel*" until they have received cream, a plot element that is emphasized through numerous close-ups of the cream itself. The milk/cream is Freud's "delicious bread," and Shosanna (and the daughters of the dairy farmer) are the "girl cousin" who is simultaneously innocent as milk and ready to be "plucked." The screen memory refracts a variety of male memories and fantasies, giving us a rare window into Landa's soul.

Shosanna's escape scene is not only strikingly reminiscent of Freud's famous screen memory text, but it is shot in a manner that slows and almost freezes the moment. The camera cuts between Landa and Shosanna, tracking slowly in to Landa's face, a move that invites the spectator to try to gain access to the inner emotions of the character. Shots of Shosanna reveal her from a distance, running by a shed (reminiscent of Freud's cottage) and in close-up from the side, running for her life. The long shots of Shosanna running by the shed, intercut by shots of Landa's face, reveal a complex temporality, reminding us of the multiple temporalities contained within the screen memories and the film itself. During the numerous cross cuts, Shosanna runs from behind the shed and passes it. However, the inclusion of a shot of her running before she passes the shed actually stretches the time it would take her in real time to pass the shed. Hence, the moment becomes extended, reminding us of its importance and indicating a mode of temporality that deviates from traditional linearity. The temporal languor emphasized in the tracking shots slowly approaching Landa's face and the editing that stretches the time of Shosanna's escape codes Shosanna, like the milk and cream, as a fetish. In her seminal essay, "Visual Pleasure and Narrative Cinema," Laura Mulvey taught us that the fetish arrests film time, inviting pleasures that have nothing to do with narrative. Within the multiple screen memories of the film, Shosanna slows time. Already in the opening credits of the film, Shosanna is marked in this manner, as an interruption of the linear progression of the narrative and a fetish that slows the action of the characters and the film itself.

Revenge is not modern: male revenge, female revenge

The multiple temporalities that reflect the multiple screen memories contained within Tarantino's film point to the temporal "problem," so to speak, of the film's revenge fantasy of imposing punishment upon those most responsible for the Nazi crimes against humanity. The film begins in 1941, yet the script "1941" appears in the frame that follows the opening frame of the movie, in which the inter-title reads first "Chapter One" and then, after a short pause, "Once Upon a Time, in Nazi Occupied France ... " The temporal marker of 1941 is, hence, not a firm one, as the film is framed as a novel or fairy tale ("once upon a time") taking place at some time in the past. Already in the first two frames of the film, Tarantino has revealed his engagement with history as screen memories. In "Chapter Two," the *Inglourious Basterds* are introduced, a powerful bunch of Jewish-American soldiers led by Aldo Raine (Brad Pitt) who are on a mission to kill and torture Nazis. Here, screen memory is revealed as both wish fulfillment and temporal displacement, as the dramatic revenge fantasies of these soldiers (fulfilled to a large degree in brutal killings, torture and tattooing of German soldiers) seem to reveal a historical knowledge on their part of the crimes of the Nazis that could only have been gained after the war. The revenge fantasies played out in the film precede the full knowledge of Auschwitz and the other camps, yet the actions of the "Basterds" seem to be informed by contemporary knowledge about the atrocities committed by the Nazis. The "Inglourious Basterds" of Tarantino's film are likely modeled in part after the famous "Ritchie Boys," a group of German Jewish-American G.I.s who had escaped Nazi Europe and were sent back to help undermine the efforts of the Nazis.[6] Like Chapter One, Chapter Two clearly also takes place in the early 1940s, but the actions of the "Basterds" are likewise embedded within the temporality of "once upon a time," a past that is always informed by the knowledge and desires of the present.

Whereas male revenge, both historically and in Tarantino's film, is generally represented literally as violence and torture, female revenge is potentially more complex, refracted through projections of and assumptions about femininity. The "Basterds" inflict physical pain and torture on their victims in a manner that literally symbolizes their backgrounds and the crimes of those they are punishing: the "Basterds" scalp their victims, symbolically re-enacting the righteous revenge of "the Apache" Aldo Raine, and they carve swastika tattoos into their victims' foreheads, marking them as victims of their own system. These modes of punishment invite a sense that violence can be just and, in some sense, rational. The swastika tattoos are reminiscent of the torture machine in Kafka's "In the Penal Colony." In Kafka's narrative, the prisoner's crime is written out and cut into his body as a tattoo, suggesting that the punishment reflects the crime. Of course, the illegibility of the words and the gruesome result of this "rational" form of murder (the bloody corpse of the criminal) remind us that there is no equilibrium possible between crime and punishment: the attempt to introduce reason into the act of vengeance is futile. Yet this is precisely the mode in which male acts of revenge such as war are usually narrated.

Francis Bacon famously called revenge a "wild justice."[7] It is not rational. As John Kerrigan shows, revenge motives keep wars going. Citing Vietnam War memoires, Kerrigan highlights the fact that revenge often structures war narratives:

> In *A Rumor of War* (1977), Philip Caputo writes about 'the reality of battle' that left him scarred but unable to settle away from combat. Withdrawn to base-camp he craved 'Revenge' for the men he had seen killed. After an ambush at Giao-Tri, his troops 'destroy with uncontrolled fury ... an act of retribution.'[8]

Even Augustine, Kerrigan points out, disseminated an idea of just war based on revenge: "*justa bella ulciscuntor injurias.*"[9] However, war can never be "reciprocal"; it is, rather, "cumulative": "Where no single blow can be conclusive, forces engage in a dialectic through which not merely the wrongs which precipitated conflict must be avenged but a mounting heap of injuries."[10]

Kerrigan argues that Hitler's attack on the Jews was articulated as a just "revenge":

> The name of the state, 'The Third Reich', derives from medieval interpretations of the Apocalypse of St. John; and, in the bombastic *Das dritte Reich* of Arthur Moeldder van den Bruch, Nazis found pseudo-historical grounds for their millenarian project. Goebbels believed that the thousand-year Reich would be born out of apocalyptic struggle between good Aryans and Jewish 'demons'. In punishing the Jews, National Socialists were instruments of the divine will and Adolf Hitler an incarnate symbol of Christ militant and victorious.[11]

Walter von Reichenau, an ardent Nazi and a "*Generalfeldmarschall*" under Hitler, called the Eastern Front soldiers an "'avenger of all bestialities inflicted on the German people' imposing 'a severe but just atonement on Jewish sub-humanity.'"[12] The discourse of revenge seeks to purify violence, lending war a biblical tone of justice and moral rectitude.[13]

High technology warfare exacerbates the failure of vengeance equivalencies, but, ultimately, revenge in any form cannot produce equivalence. As Simone Weil puts it, "The desire for vengeance is a desire for essential equilibrium ... The search for equilibrium is bad because it is imaginary. Revenge. Even if in fact we kill or torture our enemy it is, in a sense, imaginary."[14] There is no eye for an eye: each eye is unique, each situation different. The "Basterds" in Tarantino's film utilize simple weapons in their violent performances of punishment, but this does not mean that they are producing equilibrium. Indeed, as Kerrigan points out, "It might seem a dramatic weakness that, the more disablingly violent an initial attack, the less likely it is that the victim can come up with an appropriate response."[15] Revenge is, as Weil states, "imaginary," an emotion that can only be translated in the most imprecise manner into action.

Pier Paolo Pasolini focused on revenge in a number of his films, most notably in *Medea* (1969), a tragic tale of female revenge and self-destruction. Yet he pointed out that revenge narratives are never linear; ultimately, they are not modern: "The barbarians that I depict are always outside of history, they are never *historical*. In my films, barbarism is always symbolic; it represents the ideal moment of mankind."[16] Revenge tragedy questions the notion of progress. As Kerrigan puts it: "A revenge plot undoes modernity, establishing a 'regeneration of time' ... in the space before history starts."[17] Revenge is rather predicated on repetition than movement. Indeed, the realization that revenge is precisely unjust and irrational, outside of the temporal logic of modernity, suggests an inherent critique of the presumed rationality of the Enlightenment. We might say that the modern revenge tragedy precisely achieves its ends when it reveals its own failure, its inability to produce equilibrium in an unjust world.

Female vengeance, or what Shosanna can teach us

Whereas the male-dominated revenge scenario of war preserves the pretense of a just equilibrium, female vengeance understands that there is no equivalence when it comes to pain and suffering. Revenge heroines are keenly aware of the ultimately futile nature of their vengeance plans, and the enactments of these plans often involve self-destruction, a turn inward, reflecting the realization that the revenge act itself has very little to do with the original crime and much to do with an open wound that cannot be healed. The great female vengeance figures of the Western tradition perform their revenge acts knowing no equilibrium is possible and that the end result will also produce great loss to them.

The mythical queen of revenge is Medea, the figure who was wronged by Jason and who killed not only his new bride but also her own children. In Euripides' version of the myth, Medea sends a poison cloak to Glauce, Jason's new bride, killing the new couple; she then returns home and kills her two children before fleeing. Numerous variations on the Euripides version have suggested that Medea accidentally kills her children, or that, as in the 1797 opera by Cherubini, she commits suicide in the end of the play. As Kerrigan puts it, "Her suicide defies a call for vengeance, yet surreptitiously fulfils a desire for it."[18] Hence, suicide can also be seen as a form of vengeance, a punishment to those who survive and to the self. Ultimately self-destructive revenge narratives like those of Medea and Dido (who choreographs what Kerrigan calls "revenge suicide" against Aeneas[19]) reveal, I suggest, the impossibility of equivalence.[20] Medea may achieve revenge, but she also symbolically cuts off her own limbs by killing her children and the man she had once loved. Even suicide can be seen as a form of feminine revenge in taking away the object of love from the guilty party. Sarah Gates' fascinating analysis of another classic revenge play, Shakespeare's *Hamlet*, shows that Ophelia, too, enacts her revenge in the play. Indeed, as Gates puts it, Ophelia choreographs the perfect act of revenge by killing herself, thereby punishing her lover Hamlet who was responsible for the death of her father.[21] In this way, female revenge is less literal than male revenge, more aware of the costs of revenge and of revenge's failure to balance the books.

Shosanna's revenge in *Inglourious Basterds* is reminiscent of the Bride's epic revenge narrative in *Kill Bill: Vols. 1 and 2* (2003, 2004). The impetus for the "wild justice" undertaken by the Bride ("Beatrix Kiddo") in these two films is the massacre at her wedding. Her former lover and boss (and father of the baby she is carrying), Bill, and her former assassin colleagues arrive at the rehearsal and murder the entire wedding party, leaving Beatrix for dead. She hunts them down one by one and kills them, finding at last both Bill and her daughter. In the end, she kills Bill, but she cries while doing so, aware that she is killing a man she loves. Her mode of murder is the "Five-Point-Palm-Exploding-Heart" technique taught to her by Pai-Mei, a revered Chinese martial arts master. Beatrix simply performs a complex movement with her hand in the vicinity of Bill's heart, presumably accompanied by an iron will, and Bill's heart literally explodes. His body fails him, and he slowly dies. Beatrix's mode of killing her beloved does not attempt to replay the brutal acts of violence committed against her and others at her wedding rehearsal. Rather, this method of killing performs the internal nature of violence, revealing the pain of loss that all violence causes.

In her analysis of gendered revenge in *Kill Bill*, Lisa Coulthard shows that, despite the radically violent nature of Beatrix's revenge, the film is nonetheless predicated upon a traditional notion of maternal love, the lioness protecting her cubs. In the end of the film, Beatrix is reunited with her daughter B.B., who had been in Bill's care, and this rediscovered "maternal wholeness" constitutes the true meaning of Beatrix's wild hunt for justice throughout the films.[22] Female violence is, Coulthard contends, often neither disruptive nor subversive, and in her reading of *Kill Bill* she points to the "drive toward increasing domesticity that carries the final acts of the film."[23] Is the film, then, somehow traditional in its representation of female vengeance? As Judith Franco argues in her analyses of the film *Baise moi* (Virginie Despentes, 2000) and Madonna's video for the song "What it Feels Like for a Girl" (2001), female violence is usually predicated on a trauma in the nuclear family and the attempt to reconstitute this family. Yet Franco shows that neither of these factors is at play in the film and video she analyzes. The female figures in *Baise moi* and in Madonna's video perform violent acts for pleasure and without any clear motivations, suggesting that female violence might be imagined outside of the age-old maternal trope.

As Coulthard and Franco point out, one is nevertheless hard pressed to find representations of female vengeance that do not seek to reassert the nuclear family at the center of the narrative or that do not concern mothers. The famous story of Margaret Garner, a slave who attempted escape from bondage in January 1856 with her husband, his parents, their four children, and nine other slaves, is a case in point. After reaching Ohio, Margaret's family separated from the other slave families but was then discovered at the home of a relative:

> Trapped in his house by the encircling slave catchers, Margaret killed her three-year-old daughter with a butcher's knife and attempted to kill the other children rather than let them be taken back into slavery by their master, Archibald K. Gaines, the owner of Margaret's husband and of the plantations adjacent to her own home.[24]

Margaret was put on trial for the murder of the daughter whom, as she put it, "she probably loved best,"[25] and was eventually sent to the slave market in New Orleans. When the slave catchers entered the house in which Margaret and her family were hiding, her husband, Simon Garner, Jr., fired several shots at the pursuers. Margaret, on the other hand, was reported to have killed her youngest child and then to have begged her mother-in-law for assistance in killing the other children. The mother-in-law confessed that she neither encouraged nor discouraged her daughter-in-law, "for in similar circumstances she should probably have done the same."[26] In their analysis of the case, abolitionists pointed out that Margaret was impelled by a "calm determination that, if she could not find freedom here, she would get it with the angels ... Margaret had tried to kill all her children, but she had made sure of the little girl. She had said that her daughter would never suffer as she had."[27]

Paul Gilroy asks a pointed question here: "What are we to make of these contrasting forms of violence, one coded as male and outward, directed towards the oppressor, and the other, coded as female, somehow internal, channeled towards a parent's most precious and intimate objects of love, pride, and desire?"[28] Yet he has no answer for this question. Margaret Garner's tragic tale of revenge reminds us of the ways in which violence is interpreted along gender lines not only in myths but also in real-life cases: female vengeance is often driven by maternal love; it is both destructive and self-destructive, even masochistic in its destruction of beloved ones. Is this mode of vengeance weak in its inability to extract an "eye for an eye," or does it rather reveal the impossibility of exacting a just revenge? I would assert the latter, though this does not mean that all female violence is subversive. Even the final installment of Chan-wook Park's cinematic revenge trilogy, *Lady Vengeance* (2005), reminds us of the complexity in the relationship between violent female vengeance and subversion of traditional norms. The first two films of the trilogy, *Sympathy for Mr. Vengeance* (2002) and *Oldboy* (2003), are primarily concerned with male revenge fantasies in which gruesome acts of violence are committed. Each film ends without a mode of reconciliation: rather, revenge and violence have produced more death as well as bizarre relationships between the characters that can ultimately only lead to more pain. Like *Kill Bill*, *Lady Vengeance* complicates the presumption that violent revenge is a man's purview; the violence committed by Geum-ja Lee (Yeong-ae Lee) against the man who set her up to be falsely imprisoned for a crime is brutal and visceral. Yet in the end, as in *Kill Bill*, Lee is reunited with her daughter who was sent away to a foster home while she was imprisoned. The final scene presents the new-found love between the two, rounding out the revenge trilogy with a decidedly more traditional narrative than one would have expected from Park based on the first two films in the trilogy.

Ghostly laughter: Shosanna's giant face

Is female vengeance always also self-destructive? Is it always maternal? How does Shosanna's revenge narrative figure in to the discussion of female revenge as internal, self-destructive, and aware of the impossibility of avoiding pain? Tarantino teaches us during the rolling of the credits in the beginning of the film that Shosanna is special. She slows time, and the screen memory that depicts her escape from Landa is likewise stretched temporally, reminding us that she will figure in important ways in the film. Tarantino's filmmaking style is famously postmodern: one could even assert that he is the most postmodern of all contemporary Hollywood filmmakers. Georg Seeßlen fills his book with film citations in *Inglourious Basterds* alone, and there are always more to be discovered. As Fredric Jameson has taught us, postmodern style is based on pastiche, on the production of a constellation consisting of art forms and styles from a variety of historical periods and contexts. Pastiche is, in this sense, not "new." Whereas modernism attempted to represent the "New" as something not yet experienced formally, postmodernism relishes citationality for its own sake. And, certainly, Tarantino's films can be classified in this manner. Yet what of the figure of Shosanna? Even Jameson points to postmodernism's failure to cease engaging with the "New."[29] And there is, to my mind, something new about this mode of representation of female vengeance, despite the numerous screen memories represented in scenes containing Shosanna. Shosanna is, for one, not a mother. Her vengeance is not inspired by maternal instincts; nor does she kill her children in a kind of self-destructive orgy in order to protect them from worse fates. Indeed, she has no children. We see her escaping from Landa, embodying his screen memories and fantasies, and the next scene in which she appears pictures her at the cinema she has taken over from her aunt and uncle. As in much of the film, she is dressed not as a femme fatale but as an androgynous girl, in slacks and a hat. She has one friend, who is also her lover, the black projectionist, Marcel (Jacky Ido). And her act of revenge, in which Marcel burns down the cinema containing Hitler and his cronies while the projection of her face speaks "Jewish vengeance" on the screen, is both self-destructive and historically more significant than even the crimes committed against her family by the Nazis.

That Shosanna's revenge scenario exceeds the logic of equilibrium is emphasized by the title of Chapter Five: "Revenge of the Giant Face." This chapter begins with Shosanna putting on her "war paint" (literally, in the form of red rouge lines drawn on her cheeks) while the soundtrack plays David Bowie's "Cat People: Putting out Fire," the theme song for the 1982 remake of *Cat People*. The wild nature of the heroine in *Cat People*, a woman who stems from a community of wildcats and who ultimately returns to these cats, reminds us of the "wild justice" that Shosanna is planning to execute by burning down the cinema she treasures (along with herself and the only human being whom she loves, Marcel). Shosanna's "war paint" scene finishes as she positions a black veil over her face, a kind of widow's veil that seems oddly juxtaposed with her fire-red dress and lips. The lyrics of the song, "Putting out fire with gasoline," remind us of the lesson only Shosanna teaches us in this film: that there is no equivalence; revenge is like putting out fire with gasoline, producing excess violence and pain beyond anything originally imagined. Pasolini called film itself a "monstrum" (Kerrigan, 108), and the nitrate film used to burn down the theater recreates a hellish nightmare, as the monsters of history burn together with their victims.

Excess is the name of the game in this chapter, and Seeßlen rightly notes that the double murder plans are enacted entirely independently of one another.[30] Shosanna's plan, however, is the only one that succeeds without anyone's knowledge beyond that of Marcel. The plan of the "Basterds" succeeds due to Landa's indulgence for his own purposes. In this sense, only Shosanna's revenge is truly subversive. The result, however, is excess: double murder and destruction. Even the murders of Shosanna and Frederick Zoller are redundant, as both would likely have died in the fire or explosions, had they not shot one another. It is, of course, Shosanna's sudden compassion for Frederick that causes her death (as he takes this opportunity to shoot her). She is temporarily caught in the identificatory web of the cinema, likely responding empathetically both to Zoller's physical pain and to his character's loneliness in the film that screens in the background. But we should not oversimplify Shosanna's character as a compassionate female figure. She is also tough as nails, threatening a professional film developer and his family if he refuses to develop the film she has created for the Nazi bloodbath. In this sense, Shosanna defies simple categorizations as a female vengeance figure, revealing that Tarantino may indeed have produced something new in the orgy of citationality that is *Inglourious Basterds*.

Seeßlen connects the "giant face" of the chapter title and the film that Shosanna plays while the cinema burns to Charlie Chaplin's "big face" in *The Great Dictator*. For Seeßlen, Shosanna's appearance on the screen undermines the fascist aesthetic of *Stolz der Nation* in a manner reminiscent of Chaplin in the Hitler/Nazi-parody: "the individual behind the mask becomes visible."[31] This is precisely what fascist aesthetics wish to avoid at all costs: revealing the truth behind the spectacle. However, the "giant face" of Shosanna that appears on the screen as Marcel lights the nitrate film reels behind the screen is subversive not only in its size but also in its laughter. The black-and-white close-up of Shosanna's face recalls a similar shot of Anna Karina's face in Jean-Luc Godard's *Vivre sa vie* (1962) as she sits in the cinema watching Carl Dreyer's *The Passion of Joan of Arc* (1928). Karina cries as she views the intense pain revealed in Joan of Arc's face, also pictured in close-up. Seeßlen points out that Tarantino's script calls for French New Wave black-and-white in Chapter Three, the chapter in which Shosanna and Marcel make the film they splice onto the Nazi film screening on the night of the fire. Hence, the close-up of Shosanna's face in the burning theater invites us to remember New Wave heroine Anna Karina's emotional response to the cinematic representation of pain. And while Shosanna is shown in black-and-white close-up, she is neither crying nor expressing pain. Rather, she laughs.[32] Shosanna's laughter defies the film history of self-destructive vengeance goddesses. Here is her subversion of gender roles, a performance that marries self-destruction with epic, excessive violence.

Laughter is a mode of expression outside of logic and reason. There is no controlling it, and there is no ending it. It exceeds any rational comprehension and hence mirrors the excess of the triple destruction (if we include the mutual murders of Shosanna and Frederick) of the final chapter of the film. What is more, Shosanna's laughter on the projection screen as she cries "This is the face of Jewish vengeance" represents a temporal ghostliness, an arresting fetish within the narrative of the film. Recalling the close-ups of beautiful actresses that precede (and succeed, if we momentarily consider the presumed year of the scene to be 1944) her, Shosanna's face simultaneously resembles those of the victims of the Nazis in images that became available to the world after the war: her hair is pulled back as if it were shorn, and she wears no make-up.

Shosanna's close-up transfixes time in a manner that transcends linearity. As in the scene from Chapter One, she is the fetish that stops time, the pause that reminds us of the fallacy of linearity and equivalence. Laura Mulvey's analysis of the female body as fetish, as an arrester of linearity, is absolutely relevant here.[33] Tarantino consciously cites the cinema's use of the female body, nevertheless offering us something new here: a fetish as historical pause, the androgynous female face in close-up laughing incomprehensibly. As in earlier scenes, Shosanna represents the pause that reminds us of the impossibility of equilibrium. As the movie theater burns down, so does the projection screen. The final shots of the scene show Shosanna's face seemingly remaining in projection form despite the burning of the screen, as a ghostly specter. Impossibly, the female face as fetish exceeds even the laws of physics within the film narrative. As an ultimately impossible figure in the annals of film history, Shosanna resists her entrapment within the screen memories of the film's characters and its cinephile spectators, utilizing the conventions of gendered representation to reveal the impossibility of rationally measured revenge.

Why didn't Tarantino end the film here with the ghost of Shosanna exceeding the time–space continuum of the film world? Why does the film end with the comical scene in which Aldo Raine carves a swastika tattoo into Colonel Landa's forehead? Perhaps the radical nature of the previous scene needed to be contained in some manner? After carving the swastika into Landa's forehead, Raine speaks the final line of the film: "I think this just might be my masterpiece." The grotesque humor of this scene aside, the line is clearly an allusion to the director's own satisfaction with his film project. Yet Tarantino's genius may rather be located in his radically new representation of female vengeance as laughing fetish, as a ghostly pause that reminds us of the impossibility of balancing the books of history.

Notes

1 Rafael Seligman, "Juden sind keine besseren Menschen,"
   Stern, August 19, 2009. http://www.stern.de/kultur/film/
   rafael-seligmann-ueber-inglourious-basterds-juden-sind-keine-
   besseren-menschen-1504002.html (accessed February 4, 2011).

2 Georg Seeßlen, *Quentin Tarantino gegen die Nazis: Alles über
   Inglourious Basterds*. (Berlin: Bertz+Fischer, 2009).

3 Sigmund Freud, "Screen Memories," in *The Freud Reader*, ed. Peter
   Gay. (New York: W. W. Norton, 1989), 119.

4 Freud, 119.

5 Freud, 119.

6 *The Ritchie Boys*. Dir. Christian Bauer. Canada/Germany, 2004.

7 Quoted in John Kerrigan, *Revenge Tragedy: Aeschylus to
   Armageddon*. (Oxford: Clarendon, 1996), vii.

8 Kerrigan, 293.

9 Kerrigan, 305.

10 Kerrigan, 305.

11 Kerrigan, 304.

12 Kerrigan, 304.

13 The discourse of a "just war" predicated upon the old rules of
   vengeance falls particularly short in light of modern warfare
   technologies. Just as Kafka reveals the failure of equivalence in the
   punishing machine in "In the Penal Colony," so, too does machine
   warfare complicate the narrative of revenge. See also Kerrigan, 310.

14 Quoted in Kerrigan, 10.

15 Kerrigan, 7.

16 Cited in Kerrigan, 104.

17 Kerrigan, 110.

18 Kerrigan, 99.

19 Kerrigan, 100.

20 Here I differ from Kerrigan, who sees Medea's and Ariadne's wishes
   for revenge as "eye for an eye" demands (99).

21 Sarah Gates, "Assembling the Ophelia Fragments: Gender, Genre,
   and Revenge in *Hamlet*," *EIRC* 34.2 (Winter 2008): 229–47.

22 Lisa Coulthard, "Killing Bill: Rethinking Feminism and Film
   Violence," in *Interrogating Postfeminism: Gender and the Politics of*

Popular Culture, (eds) Yvonne Taster and Diane Negra. (Durham, NC: Duke University Press, 2007), 165.

23 Coulthard, 165.

24 Gilroy, Paul, *The Black Atlantic: Modernity and Double Consciousness*. (Cambridge, MA: Harvard University Press, 1993), 65.

25 Gilroy, 65.

26 Gilroy, 66.

27 Gilroy, 67.

28 Gilroy, 66.

29 In *A Singular Modernity: Essay on the Ontology of the Present* Jameson admits, in contrast to his arguments in *Postmodernism, Or the Cultural Logic of Late Capitalism*, that "the New ... cannot be fully eradicated" from the postmodern: "And this is indeed no small or insignificant contribution for postmodernity, which is unable to divest itself of the supreme value of innovation (despite the end of style and the death of the subject), if only because the museums and art galleries can scarcely function without it. Thus, the new fetish of Difference continues to overlap the older one of the New, even if the two are not altogether coterminous" (5). Fredric Jameson, *A Singular Modernity: Essay on the Ontology of the Present*. (New York: Verso, 2002).

30 Georg Seeßlen, *Quentin Tarantino gegen die Nazis: Alles über "Inglourious Basterds."* (Berlin: Bertz + Fischer, 2009), 152.

31 Seeßlen: "Das Einzelne hinter der Maske wird sichtbar." 155.

32 Seeßlen reads this laughter as the mimicry of the laughter of the Nazis while watching Frederick Zoller kill the enemies in *Stolz der Nation*, 93.

33 Laura Mulvey, "Visual Pleasure and Narrative Cinema," *Screen* 16.3, (1975), 6–18.

Works cited

Cat People. Directed by Paul Schrader. USA, 1982.

Coulthard, Lisa. "Killing Bill: Rethinking Feminism and Film Violence." In *Interrogating Postfeminism: Gender and the Politics of Popular Culture*, edited by Yvonne Taster and Diane Negra, 153–75. Durham, NC: Duke University Press, 2007.

Franco, Judith. "Gender, Genre and Female Pleasure in the
Contemporary Revenge Narrative: *Baise moi* and *What It Feels Like
For A Girl.*" *Quarterly Review of Film and Video*, 21, 2004, 1–10.

Freud, Sigmund. "Screen Memories." In *The Freud Reader*, edited by
Peter Gay, 117–26. New York: W. W. Norton, 1989.

Gates, Sarah. "Assembling the Ophelia Fragments: Gender, Genre and
Revenge in *Hamlet.*" *EIRC*, 34.2, Winter 2008, 229–47.

Gilroy, Paul. *The Black Atlantic: Modernity and Double Consciousness.*
Cambridge, MA: Harvard University Press, 1993.

Inglourious Basterds. Directed by Quentin Tarantino. USA/Germany,
2009.

Jameson, Fredric. *A Singular Modernity: Essay on the Ontology of the
Present.* New York: Verso, 2002.

—*Postmodernism, or, The Cultural Logic of Late Capitalism.* Durham,
NC: Duke University Press, 2002.

Kafka, Franz. "In the Penal Colony." In *The Metamorphosis, In the
Penal Colony, and Other Stories*, translated by Joachim Neugroschel.
New York: Schocken, 2000, 191–231.

Kerrigan, John. *Revenge Tragedy: Aeschylus to Armageddon.* Oxford:
Clarendon, 1996.

Kill Bill: Vol 1. Directed by Quentin Tarantino. USA, 2003.

Kill Bill: Vol 2. Directed by Quentin Tarantino. USA, 2004.

Lady Vengeance. Directed by Chan-wook Park. South Korea, 2005.

Medea. Directed by Pier Paolo Pasolini/ Italy/France, 1969.

Mulvey, Laura. "Visual Pleasure and Narrative Cinema." *Screen*, 16.3,
1975, 6–18.

Oldboy. Directed by Chan-wook Park. South Korea, 2003.

The Ritchie Boys. Directed by Christian Bauer. Canada/Germany, 2004.

The Searchers. Directed by John Ford. USA, 1956.

Seeßlen, Georg. *Quentin Tarantino gegen die Nazis: Alles über
Inglourious Basterds.* Berlin: Bertz + Fischer, 2009.

Seligman, Rafael. "Juden sind keine besseren Menschen." *Stern*, August
19, 2009 http://www.stern.de/kultur/film/rafael- seligmann-ueber-
inglourious-basterds-juden-sind-keine-besseren- menschen-1504002.
html (accessed February 4, 2011).

Sympathy for Mr. Vengeance. Directed by Chan-wook Park. South
Korea, 2002.

Vivre sa vie/My Life to Live. Directed by Jean-Luc Godard. France,
1962.

8

Reels of justice: *Inglourious Basterds, The Sorrow and the Pity,* and Jewish revenge fantasies

Eric Kligerman

In his 1978 film *Annie Hall*, Woody Allen plays a Jewish *Pygmalion*, Alvy Singer, who tries to educate his gentile girlfriend by introducing her to literature, psychoanalysis and foreign films. In perhaps the film's most memorable scene, after turning up two minutes late to a Bergman film, Alvy takes Annie to see yet again Marcel Ophüls' four-hour Holocaust documentary *The Sorrow and the Pity*: the film becomes a running joke throughout *Annie Hall*. In one of the film's many postmodern moments, while standing in line Alvy suffers through an academic's critique of the aesthetic techniques in the works of Fellini and Beckett. As the professor begins discussing Marshal McCluhan, Alvy steps out of line and introduces McCluhan, who informs the professor that he knows absolutely nothing about his work. Alvy turns to the camera and remarks, "Boy, if life were only like this." That is, only through art can one have control over reality and hope to re-configure it. But the fantasy is fleeting as the scene flashes to Ophüls' film and we hear: "June 14, 1940 the Germans occupy Paris. People are hungry for news." In stark contrast to Alvy's fantasy, we see how life actually is; with the appearance of the title, Ophüls' film shatters Alvy's fantasy, bringing him (and us) back to reality.

After Ophüls' documentary, the scene cuts to Alvy and Annie getting ready for bed. As Alvy praises the heroism of the French Resistance, the two banter about the Gestapo and torture. Annie declares, "That movie makes me feel guilty," and Alvy responds, "It's supposed to." *The Sorrow and the Pity* serves not only as an instrument in Annie's cultural development (a Jewish education comprised of neurosis, Holocaust memory and guilt), but the film also becomes a form of punishment. By compelling her to watch the film, Alvy, the paranoid Jew who detects anti-Semitism in the sound of a sneeze, turns film into a tool of revenge. Although by the end of the film Alvy is no longer with her, he tells us that the last time he ran into Annie, she was taking her new friend to see Ophüls' film. Thus, there is a perpetuation of the passing on of guilt.

In addition to observing how film becomes an implement of punishment, the above scene also illustrates how directors occupy the films of others. While Allen turns to Ophüls, the structure of *The Sorrow and the Pity* relies on Ophüls taking possession of German and French film to probe Germany's occupation of France. My use of the term "occupation" derives from the connotations of the German word *Besetzung*. The word connotes not only military occupation, but it is also Freud's term that is translated into English as *cathexis*: the concept which is central to the analysis of the subject's identity construction and refers to the process in which an individual invests psychic energy in a person, object or idea. During the process of cathexis, the blocked energy behind the subject's libidinal drives involves their discharge through their transformation into acts of sublimation.

Ophüls' film, however, exemplifies the process of a counter-cathexis. Within the context of the French cultural imaginary

The Sorrow and the Pity shatters the fantasy regarding how France responded to the German occupation during the war and its aftermath; he attempts to break France's attachment to the one-dimensional historical narrative of a heroic French Resistance to National Socialism. Thirty years after *Annie Hall* and Alvy Singer's legacy as the iconic image of the weak (albeit existentially triumphant) Jew, there has been a re-occupation of another narrative archetype, where alternative representations of Jewish resistance have arisen, as depicted in dramatic films like *Munich* and *Defiance*, and comedic ones such as *Don't Mess with the Zohan*. In Paul Feig's comedy *Knocked Up* the character Ben Stein tells his Jewish friends at a bar, "Every movie with Jews, we're the ones getting killed. 'Munich' flips it on its ear—we're capping motherfuckers. Any of us get laid tonight, it's because of Eric Bana and *Munich*."[1] Again, not only is there a formation of filmic consciousness through self-referentiality within this scene, but similar to Alvy's own sexual arousal after watching the heroics in *The Sorrow and the Pity* (he makes advances to Annie in the next scene), scenes of Jewish empowerment and vengeance give way to sexual vitality.

Most recently, Quentin Tarantino's *Inglourious Basterds* "flips on its ear" not simply the narrative of Jewish victimization but history itself. At the film's fantasy climax that re-imagines an alternate ending to the Third Reich, as we watch the Nazi leadership machine-gunned and incinerated in the flames of a locked movie house, Tarantino prompts the spectator to muse—to borrow Alvy's words—"Boy if life were only like this." Despite intersections that open up between *Inglourious Basterds* and contemporary depictions of Jewish resistance in fictional films, I am interested in the continuities unfolding between *Inglourious Basterds* and *The Sorrow and the Pity* that revolve around a series of conceptual and thematic intersections that include the double connotation of *Besetzung*, resistance, justice, the technique of framing films within a film, and the introspective gesture of cinema's power as seen in Ophüls' and Tarantino's analyses of propaganda, all of which open up a fruitful space for critical analysis between the films.

While Ophüls' objective is to deconstruct—or break one's cathexis to—the dominant narrative of French Resistance, Tarantino provides a fantasy space to construct a fairy tale out of history by re-imagining an alternate ending to the history surrounding the Shoah. Whereas Ophüls explores revisionist French history, compelling his audience to acknowledge the limits to the national myth of resistance, Tarantino asks his audience to imagine an alternative history to the one that actually unfolded: imagine if a group of American-Jewish commandos ("The Basterds") hunt down and brutalize German soldiers in France, while a French-Jewish woman named Shosanna Dreyfus, who had witnessed the extermination of her family, plots a similar path of revenge; both trajectories culminate in the conflagration of a movie theater housing the Nazi elite including Hitler.

I would like to turn to one of the more negative, albeit provocative, reviews that describes Tarantino's "failure of imagination and morality." Liel Leibovitz writes, "The desire to turn film into a literal, blunt instrument of revenge drains it of the terrific power it has as a sharp tool with which to cut through myopia, forgetfulness, and denial." Turning to Ophüls' *The Sorrow and the Pity* and Lanzmann's *Shoah*, Leibowitz argues that "they use film not in order to set ablaze heaping mounds of flesh, but in order to understand the complicity that led Europe to its benighted state ... *It's no coincidence that these filmmakers are Jewish. Theirs is the Jewish way.* Rather than burn film, they develop it into art. They are Talmudic, offering endless interpretations of our seemingly endless capacity for evil."[2] With his emphasis on the literal use of film as a tool of memory and hermeneutic analysis, Leibovitz presents what he means by a "Jewish way" to cinema: one devoid of violence. Although Jeffrey Goldberg presents a more positive review of *Inglourious Basterds*, he still maintains that there is a "Jewish way" to cinema and writes, "Only a non-Jew could have made this film."[3]

If Jewish films on the Holocaust are Talmudic, as Leibovitz claims, in their ability to open up an imaginary space to probe moral questions in relation to historical violence, then I would argue that the filmic structure and content of *Inglourious Basterds*—in the style of *The Sorrow and the Pity*—can itself be considered Talmudic in its approach to the catastrophic history of the Shoah's legacy in the cultural imaginary of cinema. I would place Tarantino's filmic style in the very tradition of a Jewish hermeneutics that Leibovitz and others deny to him. There is indeed something Talmudic in Tarantino's approach to the interplay between the Shoah and cinema. My use of the term Talmudic refers to an interpretation of history and its hermeneutic structure and not to any question pertaining to religious law. Similar to the design of the Talmudic page, which involves multiple voices set around a central text, whereby the borders of the page function as a polyphonic space in which contradictions and tensions regarding the original text open up across time, both films use cinematic insertions to render an interpretation of the Holocaust in German-occupied France.

While Ophüls wishes to break the attachment to the dominant narrative of French Resistance and expose an historical erasure, Tarantino's aim is to break the narrative paradigms and components that are constitutive of Holocaust cinema. Through his brazen presentation of a counter-narrative to the Shoah and representations of Jews during the Holocaust, Tarantino dismantles the structures of Holocaust discourse, the reified modes of representing catastrophic history and Jews themselves, and provokes the spectator to think anew questions pertaining to these representations. As he remarked, his film "goes against all the ponderous, anti-war, violin-music diatribes that we've seen in war movies since the '80s."[4] Resisting sacrosanct interpretations of the Shoah, Tarantino rejects any mimetic approach to history through his Brechtian-like strategies, comprised of his signature marks of terror mixed with laughter and visceral shock.

On a cursory glance one might argue that Ophüls' and Tarantino's analyses of the relations between justice, revenge and violence are diametrically opposed to one another; that a highly acclaimed documentary film diverges from Hollywood fiction with ambivalent reviews. However, I would argue that both filmmakers have similar approaches to using filmic space to probe the tensions regarding film's relation to justice. Turning to Yosef Yerushalmi's reflection that the opposite of forgetting is not memory but justice, I am claiming that both directors examine cycles of violence to underscore the tenuous relation between justice and memory.[5] I would like to return to Tarantino's oft-repeated description of his film's reliance on Spaghetti Western justice and 1970s B-movie revenge fantasies. Tarantino's conjoining of these two genres, while using the Holocaust as his backdrop, is for many critics incompatible with a concept of Jewish justice. But Ophüls too invokes the Western structure behind *The Sorrow and the Pity*, describing it as "a bias film in the right direction as biased as a Western with good guys and bad guys. It is not as easy to choose a good guy as

in an anti-Nazi film with Alan Ladd in 1943."[6] While it is not in
the scope of this analysis to explore what might be meant by Jewish
justice, as if a fluid narrative could be traced from Job through
Maimonides, Kafka, Arendt and Levinas, Tarantino's Spaghetti
Western justice juxtaposed to the Shoah raises the very questions
behind Yerushalmi's link between justice and memory.

I will turn briefly to one prominent figure in the debate on
justice and the Shoah. Although the limit of justice in relation to
the Holocaust finds its model in Hannah Arendt's *Eichmann in
Jerusalem*, even before her philosophical account Arendt delineated
the frustration behind the Nuremberg trials. Describing how Nazi
crimes "explode the limits of the law," Arendt argued that what
makes these crimes "monstrous" is that a courtroom could never
find proper punishment for those who carried out the atrocities.
Frustration arises from a lack of balance and Arendt writes, "It
may be essential to hang Goering, but it is totally inadequate. This
guilt, in contrast to all criminal guilt, oversteps and shatters all
legal systems. This is why the Nazis in Nuremberg are so smug.
We are simply not equipped to deal, on a human, political level,
with a guilt that is beyond crime."[7] Shattering the trope of the
scales of justice, the guilt left behind by genocide breaks the legal
frame needed to carry out juridical justice. Returning in 1961 to
this dilemma during Eichmann's trial, Arendt discussed how critics
opposed Eichmann's execution for being "unimaginative": it failed
to return in proper measure the violation of the law.[8] In his juxtaposition of film with genocide, Tarantino attempts to satisfy the
frustration of his audience by transferring guilt and punishment
into a fantasy realm. However, visceral satisfaction in watching
the killing of Nazis comes with a price: questions of justice will
also challenge us to probe our own specular relation to violence in
contemporary history.

The Sorrow and the Pity

Before turning to Tarantino, I will explore Ophüls' use of layering
documentary and filmic traces to form a space of justice. In one of
the opening sequences to *The Sorrow and the Pity*, Ophüls stands
in the verdant countryside of Auvergne with two farmers (Alexis

and Louis Graves) who were members of the French Resistance and asks them if they thought much of their hometown, Clermont-Ferrand, during their imprisonment in Buchenwald. Louis Graves responds, "No. You thought only of yourself. Only afterward about others. Afterwards ... "[9] These revealing lines will echo throughout the film, as Ophüls constantly asks the interviewees (German soldiers, Resistance fighters, collaborators and Jews) what they thought of the other. Shortly before the film's ending, Ophüls asks the brothers if they knew who turned them in and they reply "yes."[10] Responding to Ophüls' question, "You were denounced. Did you ever want to take revenge?" Louis Grave remarks, "What's the use? If I wanted to get even, I would have by now. You never forget. It stays engraved in your memory ... But what can you do? Nothing."[11] Their opening and closing interviews provide a frame in relation to questions of revenge and justice, calling into question the very settling of accounts, of a balancing of justice through acts of revenge.

I would like to focus on the last section of part I in *The Sorrow and the Pity*, which illustrates the interplay between anti-Semitism, propaganda, the Vichy film industry and three spaces of compromised juridical justice: the trials of Pierre Mendes-France, Bernard Natan and the inclusion of the German propaganda film *Jud Süss*.[12] In a complex montage of shifting scenes that centers on Mendes-France's trial, Ophüls' probing of the link between the courtroom and cinema reveals how the injustices inherent in both of these spaces are permeated with reverberations of anti-Semitism. While the trials become spectacles fueled by the undercurrents of xenophobia and anti-Semitism in the Vichy press, we also see how film is a tool that persecutes Jews. By returning to the testimonial archive of film and interweaving three trials, Ophüls constructs a retroactive justice to indict French complicity in Jewish persecution. With the specter of Alfred Dreyfus ever present throughout these scenes, Ophüls lays bare how the history of French anti-Semitism long preceded the German occupation. After the capitulation, anti-Semitism moved into the open as seen in the establishment of the institution for the study of the Jewish Question, propaganda exhibitions and screening of Nazi films. As Mendes-France declares, the German and French bond was strengthened through anti-Semitism, culminating in the Judeocide. Describing the climate of anti-Semitism in the courtroom, Mendes-France compares his trial to a film, where people bought admission cards "more expensive than the movies" and sat in the room "filled with hate." In his opening statement to the hostile court, invoking the legacy of Alfred Dreyfus, he states, "I am a Jew, and a freemason, but not a deserter. Now let the trial begin."[13] By professing his Jewish identity Mendes-France makes explicit why he is on trial and confronts the audience with the true ground of his arrest: he is a Jew.

In the next sequence where Ophüls inserts French newsreels of Bernard Natan's trial, one of the most important figures in the French film industry, the interplay between film, courtroom and anti-Semitism becomes even more evident. Now it is the camera that turns the trial into spectacle. Natan was accused not only of fraud but also of hiding his Jewish-Romanian background by changing his name. As the commentator keeps referring to "Natan the Jew," the newsreels reveal how the camera's invasive gaze tormented Natan in the courtroom. Slowly, those who had contributed to French film are excised from it; Mendes-France discusses how Jewish actors and directors were erased from credit titles. Thus, textual erasures prefigure the eventual physical removal of Jews. As we will see later on, in a counter move in *Inglourious Basterds*, Dreyfus deconstructs German cinema, taking down the marquees of Riefenstahl's film *The White Hell of Pitz Palu* leaving only the word "Hell" in the title. French officials eventually handed Natan over to the Gestapo and he was murdered in Auschwitz. One of the most significant contributions from Natan was his introduction of the anamorphic lens to French cinema, which increases the perspective of the frame. Ophüls' historical optic is itself anamorphic, that is, he re-frames the distortions of French history to give a more inclusive narrative of the events.

Returning to the archive in order to explore the extent to which the Third Reich's exploitation of mass culture fueled racist hatred in the French audience, Ophüls inserts one of the most disturbing excerpts from German propaganda directed by Veit Harlan, *Jud Süss/The Jew Suess* (1940). Although Ophüls' montage seems to disclose a verdict—films were not needed for the hostility was already present—his selection of scenes (the trial and execution) serves another function. Ophüls re-appropriates the scene of racial hatred not only to invoke sympathy for the Jewish victims, but also to stress the link between law and extermination; the French anti-Semitic laws were even more severe than those from Germany's 1935 Nuremberg Laws. The next scene transition is the most damning, for it explicitly discloses France's link to the Shoah. In a complex interweaving of material, Ophüls juxtaposes *Jud Süss* to footage of French actors going to Germany "For the good of art." Ophüls then cuts to a newsreel that discusses Heydrich, Himmler, and the institution of Jewish affairs in Paris. We hear, "Heydrich is president of the international police commission. France has always been represented in this commission."[14] Challenging the film's suggestion of France upholding international law, Ophüls places the architects of extermination within a French context. Although film is associated with both extermination and the forgetting of this past, the reels of cinema from the 1940s return in 1969 to depict not simply the return of the repressed but the potential space of justice. Ophüls takes hold of this propaganda to both re-occupy cinematic space and break the myth of a heroic French Resistance.

The figure of the film reel metaphorically returns at the film's conclusion, where Ophüls describes the cycles of violence that followed in the immediate post-occupation period; there is a perpetuation of retribution consisting of the killing and torturing of French collaborators. Even the Resistance comes under scrutiny as we hear how its members enacted vengeance on collaborators. Ophüls inserts documentary material that exclaims, "Let the heads of traitors roll—that is justice." What befell the captured Resistance fighters is now played out on the bodies of the collaborators and occupiers; justice becomes a balance of punishment. In one interview, a lawyer describes "the summary sort of justice" after war and we are shown pictures of men shot on the spot.[15] In one graphic tale, the lawyer, speaking about judgment and justice, describes how members of the Vichy police who had been arrested and admitted to rounding up young maquisards, plucking out their eyes, inserting live May bugs in the sockets and sewing them up. He states, "Judgment was reached quickly ... At the time such things could not be forgiven."[16] But it is this very cycle of violence that the film both critiques and wishes to disrupt. It is telling that the last act described in the film is that of a Resistance fighter, Marcel Verdiers, sparing the life of a German soldier. Instead of shooting the German, he describes how he looked at him with pity and turned away.

What, then, is justice for Ophüls? In addition to breaking one's attachment to an imaginary history, that is, to provide a space for a counter-cathexis to a historical narrative through the re-occupation of cinema, justice is constituted by the need to imagine the other albeit belatedly. Ophüls emphasizes the failure to imagine the other in relation to both the violence of extermination and during the aftermath of collaboration. As the French aristocrat turned SS member says to Ophüls, "I knew the Jews were being arrested. I never knew that, I never imagined extermination ... " Ophüls completes the exchange, "That it all ended in Auschwitz."[17] Similarly, in her response to Ophüls' question whether she ever thought that the suffering she endured after liberation others had suffered at the hands of the Nazis, Solange, the hairdresser and collaborator, responds, "I don't know. I didn't try to look so far ... "[18] Both of these failures to imagine the other extend to Ophüls' audience, whereby the retroactive justice of cinema compels the spectator to acknowledge degrees of culpability: their own failure to imagine or think through the aims of National Socialism. Ophüls' anamorphic gaze, conveyed through his contrapuntal editing, requires the spectator to re-construct the between of montage of material that was present in 1940. Film beckons acts of self-reflection through the re-imagining of the other's erasure that occurs in the gaps of cinema. Ophüls uses montage and polyphony of voices to confront the audience with a difficult history and to trigger unease; specular satisfaction arises through one's recognition that film captures someone's guilt or responsibility. Yet these moments come at a cost for his French audience who must acknowledge the degree to which the national narrative of heroic resistance is a fantasy.

Inglourious Basterds

Similar to Ophüls, one of the most compelling facets of *Inglourious Basterds* is Tarantino's own use of textual juxtapositions and his reliance on structures of interrogation. From its opening scene where SS officer Hans Landa interrogates the French farmer LaPadite, each of the five chapters features narratives infused with an interrogative mode. Yet it is Tarantino's own interrogation of film through other films that is key to his Talmudic approach to cinema and which he transfers to the spectator, who must ultimately assume the role of an investigator to unravel the film's intricacies. Central to its Talmudic structure, Tarantino's dense layering of filmic intertextuality creates a polyphony of voices analogous to the "contrapuntal montage" used to describe Ophüls' technique. Like Ophüls, Tarantino anamorphically probes the historical complexities between present and past in relation to shifting sites of violence.[19]

Furthermore, the film's Talmudic structure operates through the mechanics of a condensation contained in Tarantino's *mise en scène*. Moreover, this layering effect is itself constitutive of the pleasure and frustration ascribed to his use of images. The film's multivalent structure also contributes to such diverse readings of it being guilty of Holocaust revisionism to being a hyper-Zionist fantasy. One particular resonance embedded within a frame might snag the spectator without opening up other layers. In the frame's verticality Tarantino leads us through a history comprised of both high and "low" cinema, where we become witnesses to the condensation of filmic history; one frame recalls a series of other frames within the architectonic of cinema. In turn, we cannot overlook the risks that this archive poses for the critic/analyst of the film, whereby the text entraps us in a hermeneutic labyrinth. While interpretive acts and recognizing visual citations are a source of pleasure, the dense layering potentially takes us to unanticipated traumas from both history and film. There are several instances of a Talmudic-like condensation of the frame that I would like to approach in this analysis, including the projection of Dreyfus' face on the screen in her theater, the film *Nation's Pride*, and the final *mise en scène*, where Aldo the Apache disfigures Landa in the forest.

Tarantino's transformation of cinema into a place of resistance relies on his re-occupation or *Beseztung* of cinematic history to dismantle specific historical narratives. His subversions are not aimed at the history of WWII, but rather at the medium of film itself. Constantly breaking down the fourth wall to draw attention to his interrogation of the interplay between filmic and historical violence, Tarantino also underscores our specular relation to the violent narratives unfolding on the screen. Yet *Besetzung* also involves the question of affect. One of the most intriguing aspects of the debates around *Inglourious Basterds* is a similarity in numerous Jewish responses: there is a sexual charge engendered by Tarantino's portrayal of Jewish resistance and violence. As Tarantino remarked, "People might say I've gone too far, but I know for a fact Jewish people have been waiting for a WWII Jewish revenge movie for a long time." Calling the film "Kosher porn," Eli Roth, who plays the Bear Jew, described his act of machine gunning Hitler as "orgasmic"; the film's producer Lawrence Bender said to Tarantino, "As a member of the Jewish tribe, I thank you. This is a fucking Jewish wet dream"; Goldberg goes one step further and describes the film as an "unabashed wet dream of vengeance." The transformation of images of Jewish revenge into metaphors of sexual discharge and libidinal energy in the spectator reaffirms the concept of cathexis and fantasy identity formation for the Jewish (albeit essentially male) spectator.[20]

In one of the most critical responses to *Inglourious Basterds*, Daniel Mendelsohn would disagree with this claim.[21] Mendelsohn, acclaimed author of the Holocaust memoir *The Lost* wrote, "Tarantino indulges this taste for vengeful violence by turning Jews into Nazis. In history, Jews were repeatedly herded into buildings and burned alive ... the Nazis made sport of human suffering; Nazis carved Stars of David into the chests of rabbis before killing them; Tarantino, invites his audiences to applaud this odd inversion, to take a deep satisfaction in turning the tables on the bad guys. Do you really want audiences cheering for a revenge that turns Jews into carbon copies of Nazis, that makes Jews into "sickening" perpetrators?"[22] Mendelsohn continues by asserting that the "Jewish" way—one that relies on the refrain of "never again"—would be morally superior through its preservation of memory. Whereas Mendelsohn believes in the mimetic ability of film to mirror reality, Tarantino rejects any mimetic approach to history via film; his film never intends to be anything other than fantasy. While Mendelsohn's critique falls back into the cliché "never again," it is the visual equivalents of such reified turns of speech that Tarantino wishes to undermine. Moreover, Mendelsohn leaves an important feature out of his analysis. Tarantino's cinematic insertions are central to an understanding of the film. *Inglourious Basterds* should be approached from the intersection between historical catastrophe and cinematic history; the inversions that Mendelsohn stresses are bound to the structures of revenge films, where the tables are turned on the initial perpetrators. Tarantino's images are layered. As I will examine later, carving up the body may be an act of Nazi brutality, but it is also an image Tarantino appropriates from Wes Craven's *Last House on the Left*. While locking the doors and setting a building aflame may recall the crematoriums, it gestures as well to Brian De Palma's *Carrie*.

Similar to how the horror genre from the late 1960s and 1970s reacted symptomatically to the Vietnam War and America's racial tensions, Tarantino's employment of the cultural imaginary of Hollywood horror films reflects on contemporary political and social unrest. The director Joe Dante has designated this wave of films as "Abu Ghraib movies."[23] By referencing these genres and films, Tarantino confronts his audience with the historical and political tensions in the present. In the displacement of history with popular culture, the spectator needs to read, hear and interpret these phonic cues. Although Tarantino invites us to engage in the pleasure of violence, it is the spectator who is juxtaposed to the Nazis in the movie theater who cheer each time an American soldier is shot on-screen. Tarantino's fantasy space of revenge places the spectator in the position to interrogate the complexities behind the ethical relation to where historical violence and cinematic violence merge. *The Sorrow and the Pity* enters into the memory debates in French culture as De Gaulle reasserted his power, the violence in Vietnam was reaching its climax and the aftermath of France's colonial occupation of Algeria haunted national consciousness. We cannot therefore overlook the relevance of *Inglourious Basterds* in relation to America's wars in Iraq and Afghanistan; the film was released the same week as the C.I.A. report on the torture of prisoners in Guantanamo and Abu Ghraib was made public.

The complex layering behind *Inglourious Basterds* can be analyzed in the film's opening sequence, which captures in fifteen minutes what Ophüls develops over four hours. Beginning with the chapter title "Once Upon a Time ... Somewhere in German-occupied France," the scene displays the exterminationist drive behind Nazi anti-Semitism. The structure of the title that is comprised of allusions both to Grimms' fairy tales and the Spaghetti Western genre—an indefinite location (somewhere) and a spatial/temporal marker of a specific history—crafts the tensions inherent to Tarantino's engagement with the Shoah. The ambiguous "somewhere" gives way to a definitive point: Vichy France during WWII. Tarantino has located in this elliptical space that juxtaposes

Grimms' fairy tales, Spaghetti Westerns and an unsettling historical period a site for reflection and interrogation.

Inglourious Basterds begins in a countryside farmhouse and we hear the Italian composer Ennio Morricone's score "The Verdict" from the film *The Big Gundown*. The scene commences with multiple forms of artistic occupation including Tarantino's use of the Spaghetti Western and Grimms' fairy tale motifs, and Morricone's turn to German classical musical: his score is derived from Beethoven's *Für Elise*. Despite the fairy tale-like opening, *Inglourious Basterds* is steeped in history; the Jewish extermination is juxtaposed to other instances of American and French historical violence including the colonialization of the West, the genocide of Native Americans, the history of racism and slavery, oblique references to the Vietnam War and the current war on terror. In a later sequence Tarantino turns to Morricone's score from *The Battle of Algiers*: Gillo Pontecorvo's film on French colonialism, torture and Algerian resistance that eventually turns into a reflection on what constitutes terrorism.[24] Finally, by naming the Jewish heroine Dreyfus, Tarantino underscores French anti-Semitism and forms a trajectory connecting Nazi extermination to French history. Although the Shoah is placed in a larger frame of historical violence, Tarantino is not reducing these events but creates a vertiginous layering to unsettle the viewer and beckons us to explore the implications of historical violence and its repression via film, pop culture imagery and historical iconography.

Despite its numerous overt and hidden references to cinema, at the center of *Inglourious Basterds* lies Tarantino's analysis of film's relation to violence as conveyed in his references to Riefenstahl, Goebbels and the inclusion of the fictional docu-drama *Nation's Pride*. The exterminationist ideology behind Nazi propaganda films is embodied in Hans Landa's words, "the Jew Hunter," during his interrogation of the French farmer LaPadite, who is suspected of hiding a Jewish family. The farmer's name encodes Ophüls' film: LaPadite conveys the pity (*la pitié*) for the other sought by Ophüls. Borrowing the rhetoric espoused in German propaganda films, Landa compares Jews to rats and his description mirrors one of the most infamous scenes from Fritz Hippler's *The Eternal Jew*, where images of rats running through sewers are set next to Jews spreading across the world. Tarantino seems to adapt the following lines from *The Eternal Jew*: "Where rats turn up, they spread diseases and carry extermination into the land ... the Jews infect the races of the world." In a chilling passage from his diary after *The Eternal Jew* was shown to Nazi officials, Goebbels wrote: "A very large audience with almost the entire Reich Cabinet. The film is an incredible success. One hears only enthusiastic responses. The whole room raves. That's what I had hoped for."[25] During the climax of *Inglourious Basterds*, Tarantino captures this very enthusiasm of Nazi officials viewing *Nation's Pride*. But while the German audience becomes ecstatic watching a German sniper shooting Americans, Tarantino eventually reverses the direction of visual pleasure as we replace those in the theater and view the Third Reich's destruction through burning reels of film. Yet this inversion is more complex than Germans placed in a crematorium. As I will examine later the reversal involves our own seduction by filmic representations and our specular relation to violence.

The mounting terror in the opening scene arises through the interplay of music, camera movement and dialogue. When we first see LaPadite, he wields an axe against a tree trunk and projects an image of strength. Landa's interrogation of the farmer, like so many other pivotal scenes in Tarantino's films, is set around a kitchen table and involves an act of interpolation. One might recall the opening scene of *Reservoir Dogs* when Mr. Pink and the other bank robbers deconstruct Madonna's video *Like a Virgin*. Similarly, during the Mexican stand-off in the restaurant at the end of *Pulp Fiction*, Jules the hitman interprets the meaning of his Ezekiel passage. In Landa's tension-laden interrogation regarding the whereabouts of the Dreyfus family, the camera descends slowly from the table to beneath the floor. In the claustrophobic space we see looks of terror in the family's eyes as they try to peer through the cracks. As the camera moves upward to the table, we are now privy to LaPadite's secret.

Sitting at a table with ink and paper, Landa evokes an image of Eichmann: a totalitarian bureaucrat who revels in speaking clichés and the "officialese" of the Nazi apparatus. However, while Landa recognizes the banality of his task of rounding up and exterminating Jews, he is far from banal. Arendt will say of Eichmann that he is neither Macbeth, Iago nor a monster, but evokes a banality of evil.[26] But while Landa recognizes the banality of his task of rounding up and exterminating Jews, he is far from the banality of evil. Although Arendt underscores how Eichmann was devoid of the moral imagination required to think from the position of the other and to grasp the moral rupture of his actions, the cultured ' Landa, who converses in four languages and eventually participates in the carrying out of the Third Reich's destruction, revels in his ability to think like a Jew. Yet this skill is not used to form a moral judgment regarding his actions but instead is effectively employed to track down Jews. His eventual decision to cut a deal with the Allies and make "Operation Kino" a success is motivated through self-interest, not any moral imperative to halt the war.

But as the scene's tension mounts, Tarantino disrupts the horror behind Landa's words with comic relief. Landa the detective takes out an absurdly large Sherlock Holmes-like pipe. In this flash of levity that dispels anxiety, Tarantino reminds the spectator of cinema's inauthenticity. However, the terror in Tarantino eventually resumes with the family executed beneath the floorboards. We do not see their bodies, but instead watch machine guns rip holes through the wood, as LaPadite recoils in horror. The moral complexity of the scene relies on our specular relation to what unfolds upon LaPadite's face. As the audience admires his act of resistance, anxiety escalates as we watch his responses to Landa's sadistic game of cat and mouse. Once Landa reveals that he knows the location of the Jews, LaPadite concedes, hoping he and his daughters will avoid punishment. The camera lingers on his anguished face as tears stream down his cheeks. Specular identification is directed not toward those beneath the floorboards, but toward the French farmer's nonviolent resistance of hiding Jews.

The trademark scenes of violence in Tarantino's films arise in the second chapter, titled "The *Inglourious Basterds.*" The scene begins with Lt. Aldo "the Apache" Raine, who describes himself as part Apache Indian from Tennessee, explaining to his Basterds their mission. His words should also be construed as a warning to the audience of the violence that will come.

> We will be cruel to the Germans. And through our cruelty, they will know who we are. And they will find the evidence of our cruelty in the disemboweled, dismembered and disfigured bodies of their brothers we leave behind us. And the German won't be able to help themselves but imagine the cruelty their brothers endured at our hands, and our boot heels and the edge of our knives … And when the German closes their eyes at night and

they're tortured by their subconscious for the evil they have done, it will be with thoughts of us that they are tortured with.

The depictions of provoking fear in the German imagination and the haunting of the unconscious in the Germans are not tied to the crimes committed against the Jews, but rather the retribution that awaits them. The affect is not one of guilt, but fear. The question of justice is transformed into a haunting without end and Aldo tells his men, "We will not let them sleep at night." With its Spaghetti Western justice evocative of Clint Eastwood in *Hang 'Em High*, who seeks revenge against the men who attempted to lynch him, the ones who mete out justice might already be dead, coming from beyond the grave. Our introduction to Aldo begins with a close-up shot of the scar around his neck from a possible lynching. While the dismembered bodies are meant to provoke terror and occupy the unconscious of the German soldiers who encounter these traces, the interplay between disfigurement, imagination and the unconscious operates on another level as well: that of a filmic and historical unconscious directed at the spectator. The mark of the scar on the neck of a southerner who is fighting injustice in Europe points to a possible backstory of his similar actions in America.

Nonetheless, Aldo's men owe him a debt as well. At the conclusion of his speech, he tells his soldiers: "When you join my command, you take on debit. A debit you owe me, personally. Each and every man under my command owes me 100 Nazi scalps. And I want my scalps." I wish to suggest that we should try to understand this debt around which the film revolves in terms of the German word *Schuld*, which translates into both *debt* and *guilt*. On one level the film illustrates the problems between justice, guilt (*Schuld*) and punishment in relation to genocide. How do we approach this mechanism of a debt within the context of justice sixty-five years after the Shoah if the structures of juridical justice are inadequate? But Tarantino is addressing his audience as well. Specular pleasure of a fantasy will come with a price.

After Aldo's speech, the scene immediately switches to the aftermath of a battle scene and through a graphic close-up shot, we see the Basterds indeed removing the scalps from the bodies, peeling them from the skulls and leaving the viscera exposed. It is as if Tarantino uses anti-Semitic stereotypes and propaganda—Shylock's pound of flesh—as a weapon against those who persecute Jews. If his men owe him the scalps, what is the debt of Tarantino's audience? Where is the spectator's moral consciousness situated in relation to this fantasy? At this potential moment of pleasure mixed with revulsion, the spectator's satisfaction before the shocking image is balanced by a gesture to recollect another scene of genocide: that of Native Americans.

Perhaps the most disturbing figure in the film is Eli Roth's depiction of the Bear Jew: a baseball bat-swinging psychopath who bludgeons Nazis to death with his Louisville Slugger. When a German officer refuses to reveal the position of enemy troops, Aldo threatens to call out the Bear Jew, adding that watching him bash in heads "is the closest we get to going to the movies." When violence erupts, the camera places the spectator in the role of the German soldier and there is no vicarious thrill of swinging the bat, of occupying the executioner's position. In a graphic close-up shot, we see the bat smash in the German's head. But then the perspective immediately moves to a bird's-eye view above the trees as the Bear Jew continues hitting the head. Although we still see the carnage, we now watch from a distance that obscures the details. Instead it is the repetitive sound of the bat that clearly resounds through the scene. Despite Jeffrey Wells' description that this scene is "morally disgusting," I contend it operates by means of a moral complexity that implicates our spectatorship.[27] While the spectator may be drawn to a film whose trailer exclaims "we will be doing one thing only ... killing Nazis," the satisfaction of vengeance is compromised by the visceral affect of horror or repulsion that is part of the debt owed for our spectatorship.[28]

Whereas Dreyfus will cut into Goebbels' film, Aldo literally cuts the iconic symbol of National Socialist terror and its crimes into the German body, leaving his signature behind. These flesh-inscribed swastikas not only constitute an act of writing but, like a message in a bottle, the disfigured bodies are meant to trigger acts of reading and recollecting in those who come across the marked soldiers, whose survival comes at a price—the cut. It is not only a reminder to the perpetrator who intends to hide behind civilian clothes after the war, but to all those who wish to forget the past: this history cannot be concealed.

Articulating both a debt and guilt that can never be erased, Aldo's mark becomes an act of resistance to forgetting. His ritual cutting of German troops—the scalping of the dead and sparing one soldier with the inscribed forehead—reminds one of God's marking of Cain after the murder of Abel: God's warning to others that Cain was not to be touched but forced to live in exile. Yet the Hebrew word translated as Cain's "mark" (*'owth*), a word that conveys both sign and remembrance, is the same word used for "circumcision." Thus, the ritual of marking the Jewish body as a sign of identification is transferred to the German, where the swastika forever identifies him as a member of Hitler's regime. Like Arendt who stresses that the court judged correctly that Eichmann must be removed from humanity, Tarantino proposes another manner in which this removal is to be carried out, albeit in a space outside the law that imaginatively fulfills this removal via the mark.

Prompting us to question our own position of looking at violence in relation to the affect it induces within us, Tarantino constructs parallels throughout the film's climax, which takes place in a movie theater, between his audience and what is occurring on the screen as the Germans watch *Nation's Pride*. The inversions transpiring in the film are more complex than a simple reversal of punishment between victims and perpetrators, where Nazi brutality is inverted via fantasy acts of retribution. Although visual pleasure behind the fantasy is conjoined to unease in recognizing within the reversal that these acts were carried out upon Jewish bodies, we need to realize that our subject position throughout the film is analogous to that of the Germans watching *Nation's Pride*.

Perspectives shift throughout the final scene: Dreyfus in her projection booth, the Germans in the theater, the war hero Private Frederick Zoller atop his bell tower on the screen and in the balcony alongside Hitler and Goebbels. Our own specular position needs to be read next to theirs. Similar to the Basterds cheering as they watch the Bear Jew kill German soldiers, Hitler and Goebbels applaud each death depicted in *Nation's Pride*. Likewise, Tarantino invites his audience to cheer. However, Tarantino shows how the cinematic experience goes beyond sheer pleasure, when Zoller encounters his own image on the screen in the film. Comparing himself to *Sergeant York*, Zoller stars in a film about his exploits as a sniper in which he shot over 200 American soldiers. Zoller, however, does not celebrate what he is watching, but rather we observe a moment of enlightenment upon his face in relation to the violent scene he both enacted and acted out before the camera. As we witness his agonized reactions to the re-creation of violence on the screen, it is as if the filmic medium brings to consciousness the horrors of the event.

Again, the trope of occupation dominates this scene. Directing the propaganda sequence *Nation's Pride*, Eli Roth occupies Tarantino's film. There is a complexity behind the *mise en scène* of Roth's *Nation's Pride*, and like Tarantino, Roth cites a series of films including Sergei Eisenstein's iconic image of a solder shot in the eye from the Soviet propaganda film *Battleship Potemkin*, Howard Hawks' *Sergeant York*, and Peter Bogdanovich's crazed sniper in *Targets*. The most revealing of these citations is the 1968 *Targets*, which tells the story of a Vietnam veteran who murders his family and then goes on a shooting spree. Based loosely on the story of a Vietnam veteran, Charles Wittman, who went atop the University of Texas bell tower and shot sixteen people, *Targets'* climax occurs in a drive-in movie theater where the sniper shoots through the screen at spectators who are watching a horror film. Similar to how Private Zoller is unsettled when he sees himself on the screen, the sniper in *Targets* succumbs to the doubling of Boris Karloff's character, which is featured on both the screen and in the audience. In this uncanny blur of fantasy and the real, violence again crosses the screen, as Karloff subdues the sniper with his cane. Replacing the genre of Victorian horror with the horrors of Vietnam coupled with the violence seething within suburbia, Bogdanovich uses as his last image on the drive-in screen the scene of a massive fire consuming the gothic castle in Karloff's film.

But it is Dreyfus who ultimately interrupts the cinematic experience as she cuts and inserts her film within *Nation's Pride*. When we first see Dreyfus preparing for her task, she applies rouge to her face like war paint, thus merging with Aldo the Apache. Moreover, like Aldo who possibly comes from beyond the grave as his scar indicates, Dreyfus too will speak from beyond the grave to exact revenge. In his tower on the screen, we see Zoller carving a swastika into the wood—thereby alluding to the mark left on the heads of Germans designed to haunt those back home—and he screams to the American troops below, "Who wants to send a message to Germany?" At this moment Dreyfus does her own act of cutting and inserts herself in the film, responding, "I do." Re-occupying the space of film through her cutting, Dreyfus asserts her Jewish identity and exclaims, "Look deep into the face of the Jew" who is going to kill you. The screen explodes in flames, as her face now illuminates the smoke. As the leaders of the Third Reich are consumed in the inferno, the face of Dreyfus killed moments earlier appears from beyond the grave. Having spliced herself into Goebbels' film—an act signifying the re-occupation of cinema and her movie house—her mocking face exclaims to those trapped in the flames, "This is the face of Jewish vengeance."

The striking image of the French-Jewish heroine's wraithlike face projected onto the surface of smoke and fire is Tarantino's own filmic gesture to the history of cinema. Opening up a series of interpolations, Dreyfus' "giant face" contains within it a filmic archive of classic Hollywood (*The Wizard of Oz*) and Weimar German (*Metropolis*) cinemas, European *avant garde* (*Persona*), contemporary horror (*Carrie*) and popular culture (*Raiders of the Lost Ark*). In effect, Dreyfus assaults the Third Reich with a film aesthetic they reproached: Expressionism. Like the mechanism behind cathexis, Dreyfus' disembodied head becomes a projection of our own desire for revenge. By crossing from the space of film and fantasy into the real, Dreyfus not only breaks the fourth wall, but her uncanny figure and voice embody the return of the dead. Moving within the flames out from the screen, Dreyfus bears as well an uncanny resemblance to the specters in De Palma's *Carrie* and Spielberg's *Raiders of the Lost Ark*. The turn from a laughing audience to a demonic wraith exacting revenge through fire is Tarantino's homage to De Palma's own tale of vengeance. In addition, while Tarantino may reject the somber violins that accompany Jews going to their deaths in Spielberg's *Schindler's List*, he invokes the fantasy of divine revenge emanating from the ark in *Raiders*, where Nazis are incinerated by a beautiful spirit that transforms into the angel of death. It is not so much the method of punishment—the inversion of theater into furnace—but rather how the dead continue to collect on the *Schuld* that consti-tutes the uncanny justice in this film.

Contrary to Alexander Kluge's concern that Tarantino's film might obscure history through his distortions, they take us repeatedly to the specters of other political catastrophes which are interspersed iconically and phonically throughout *Inglourious Basterds*.[29] For instance, a Gestapo officer deconstructs *King Kong* as an allegory for American slavery. Goebbels excoriates the success of black American Olympians as a sign of slavery. Aldo the Apache recalls the legacy of Native American genocide, while his scar points to the history of lynching. Contrary to a reduction of history, the aim of juxtaposing shifting moments of historical catastrophe turns the question of specular affect back on the spectator, who must untangle the oscillation between fantasy and history, along with the affects of pleasure and unease.

Tarantino conveys this uneasiness mixed with pleasure when he describes what his goal was in the film's climax: "I set up the scenes and I jerk you off to have a climax. And in this movie I jerked you off and I fucked with the climax ... at some point those Nazi uniforms went away and they were people being burned alive. I think that's part of the thing that fucks with the catharsis. And that's a good thing."[30] Like the sexual descriptions used by Roth, Bender and Goldberg, Tarantino reinforces the libidinal charge behind this explosion of violence. However, the payoff—the money shot of the Bear Jew obliterating Hitler's face with a machine gun—entails a debt too. I would claim that the moment of failed catharsis is actually an interrupted cathexis designed to subvert specular pleasure. We can see this more clearly in the film's last shot.

At the film's conclusion, Aldo exudes frustration as he listens to Landa work out a deal with an American commander for his conditions of surrender. Even though Landa insists that he will not find himself in front of a "Jewish tribunal" at the war's end, that he will take off his uniform, blend into America and conceal his past, it is Aldo who re-occupies Landa's intended narrative of deception by marking him. The most striking aspect of the ending again concerns specular identification. While the earlier scene of cutting was shot from the soldier's perspective, we now occupy Aldo's position and see every incision from his knife on Landa's forehead.

However, the last act of framing returns to the low angle camera perspective of Landa looking up at Aldo. The final scene again entraps the spectator in a multiplicity of references that include the brutal rape and murder scene in Wes Craven's *Last House on the Left*—a revenge fantasy that reworks Bergman's *The Virgin Spring*—and allusions to the ominous forest landscape in the Coen brothers' *Miller's Crossing*. Aldo's hovering over Landa with his knife invokes Craven's figure of the killer-rapist who carves his name in his victim's chest. Within this layering of the forest's *mise en scène*, Tarantino collapses spaces of violence and revenge (*Last House on the Left* and *Virgin Spring*), mercy (*Miller's Crossing*) and eventually redemption (*Virgin Spring*). Although Aldo's opening speech of vengeance to the Basterds hearkens back to Jules' Ezekiel passage in *Pulp Fiction*, counter to Jules' final act of mercy Aldo instead fulfills Jules' concluding line, "And you will know my name is the Lord when I lay my vengeance upon thee." Aldo's cut reinforces the specter of divine retribution as Landa forever carries upon his body the pariah's mark of exile.

Acknowledging his own contribution and iconic place in film, Tarantino also employs his oft-used low angle shots from inside car trunks: a perspective meant to disempower the spectator.[31] Looking up at Aldo, who pronounces the final words, "This could be my masterpiece," we too are cut by the film. The mark left by Tarantino within the spectator is an affective trace meant to thwart a therapeutic catharsis or cathexis. Incomplete cathexis—similar to the postponement of justice—elicits a psychic tension through the absence of equilibrium. Although Tarantino may situate his audience in a liminal space between history and fantasy, we are simultaneously placed on a borderland of specular affect between pleasure and unease.

By leading us into the theater with a promise of vengeance, Tarantino subverts our specular pleasure in an imaginary justice by placing us into another theater alongside cheering Nazis. Despite the claim that *Inglourious Basterds* lacks moral imagination—the same term used by Arendt to describe Eichmann's failure to imagine the other—Tarantino turns the question of moral imagination back onto the spectator.[32] While the film may appeal to a desire for revenge, to satisfy one's juridical frustration through fantasies of inversion, Tarantino situates the spectator in a position from which to reflect on his/her ethical relation to the intersection between historical and cinematic violence, holding up other scenes of political violence that resonate within our own cultural imaginary.

I would like to conclude with another documentary mentioned earlier in this analysis. At the end of his nine-hour documentary *Shoah*, Claude Lanzmann turns to modern-day Israel and focuses on survivors of the Warsaw Ghetto uprising. Although *Shoah* may gesture toward a possible tale of triumph by giving the last word to survivors from the iconic place of Jewish resistance, there is nothing uplifting nor heroic in their stories. The film's concluding image—devoid of resistance or justice—is comprised of a low angle shot of train wheels rolling infinitely toward a blackened vanishing point. Similar to the reels of justice and cycles of violence that are present in Ophüls and Tarantino, Lanzmann ends with the image of circular movement, yet it is not one of retribution but rather signifies the indestructibility of the Shoah itself. Fulfilling his obsession of putting last Jews before the camera to testify to the destruction of Eastern European Jewry, Lanzmann transforms the tale of Jewish resistance into a ghost story, where survivors from the Warsaw Ghetto are juxtaposed to the inescapable machine of annihilation, the train, moving toward an unreachable vanishing point. Subverting the commemorative tale of resistance, Lanzmann's final shot of the train reveals that there is no fixed relation between law, violence and justice; rather, they are bound by hermeneutic shifts in history. Dreyfus and Aldo's appearance from beyond the grave—similar to the return of archived film in Ophüls and Lanzmann's insertion of ghostly figures—points to the mechanism of an uncanny justice. As Tarantino seduces us with promises of revenge, a debt of judgment is passed on to the spectator, who must deconstruct the film's semiotics haunted by other filmic cues as well as historical scenes of violence.

Notes

1   A. O. Scott, "Jewish History, Popcorn Included." http://www. nytimes.com/2009/10/04/movies/04scot.html

2   Liel Leibovitz, "Inglourious Indeed Tarantino's '*Inglourious Basterds*,' *Tablet Magazine*, http://www.tabletmag.com/ arts-and-culture/14057/inglourious-indeed/

3   Jeffrey Goldberg, "Hollywood's Jewish Avenger," www.theatlantic. com/doc/200909/tarantino-nazis/2; Andrew O'Hehir, "Is Tarantino Good for the Jews?" http://www.salon.com/entertainment/movies/ beyond_the_multiplex/feature/2009/08/13/basterds; Karine Cohen-Dicker, "Jewish Revenge Porn" in *The Jewish Daily Forward*, http:// www.forward.com/articles/107073/

4   See Tarantino's interview with Tom Huddleston, http://www.timeout. com/film/features/show-feature/8395/quentin-tarantino-interview.html

5   "Only in Israel and nowhere else is the injunction to remember felt as a religious imperative to an entire people ... Is it possible that the antonym of 'forgetting' is not 'remembering', but *justice?*"

(Yerushalmi, cit. Derrida, *Archive Fever*. Chicago: University of Chicago Press, 1998, 76–7.

6 Annette Insdorf, *Indelible Shadows: Film and the Holocaust*. Cambridge: Cambridge University Press, 1989, 230.

7 Hannah Arendt and Karl Jaspers, *Correspondence 1926–1969*, eds. Lotte Kohler and Hans Saner, trans. Robert and Rita Kimber. New York: Harcourt Brace Jovanovich, 1992, 54.

8 Hannah Arendt, *Eichmann in Jerusalem: a Report on the Banality of Evil*. Penguin Classics, 2006, 250.

9 Ophüls, Marcel. *The Sorrow and the Pity*. New York: Berkley Windhover Books, 1975 [English translation/appendix by Mireille Johnston and introduction by Stanley Hoffmann], 7. I will include page numbers from this text directly after the citation.

10 Ophüls, 169.

11 Ophüls, 169.

12 Pierre Mendes-France was a French Jew who fought with the Allies during the war after he escaped from a French prison, where he was being held for desertion. He also served as Prime Minister of France from 1954–1955. Bernard Natan (born Natan Tannenzaft) was a Romanian Jew who immigrated to France in 1921 and was a key figure in the development of the French film industry.

13 Ophüls, 62–4.

14 Ophüls, 82–3.

15 Ophüls, 166.

16 Ophüls, 166–7.

17 Ophüls, 149.

18 Ophüls, 165.

19 Brett Bowles "'Ça fait d'excellents montages': Documentary Technique in *Le chagrin et la pitié*" in *French Historical Studies*. http://fhs.dukejournals.org/cgi/reprint/31/1/117.pdf

20 Goldberg, "Hollywood's Jewish Avenger".

21 David Denby, "Americans in Paris: *Inglourious Basterds and Julie & Julia*." "Tarantino may think that he is doing Jews a favor by launching this revenge fantasy ... but somehow I doubt that the gesture will be appreciated." http://www.newyorker.com/arts/critics/cinema/2009/08/24/090824crci_cinema_denby

22 Daniel Mendelsohn, "*Inglourious Basterds*: When Jews Attack," http://www.newsweek.com/2009/08/13/inglourious-basterds-when-jews-attack.html

23 See Stephen Applebaum's interview with Joe Dante, http://
    stephenapplebaum.blogspot.com/2007/01/joe-dante-i-see-it-as-
    dissolution-of.html

24 After Landa captures Aldo he remarks that some might consider
    his Operation Kino "mission" a "terrorist plot". Aldo and another
    Basterd (Private Utivich) have hoods placed on their heads prior to
    their interrogation, and Tarantino invokes images of Abu Ghraib.

25 Eric Rentschler, *The Ministry of Illusion: Nazi Cinema and its
    Afterlife*. (Harvard University Press: Cambridge, 1996), 149.

26 Hannah Arendt, *Eichmann in Jerusalem: a Report on the Banality of
    Evil*. (Penguin Classics, 2006), 287.

27 Jeffrey Wells, "Jew Dogs," http://hollywoodelsewhere.com/2009/08/
    jew_dogs.php

28 The filmic layers are not only reserved to scenes and images, but
    to characters as well. Donnie Donowitz, who is configured as a
    Golem, is played by *Hostel* director Eli Roth, whose film spurred
    the description of "torture porn." By casting Roth in the brutal
    role of the Bear Jew, Tarantino links his character back to Roth's
    controversial genre.

29 Assaf Uni, "The Holocaust, Tarantino-style: Jews scalping
    Nazis," http://www.haaretz.com/jewish-world/news/
    the-holocaust-tarantino-style-jews-scalping-nazis-1.255095

30 Julian Sancton, "Tarantino Is One Basterd Who Knows How to
    Please Himself," http://www.vanityfair.com/online/oscars/2009/08/
    tarantino-is-one-basterd-who-knows-how-to-please-himself.html

31 This shot re-appears in *Reservoir Dogs*, *Pulp Fiction*, *Jackie Brown*
    and *Kill Bill: Volumes 1 and 2*.

32 Arendt, *Eichmann in Jerusalem*; 55–9.

Works cited

Annie Hall. Directed by Woody Allen. USA, 1977.

Applebaum, Stephen. http://stephenapplebaum.blogspot.com/2007/01/
    joe-dante-i-see-it-as-dissolution-of.html

Arendt, Hannah. *Eichmann in Jerusalem: a Report on the Banality of
    Evil*. Penguin Classics, 2006.

Arendt, Hannah and Jaspers, Karl. *Correspondence 1926–1969*, edited
    by Lotte Kohler and Hans Saner; translated by Robert and Rita
    Kimber. New York: Harcourt Brace Jovanovich, 1992.

The Battle of Algiers. Directed by Gillo Pontecorvo. Italy/Algeria, 1966.

Battleship Potemkin. Directed by Sergei M. Eisenstein. USSR, 1925.

The Big Gundown. Directed by Sergio Sollima. Spain/Italy, 1966.

Bowles, Brett. "'Ça fait d'excellents montages': Documentary Technique in *Le chagrin et la pitié*" in *French Historical Studies* at http://fhs. dukejournals.org/cgi/reprint/31/1/117.pdf

Carrie. Directed by Brian De Palma. USA, 1976.

Cohen-Dicker, Karine. "Jewish Revenge Porn." *The Jewish Daily Forward*, June 12, 2009. http://www.forward.com/articles/107073/

Defiance. Directed by Edward Zwick. USA, 2008.

Denby, David. "Americans in Paris: *Inglourious Basterds and Julie & Julia*." http://www.newyorker.com/arts/critics/cinema/2009/08/24/090824crci_cinema_denby

Derrida, Jacques. *Archive Fever*. Chicago: University of Chicago Press, 1998.

Don't Mess with the Zohan. Directed by Dennis Dugan. USA, 2008.

The Eternal Jew. Directed by Fritz Hippler. Germany, 1940.

Goldberg, Jeffrey. "Hollywood's Jewish Avenger." *The Atlantic*, September 2009. www.theatlantic.com/doc/200909/tarantino-nazis/2

Hang 'Em High. Directed by Ted Post. USA, 1968.

Huddleston, Tom. In *Timeout London*, August 13, 2009. http://www.timeout.com/film/features/show-feature/8395/quentin-tarantino-interview.html

Inglourious Basterds. Directed by Quentin Tarantino. USA/Germany, 2009.

Insdorf, Annette. *Indelible Shadows: Film and the Holocaust*. Cambridge: Cambridge University Press, 1989.

Jud Süss. Directed by Veit Harlan. Germany, 1940.

King Kong. Directed by Merian C. Cooper and Ernest Schoedsack. USA, 1933.

Knocked Up. Directed by Judd Apatow. USA, 2007.

The Last House on the Left. Directed by Wes Craven. USA, 1972.

Leibovitz, Liel. "Inglourious Indeed Tarantino's '*Inglourious Basterds*,'" in *Tablet: A New Read on Jewish Life*, August 21, 2009. http://www.tabletmag.com/arts-and-culture/14057/inglourious-indeed/

Mendelsohn, Daniel. "*Inglourious Basterds*: When Jews Attack." *Newsweek*, August 14, 2009. http://www.newsweek.com/2009/08/13/inglourious-basterds-when-jews-attack.html

Metropolis. Directed by Fritz Lang. Germany, 1927.

Miller's Crossing. Directed by Joel and Ethan Coen. USA, 1990.

Munich. Directed by Steven Spielberg. USA/Canada/France, 2005.

O'Hehir, Andrew. "Is Tarantino Good for the Jews?" *Salon*, August 13, 2009. http://www.salon.com/entertainment/movies/beyond_the_multiplex/feature/2009/08/13/basterds

Persona. Directed by Ingmar Bergman. Sweden, 1966.

Pulp Fiction. Directed by Quentin Tarantino. USA, 1994.

Raiders of the Lost Ark. Directed by Steven Spielberg. USA, 1981.

Rentschler, Eric. *The Ministry of Illusion: Nazi Cinema and its Afterlife*. Harvard University Press: Cambridge, 1996, 149.

Reservoir Dogs. Directed by Quentin Tarantino, USA, 1992.

Sancton, Julian. "Tarantino Is One Basterd Who Knows How to Please Himself." *Vanity Fair*, August 20, 2009. http://www.vanityfair.com/online/oscars/2009/08/tarantino-is-one-basterd-who-knows-how-to-please-himself.html

Schindler's List. Directed by Steven Spielberg. USA, 1993.

Scott, A. O. "Jewish History, Popcorn Included." *New York Times*, October 1, 2009. http://www.nytimes.com/2009/10/04/movies/04scot.html

Sergeant York. Directed by Howard Hawks. USA, 1941.

Shoah. Directed by Claude Lanzmann. France, 1985.

The Sorrow and the Pity. Directed by Marcel Ophüls. France/Switzerland/West Germany, 1969.

Targets. Directed by Peter Bogdanovich. USA, 1968.

Uni, Assaf. "The Holocaust, Tarantino-style: Jews scalping Nazis." *Haaretz*, October 7, 2008. http://www.haaretz.com/jewish-world/news/the-holocaust-tarantino-style-jews-scalping-nazis-1.255095

The Virgin Spring. Directed by Ingmar Bergman. Sweden, 1960.

Wells, Jeffrey. "Jew Dogs." *Hollywood Elsewhere*, August 11, 2009. http://hollywood elsewhere.com/2009/08/jew_dogs.php

The White Hell of Pitz Palu. Directed by Arnold Fanck and G. W. Pabst. Germany, 1929.

The Wizard of Oz. Directed by Victor Fleming, et al. USA, 1939.

9

"Fire!" in a crowded theater: liquidating history in *Inglourious Basterds*

Sharon Willis

Quentin Tarantino maintains a consistent obsession with the cinema as cinephilia, which he invites his audience to share, in his work's explicit and ironic play with film history. His films present us with clever, wry, and often breathtaking thrills and shocks as film genres and citations collide and reshape each other. Beginning with its title, borrowed from Italian director Enzo Castellari's 1978 WWII action film, *The Inglorious Bastards*, a camp version of *The Dirty Dozen* (Robert Aldrich (1967), *Inglourious Basterds* (2009) exhibits these tendencies in overdrive.[1] This film overheats—literally in a conflagration—as it joins Tarantino's preoccupations into a grandiose and troubling reading of History as screen memory. *Inglourious Basterds* screens a fantasmatic play with and on History, cast as the inventory of film genres and historical references it deploys. Film history seems to effect and to authorize, however ironically, its final lugubrious pyrotechnic display.

Projected on this history-as-screen, the filmmaker's familiar preoccupations emerge in the grotesque brutality of the "Basterds," Jewish guerrillas-cum-terrorist thugs who behave much like fascist brown shirts. Both visually and aurally, the film luxuriates in the brutal exploits of this team, led by an emphatically non-Jewish Lt. Aldo Raine (Brad Pitt), whose name pays homage to actor Aldo Ray, of course. Operating in France, they gleefully pursue their mission to kill and mutilate as many Nazis as they can. Although this "posse" recalls popular action-adventure revisions of WWII, like *The Dirty Dozen* and *The Guns of Navarone* (J. Lee Thompson, 1961), it also bears the director's sadistic stamp.

Think, for example, of the first grisly episode where we see the Basterds in action. A sickening point of view shot briefly aligns us with a German officer who awaits his execution. From this angle we look up at Private Donny Donowitz (Eli Roth) who winds up for the first baseball bat blow to the German's skull. Abruptly zooming back to a long shot, the film carries us out of harm's way and situates us among the jubilant crowd of Basterds who watch this lethal beating. Chuckling, whistling, and cheering, they sound much like a bunch of adolescents glorying in the gore of a horror movie—or much worse. But aggressive obsessions also emerge from the terribly slick Nazi Colonel Landa's (Christoph Waltz) gleeful psychological sadism. They also swirl around Shosanna Dreyfus (Mélanie Laurent), the Jewish theater owner who has escaped Landa's massacre of her family, and who manages to immolate the entire Nazi high command at a private screening in her auditorium. Surely it is no coincidence that part of her plot entails her making a film of her own?

A fantasy that cinema might intervene materially in history literalizes the power of the cultural archive that provides this film's architecture. *Inglourious Basterds'* cinephilic playfulness intersects with the concerns of contemporary film scholars and archivists as it explores the film medium's fascination with its own materiality as well as its archival impulses. Through its climactic conflagration, this film imagines concretizing the ambivalent— fearful and desiring—fascination with destruction that grounds the archival impulse. In *Archive Fever* Jacques Derrida contemplates "a death drive without which there would not in effect be any desire or any possibility for the archive."[2] "There would indeed be no archive desire," he writes, "without the radical finitude, without the possibility of a forgetfulness which does not limit itself to repression ... there is no archive fever without the threat of this death drive, this aggression and destruction drive."[3]

Such a death drive haunts archivists as much as it does the archive, most particularly in the digital age. In *The Death of Cinema*, film historian and archivist Paolo Cherchi-Usai offers provocative speculations on the relentless decay of the material film object and on the consequences of digitization. "Cinema," he asserts, "is the art of destroying moving images."[4] For Cherchi-Usai, all moving images are "disgraced," since they degrade in each performance. Film's exhibition promotes its extinction. Its very means of coming into being for spectators, our primary means of knowing it, becomes the agent of its wearing away into ruin. Put otherwise, physically, film consumes itself. But Cherchi-Usai also links the paradoxical nature of the archive to film history itself. "The subject of film history being the destruction of the moving image, its primary goal is to recapture the experience of the first viewers, an empirical impossibility." "If put into practice," he contends, "such reconstruction would lead to the obliteration of film history."[5]

Film's material fragility and the inevitable decay of its matrices— silver nitrate and acetate—haunt the work of the archives, of course. Nitrate becomes explosive with age, and acetate succumbs to vinegar syndrome, a chemical breakdown. These delicate and volatile substrates can also make themselves known in projection: scratches, discolorations, splices inscribe the film's age and history. A failure of the projection apparatus introduces the object's materiality in more shocking ways, as when the frame freezes, or the film breaks, melts, or catches fire. (Two films that represent this effect come to mind: Ingmar Bergman's 1966 *Persona* and Monte Hellman's 1971 cult classic, *Two-Lane Blacktop*). Surely, such projection events inflect Tarantino's vision here.

In the contemporary moment, in our institutional and personal archives, digitization aims to rescue our film heritage from its analog materiality. Its technology introduces new viewing practices, even as it produces an unprecedented access and seemingly boundless circulation of its objects. Such conditions promote cinephilia on new terms. As Laura Mulvey writes in *Death at 24x a Second*, digital technologies deliver film as a radically different object, one whose flow we can stop, interrupt, reverse—in short, edit to our own measure. Technology sustains new forms of cinephilic fetishism. We can attack our object, cut it up, reorder it. In its theatrical projection, of course, the exhibition apparatus itself forecloses such interventions, respecting the object's irreversible forward drive. In a film's digitally malleable form, then, Mulvey indicates, "some detail or previously unnoticed moment can become at least as significant as the chain of meaning invested in cause and effect."[6] We can, in other words, produce the arresting effects of the close-up through our own technological interventions in our objects.

Thomas Elsaesser provides another angle on contemporary cinephilia, one that aptly describes the tone and structure of Tarantino's films. Discussing contemporary cinephilia, Elsaesser contends that it confronts the problem that its "attachment to the unique moment and to that special place—in short, to the quest for plenitude, envelopment and enclosure—is already ... the enactment of a search for lost time, and thus the acknowledgment that the singular moment stands under the regime of repetition, of the re-take, of the iterative, the compulsively serial, the fetishistic, the fragmented and the fractal."[7] "Nowadays," he continues, "we know too much about the movies, their textual mechanisms, their commodity status, their function in the culture industries and the experience economy, but—equally important, if not more so—the movies also know too much about us, the spectators, the users, the consumers" (40). This is precisely the ground on which Tarantino's film approaches us, luring us to match our film historical knowingness to its own.

A polyglot film

On the occasion of the 2009 Cannes Festival, *Cahiers du Cinéma* published an interview with the director, in which he observes that he continually works on genre; or perhaps, more properly, reworks genres. His films frequently break down into chapters that represent sharply distinct genres. "In *Inglourious Basterds*," he asserts "the genres are latent, but the first two chapters have the tonality of

Westerns, even of Spaghetti Westerns, and the third would be a French film. From Chapter Four, it's the mission film."[8] In an earlier interview, the director describes this effect in *Pulp Fiction*'s structure: "You're following these two guys, you're following them, then suddenly they turn a corner and BOOM! They're in the middle of another movie! How the fuck did they get in there? They don't know and you're just as confused as they are."[9] Disorienting us in its leaps from genre to genre, *Inglourious Basterds* rewards us with the pleasures of recognition and recollection that emerge. And in the process it celebrates a certain cosmopolitanism through its fluency in genres.

What's odd, here, in Tarantino's segmentation of his film, is the classification of "French" film as a genre. No doubt, he means to indicate that this segment largely eschews action, relying instead on words, gestures, and anxious or suspicious glances to drive the plot. In tense scenes organized around Shosanna, we explore her negotiations with the German soldier who admires her, Frederick Zoller (Daniel Brühl), and Hans Landa. Verbal sparring and probing shape suspenseful encounters which play out as dramas of knowledge: who knows what about whom? But they also showcase the actors' linguistic facility as the Germans converse fluently in French. Indeed, almost all the principals in this story speak two or more languages. Their diegetic multilingualism produces a striking analogy with the film's formal transcultural citation and translation of cinematic genres, styles, and works.

In her analysis of contemporary cinephilia, Jenna Ng celebrates Tarantino as the case par excellence of the "strategies of cinematic tributes" that "effortlessly fuse love with diversely cross-cultural references, a delivery of the fluid transcultural expressions with which contemporary cinephilia traverses the globalized, amalgamated world of the twenty first century."[10] She cites the *Kill Bill* series for "its fluency of transcultural film literacy, one manifestation of which lies in today's plethora of cross-cultural filmic intertextuality, born from a diversity of film culture experiences."[11] Interestingly, Ng also notes the limitations of this cosmopolitanism, which the film self-consciously inscribes in language, as Beatrix Kiddo receives criticism for her poor command of Mandarin. For her, this amounts to a "self-reflexive acknowledgment of a limited love, always to be curbed by translations, prisms of understanding, limitations of assimilation, and cultural barriers."[12]

A similar nod to linguistic limitation occurs in a key scene in *Inglourious Basterds*. When Aldo and his comrades gather with German actress Bridget von Hammersmark (Diane Kruger) at the premiere of Goebbels' film, *Nation's Pride*, Landa joins the group. She introduces them as Italians who have no German. But when she speaks to them in Italian to introduce Landa, their expressions indicate only uneasy incomprehension. When Landa surprises them—and us—by switching into Italian, the awkward embarrassment is complete. As he prods them into repeating their names, our amusement at their hideous pronunciation grows with the suspense the sequence generates. And, of course, the accents give them away. Amusing as this moment of apparent self-deprecation on the director's part may be, it ultimately hints at a more self-satisfied American exceptionalism expressed as obstinate monolingualism.

The fate of the embarrassingly monolingual Basterds, however, contrasts with that of Lt. Archie Hicox, the British member of the Operation Kino planning team, who works as a film critic. He is bilingual, like the German/Irish actor Michael Fassbender who plays him. Once the Kino team has assembled in a French village café, Hicox's accent draws suspicion from the Nazi customers around them, since they cannot match it to their dialect maps. While they can place the other native speakers, he remains unsituated. He improvises a cover story based, not surprisingly, on the movies. He announces that he hails from the Pitz Palu region, citing his appearance as an extra in *The White Hell of Pitz Palu* (1929), directed by G. W. Pabst. We, of course, have recently seen that title on the marquee of Shosanna's Gamaar Theater. What finally gives him away, however, is not his "bizarre" accent, but the way he overplays his hand: he aggressively seeks to repel the attentions of, first, a German solider, and then an officer, who plant themselves at his table, lured by the presence of the actress and British spy, Bridget von Hammersmark. Finally, he orders three drinks with a foreign gesture, holding up his three middle fingers, like a Brit or an American, rather than thumb, index and middle finger, like a German. He has missed the vernacular nuance of gestural signs.

How perfect is the irony of the film *critic* missing this crucial visual marker! But he is also a scholar and author of two books: "Art of the Eye and Art of the Mind: German Cinema of the 1920s" and "Twenty-Four Frame Da Vinci: A Subtextual Film

Criticism Study of the Work of German Director G. W. Pabst." This last incredible mouthful must amuse those cinephiles who write on Tarantino's work from an academic context, and to whom it is obliquely addressed. It is no wonder, then, that the critic blows his cover and that of his comrades, leading to all of their deaths, and jeopardizing the mission.

Generic mash-ups

In its cinephilic "sampling," or "re-mastering" of genres, *Inglourious Basterds* pointedly evokes *The Searchers* (1956), John Ford's deeply melancholy revenge narrative, as its first episode, shaped in his account as a Western, recalls Ford's film in a stunning image shot from inside a dark interior to capture the bright and empty landscape beyond its door. But, *Inglourious Basterds* invokes *The Searchers'* terms only to invert them, as Shosanna, sole survivor of her massacred family, will re-emerge later as a Nazi hunter whose efforts align with those of the "Basterds." We meet them in "Chapter Two" in a scene reminiscent of *The Dirty Dozen*, as Aldo Raine assembles a "posse" that seems to descend directly as well from iconic Western vigilante bands. Indeed, Tarantino tells *Cahiers* that Aldo chooses Jewish combatants, so that "he can transform anti-Nazism into a *holy war*."[13]

In this film's spectacular climax, Shosanna Dreyfus and her Afro-French projectionist, Marcel (Jacky Ido), succeed in incinerating the entire Nazi high command, locked in the auditorium where Goebbels' production, *Nation's Pride*, is screening. Nothing more or less than the Gamaar cinema's own material archive provides the source and the medium of this conflagration, which ignites when footage of Shosanna appears on-screen.[14] Marcel sets fire to the reels, piled behind the screen, on a cue that comes from within the projected film itself. Flames burn through the screen to engulf the space, and the audience finds itself within the spectacle. As the spectacle jumps from the screen into the diegetic real, Shosanna's face, held in enormous close-up, floating above the flames that crackle around it, powerfully recalls Carl Dreyer's *The Passion of Joan of Arc* (1928), in its monumentalized expressive facial detail. It is as if *both* the most frequently represented female martyr in history and classic early cinema itself were underwriting the film's vision.

Asserting the deliberateness of this citation, Tarantino tells *Cahiers* that he originally imagined Shosanna as a "Jewish Joan of Arc," much more "bad ass," than she appears in the final version of the script. These giant close-ups, then, remain as a residue of that "bad ass Joan." But Tarantino emphasizes their ambiguity, "at the same time, it's the devil, Big Brother" (10). This particular construction of the avenging martyr produces some significant displacements from Dreyer's figure. While Shosanna fails to emerge as a full-fledged action hero, this does not diminish the potency of the effects that condense in and around the residual image of *The Passion*'s Joan.

In its spectacle of the face engulfed in flames, Tarantino's film also evokes another version of that most cinematic of historical heroines, Luc Besson's *The Messenger* (1999). Unlike *The Passion of Joan of Arc*, which concentrated exclusively on Joan's imprisonment and trial, this Franco-American (Gaumont/Columbia) co-production provides equal attention to the bloody spectacle of battle. *The Messenger* emphasizes Joan's nationalist fury and links it to the childhood trauma of witnessing her sister's rape and murder by an English soldier. Besson's film revels in the hysterical brutality unleashed in battle, and in extended views of dismembered corpses. Even as it emphatically repeats the monumental close-ups that dominated Dreyer's film, this iteration of Joan of Arc presents her as an action hero, a compulsive killing machine. In her relentless drive to kill, she closely resembles both the heroine of Besson's *La Femme Nikita* (1990) and Tarantino's own recent female action hero: The Bride/Beatrix Kiddo (Uma Thurman) of the *Kill Bill* franchise (Vol. 1, 2003; Vol. 2, 2004). Like Tarantino's Bride, Besson's Joan (Milla Jovovich) ruthlessly pursues vengeance. Shosanna Dreyfus, then, emerges as a new version of this Joan, a brutal avenger propelled by a nationalist passion and a revenge scenario.

"Primitive" cinema

But as this film deploys Joan of Arc it also recalls the work of another cinephile to whom Tarantino regularly pays homage,

Jean-Luc Godard. His homage often takes the form of quotation, but it never rises to the level of Godard's own dizzying art of citation. In Godard's films, visual and verbal citations work on and against each other, cutting into the forward flow, brusquely and urgently calling our attention to the meanings that are escaping us. This rigorous conceptual "montage" demands an analytical spectator, vigilantly reflecting and remembering. By contrast, Tarantino's citations most often reward us by confirming our own "knowingness." As Dana Polan describes the effect of the flow of allusions in *Pulp Fiction*, "for the spectator, there's little major intellectual work to be done here ... you either get the reference or you don't."[15] "Getting the reference," he continues, "allows entry into a private club, this being one of the functions of cult culture."[16]

Inglourious Basterds refers to Godard's fascination with the movie theater itself. His work regularly treats the theater as ambiguous liminal site, often a site of passage, where fugitives take refuge, and where a variety of illicit activities take place. In *Vivre sa vie/My Life to Live* (1962), Anna Karina's Nana attends a screening of *The Passion of Joan of Arc*. At first it appears she's seeking respite from the grinding pace at which she turns tricks, but we soon see a man placing his arm around her. On-screen unfolds the most extended exchange between the sympathetic Jean Massieu (Antonin Artaud) and Joan (Maria Falconetti), the moment when he arrives to prepare her for the stake.

As if cutting his own film into Dreyer's, Godard interrupts this prolonged exchange with two shots of Karina, also held in enormous close-up, her face starkly illuminated, thrown into relief against velvety unarticulated darkness. Positioned close to the center of the frame, only slightly to its right, Nana appears in a triangular relay with the screen gazes that seem to communicate with hers. She comes between these monumental masks, and yet, her position seems inclined to alignment with Joan's. Her eyes fill with tears in a mirror of Falconetti's, as if anticipating her own fate at the hands of the pimps who surround and constrain her: at the film's end, she will be shot in a dispute between them. This moment of cinephilia seems saturated with aggression.

Interestingly, Tarantino's theatrical conflagration finds another antecedent in Godard's *Les Carabiniers* (1963), which also includes a scene where the screen is destroyed. In this bitter allegory, composed largely of fragmented and disconnected "chase sequences," two backward, impoverished rural boys, Ulysses (Marino Mase) and Michel-Ange (Albert Juross) stumble off to war, lured by promises of wealth from the carabiniers who conscript them. Tracking their journey, the film finds them assaulting and killing civilians, molesting women, stealing from the houses they ransack. But *Les Carabiniers* trenchantly interrupts the almost slapstick episodes in this picaresque progress with stark documentary images from WWII. Battle footage repeatedly appears, as do images of slaughtered corpses. Chilling in effect, this clash of film stocks and genres arrests us in its contemplation, demands that our work of analysis match that of the editing. When the conscripts return home all the booty they have to show is a trunk full of postcards, a pile of cheap, mass-produced images—meaningless citations.

But Godard has punctuated his film with a remarkable scene that evokes his own ambivalent cinephilia and that calls attention to the primitive scenarios, like the chase, through which he recalls early cinema. Towards the middle of the film, Michel-Ange takes a break from killing and looting to make his first ever visit to the "cinématographe." This telling term refers to the Lumière brothers' invention, a camera that both recorded and projected film. Elaborating this reference, the scene that unfolds shows Michel-Ange stumbling in the unaccustomed dark of the theater and pausing to grope a woman spectator beside him. On-screen we see a train approaching a station (recalling the Lumières' train films, entering and leaving the station). As the train draws near, Michel-Ange covers his eyes and cowers, in comic evocation of well-worn stories about how cinema's first viewers reacted to the new spectacles. Offering a brief inventory of early film genres—actuality, views, pornography—this sequence exhibits Michel-Ange as "primitive" spectator.[17]

Finally, a short film entitled *A Woman of the World Takes a Bath* brings Michel-Ange out of his seat. As the woman on-screen strips, he approaches the screen. Once she has reclined in the bath, he caresses her body, ever more insistently and vigorously seeking to enter the diegetic world, until he rips the screen down. While he fumbles confusedly, we continue to watch the images now projected on the bare brick of the wall that had supported the screen.

Of course, Godard also aggressively invites us to question the smug distance contemporary viewers claim from the naive spectator of early cinema. Tom Gunning provides us with a sophisticated reinterpretation of this early spectator. Addressing the myth of the "panicked and hysterical audience" that has been central to many accounts of "the cinema's first audiences," Gunning explores the terms in which it is constructed as primitive: "the myth of initial terror defines film's power as its unprecedented realism, its ability to convince spectators that the moving image was, in fact, palpable and dangerous, bearing towards them with physical impact."[18] When we imagine early spectators as infantile this way, we assure ourselves of our own sophistication, as opposed to their primitivism.

Gunning's more nuanced approach to early film reception emphasizes the pleasure screaming spectators derived precisely from watching the illusion take place. "This vertiginous experience of the frailty of our knowledge before the power of visual illusion," he contends, "produced that mixture of pleasure and anxiety" that "founded a new aesthetic of attractions."[19] That aesthetic foregrounds display itself, highlighting juxtaposition and shock, and it recalls early cinema exhibition's roots in the fairground. What better description of Tarantino's own aesthetic might we propose than a "cinema of attractions"?[20] Just as early cinema screenings involved a succession of shorts ranging across a broad range of subjects, so *Inglourious Basterds* veers from genre to genre, jolting us with its jagged transitions.

Tarantino seems to entertain the fantasy of returning his spectators to a cinematic primal scene: shocked and awestruck, thrilled to the point of panic. And he literalizes his fantasy in the pandemonium that grips the audience in the climactic sequence of *Inglourious Basterds*, where the image on-screen invades the auditorium as flames burst through it and into real space. Thus, this scene aggressively literalizes the "primitive" spectator we like to imagine, distinguishing with difficulty between on-screen and off-screen realities/worlds. But it also seems to imagine the primitive audience of cinema's birth as childish. This is familiar ground: Dana Polan has described *Pulp Fiction* "as an infantilization" that "constructs all spectators as childlike."[21]

"French" film

Chapter Three—the "French" film—entitled "German Night in Paris," overtly introduces cinephilia into the diegetic scene, since Frederick Zoller (Daniel Brühl) approaches Shosanna through a discussion of cinema. Taking as his point of departure her theater's marquee, he engages her in a critical discussion of *White Hell of Pitz Palu* (G. W. Pabst, 1929), starring Leni Riefenstahl. While she expresses her distaste for the actress, she admits to admiring Pabst, explaining, "I'm French. We respect directors in our country ... Even Germans." What this amateur critic does not yet know, and what she will learn in the next sequence, is that Zoller is himself a film star. This "German Sergeant York" has become a national hero through his exploits as a lone sniper, and has, like his American predecessor, played himself in a film, Goebbels' *Nation's Pride*.

Goebbels (Sylvester Groth) becomes central to this segment, since Zoller aims to convince him to hold his film's special premiere for a Nazi audience in Shosanna's theater. This plan leads to her involuntary visit to a luxury restaurant, where she submits to questioning about the security of her facility. Her interrogator turns out to be none other than Hans Landa, who toys with her over strudel and cream, ordering for her a glass of milk which looms large in the frame, evoking Hitchcock's oversized glassware, and the menacing glass of milk Cary Grant brings to his wife (Joan Fontaine) in *Suspicion* (1941). Even more striking may be the resonance with Alicia Huberman's (Ingrid Bergman's) poisoned cup of coffee in *Notorious* (1946), which also starred Grant. Alicia, we remember, posed as a Nazi—and even married one—in order to infiltrate a group of Nazi exiles in South America. Alicia, then, bears some resemblance to Bridget von Hammersmark and her cohort.

Laying the foundation for Shosanna's plot to burn down her theater and annihilate its audience, this sequence also establishes some echoes with the Basterds' parallel plot, "Operation Kino." "Film people" emerge as the principals in both. The theater owner becomes a director and editor, and she carries out her plan in parallel to the Basterds' mission, which involves Bridget von Hammersmark, the German actress and British spy and the British film critic, Lt. Archie Hicox.

But this chapter also introduces a jarring effect. After its title appears on-screen, we read the words "1944," "June," across the establishing shot of the Gamaar theater. This relatively precise temporal marker, which places us some three years after Shosanna's escape from Landa, actually displaces the very history we might expect it to recall. D-Day happened in June of 1944, on the 6th, to be exact. And that month was punctuated by the slow Allied advance: Cherbourg was finally liberated on June 27; and Paris waited until August 25 of that year. To zero in on this precise month, while leaving days unspecified, seems a gesture of displacement—if not erasure—of History in favor of the fantasy scenario which will emerge. Perhaps the film here evokes a cinematic memory as well: Darryl Zanuck's *The Longest Day* (1962), which confined itself to the first twenty-four hours after the D-Day landing, another polyglot co-production, like *Inglourious Basterds*, that divides into episodes that feel like completely different films. No doubt this is because it employed three credited directors: Ken Annakin, Andrew Marton, and Bernard Wicki. Moreover, its all-star cast produced dizzying collisions of pop cultural intertextuality.

In the course of this episode's unfolding we find a significant contemporary film, and the one French release to appear on the Gamaar's marquee: Henri-Georges Clouzot's *Le Corbeau/The Raven* (1943). This is perhaps the most famous film to emerge from Continental-Films, the German studio created in Paris under the Occupation. It was certainly the most controversial, sparking bitter criticism both upon its release and during the *purges* that followed the Liberation.[22] *Le Corbeau* concerns the disruption of a small village by a series of anonymous "poison pen" letters denouncing several of its inhabitants. As the circulation of these letters escalates, the town is thrown into a chaos of mutual suspicion and increasingly hysterical collective efforts to establish their author's identity. Among the prominent suspects are the doctor who emerges as the film's protagonist, Rémy Germain (Pierre Fresnay) and his lover, Denise Saillens (Ginette Leclerc). Dr. Germain has newly arrived in the village, and his past remains mysterious. We suspect he performs abortions, since he avows that he always places the life of the mother ahead of the fetus. Denise, a vampish manipulative semi-invalid, is also afflicted with a slight congenital limp. These thoroughly ambiguous figures certainly present a provocation to Vichy's fascist moralism.

From the cycle of increasingly bitter and ugly recriminations that lead to the film's climax in murder, these two characters emerge as the only ones with any integrity in a world of cowardice and corruption. It is not so surprising that some saw this bitter film as promoting or embracing a German/Nazi view of the degeneracy of the French nation. But one can also see that the film's catalyst, the anonymous letter, seems most potently to evoke the letters of denunciation so commonly written by collaborators. This pointed image disturbingly recalls the sharp fissures in French society under the Occupation.

Inside the Gamaar theater, *Inglourious Basterds* reminds us again of Clouzot through repeated views of a poster for his first film, *L'Assassin habite au 21*, also starring Pierre Fresnay, and also made under the auspices of Continental-Films. Propaganda Minister Goebbels appointed Alfred Greven, a German film buff, to run this enterprise, and most reports indicate that he granted some measure of creative freedom to the well respected film personnel he retained there. His role remains ambiguous: his filmmakers avoided Vichy censorship; he is reputed to have known that one of his screenwriters, Jean-Paul Le Chanois, was Jewish; he ran afoul of Goebbels over Christian-Jacque's *La Symphonie fantastique*.[23] Greven certainly read Clouzot's film as alluding pointedly to the practice of informing that haunted occupied France, and he promptly fired the director. Nonetheless, at the Liberation, Clouzot was condemned by a committee of film professionals, even as directors René Clair, Marcel Carné and Jacques Becker joined such intellectuals as Sartre and De Beauvoir in defending him.

Le Corbeau's moral ambivalence and ambiguity transferred to the person of its director, who had, after all, continued to work for the German controlled studio. And this figure seems curiously sympathetic to the universe of *Inglourious Basterds*. How to weigh this allusion against Tarantino's film: does it point to his own sense of nihilism? Does it inflect his film with further ambiguity? How are we to take the film's fascination with its own film buff, Goebbels? Do the references to Clouzot's films also playfully allude to *Inglourious Basterds*' status as a co-production? It was shot at the UFA Studio in Potsdam-Babelsberg. This largest and most important of the Berlin production companies of the Weimar era was nationalized and came under Goebbels' control in 1933, producing the most prestigious projects in Nazi cinema until 1945.

How might *Inglourious Basterds* be attempting—or not—to reflect on the paradox of this studio's history as the site for its own Nazi-themed fantasies?

But in its emphasis on the archive and its destruction, as well as on cinephilia, *Inglourious Basterds* also reminds us of Henri Langlois, founder of the Cinémathèque Française. During the Occupation, Langlois succeeded in rescuing a substantial number of films that the Nazis had confiscated for destruction—by fire, of course. In this semi-clandestine enterprise, he was abetted by Frank Hensel, an officer and film connoisseur, who was then president of FIAF (Fédération Internationale des Archives du Film), and who had had been appointed director of the Reichsfilmarchiv (Reich's Film Archive) in Paris. Many of the films Langlois was able to save thanks to Hensel's practice of "counterseizure" survived the war in the basement vaults of the Palais de Chaillot, which had been requisitioned for FIAF. This site later became the Cinémathèque where Godard and Truffaut acquired their film education.[24] Historians generally acknowledge the uneasy paradox that the Cinémathèque benefitted significantly from this unusual German collaboration; it had its inception in a kind of "co-production."

Watching us

Chapter V, "Revenge of the Giant Face," explodes in a frenzy of violence. But its violent eruption comes only after a sustained montage of highly aestheticized shots that present a prolonged meditation on cinema and spectatorship. This sequence begins with Shosanna leaning against the frame of a bull's-eye window through which we see a poster for a Bridget von Hammersmark film. Shosanna is doubled by her own reflection and superimposed on the actress's face. This play of reflections shifts slightly as a slow montage sequence reframes her, from long shot, to medium shot, to medium close-up, to close-up. Reframing this gorgeous image, the camera emphasizes the echo her dress strikes with the red borders on swastika banners that hang in the lobby. We note that this window, with a circle in the middle of its frame—the bull's eye—resembles an aperture, as well as a target. It also recalls a camera lens, and it anticipates the aperture through which Shosanna will watch the film she projects to the Nazi audience.

A cut denotes an ellipsis, and we see her in extreme close-up, still looking off-screen right. She slowly applies her make-up, silhouetted in profile against the red banners we see through the window, but now no longer in focus. The Nazi banners have become abstracted and aestheticized as a pattern of red and black. This sensuous sequence offers lingering close-ups of the make-up itself and of its application. In its luxurious fetishization of feminine masquerade, this sequence clearly recalls countless film noir femmes fatales. It culminates when Shosanna seductively lowers a black veil very much like Barbara Stanwyck's in *Double Indemnity*, the 1944 release by Austrian émigré director, Billy Wilder.

Significantly, this sequence directly cites another—exaggeratedly literal—femme fatale, the protagonist of *La Femme Nikita* (1990), another of Luc Besson's spectacularly violent heroines. Nikita (Anne Parillaud), a former delinquent, has been conscripted by a secret government agency and trained to operate as an assassin under its control. Her "cover" includes an extreme version of feminine masquerade: body hugging mini dresses and impossibly high stiletto heels. A central scene in Nikita's re-education, captured in obsessive close-up attention to detail, finds her receiving instruction in feminine artifice from a mentor played by the iconic actress, Jeanne Moreau, who presides over the ritual of applying make-up. Recalling Nikita's stunning wardrobe, Shosanna's form-fitting red gown completes her transformation into the femme fatale. Marcel, however, produces a contemporary film reference upon seeing her: Danielle Darrieux. That actress presents another ambiguous figure: she aroused suspicion among many of her countrymen for participating in a Nazi sponsored French celebrity tour of Germany during the Occupation.

Parallel editing brings three "plots" to intersection in the theater. Shosanna and Marcel prepare to immolate the auditorium as, simultaneously, the Basterds wait to set off their explosives and open fire on the crowd. Meanwhile, Aldo and his comrade, Utivich (B. J. Novak), given away by their hopelessly defective linguistic skills, have been captured by Hans Landa. Through intercut sequences, they carry out a long negotiation through which Landa endorses and joins the Operation Kino plot. Indeed, he becomes a kind of director here, writing himself into its scenario through his elaborate negotiations with U.S. authorities. We are reminded of Tarantino's comment to the editors of *Cahiers du cinéma*: "Landa is a director. Someone pointed out that he's a little like my stand-in, he's a showman, a storyteller."[25]

These three plots intersect across the literal film projection in its alternating attention to the screen and the spectators. Shosanna's plot takes us into the cinematic apparatus itself, beginning with the production process that precedes projection. In flashback we watch as she splices her footage into *Nation's Pride*, meticulously cutting and gluing. It is as if the film we are watching is watching itself come into being. When Shosanna places her filmstrip beside *Nation's Pride*, we see that the dimensions of the still close-ups of her face exactly reproduce those of Zoller's. She is creating a perfect graphic compositional match in this montage.

This scene inevitably recalls Dziga Vertov's 1929 *Man With a Movie Camera*, a documentary that starred his cinematographer brother, Mikhail Kaufman, and featured his wife and editor, Elizaveta Svilova. In that film's most spectacularly memorable sequence, the movement of horse and carriage abruptly arrests. A cut carries us into the editing room, where Svilova examines several filmstrips, holding them up to the light, just as Shosanna does. She splices a sequence, and then, movement flows back, gorgeously animating the still images we have been contemplating. Vertov here both insists on the materiality of the film medium and reproduces the magic of early cinema exhibition, which often produced this thrilling shock, setting stillness into motion.

At the end of this flashback, we're back in the mission plot. Perhaps a bit anxiously, *Inglourious Basterds* seems in this sequence to richly appreciate the Nazi spectacle deployed in the theater; but the mission plot absorbs and redirects our anxiety. Shosanna and Marcel act in counterpoint to the film screening, *behind* the image, in the space of its material support in the projection booth, and literally, behind the screen itself. They have calibrated their operation to the physical medium as well; their schedule is timed to the literal unspooling of the film's reels on the projector.

In the screening sequences, we find *Inglourious Basterds* staging an infantile fantasy of omnipotence: what if, or if only, looks— or wishes—could kill. And this fantasy links to another sadistic fantasy: that of terrorizing people with a false cry of alarm, yelling "Fire!" in a crowded theater. As the screening begins, we see Shosanna and Marcel, each in close-up, facing screen right, illuminated by the whirring projector. An image of the film on-screen is set in a shot/reverse shot structure with the audience, from the screen's own point of view. It is as if the film itself is watching its spectators; and here the extra diegetic world we occupy fantas-matically merges into the diegesis. Preoccupied with the fantasy of watching its spectators watching it, *Inglourious Basterds* seems almost to watch *itself* with fascination, as its aggressive machinery bears down upon us.

Giant faces

Zoller appears in medium close-up from a low angle, pointing his rifle right at the diegetic spectator. A series of cuts links close-ups of Goebbels in profile watching the film and Shosanna facing in the same direction. The next cut establishes a graphic match with Zoller, uneasily contemplating his own image and replicating Shosanna's position in the frame. As music and cutting rhythm recall *Mission Impossible*'s structure of simultaneous actions unfolding, Shosanna threads the final reel onto the projector as Marcel sets about barricading the audience in the theater. We follow him to his post behind the screen, where he gazes at the close-up of an enormous pile of shell casings that appears against the shimmering reels of silver nitrate film.

After the camera closely observes Shosanna threading the third reel, Zoller—who apparently can no longer bear watching his film—bursts in upon her. She shoots him and then goes back to watching the film for a bit. This moment suggests that it holds some allure for her. Perhaps, *Inglourious Basterds* seems to imply—neutralizing historical specificities—she identifies with this crudely drawn solitary hero battling legions of adversaries against the odds. While she turns to examine the fallen Zoller, we continue to look through the projection aperture to see him on-screen, still firing his rifle. Moments later, the wounded Zoller arises to blast Shosanna back against the wall. As in *Bonnie and Clyde* (1967), her death is highly aestheticized, captured in slow motion; her flesh is blasted apart, and her dress, lipstick, and blood rhyme in an overall crimson tonality.

Meanwhile, intercut footage shows Hitler (Martin Wutke) and Goebbels reacting with increasingly hysterical glee to Zoller's slaughter of enemy troops. Captured in close-up and luridly lit, their enormous, grotesque faces, mouths gaping open in laughter, remind us again of the "Giant Face." Across the relay the montage produces, three referents emerge for this term. From Marcel's vantage point we watch as the film replicates its treatment of Shosanna at the beginning of this segment, cutting three times, from medium close-up, to close-up, to extreme close-up of Zoller's eyes. In its predominance of close-ups on Zoller, *Nation's Pride* figures him visually and psychologically as Shosanna's double. At the same time, *Inglourious Basterds* matches its treatment of Hitler and Goebbels to that of these twinned "film stars." This is the volatile ambiguity that governs the sequence—who, after all, is the "giant face"? Since the rhythm of cutting places us among the diegetic film audience, what is our relationship to this shifting figure?

When Zoller speaks for the first time directly to the camera, he demands in English: "Who wants to send a message to Germany?" Shosanna, that skilled editor and now actress, replies in English: "I have a message for Germany: that you are all going to die." Hitler rises screaming as the projection drives forward: "I want you to look deep into the face of the Jew who's going to do it." Her spectral face fills the screen, as she speaks from beyond death. Finally, we see only her mouth in enormous close-up. Marcel's lighted cigarette flies across the frame in gorgeous extreme close-up to ignite the silver nitrate. Shosanna laughs demonically in a shot/reverse shot with Hitler's face, and the camera zooms in on him from a low angle. As the diegetic border collapses in the theater, we viewers are absorbed into the Nazi crowd. Terrified spectators scramble desperately, battering at the barred doors, and flames consume both image and screen, leaving us to look through the rectangle it had occupied into the storage space behind the stage. Shosanna's voice persists beyond the image's disappearance; it continues to project over the scene: "This is the face of Jewish vengeance."

Through her film and her appearance as a "Giant Face," this victim turned aggressor enacts a punishment perfectly matched to the criminals it targets. But that is the problem: this fantasy of a cosmic superego reverses and mirrors the atrocity of the perpetrator it treats as cosmic id. Saul Freidlander has identified what he terms "a malignant inversion," in representations of Nazism, which he finds remain marked by "its phantasms, images, and emotions."[26] "More precisely," he argues, "beneath the visible themes one will discover the beginning of a frisson, the presence of a desire, the workings of an exorcism."[27] Such a "frisson" clearly contributes to the visceral energy that animates this conflagration scene.

In *States of Fantasy*, Jacqueline Rose argues that "as soon as justice becomes its own ultimatum, it gets vicious, hell-bent on fulfilling itself."[28] By this she means to contend that vengeance can never be more than its own source and end. Discussing the problem of political vengeance in a psychoanalytic frame, she reminds us of the collusion involved in internal psychic struggle: "The superego draws its energies from the same unconscious impulses it is intended to tame; it turns against the ego the very force with which the ego strains to reject its commands ... Superego and unconscious are antagonists, but they also have the most intimate, passionate relationship with each other: dedicated combatants, tired and devoted cohabitees."[29] Thus, these adversaries remain bound together in intimate mirroring aggression. Similarly, the avenging force of *Inglourious Basterds* is locked into a volatile structure of reversibility with its enemy, and displaced across the relay of close-ups that organize this screening sequence.

Much has been written about the power of the close-up, and of its centrality, in turn, to cinema's own power. Many writers focus on its embodiment of opposing tendencies—the affective/expressive and the analytical. Jean Mitry reminds us that this effect of extreme magnification is as old as cinema itself.[30] For him, this shot tends towards abstraction: "the close-up provides a tactile, sensuous impression of objects. However, in isolating them, to some extent it turns them into symbols."[31] "The close-up which isolates the detail, removing it from everything but its quality as an ephemeral *sign*," Mitry writes, "can really be applicable only to epic films or subjective analyses, to anything more or less directed toward trans-forming reality into symbols."[32]

In *Watching: Reflections on the Movies*, Thomas Sutcliffe continues this line of analysis. "Like mental concentration," Sutcliffe writes, "the close-up is crucially a combination of enhancement *and* exclusion ... as the zoom proceeds, what is extraneous and peripheral is visibly forced outwards from the edge of the frame to permit the centre of the image to grow in potency."[33] He goes on to assert its volatility: "there can also be a kind of weightlessness to the extreme close-up—a sense that when objects are detached from their implication in the world they float free, ready to absorb whatever meanings we wish to attach to them."[34] In its instability and isolation, the close-up functions, for Sutcliffe, much like the cinematic "attraction": "The more 'poetic' a close-up, in the sense of being detached from the prosaic purposes of the film, the more we are returned to a kind of delirium of seeing, in which the magnification becomes less an analytical dissection of its qualities than an opportunity to revel in what it can be made to mean."[35] Certainly, Tarantino maximizes this resource. Detached and abstracted from context, the image becomes susceptible to multiple and unstable meanings.

Not surprisingly, many analysts of the close-up turn to *The Passion of Joan of Arc*. Released in 1928, on the verge of the sound revolution, this film is much cited for its exploitation of silent cinema's features. André Bazin falsely remembers this film as "shot entirely in close-up."[36] For him, the film's "aesthetic secret" lies in the close-up: "the systematic use of close-ups and unusual angles is well calculated to destroy the sense of space."[37] Speaking specifically of *The Passion* in his 1945 essay, "The Face of Man," Béla Balász describes the drama of its interrogation scenes: "We neither see nor feel the space in which the scene is in reality enacted."[38] He takes great care to distinguish the face from any other object magnified in isolation: "Facing an isolated face takes us out of space, our consciousness of space is cut out and we find ourselves in another dimension: that of physiognomy."[39] In close-up, he writes, "the single features, of course, appear in space; but the significance of their relation to one another is not a phenomenon pertaining to space ... "[40]

Interestingly, in *The Movement-Image*, Gilles Deleuze echoes these readings of *The Passion*: "the event itself, the affective, the effect, goes beyond its own causes, and only refers to other effects, while the causes for their part fall aside."[41] This referential chain is produced by "affective cutting," which, Deleuze explains, "proceeds by what Dreyer himself called 'flowing close-ups.' This is ... primarily a way of treating the medium shot and the full shot *as* close-ups—by the absence of depth or the suppression of perspective."[42] This "suppression of perspective," for Deleuze, relates to the notion of "unframing" he borrows from

Pascal Bonitzer, which "designate(s) unusual angles which are not completely justified by the requirements of action or perception."[43] We might see the "giant face" sequences in *Inglourious Basterds* as accomplishing a kind of "unframing," which works to suppress or disrupt our sense of perspective in a relentless relay of colliding effects.

In an explicitly politicized reading of this unframing effect, Siegfried Kracauer links the spatial abstraction of Dreyer's film to an abstraction from history: "Isolated entities," he writes, "the faces he lavishly displays resist being localized in time so stubbornly that they do not even raise the issue of whether or not they are authentic ... " This film, Kracauer concludes, "unfolds in a no-man's land which is neither the past nor the present."[44] Such an historical no-man's land seems precisely the terrain on which *Inglourious Basterds* stages its fantasies.

Film history with a vengeance

In another telling film historical allusion, Enzo Castellari, director of *The Inglorious Bastards* (1978), appears here in cameo to yell "Fire!" as the conflagration begins. This ironic playfulness displaces yet again our frame of reference for this horrific scene pulling us out of the scene at hand—the immolation of the diegetic archive—and back into the director's own archive. As the image becomes performative, igniting the auditorium, we lose perspective in a dizzying play of surface and depth. When the screen bursts, its rectangular surface gives way to striking depth behind its frame. Calling unexpected attention to the flatness that the illusion of motion pictures conceals, this luminous rectangle draws our attention away from the hysterical crowd. Fascinated by this dazzling image, abstracted from narrative context, we have returned to the emergence of a cinema of attractions in the fairground's array of astonishing spectacles, including, of course, pyrotechnics. This is a cinematic world that perfectly matches the one Dana Polan finds in *Pulp Fiction*. "The universe is not to be seen as meaningful but is, to put it bluntly," he contends, "simply *to be seen*—to be experienced as sheer dazzle, to be lived in the superficiality of its affective sights and sounds."[45]

Shot through with affect that displaces meaning, ultimately, this theater sequence exhibits an exhilarating fantasy: film becomes a literal weapon, intervening directly in History. But can these playful evocations of cinema's history screen out this horrific spectacle of a frantic crowd, trapped in a large room, facing their own immolation, or its previous display of sadistic violence perpetrated by the Jewish guerrillas? These images cannot fail to echo powerful memories of the WWII era.

This climactic sequence presents a scene that, for this spectator at least, horrifically evokes and also *condenses* images of the gas chamber and the crematorium. In this staging of the Nazis' victim triumphing over the perpetrators, Shosanna's vengeance reveals a perverse underside of fantasmatic reversal. Imagining Nazis placed in the position of their death camp victims may conceal a powerful identification with the aggressor. That identification effects a degraded and degrading reversal that redounds upon the spectator. And it reduces reactions to historical Nazi atrocities to the privatized, narrow moral framework of a revenge fantasy. In the 1980s Friedlander posed a pointed question about "Nazism" as an "obsession" for "the contemporary imagination," and it is one that seems apt to ask about this film." Is such attention fixed on the past only a gratuitous reverie, the attraction of spectacle, exorcism, or the result of a need to understand; or is it, again and still, an expression of profound fears, and, on the part of some, mute yearnings as well?"[46]

In the midst of the archival pleasures with which it has lured the cinephile spectator, *Inglourious Basterds* has not so slyly obliged us into a position of identification with the Nazi audience. With obvious satisfaction Tarantino characterizes this effect in his interview with *Cahiers*: "That's my sadistic side: in the theater, you are in the same situation as the Nazis before the film ... I trap you in a cinema and show you a theater on fire. I would like the spectators to look around and say to themselves: "It would be crazy if that happened now!"[47] When it comes to History, he recognizes that "We all know that Hitler didn't die in a cinema fire."[48] However, he offers by way of explanation, "my characters don't know that they are participating in History ... "[49]

"Once I've plunged them into History, it is modified," he continues grandiosely.[50] "What is History? Facts known through the writings of historians. The film shows that, in the end, History will only retain the hero of this adventure, that's Hans Landa—it's his plan, he's the hero of it."[51] So this film's gleeful violence takes aim at History itself. Framed as a series of fictional "attractions," History becomes a parade of shocks rendered—or administered— as highly aestheticized spectacles.

But the film's escalating aggression also increasingly targets its spectators, and its sadism culminates in its insistence on aligning us with doomed and dead Nazis. In his construction of Hans Landa, with his cultivated expertise in catching fugitive Jews and his willingness to abet the Basterds' plan to destroy the theater, Tarantino sustains his film's brutal, if ambivalent, identification *with* Nazi aggression through to its conclusion. This film's last "take," its final image, means to take us in, quite literally. In the previous projection scene, where we have found ourselves inescapably positioned at times with the Nazi audience, the camera's point of view has also circulated among the Basterds and Shosanna watching the film as well. But at its end, the film locks us into Landa's point of view, gazing up at Aldo and Utivich, as Aldo admires his perfection of his craft in the swastika he has carved into Landa's flesh. In its insistence on the visible marking of identity, the film plays on—but also *shares*—another Nazi preoccupation.

Since *Inglourious Basterds* revels in Landa's cleverness, his stunning polyglot verbal agility, his masterful orchestration of traps, and his knowing manipulation of his victims, another powerful reversal asserts itself. As aggressor becomes victim, the film visually imposes identification with him. It is as if this final identification punishes and exonerates all previous moments of identification with his sadistic power and aggression. But a simple reversal undoes nothing. This final ironic twist at the spectator's expense cannot contain the film's previous excesses; it cannot guarantee we will accept that its director has earned the right to deploy his punitive fantasies before and upon us.

Nor can irony screen out collective memory and historical trauma in the perverse intersections of fantasy and history that *Inglourious Basterds* produces through its cinematic citations. In this cinephile world, film's only referent is itself; its own film archive displaces History.[52] Despite its fascination with film historical detail, the central referent of *Inglourious Basterds* seems to be the *auteur*'s own oeuvre, from *Reservoir Dogs* to the *Kill Bill* franchise. Its fantasy of film's intervention in material history finally projects the director's fantasy of making his mark within History reduced to *film* history, like Shosanna, inserting his own footage into its unfolding.

Notes

1 Tarantino's interest in *The Inglorious Bastards* led to its re-release in—deluxe—DVD format. When Castellari appears in *Inglourious Basterds*, yelling "Fire!" in the crowded theater, he joins several other "ghosts," actors who embody Tarantino's film references.

2 Jacques Derrida, *Archive Fever: A Freudian Impression*. Chicago and London: University of Chicago Press, 1996, 29.

3 Derrida, 19.

4 Paolo Cherchi-Usai, *The Death of Cinema*. London: British Film Institute, 2001, 7.

5 Cherchi-Usai, 25.

6 *Death at 24x a Second*. London: Reaktion Books, 2006, 28.

7 "Cinephilia or the Uses of Disenchantment," *Cinephilia: Movies, Love and Memory*, eds. Marijke de Valck and Malte Hagener. Amsterdam: Amsterdam University Press, 2005, 39.

8 *Cahiers du cinéma* editors, "Entretien avec Quentin Tarantino: On n'a pas besoin du dynamite quand on a de la pellicule." *Cahiers du cinéma* 646 (2009): 10. Translations are mine.

9 Cited in Dana Polan, *Pulp Fiction* (London: BFI/Palgrave/Macmillan, 2000), 29.

10 Jenna Ng, "Love in the Time of Transcultural Fusion: Cinephilia, Homage, and *Kill Bill*," in *Cinephilia: Movies, Love and Memory*, (67).

11 Ng, 67.

12 Ng, 74.

13 *Cahiers du cinéma*, 14.

14 Tarantino pointedly calls our attention to the medium's material history and makes another self-reflexive reference when he inserts a voiceover, recognizable as Samuel L. Jackson, that details silver nitrate's properties.

15 Polan, 18.

16 Polan, 18.

17 Elsaesser also makes mention of this scene in "Cinephilia or the Uses of Disenchantment," writing that "the naked brick wall that remained in Godard's film is as a good a metaphor for this disenchantment I am speaking about as any" (39). What he means by "disenchantment" here is the "anxious" pre-video, pre-digital spectatorship "trying to seize the cinematic image, just as it escaped one's grasp," in theatrical viewings, however often repeated.

18 Thomas Gunning, "An Aesthetic of Astonishment: Early Film and the (In)Credulous Spectator," in *Film Theory and Criticism*, eds. Leo Braudy and Marshall Cohen. New York and Oxford: Oxford University Press, 2009, 737.

19 Gunning, 743.

20 A similar notion seems to motivate Dana Polan's description of *Pulp Fiction*: "If *Pulp Fiction* and Disneyland are constructions of imaginary universes that in postmodern style make manifest their artificial nature, we might even directly compare the experience of watching *Pulp Fiction* to visiting a theme park. There is in both activities the sense that the trajectory one follows is made up of a series of individual attractions, each of which sets out to surprise and dazzle. Certainly, many of the moments in *Pulp Fiction* set themselves off from the plot to become stand-alone bits of virtuosity either in the craft of the dialogue or the weirdness of the action ... " (76).

21 Polan, 47.

22 "Not only was the film banned after the Liberation," writes Alan Williams, "but almost everyone involved in its production received some sort of punishment for their participation; there were even some calls for the death penalty for its principal creators" (*Republic of Images: A History of French Filmmaking*. Cambridge, MA and London: Harvard University Press, 1992, 259).

23 See Williams 256–7. See also Bertrand Tavernier, "An Alliance of Forgetting," on *Le Corbeau* Criterion Collection DVD. Tavernier's film, *Laisser Passer/Safe Conduct* (2002) elaborates a fictionalized account of the studio and its personnel.

24 For a fuller account of these events, see Richard Roud, *A Passion for Films: Henri Langlois and the Cinémathèque Française* (Baltimore and London: The Johns Hopkins University Press, 1999), 47–54.

25 *Cahiers du cinéma*, 15.

26 Saul Freidlander, *Reflections of Nazism: An Essay on Kitsch and Death* (Bloomington and Indianapolis: Indiana University Press, 1993), 14–15.

27 Freidlander, 18.

28 Jacqueline Rose, *States of Fantasy*. London: Oxford University Press, 1996, 91.

29 Rose, 91.

30 "The 'big heads' ('*grosses têtes*'), as they were then called, suddenly appearing in the midst of a uniform sequence of long shots, had been used by Méliès in his films around 1901 ... the big heads, however, whose sudden appearance constituted an effect of surprise, were more associated with the 'animated portrait' than with film expression." Jean Mitry, *The Aesthetics and Psychology of Cinema* (Bloomington and Indianapolis: Indiana University Press, 1997), 69.

31 Mitry, 130.

32 Mitry, 296.

33 Thomas Sutcliffe, *Watching: Reflections on the Movies*. (London and New York: Faber and Faber, 2000), 80–1.

34 Sutcliffe, 100.

35 Sutcliffe, 100.

36 André Bazin, *What is Cinema?* (Berkeley, Los Angeles and London: University of California Press, 2005), 103.

37 Bazin, 109.

38 Béla Balász, In *Film Theory and Criticism*, eds. Leo Braudy and Marshall Cohen, (New York and Oxford: Oxford University Press, 2009), 281.

39 Balász, 276.

40 Balász, 276.

41 Gilles Deleuze, *The Movement-Image* (Minneapolis: University of Minnesota Press, 1986), 106.

42 Deleuze, 107. Likewise, in his book, *La Passion de Jeanne d'Arc*, David Bordwell contends that "the very principle of the close-up ... is an *abstracting* one." (Bloomington and London: Indiana University Press, 1973), 25. "What, then," he asks, "is abstraction but an emphasis on the shot as image, as the destruction of the time–space continuum, the construction of the shot as a closed world, and the creation of a schematic flatness—of, in short, a tendency to free the image from denotation?" (23).

43 Deleuze, 107.

44 Siegfried Kracauer, *Theory of Film: The Redemption of Physical Reality*. (Princeton: Princeton University Press, 1997), 80.

45   Polan, 79.

46   Freidlander, 19.

47   *Cahiers du cinéma*, 15.

48   *Cahiers du cinéma*, 15.

49   *Cahiers du cinéma*, 14.

50   *Cahiers du cinéma*, 14.

51   *Cahiers du cinéma*, 15.

52   This effect becomes especially puzzling in light of his stated commitment to rigorous historical accuracy in the selection of posters for display in his film. He reports with some bravado that he fired a props master for choosing posters of films the Nazis had banned, telling the *Cahiers* editors that "They preferred pretty props to true/accurate props" (13).

Works cited

Balász, Béla. "The Face of Man." In *Film Theory and Criticism*, edited by Leo Braudy and Marshall Cohen. New York and Oxford: Oxford University Press, 2009, 275–81

Bazin, André. *What is Cinema?* Berkeley, Los Angeles and London: University of California Press, 2005.

Bonnie and Clyde. Directed by Arthur Penn. USA, 1967.

Bordwell, David. *La Passion de Jeanne d'Arc.* Bloomington and London: Indiana University Press, 1973.

Cahiers du cinéma editors, "Entretien avec Quentin Tarantino: On n'a pas besoin du dynamite quand on a de la pellicule." *Cahiers du cinéma* 646, (2009), 10–15.

Cherchi-Usai, Paolo. *The Death of Cinema.* London: British Film Institute, 2001.

Deleuze, Gilles. *The Movement-Image.* Minneapolis: University of Minnesota Press, 1986.

Derrida, Jacques. *Archive Fever: A Freudian Impression.* Chicago and London: University of Chicago Press, 1996.

The Dirty Dozen. Directed by Robert Aldrich. USA, 1967.

Double Indemnity. Directed by Billy Wilder. USA, 1944.

Elsaesser, Thomas. "Cinephilia or the Uses of Disenchantment." In *Cinephilia: Movies, Love and Memory*, edited by Marijke de Valck and Malte Hagener. Amsterdam: Amsterdam University Press, 2005, 27–43.

Freidlander, Saul. *Reflections of Nazism: An Essay on Kitsch and Death*. Bloomington and Indianapolis: Indiana University Press, 1993.

Gunning, Thomas. "An Aesthetic of Astonishment: Early Film and the (In)Credulous Spectator." In *Film Theory and Criticism*, edited by Leo Braudy and Marshall Cohen. New York and Oxford: Oxford University Press, 2009, 736–50.

The Guns of Navarone. Directed by J. Lee Thompson. UK/USA, 1961.

The Inglorious Bastards. Directed by Enzo G. Castellari. Italy, 1978.

Inglourious Basterds. Directed by Quentin Tarantino. USA/Germany, 2009.

Kill Bill: Vol. 1. Directed by Quentin Tarantino. USA, 2003.

Kill Bill: Vol. 2. Directed by Quentin Tarantino. USA, 2004.

Kracauer, Siegfried. *Theory of Film: The Redemption of Physical Reality*. Princeton: Princeton University Press, 1997.

L'Assassin habite au 21. Directed by Henri-Georges Clouzot. France, 1942.

La Symphonie Fantastique. Directed by Christian-Jaque. France, 1942.

Le Corbeau/The Raven. Directed by Henri-Georges Clouzot. France, 1943.

Les Carabiniers/The Caribineers. Directed by Jean-Luc Godard. France/ Italy, 1963.

The Longest Day. Directed by Ken Annakin, Andrew Marton, et al. USA, 1962.

Man with a Movie Camera. Directed by Dziga Vertov. USSR, 1929.

The Messenger: The Story of Joan of Arc. Directed by Luc Besson. France, 1999.

Mission Impossible. CBS, Desilu Productions/Paramount Television, 1966–1973.

Mitry, Jean. *The Aesthetics and Psychology of Cinema*. Bloomington and Indianapolis: Indiana University Press, 1997.

Mulvey, Laura. *Death at 24x a Second*. London: Reaktion Books, 2006.

Ng, Jenna. "Love in the Time of Transcultural Fusion: Cinephilia, Homage, and *Kill Bill*." In *Cinephilia: Movies, Love and Memory*, edited by Marijke de Valck and Malte Hagener. Amsterdam: Amsterdam University Press, 2005, 65–79.

Notorious. Directed by Alfred Hitchcock. USA, 1946.

The Passion of Joan of Arc. Directed by Carl Theodor Dreyer. France, 1928.

Persona. Directed by Ingmar Bergman. Sweden, 1966.

Polan, Dana. *Pulp Fiction*. London: BFI/Palgrave/Macmillan, 2000.

Pulp Fiction. Directed by Quentin Tarantino. USA, 1994.

Reservoir Dogs. Directed by Quentin Tarantino. USA, 1992.

Rose, Jacqueline. *States of Fantasy*. London: Oxford University Press, 1996.

Roud, Richard. *A Passion for Films: Henri Langlois and the Cinémathèque Française*. Baltimore and London: The Johns Hopkins University Press, 1999.

The Searchers. Directed by John Ford. USA, 1956.

Suspicion. Directed by Alfred Hitchcock. USA, 1941.

Sutcliffe, Thomas. *Watching: Reflections on the Movies*. London and New York: Faber and Faber, 2000.

Tavernier, Bertrand. "An Alliance of Forgetting." On *Le Corbeau* Criterion Collection DVD, 2004.

Two-Lane Blacktop. Directed by Monte Hellman. USA, 1971.

Vivre sa vie/My Life to Live. Directed by Jean-Luc Godard. France, 1962.

The White Hell of Pitz Palu. Directed by Arnold Fanck and G. W. Pabst. Germany, 1929.

Williams, Alan. *Republic of Images: A History of French Filmmaking*. Cambridge, MA and London: Harvard University Press, 1992.

10

Is Tarantino serious? The twofold image of the *Auteur* and the state of exception

Oliver C. Speck

Quentin Tarantino might be American cinema's best know *auteur*, one of the very few directors whose work is promoted in the U.S. with the "a film by" label. It is a label that, of course, the filmmaker himself tirelessly and skillfully promotes, conjuring up the image of a young man, who, growing up fatherless, provided himself with his own education in the form of countless movies as a video-store clerk, then, taking on his father's last name, conquered the world of cinema. With this narrative of origin, Tarantino puts himself into a long line of European *auteur*-directors whose affiliation with the cinema is supposed to be caused by a self-filiation: Jean-Luc Godard famously disinherited by his affluent Swiss family becomes French; Rainer Werner Fassbinder and his problematic relationship with his mother; Michael Haneke growing up with his aunt, father- and motherless, to name a few directors who claim a similar origination myth. The oedipal undertones of these (self-) images are too obvious to be pointed out, and there is no need to speculate how much here is based on truth and how much is a clever spin. However, in the work of these filmmakers, those psychoanalytical fantasies result in a twofold image of the *auteur*, as someone who is always implied and implicated in his very own creation. This image takes different forms, without doubt, but derives from the same fantasy: that of a *genuine* creation of real, serious art that is grounded in nothing but itself. This fantasy of the autochthonous lens, however, is deliberately complicated by these *auteurs* with references to history, or, more precisely, the fascist past, because it is exactly this image of wholeness that lies at the heart of fascist propaganda, the utopia of a pure community. Apart from the personal involvement, the older generation of *auteurs* is clearly fascinated by the monstrous conflation of art and politics, famously described by Walter Benjamin in his "The Work of Art in the Age of Mechanical Reproducibility." Indeed, their entire oeuvre could be seen as an attempt to deconstruct the propagandistic cinema of the fascist past, to the point of an aporetic cinema.

While Fassbinder, Godard and Haneke are certainly implicated personally by fascism, growing up in the immediate aftermath of WWII in nations that were more or less involved in the Holocaust, Tarantino belongs to another generation and another culture, that is, he taps into a different collective memory. Nevertheless, with *Inglourious Basterds* (2009) he evokes memories of WWII and films about it, referring directly and indirectly to Fassbinder's two most direct examinations of German UFA studio cinema under the Nazis, *Lili Marleen* (1981) and *Die Sehnsucht der Veronika Voss / Veronika Voss* (1982).[1]

Tarantino's female characters, Bridget von Hammersmark and Shosanna Dreyfus, are clearly amalgams of Fassbinder's heroines. And Fassbinder's ingenious way of copying the stylistics of classic UFA productions in order to show the power of these images is, in turn, taken up by Tarantino. The ending of *Inglourious Basterds* proves that Quentin Tarantino's film is also a meditation on the power of images, an attempt to fight one image with another: Shosanna Dreyfus' face is projected onto the smoke of the burning movie theater, taunting the audience, while Hitler's face is shot into pieces, thus showing the revenge-fantasy *as* pure fantasy, that is, as a projection. The *Führer*'s all-powerful image is destroyed, uncovered as a *Wizard of Oz*-construction of smoke and mirrors by another Wizard of Oz, while the collective memory of one "burnt sacrifice" is countered by another. Here, the American Tarantino openly dares what the older generation of *auteurs* would never have dared: he creates a pleasurable revenge fantasy linked to memory of the extermination camps. In other words, the aporetic, complex counter-cinema of the European *auteurs* is, in turn, countered by an image of wholeness.

As this brief introduction implies, there are several competing images at work: the image of the *auteur*, the image of history as it appears in collective memory and the image of the film, linked intertextually to many other films, causing pleasure or disgust. The important question is how these images provide a political analysis. In the following, I will trace this image of the *auteur* in Tarantino's *Inglourious Basterds*, linking it to his politics, discussing his *politique des auteurs*. As a counterpoint to this *politique*, I will refer to the political philosopher Giorgio Agamben's *Homo Sacer* project where strikingly similar points are discussed.

The *auteur* and the reader

Godard's latest film at the time of this writing—*Film Socialisme*, announced to be his last film—is a complex intertextual network of competing voices, including the English subtitles, which are written in a type of pidgin, evoking the rudimentary English of Hollywood-Indians. True to the image of the eternal outsider, Godard did not show up at the Cannes film festival for the press conference, instead sending a cryptic message hinting at his imminent death.[2] Fassbinder, forever the *enfant terrible* of West German cinema, deliberately blurred the boundaries between reality and fiction, famously casting his own mother in crucial roles and inviting comparisons between his films and his private life.[3] The Austrian director Michael Haneke, to stay with the example, carefully controls his public image of the "bearded prophet,"[4] promoting similar-looking headshots that show him as a stern, forbidding father figure. While Haneke never appears in his own films, like Fassbinder and Godard, the *auteur*ial presence is always palatable in his work. Tightly framed shots that run against the norm of Hollywood and long, uninterrupted takes that abruptly begin and end in the middle of a movement constantly remind the viewer of the creative force *hors cadre*.

It would, of course, be completely wrong now to accuse the three directors that serve as examples here of creating a cult of their own genius, thus aiming for the establishment of a position that serves as a signifying center. On the contrary, as post-war European films created in the wake of totalitarian propaganda, the films of Godard, Fassbinder and Haneke show an astute awareness of the perils of any totalizing force, any appeal to transcendence. Given the seemingly apolitical nature of most propaganda films, which, for the most part, come in the guise of entertainment films, it is no surprise that these directors opted for a mode of filmmaking that can only be called "unpleasurable." Paul de Man points out: "The aesthetic is, by definition, a seductive notion that appeals to the pleasure principle, a eudaemonic judgment that can displace and conceal values of truth and falsehood likely to be more resilient than values of pleasure and pain."[5] The unpleasure that a film by a European *auteur* creates, thus serves as an antidote to the seductiveness of propaganda. While the strategies certainly vary in the individual work, *auteur* films generally display no psychological realism, thus discouraging an identification with the characters, openly formulate their political claims and, by using various references and intertexts, create a mode of confusion and avoid any type of closure. Notably, Godard turned away from his more playful films which, while featuring characters that appeared completely artificial, still showed a caustic sense of humor. It is the modernist strategy of an ever-evolving play of pre-texts and intertexts, laid out by an *auteur*, in combination with the carefully promoted public image as self-made artist that all three have in common. All three directors, then, evoke the image of the romantic genius, only to undermine it by questioning the possibility that an authorial authority actually exists that can serve as a guarantor to make sense of this constant play of texts and intertexts.

From this perspective, Godard appears as the *über-auteur* upon whom these textual, that is, inter- and extratextual, strategies are modeled. Quentin Tarantino, as is well-known, named his own production company "A Band Apart" after one of Godard's films from his "cool" phase, *Bande à part/Band of Outsiders* (1964).

Bande à part, in turn, is a reaction—sometimes an homage, sometimes a spoof—to François Truffaut's famous *Jules et Jim* (1962), a film that—like *Inglourious Basterds*—features dialogues in English, French and German. However, contrary to the late Godard, to Fassbinder and to Haneke who promise the displeasure they create, Tarantino's films refer mostly to popular genres that provide rather base pleasures. Indeed, Tarantino, as positive and negative reviews alike do not fail to point out, "favors low-budget 'grindhouse' material: martial arts films, 'blaxploitation' works from the 1970s, 'midnight movies' and spaghetti westerns." These low-brow sources, as the appalled critic continues, are "treated entirely uncritically."[6] Indeed, measured by the standards of the other three *auteurs* that serve here as prototypical examples, Tarantino seems to fully embrace the racism and sexism inherent in the respective genres as an authentic voice without any critical distance. If we take the *politique des auteurs*, invoked earlier as refusal of closure and totalization, as a call to arms and incitement to destroy hegemonizing strategies of representation, Tarantino appears as its worst imitator and detractor, fully giving into postmodern relativism with his retro-chic. Thus he arms himself against any criticism with the postmodern twist that this is all just a simulacrum, a tongue-in-cheek celebration of a long lost time when a young white male viewer could still indulge in violent fantasies of fullness, unhindered by today's political correctness.

What most critics and even the fans seem to miss, though, is that Tarantino takes his own *auteur*ship quite seriously. Comparing Tarantino to Steven Spielberg can quickly show this: films such as *Saving Private Ryan* (1998) and *Schindler's List* (1993) openly embrace humanism as a countermeasure against the atrocities committed by the Nazis. The latter film's motto is even "Whoever saves one life, saves the world entire." And *Private Ryan* ends, right after Captain John Miller's emotional death scene, with James Ryan asking the audience to consider if they are worthy of the sacrifice of the "Greatest Generation": "Tell me I have led a good life ... Tell me I'm a good man." While Spielberg's intentions are certainly beyond reproach, the point of contention for Godard, who railed against Spielberg on many occasions, lies in the division of form and content, the implicit assumption that the meaning of a text is completely separate from the way it is told. To wit, with roles reversed, the entire *Saving Private Ryan* could be imagined as a perfect Nazi-propaganda film, where a motley band of German soldiers bravely searches for a *Landser*—a private in the *Wehrmacht*—behind enemy lines: the role of the cowardly German who later shoots a fleeing G.I. in the back would now be filled by an American, the brave Captain Miller would now be Müller, philanthropic teacher in his private life, etc .... As Claude Singer has shown in his study on *Jud Süss/The Jew Suess* by Veit Harlan (1940), the Nazis carefully studied other films, adopted their rhetoric and distorted their message, effecting just such a switch. In the case of the Nazis, it was the British film *Jew Süss* by Lothar Mendes from 1934, based on Lion Feuchtwanger's successful novel *Jud Süss* from 1925, banned in 1933 in Germany, which Harlan changed from a film of sympathy and tolerance into an instrument propagating racial hatred.[7] In other words, any genre—a war film to stay with the example—can easily be turned around by assigning the positive values to the German and portraying his adversaries as cruel and inhuman. The insertion of the "film-within-the film," *Stolz der Nation*, clearly shows that Tarantino has understood this reversibility that results from the division of form and content as a problem. Judging by his looks and background story, the character of Pvt. Fredrick Zoller (played by the boyish Daniel Brühl) obviously refers to Audie Murphy, who became famous as the most decorated combat soldier of the Second World War and who played himself in a cinematic portrayal of his heroic deeds, one of which was single-handedly killing scores of enemy soldiers.

The thematization of the form/content divide is nothing new in Tarantino's oeuvre. A clear sign of this is his inclusion of irreverent readings, namely interpretations of popular culture against the grain. Already in Tarantino's first feature, *Reservoir Dogs* (1992), the character of Mr. Brown, significantly played by the director himself, provides a reading of Madonna's song, "Like a Virgin." Instead of the common, metaphoric reading of the topic being true love, Mr. Brown argues that the pop song is to be taken literally: it is actually about a promiscuous woman who finally encounters a man with a penis large enough to cause her pain: "The pain is reminding a fuck machine what it was like to be a virgin. Hence, 'Like a Virgin'." Apart from the juxtaposition of the coded language of romance with crude slang (which might strike some critics as juvenile) in order to drive the point home that language is always "about" something else, Mr. Brown as a reader forgoes the tempting metaphoric interpretation for the metonymic relation between sexual intercourse, pain and memory. Tarantino thus reveals Madonna's performance, often praised as a subversive, feminist celebration of fun, as yet another confirmation of phallologocentric power—of course, in our society, woman does not exist; there are only "fuck machines" or virgins. In other words, these irreverent readings position a critique of ideology.[8]

These metonymic/allegoric readings occur throughout Tarantino's oeuvre, often performed by characters that are unceremoniously and quite suddenly killed. The character of Mr. Brown never makes it into the warehouse. In *Jackie Brown* (1997), Melanie Ralston (Bridget Fonda) is able to astutely read the character of Ordell Robbie, providing a complex psychological map of a man who seems to be far more powerful than she. And in *Pulp Fiction* (1994), the easygoing Vincent Vega (John Travolta) is equally able to analyze his colleague's rhetoric with astonishing insight. The importance that Tarantino bestows on those readers can be found, again, in *Inglourious Basterds*, where the topic of writing and reading is prominently featured. Here, the German SS officer immediately wins the game of "who am I," not only quickly guessing the fictional character, King Kong, but also by pointing out that the film is an allegory of "the plight of the Negro in America." Not surprisingly, the observant officer immediately picks up on the strange accent and the wrong hand gesture of his British opponent. While the Americans are unable to even briefly pose as Italians, the multilingual Hans Landa, nicknamed "The Jew Hunter," is a skilled detective and narrator. The figure of the suave, multilingual foreigner is, of course, a stock character in American popular imagination, and it is precisely these traits that make Landa the ideal hunter. Indeed, Carlo Ginzburg, in his seminal article on "Clues," links the emergence of the hunter to the invention of narration itself:

> [T]he data is always arranged by the observer in such a way as to produce a narrative sequence, which could be expressed most simply as "someone passed this way." Perhaps the actual idea of narration ... may have originated in a hunting society, relating the experience of deciphering tracks.[9]

The "Cinderella-sequence" at the film premiere in which Bridget von Hammersmark is presented the shoe she lost during the tavern shootout underscores Landa's deductive abilities. While searching for clues, he creates a narrative that quickly reconstructs the events. "I'm a detective," he later proudly tells Lt. Aldo Raine.

Reading and writing

Compared to the linguistic and hermeneutic skills of the Germans, the Americans must appear as simpletons. Unable to be anything else than himself, Raine is the clichéd straightforward American, a country boy who cannot hide his thick hillbilly accent. Compared to his flamboyantly intellectual opponent, Raine appears as a simple craftsman, whose ability to read and write is limited to a primitive form of writing, that is, the carving of swastikas on his prisoners' heads with a Bowie knife. What American and German officers have in common, however, is a complete disregard for any form of morality, instead clinging to a type of professional ethic. The first time we see the Basterds in action, the camera pans over scalped bodies, underlining that Raine literally means what he says. The interrogation scene afterwards makes clear that the troupe of Americans does not follow any rules laid out by the Geneva Convention; indeed, their actions certainly fulfill the legal definition of a war crime. It is noteworthy that the German officer would rather die a horrible death than become a traitor, just as the "Mexican stand-off"[10] in the basement bar is handled by both the SS officer and his enemies in the most gentlemanly way possible. Nobody attempts to flee, and nobody shows any sign of fear. There is even time for a toast and a whiskey tasting before facing certain death. After the shootout, which leads to the death of nearly everybody in the basement, another stand-off is diffused by Raine, who promises to spare the life of the last remaining German. As Raine and the German soldier point out, a Mexican stand-off can only be resolved by trust, and Raine is clearly not pleased by Bridget von Hammersmark's killing of this young soldier, as he intended to keep his promise. The following brutal interrogation, or rather sublimated penetration—Raine pokes his finger in von Hammersmark's bullet wound—shows that he does not trust her.

In terms of film history, Landa is a fascinating take on the above-mentioned stock character of the charming Nazi. Asked about films that inspired *Inglourious Basterds*, Tarantino states:

I was very influenced by Hollywood propaganda movies made during World War II. Most were made by directors living in Hollywood because the Nazis had taken over their countries, like Jean Renoir with *This Land Is Mine*, or Fritz Lang with *Man Hunt*, Jules Dassin with *Reunion in France*, and [Anatole Litvak's] *Confessions of a Nazi Spy*—movies like that. Almost all these movies, by the way, starred George Sanders.[11]

Tarantino mentions only four films here (three indeed starred George Sanders), but he must have also had Alfred Hitchcock's *Foreign Correspondent* (1940) in mind, where Sanders plays the whimsical British agent ffolliott.

George Sanders' character in Lang's *Man Hunt* (1941), the perverted aesthete Quive-Smith, perfectly at ease in German and English, appears to provide the most direct inspiration for Landa. The story of *Man Hunt* is worth recalling: shortly before the German attacks on Poland and France, Alan Thorndike (Walter Pidgeon), a hunter so unerring that he now stalks but never shoots, sets out to get Hitler in the sight of his gun, just to prove that it can be done. Caught in the act, he is brought to Major Quive-Smith. The aristocratic Quive-Smith, also a passionate hunter, indeed believes that Thorndike just followed his whimsical idea of sportsmanship. However, Quive-Smith, who "gave up hunting for politics," as he declares, intends to use the incident to discredit Great Britain and demands Thorndike to sign a confession that he wanted to assassinate Hitler. Thorndike refuses. After being badly beaten, Thorndike is able to escape and becomes the Nazis' prey. He is followed to London, where he encounters Jerry Stoke (Joan Bennett), a low-class girl who shelters him. Her love for him proves to be her doom. Even under torture, she does not reveal Thorndike's whereabouts. Because of a mistake, Thorndike's hiding place is revealed nevertheless and Quive-Smith can trap him in a cave, taunting him with a cheap trinket—a small arrow—that Thorndike gave to Jerry. Thorndike, realizing that the girl has sacrificed her life for him, fashions a weapon out of the arrow and manages to kill Quive-Smith, although he is wounded in the process. The coda, more fit for a comic book and certainly appealing to Tarantino, starts out with newsreel footage of Hitler, rolling German tanks and London after a bombardment, and ends with a cheap-looking back-projection of the parachuting hero while a newsreel voiceover in staccato assures us that "from now on, somewhere within Germany, there is a man with a precision rifle and the high degree of intelligence and training that is required to use it, and this time he clearly knows his purpose, and, unflinching, faces his destiny." The ending of Lang's *Man Hunt* is especially interesting because its fantastic idea and strangely blatant style hints that it might be a vision of the dying hero, just as Shosanna's ultimate filmic revenge appears more like a nightmarish vision than a wish fulfillment.

The basic plot of *Foreign Correspondent* is quite similar to Lang's *Man Hunt*, a film that was released one year later and that also shows some similarities to Renoir's *This Land Is Mine* (1943). The point of all these films was, of course, to convince the American public that the United States had to intervene in the war overseas. Aiming at overcoming the United States' isolationism, they show the Nazis as formidable foes, charming and seductive, unlike post-war films that gave rise to the cliché of the heel-clicking German blinded by slavish obedience to rules. While the stock character of the cultured Nazi certainly became a cliché in Hollywood films and might have its roots partially in an American strain of anti-intellectualism, it should be noted that the character in its original formation is that of an educated professional who sells his talents to the ruling party. Apart from Quive-Smith, the well-read Major Erich von Keller (Walter Slezak) in Renoir's *This Land Is Mine* is just such a character, and Orson Welles will revisit this type in his *The Stranger* (1946), where a Nazi criminal can easily pose as an American college professor, and, of course, in the character that he famously plays in Carol Reed's *The Third Man* (1949). In the context of these Hollywood propaganda movies, the wily Gestapo Inspector Alois Gruber (Alexander Granach) in the justly-famous Fritz Lang/Bertolt Brecht cooperation, *Hangmen Also Die!* (1943), appears as a direct predecessor to Hans Landa.

The heroes in the pre-war films are always accidentally put in a position where they have to decide to give up their status as amateurish observers and intervene; in other—that is, Tarantinian—words, they must "go pro." Most crucially, the heroes are virtual doppelgangers of their Nazi counterparts, something that Quive-Smith points out to his adversary on more than one occasion. In Jean Renoir's film, George Sanders' character is one who sells his soul to the Mephistophelian Nazi and who then can't live with the guilt. However, once these accidental heroes decide to fight on the side of good, the scales are turned and the hunters become the hunted. Not surprisingly, *Inglourious Basterds* skips the decision-making process and cuts straight to the chase, that is, the "hunting the hunters." We should keep in mind that Lt. Raine and his band of scalp-collecting "Apaches" embody the genre-typical role-reversal. As J. Hoberman recognizes in his review, "*Inglourious Basterds* basically enables Jews to act like Nazis, engaging in cold-blooded massacres and mass incineration, pushing wish fulfillment to a near-psychotic break with reality."[12] Through its provocative images, *Inglourious Basterds* indeed lends credibility to this projection, showing that there appears to be no difference between the American Basterds and the "Nazi Bastards" they are hunting.

It is now tempting to arrest the reading of *Inglourious Basterds* with the equations pointed out above: American soldiers are as ruthless as their German enemies, and the Germans are as brave as their opposites. However, the problematic figure of Hans Landa remains. Again, we need to return to the sequence of the Basterds in action, in order to understand the meaning of the character of the treacherous Landa who appears to be the odd one out in this equilibrium.

Interrogating a captured officer, Raine establishes first that he means business: "We ain't in the prisoner-taking business; we are in the Nazi-killing business!" Establishing the clearing as a place of professional conduct, he thus establishes a code of trust—he would not kill the German if his demands were met. On the other hand, no moral qualms would stop him from executing an unarmed prisoner of war, because there is nothing personal in this business transaction. When Lt. Raine invites Hugo Stiglitz to join the Basterds, the renegade German is told that he could channel his hatred for authority figures and "go pro." Given the clear choice by Lt. Raine, betray your comrades or die, the German officer, Werner Rachtmann (Richard Sammel)—fully aware that he just condemned himself to a gruesome death—answers, while putting his hand on his heart, "I respectfully refuse, Sir!" This gesture is obviously meant to refer to the oath that he has sworn as a soldier. An oath, we should not forget, that was after all bound to Hitler and not the German nation. Stoically awaiting his death, the officer is asked whether he received the Iron Cross that he is wearing "for killing Jews." Before his head is bashed in with a baseball bat by the "Bear Jew," he defiantly answers "for bravery." The camera, in this sequence often centered on the German at eye-level, clearly portrays the officer as a heroic man. Raine even refers to this macabre spectacle self-referentially as a movie. The provocative move of showing Germans to be as courageous as their counterparts is certainly a strong factor here. This appears to be directed against Spielberg's *Saving Private Ryan* and its character of the spineless German prisoner who is spared by the idealistic Captain Miller. However, we should not forget that in the immediate aftermath of this slaughter, the surviving young private immediately betrays the German position and, although rewarded with his life, receives the carved swastika, just as Hans Landa is marked for life at the end of the film. The swastika, written in the flesh, is thus not simply a sign designating a former Nazi, but curiously becomes a sign for those who are too cowardly to die for their country, or, to be precise, a sign of those who do not honor their oath.

Here, we can finally pinpoint the above-mentioned imbalance in the "equation": the professional "ethos," if it can be called that, demands a strict adherence to the basic principle of business. That is, there is nothing personal to consider as only the job counts. Hans Landa, the hunter-detective, is the only main character who does not play by the professional rules. He changes loyalties as soon as he finds himself on the losing side. Here, it seems, lies the true monstrosity of his crime: by not holding firm to his oath of absolute loyalty, he does not behave like a professional, but rather an amateur. In other words, Landa cannot be trusted.

What appears first as a simple role reversal—let's treat the Nazis the way they treat others—is actually a perfect balance struck: both parties involved act strictly as professionals, only vested in their code of honor for which they are ready to sacrifice themselves. And that means that they do not recognize the other as a human being, but as a professional problem. "Nazi ain't got no humanity," as Lt. Raine declares in his recruitment speech. And he, in turn, shows no sign of humanity, either. It is at this point that Tarantino's fascinating affinity to Giorgio Agamben's *Homo Sacer* project emerges. In the following section, I will very briefly address Agamben's project, especially the relatively recently published book on the politics of the oath, in order to pinpoint these affinities.[13]

Homo Sacer and "Sovereign": a chiasmic encounter

The figure at the heart of Agamben's project, the *homo sacer*, "an obscure figure of archaic Roman law,"[14] appears to exist in a paradoxical state. Banned from the community, he has lost all value and thus cannot be sacrificed. More importantly, as an outlaw, he does not enjoy any legal protection and can therefore be killed without impunity. Rather than being a marginal figure, the *homo sacer*, as Agamben shows in his study, stands at the nexus of modern politics. Here, Agamben draws on two disparate—or so it seems at first—political concepts. The first is Foucault's notion of "biopolitics," a form of government, whose emergence is linked to modernity:

> For the first time in history ... biological existence was reflected in political existence; the fact of living was no longer an inaccessible substrate that only emerged from time to time, amid the randomness of death and its fatality; part of it passed into knowledge's field of control and power's sphere of intervention.[15]

The modern state becomes a manager of the community,[16] using all the scientific tools at its disposal "to get the job done," that of competing with other nation-states. Scientific knowledge, in the form of the quantitative analysis of its population, allows a government to control growth, prevent diseases and plan for the future, but it does, of course, also serve as a tool of repression by redirecting resources, limiting the freedom of parts of its population or even resorting to measures like incarnation and forced sterilization. Indeed, politics is here directly involved with life.

The second political concept that Agamben evokes is by Carl Schmitt, the dedicated National Socialist and controversial political theorist. While this seems, at first, a strange choice, it is Schmitt who provides, in his attempt to theoretically legitimize dictatorial rule, a definition of brilliant simplicity of the principle of sovereignty: "Sovereign is he who decides on the exception."[17] According to Agamben, the sovereign is, then, paradoxically "at the same time, outside and inside the juridical order."[18] The same foundational

momentum that creates any sovereign state (the simple performative speech act: "We lawfully declare our sovereignty, by giving
ourselves a law!") must necessarily bring about the conflation of
politics and life, because the paradoxical nature of the founding
statement implies, too, that laws can be suspended in times of crises
with the declaration of a state of exception. As Agamben points
out, the constitution of the Weimar Republic was actually never
annulled. Hitler, instead, declared a state of emergency, thus ruling
with absolute power.[19] In the absence of a legal framework, the
word of the *Führer* effectively becomes the law.

Once such a state of emergency is declared, legal protection is no
longer available. To put it bluntly, a political dissident automatically becomes an "enemy of the state," banned from the community
by having his or her citizenship revoked and being held in a camp:
"He who has been banned is not simply set outside the law and
made indifferent to it but rather *abandoned* by it, that is, exposed
and threatened on the threshold in which life and law, outside and
inside, become indistinguishable."[20] Once a person is thus stripped
of all political rights, only the "bare life," as Agamben calls it
following Walter Benjamin, remains.[21] The taking of such a "bare
life" is indeed not a crime, because the killing of a *homo sacer*
happens in the legal vacuum of the state of exception.[22] It could be
said, then, that everybody who decides if a life is valuable or not
performs this biopolitical paradigm. Here, Agamben draws our
attention to euthanasia, where the physician effectively becomes
a sovereign and makes the decision on the value or non-value of
life.[23]

From this perspective, the structural turn of "hunting the
hunters" in *Inglourious Basterds* is one of a *homo sacer* declaring
himself sovereign, now reducing the other to his bare life. One
of the most fascinating illustrations of this reversal in cinema
is, without doubt, *The Dirty Dozen* (1967) by Robert Aldrich,
which obviously influenced Tarantino. In this film, twelve inmates,
most of whom are on death row for crimes like rape and murder,
are sent on a suicide mission to kill as many Nazi officers as
possible. Already "dead men walking," their mission is not about
redemption, but about the creation of a moral vacuum where the
enemy can be exterminated like rats. In a memorable scene, the
officers and their female companions are trapped in a basement
while the "Dirty Dozen" attempt to burn them alive, just as the SS

burned churches and barns full of people. To take another filmic example, in *Man Hunt*, the cynical Quive-Smith turns Thorndike into a *homo sacer* and takes the life of the girl, only to find out that he has thereby created a hunter who now declares an exception for himself.

As mentioned above, there appears now to be no difference between Raine and his "Apaches" and the Germans, all of whom are in a chiasmic relationship of *homo sacer* and sovereign, of prey and hunter. Again, we need to return to the curious incident of the brave German and his oath to understand what is at stake. An oath is generally understood as a promise to tell the truth, warranted by god(s), whose wrath would come upon us should this oath be broken—a religious gesture that grounds a juridical act. As Agamben explains in his *The Sacrament of Language: An Archaeology of the Oath*, already the earliest meditations on the oath point out that the possibility of perjury is always present in this promise. As Agamben shows, however, citing mainly Greek and Roman sources, what is at stake is "trust (*fides*)": "Contrary to the opinion very often repeated by modern scholars, the obligatory nature of the oath does not derive from the gods, who are called only as witnesses, but from the fact that it is situated in the sphere of a more far-reaching institution, the *fides*, which regulates relations among men as much as those between peoples and cities."[24] Again, in Tarantinian terms, the Mexican stand-off is not an exception, but the model for any relation where only trust can defuse the potential bloodbath. If somebody breaks this trust, he is not punished by the gods, but instead cursed by a political curse, that is, he is excluded from the community and becomes a *homo sacer*.[25] We just need to remember Shosanna's curse not only on the Nazi leaders, but also on those who sold their talent to them—the German actors and directors who are prominently featured in the reception at the cinema sequence. The German soldiers, with the notable exception of Landa, however, are bound by their oath to the *Führer*,[26] just as the Americans swear their allegiance to Raine in the recruitment scene. As Raine puts it, again in terms of a business deal: "When you join my command, you take on debit. A debit you owe me, personally!" The amateur Landa, instead, means pleasure, not business, thereby acting unprofessionally, as was pointed out above.[27]

Here, we can finally return to the initial question concerning Quentin Tarantino's image of the *auteur*. If his European predecessors follow a strategy of a sophisticated reading, attempting to deconstruct the propagandistic cinema of the fascist past, as was pointed out above, Tarantino clearly sides with crude writers such as Lt. Raine. Again, we need to remember that all the sophisticated readers in his films meet an untimely end. In other words, if indeed the modernist *auteur* constantly questions the existence of an authorial authority, the postmodern dictator-director posits himself as the sole guarantor to make sense of this constant play of texts and intertexts. All of cinema seems for him to be a threshold situation, "not indifferent to the law but rather *abandoned* by it," to paraphrase Agamben from the quote above. It makes perfect sense, then, that the *auteur* Tarantino embraces "low-budget 'grindhouse' material: martial arts films, 'blaxploitation' works from the 1970s, 'midnight movies' and spaghetti westerns," because these works are similarly abandoned by the law, that is, the conventions of cinema that take the form of a law. Here, form and content mirror each other just as the Americans and the Germans mirror each other in their chiasmic encounter. Laws of filmmaking, such as continuity and smooth transitions are ignored, just as the film itself is only ruled by the libidinal will of its creator. And it is the adherence to this rule that we can trust.

Notes

1   The "Universum Film Agentur," or UFA, produced most of Nazi Germany's films. The majority of these films were, however, not the infamous propaganda films, such as *Jud Süss/The Jew Suess*, mentioned below, but comedies, musicals and melodramas. These movies were generally considered "apolitical" after the war, regularly appearing on television and in local cinemas. Fassbinder's intertextual dialogue draws attention to the fascist ideology that carries these films.

2   The French newspaper *Libération*, http://www.liberation.fr/culture/0101635824-a-cannes-godard-fait-defection (accessed July 29, 2010), quotes the note Godard sent to the festival director as follows: «*Suite à des problèmes de type grec, je ne pourrai être votre obligé à Cannes. Avec le festival, j'irai jusqu'à la mort, mais je ne ferai pas un pas de plus. Amicalement. Jean-Luc Godard.*» (Anon. "*A Cannes, Godard fait défection*") ["Due to problems of the Greek

type, I will not be at your disposition at Cannes. I am with the festival until death, but I won't go one step further." (Translation mine.)] Godard's pun draws a parallel to the debt crisis of Greece which shook Europe at the time of the 2010 festival and Godard's well-known evocations of Greek myths in his films.

3 The most obvious example would be *In einem Jahr mit dreizehn Monden/In a Year with Thirteen Moons*, where Fassbinder himself appears on a TV show that plays in the background of a scene. The film draws clear parallels between the main character and Armin Meier, Fassbinder's lover, whose suicide had been widely discussed in the press shortly before the film was made. *In einem Jahr mit dreizehn Monden* also features Fassbinder's own mother as a Schopenhauer-quoting Mother Superior who, in a densely-layered scene, lip-synchs a psychological reading of an orphan while the camera draws attention to itself by circling the action.

4 Scott Foundas, "Interview: Michael Haneke: The Bearded Prophet of *Code Inconnu* and *The Piano Teacher*," http://www.indiewire. com/article/interview_michael_haneke_the_bearded_prophet_of_ code_inconnu_and_the_piano1/ (accessed June 16, 2009). See also, among many such observations: Alan Riding, "The Unhappy World of Michael Haneke," http://www.nytimes.com/ 2005/11/06/movies/ moviesspecial/06ridi.html?scp=4&sq=Haneke&st=cse (accessed March 11, 2009). The journalist is astounded that Haneke can be quite jovial in private life. As anecdotal evidence for Haneke's control of his public image, I can refer to my own experience with Michael Haneke who objected very strongly to the title of my own book about his work (*Funny Frames*), fearing that the title might be understood as derogatory.

5 Paul De Man, *The Resistance to Theory*, 64.

6 Hiram Lee, "*Inglourious Basterds*: Quentin Tarantino goes to war," http://www.wsws.org/articles/2009/sep2009/bast-s01.shtml (accessed May 1, 2010).

7 Claude Singer, *Le juif Süss et la propagande nazie: L'Histoire confisquée*. Singer's informative study concludes with a chapter on the post-war career of the people involved in the making of the film. It is sad to see the failure of justice in Germany and France after the War.

8 In their *Tarantinian Ethics*, Fred Botting and Scott Wilson concentrate on the topic of pain and pleasure (66–7) in their reading of this scene. Their, mostly Lacanian, reading of Tarantino's oeuvre, touches on some topics that I cover here. However, the focus of my contribution, reading and writing, is different from what is covered

in *Tarantinian Ethics* and a thorough discussion would exceed the scope of this chapter.

9   Carlo Ginzburg, "Clues, Roots of an Evidential Paradigm," 103.

10   In cinematic terminology, a Mexican stand-off refers to a situation where two or more characters have guns pointed at each other. Made popular by John Woo's gangster films, such a deadlock situation appears in most of Tarantino's films, including the films he scripted. In addition, a generic convention dictates that the characters indulge in so-called "gunpoint banter," exchanging sarcastic witticisms, showing that they are not willing to back off. According to Botting and Wilson, "The Mexican stand-off constitutes the standard cinematic rehearsal of Hegel's master-slave dialectic in which a fight for prestige demands that the combatants either risk death or give way, acceding to the desire of the other, who becomes master" (*Tarantinian Ethics*, 112).

11   Ella Taylor, "Quentin Tarantino: The *Inglourious Basterds* Interview," http://www.villagevoice.com/2009-08-18/film/quentin-tarantino-the-inglourious-basterds-interview/2/ (accessed January 31, 2011). George Sanders plays a Nazi in *Confessions of a Nazi Spy* (1939) and in *Man Hunt* (1941), a British agent in Hitchcock's *Foreign Correspondent* (1940), and a collaborator who cannot live with his guilt in Renoir's *This Land Is Mine.*

12   J. Hoberman "Quentin Tarantino's *Inglourious Basterds* Makes Holocaust Revisionism Fun," http://www.villagevoice.com/2009-08-18/film/quentin-tarantino-s-inglourious-basterds-makes-holocaust-revisionism-fun/2/ (accessed January 31, 2011).

13   The scope of Agamben's *Homo Sacer* project (the recent *The Sacrament of Language: An Archaeology of the Oath*, that I briefly address below, appears as "*Homo Sacer II, 3*") is, of course, quite different. However, the explanatory power of Agamben's fusion of political concepts allows for a structural comparison.

14   *Homo Sacer*, 8.

15   Michel Foucault, *The History of Sexuality—Vol. 1: An Introduction*, New York: Vintage, 1990, 142; see the chapter on "The Right of Death and Power over Life": 135–45. See also Foucault's concise seminar description in Michel Foucault, "The Birth of Biopolitics," trans. Robert Hurley et al., *Essential Works, Volume I: Ethics—Subjectivity and Truth*, Paul Rabinow, ed., New York: New Press, 1997, 73–9. Agamben, whom I will discuss below, expands and reworks Foucault's notion, since biopolitics is always inscribed in the founding act of sovereignty. Hence Agamben's notion that the

site of biopolitics is the camp and not the prison. See also: Kalliopi
Nikolopoulou, "Book Review," *Substance 93*, 2000, 124–31, here:
128–31.

16　As Foucault puts it, biopolitics concerns the "question of how to
introduce economy … into the management of the state." Michel
Foucault, "Governmentality," trans. Robert Hurley et al., *Essential
Works, Volume III: Power*, James D. Faubion, ed., New York: New
Press, 2000, here: 207.

17　*Homo Sacer*, 11.

18　*Homo Sacer*, 15.

19　See here esp. HS 168–70, where Agamben links the declaration of a
state of emergency and the construction of concentration camps.

20　*Homo Sacer*, 28, italics in original.

21　*Homo Sacer*, 65.

22　See here especially *Homo Sacer*, 82–3.

23　See here *Homo Sacer*, 136–43.

24　*The Sacrament of Language*, 23.

25　See here esp. *The Sacrament of Language*, 36–8.

26　This seems to me the failure of *Valkyrie* (2008, Bryan Singer) that
solely concentrates on the actions of von Stauffenberg (Tom Cruise)
to overthrow Hitler, instead of concentrating on the role of the oath
that has to be broken.

27　In this regard, Hans Landa strongly resembles the character of
Ulrich in Robert Musil's novel *Der Mann ohne Eigenschaften* (The
Man without Qualities) 1930–42. Recognizing the relativity of all
ideologies and without spiritual home, Ulrich separates himself from
the community and indulges in a cynical observation of the world
around him (thanks to Robert von Dassanowsky for pointing out
this intertextual relationship).

Works cited

Agamben, Giorgio. *The Sacrament of Language: An Archaeology of the
Oath (Homo Sacer II, 3)*. Stanford, CA: Stanford University Press, 2011.
—*Homo Sacer. Sovereign Power and Bare Life*. Stanford, CA: Stanford
University Press, 1998.
Anon. "A Cannes, Godard fait défection." *Libération*, May 16,
2010, Culture: Festival de Cannes 2010. http://www.liberation.fr/

culture/0101635824-a-cannes-godard-fait-defection (accessed July 29, 2010).

Bande à part/Band of Outsiders. Directed by Jean-Luc Godard. France, 1964.

Botting, Fred, and Scott Wilson. *The Tarantinian Ethics*. London: SAGE Publications, 2001.

Confessions of a Nazi Spy. Directed by Anatole Litvak. USA, 1939.

De Man, Paul. *The Resistance to Theory*. Minneapolis, MN: University of Minnesota Press, 1986.

The Dirty Dozen. Directed by Robert Aldrich. USA/UK, 1967.

Film Socialisme. Directed by Jean-Luc Godard. Switzerland/France, 2010.

Foreign Correspondent. Directed by Alfred Hitchcock. USA, 1940.

Foucault, Michel, "Governmentality." In *Essential Works, Volume III: Power*, edited by James D. Faubion, trans. Robert Hurley et al. New York: New Press, 2000, 201–22.

—"The Birth of Biopolitics." In *Essential Works, Volume I: Ethics—Subjectivity and Truth*, edited by Paul Rabinow and translated by Robert Hurley et al. New York: New Press, 1997, 73–9.

—*The History of Sexuality – Vol. 1: An Introduction*, New York: Vintage, 1990.

Foundas, Scott. "Interview: Michael Haneke: The Bearded Prophet of 'Code Inconnu' and 'The Piano Teacher'." *indieWIRE* (March 29, 2002). http://www.indiewire.com/article/interview_michael_haneke_the_bearded_prophet_of_code_inconnu_and_the_piano1/ (accessed June 16, 2009).

Ginzburg, Carlo. "Clues, Roots of an Evidential Paradigm." In: Carlo Ginzburg, *Clues, Myths, and the Historical Method*. Baltimore, MD: Johns Hopkins University Press, 1989, 96–125.

Hangmen Also Die! Directed by Fritz Lang. USA, 1943.

Hoberman, J. "Quentin Tarantino's *Inglourious Basterds* Makes Holocaust Revisionism Fun." *The Village Voice*, Tuesday, August 18, 2009. http://www.villagevoice.com/2009-08-18/film/quentin-tarantino-s-inglourious-basterds-makes-holocaust-revisionism-fun/2/ (accessed January 31, 2011).

In einem Jahr mit dreizehn Monden/In a Year with Thirteen Moons. Directed by Rainer Werner Fassbinder. West Germany, 1978.

Inglourious Basterds. Directed by Quentin Tarantino. USA, 2009.

Jackie Brown. Directed by Quentin Tarantino. USA, 1997.

Jud Süss/Jew Suess. Directed by Veit Harlan. Germany, 1940.

Jules et Jim/Jules and Jim. Directed by François Truffaut. France, 1962.

Lee, Hiram. "*Inglourious Basterds*: Quentin Tarantino goes to war." *World Socialist Website*, September 1, 2009. http://www.wsws.org/articles/2009/sep2009/bast-s01.shtml (accessed May 1, 2010).

Lili Marleen. Directed by Rainer Werner Fassbinder. West Germany, 1981.

Man Hunt. Directed by Fritz Lang. USA, 1941.

Musil, Robert. *The Man without Qualities, Vol. 1: A Sort of Introduction and Pseudo Reality Prevails*, trans. Burton Pike and Sophie Wilkins. New York: Vintage, 1996.

—*The Man without Qualities, Vol. 2: Into the Millennium*, trans. Burton Pike and Sophie Wilkins. New York: Vintage, 1996.

Nikolopoulou, Kallioppi. "Book Review." *Substance*, 93, 2000, 124–31.

Pulp Fiction. Directed by Quentin Tarantino. USA, 1994.

Reservoir Dogs. Directed by Quentin Tarantino. USA, 1992.

Riding, Alan, "The Unhappy World of Michael Haneke." *The New York Times*, November 6, 2005. http://www.nytimes.com/2005/11/06/movies/moviesspecial/06ridi.html?scp=4&sq=Haneke&st=cse (accessed March 11, 2009).

Saving Private Ryan. Directed by Steven Spielberg. USA, 1998.

Schindler's List. Directed by Steven Spielberg. USA, 1993.

Singer, Claude. *Le juif Süss et la propagande nazie: L'Histoire confisquée*. Paris: *Les Belles Lettres*, 2003.

The Stranger. Directed by Orson Welles. USA, 1946.

Taylor, Ella. "Quentin Tarantino: The *Inglourious Basterds* Interview— Two decades after the severed ear of *Reservoir Dogs*, Quentin Tarantino serves up Hitler's head on a plate." *The Village Voice*, Tuesday, August 18, 2009. http://www.villagevoice.com/2009-08-18/film/quentin-tarantino-the-inglourious-basterds-interview/2/ (accessed January 31, 2011).

The Third Man. Directed by Carol Reed. UK, 1949.

This Land is Mine. Directed by Jean Renoir. USA, 1943.

Veronika Voss. Directed by Rainer Werner Fassbinder. West Germany, 1982.

The Wizard of Oz. Directed by Victor Fleming. USA, 1939.

11

Disruptive violence as means to create a space for reflection: thoughts on Tarantino's attempts at audience irritation

Alexander D. Ornella

Introduction

Quentin Tarantino's latest violent masterpiece *Inglourious Basterds* has been well yet critically received. Many reviewers have pointed out that the film is morally ambivalent the least because of the aesthetics of violence and the revised version of Europe's darkest years of the twentieth century. Dvir Abramovich, for example, criticizes the "commodification of the Holocaust" and argues that "*Inglourious Basterds* insensitively uses the Holocaust as entertainment."[1] Others, however, such as Rafael Seligmann or Georg Seeßlen, perceive it as a much needed and refreshing film—despite or precisely because Tarantino makes obvious the webs of violence.[2]

This article suggests that violence is a deliberate and important means for *Inglourious Basterds* to work. To fully appreciate the multilayered message of the film, an alternative reading of its aesthetics of violence is necessary: one that focuses on Tarantino's defiant and bold (yet intentional) use of various forms of violence to brilliantly orchestrate (or manipulate) the viewers' emotions and bodily senses. He stages violence as spectacle, but the way he uses violence is always also more than a spectacle: it serves as irritation—or better interruption—of audience perception, audience experience, and audience expectations. Instead of offering a cathartic moment or happy ending, Tarantino, in fact, refuses to offer catharsis and thus opens up a space for reflection and transformation. I will posit that media violence or on-screen violence can have a purpose and an important function in social, cultural, and media narratives. Secondly, I will review Tarantino's use of violence and provide a close "reading" of several key scenes of *Inglourious Basterds* to better understand why Tarantino relies on violence and what he tries to achieve with his unique aesthetics.

The ambivalence of media violence

The critique of media violence

Debates on media violence and representations of violence in media emerge more or less on a regular basis, usually whenever an ultra-violent film is released or following an act of murderous violence. In these debates, politicians are quick to link violent outbreaks to the ready availability of violent computer games or violent action movies in a desperate attempt to soothe the outraged public. The solutions politicians offer seem simple: ban on-screen violence and we will all live happily ever after. Real life, however, is not simple, and simple solutions all too often turn out to be simplistic rather than simple, neglecting broader socio-cultural phenomena. Violence in media is, of course, a delicate topic and thus thorough analyses and readings of the aesthetics of violence and how different parts of the audience receive it, make sense of it, and incorporate it into their (daily) lives and narratives of the self, are important.

The main sources of violence in media[3] are probably news reports, action/horror films, and violent computer games. While art house directors, such as the renowned Austrian filmmaker Michael Haneke, employ a presence/absence of violence to criticize what can be called the omnipresence of violent patterns in media, most commercial productions or Hollywood films commodify violence. In horror films such as *Hostel* (2005) or *Saw* (2004) and many other action films, physical violence is used to entertain the audience and satisfy their lust for blood, the thrill, or provide for an adrenaline kick. Violence is often conducted outside the legal framework (e.g. as vigilantism or as glorification) and without (moral or bodily) consequences (for the viewers). Violence becomes a spectacle with what seems to serve a simple purpose: to entertain and arouse the audience, to numb their senses, to cater to and play with their fears and exceed their expectations. Over the years, filmic violence has become more graphic and explicit suggesting that the audience's desire for violence can only be satisfied by an ever new and more sophisticated and explicit aesthetics of violence.

Scholars such as Margaret R. Miles criticize these developments and argue that showing and watching violent images is a "voyeuristic exploitation of suffering people. The pain of the oppressed is ultimately used for the entertainment of comfortable spectators."[4] This easy consumption of violence from a safe distance does not remain without consequences. According to Miles, one single film glorifying ultra-violent actions might not make a difference, but being exposed to on-screen violence over and over again has a subtle yet deep structural impact on our societies. The continuous exposure to violence as entertainment, the contexts of in-film violence, i.e. how violence is argued and justified, and the portrayal of violence as a perfectly valid and justified approach to solving problems and disputes, make both violence itself and violence as resource for solving problems appear normal. Over time, Miles argues, this continuous exposure to the portrayal of violent action as normal or acceptable behavior, or worse as the only way the good guys can prevail over the bad guys, desensitizes us from the pain of the other(s).[5] "Like actual violence, screen violence has been shown to anesthetize against empathy with the victim's pain."[6]

Miles offers an important contribution and perspective to the discussion of violence in media. In fact, if we presume that alternatively gendered role models on-screen might contribute to overcoming gender stereotypes in society, it is not so far off to assume that on-screen violence does have an impact on viewers' values, patterns, and behaviors. However, the question still remains what forms of on-screen violence have what kind of impact? Further, does the impact of media violence on society or the relationship between on-screen violence and violent behavior not have to be understood as multifactorial interrelationship, an interrelationship which media violence contributes to but is just one piece of the puzzle?

Is all media violence equal?

Not all media violence and representations of violence in media are equal[7] and analyses of the impact of media violence on real life usually produce mixed results. Recent studies also suggest that violent computer games, the medium most commonly blamed for a perceived increase of real life violence, need to be treated differently than violent films. While politicians generally blame the presence of violence in popular culture for massacres such as in Winnenden, Germany (2009) or Columbine, USA (1999), neuroscientific research points out that the cause and effect relationship is a more complex one. Christina Regenbogen and her colleagues, for example, suggest that the brain of a computer gamer is able to distinguish violence in a virtual environment from violence in real life better than previously thought. Their study provides evidence that suggests that the transfer processes between a virtual gaming environment and real life happen only very selectively. In order to win a game, gamers need to control their actions and analyze a new situation within seconds. It seems that transfer processes are limited to control and analytical mechanisms rather than violent behavior.[8] The example of violent computer games shows not only that more research needs to be done but that many other factors, such as risk factors for violent behavior, social rootedness/ withdrawal, game contexts, as well as behavioral and personality traits contribute to transfer processes.[9]

While long-term studies on the impact of violent games are still a desideratum, filmic violence has received more attention.[10] The results of these studies, however, remain ambivalent and even those studies designed to consider the social context of the participants showed that data gathering can be problematic because many random variables contribute to the phenomena. Studies necessarily have to choose a limited number of variables from a broad variety of factors that can or might contribute to violent behavior. The selection leads to a blind spot with regard to the causes and effects relation of the variables measured and those discarded. In his 1981 re-examination of George Gerbner's study on the influence of the time spent in front of the TV on one's fear of becoming a crime victim, Paul Hirsch tried to show how arbitrary variables, results, and links—in particular in studies employing a one-dimensional perspective—can be. Instead of the original relation fear/gender/ TV consumption, Hirsch related fear/zodiac signs/TV consumption of Gerbner's participants and found that zodiac signs were a more "reliable" indicator of one's fear than the time spent in front of the TV.[11] Hirsch's re-examination is already thirty years old, yet it shows the problems of studies that try to demonstrate a strong link between (one) particular variable(s) and a specific behavior or world view.

Studying the impact of exposure to on-screen violence on the audience's behavior, we need to keep in mind that a variety of phenomena, experiences, (power) relations, personality traits, and perceptions of oneself, the other, and the environment/ world contribute to behavioral patterns. For example, violent and aggressive experiences in the past can influence and affect people's behaviors, reactions, and perceptions.[12] While exposure to on-screen violence under certain circumstances can have an impact on (aggressive) behavior, the motivation why someone exposes themselves to filmic violence has to be considered and evaluated as well.[13] Haridakis and Rubin's study shows that the popular equation—exposure to ever more on-screen violence leads to ever more violent behavior—some studies support and policy makers use without nuance, needs to be reevaluated. "The results suggest that males who had experienced crime, watched violent programs to be entertained, and perceived the programs to be realistic, were more likely than their counterparts to be physically aggressive."[14] I am in no way implying that we remain untouched by media, yet, demonizing media and interpreting media exposure as the sole or most important factor causing aggressiveness is too simple a model to explain complex behavioral patterns. "Perhaps the most important finding is that audience characteristics often were the most important predictors of aggressive attitudes ... This finding is at odds with past research suggesting that exposure leads to aggression. Our results suggest that the psychological and social circumstances viewers bring with them to the viewing experience are more predictive of aggression than is exposure."[15]

Taking into account other influences besides exposure shifts the perspective from a one-dimensional exposure model to a plurifactorial model that opens up a space for new questions to be asked: does continuous exposure contribute to aggression and/ or are people who tend to aggressive behavior drawn to violent programming? What are the effects of different forms and expressions of filmic violence, such as news, horror films, or action films? How do identification processes with violent action or violent characters differ from individual to individual and between different audiences?[16] We have to ask how different people use different media and consume different media content. Further, it is important to consider the audience's social background and media literacy, or as Haridakis and Rubin find: "Research has shown that psychological and social factors such as loneliness ... isolation ... and lifestyle ... affect media use. This study supports the premise that they also affect the outcomes of media use."[17]

Media violence as *mysterium tremendum et fascinosum*

Despite all the criticism, the number of new films containing violent, aggressive, or explicit language and content is not decreasing; rather, we seem to be drawn to on-screen violence. We seem—to put it bluntly—to appreciate and enjoy aggressive behavior towards the other on-screen in ways we would not approve of in real life. We seem to be fascinated with violence and long for its aesthetics to be staged for us in cinema. There is a sort of *mysterium tremendum et fascinosum* in filmic violence that strangely attracts us and draws us into the movie theaters. We enjoy violence as entertainment and what Seneca wrote some 2000 years ago still seems to hold true: "satis spectaculis ex homine hominis mors est."[18] Violence has to some degree always been a spectacle, but today, this spectacle is readily available in cinemas, in our homes, on TV, and 24/7 on the internet. The question of the relationship between exposure to violent behavior on-screen and "real life" violence is, in fact, an important one, yet, we need to deal with and analyze the *mysterium tremendum et fascinosum* that lies within media violence.

I suggest an alternative reading of the aesthetics of violence and our attraction to the *mysterium* that lies in the awfully awe-ful images. This alternative reading evolves not around the question of the impact of media exposure on (violent) behavior, rather, it evolves around the question why we enjoy watching "bad things happen to good people, or ... even worse things happen to bad people."[19]

The joy in or the exposure to the other's pain is not new to stories and media of the twentieth and twenty-first centuries, but violence is an age-old sign and symbol system that has shaped power structures and religions, as well as founding myths of cultures and societies. As James Twitchell points out, "the most enduring self-contained sign system of preposterous violence in Western popular culture is the Passion of Christ, especially the Crucifixion ... While it might be sacrilegious to consider the Passion of Christ as an advertisement for the institution of the Catholic Church, there may be some provocative similarities."[20] Twitchell can of course be criticized from a theological perspective because what he calls "preposterous violence," Jesus' obedience and endurance of suffering and death, is the central mystery of salvation in Christianity. Yet, I believe Twitchell is aiming for something different. Throughout Christian (art) history, Jesus' suffering and death have not only been commemorated in liturgy, prayer, and meditation, but staged and enacted as spectacle in passion plays, impressive/horrific paintings, and film (e.g. Mel Gibson's *The Passion of the Christ*, 2004). Finding entertainment in violence has not only been a (sometimes dark, cruel, and very unfortunate) aspect of social, cultural, and human life, but has been a central aspect of stories that deal with the meaning of human life and questions that are central to human self-understanding: where do we come from, who are we, where are we heading to?

As Burkhard Gladigow and Stig Förster point out, violence is an essential ingredient in many mythical narratives of the beginning, both of the beginning of the world and of the struggle of the beginning of a nation.[21] In many creation myths, the world we live in becomes a habitable place only through and after an act of violence. Often, these violent struggles have to be permanently actualized and ritualized to prevent the forces of chaos from destroying life.[22] These myths also point out that the relation between violence, order, and chaos, and their impact on social order and human self-understanding is not a simple one. An example of the complex relationship(s) between good, evil, violence, chaos, and order as well as the diverse manifestations and appearances of violence can be found in the Babylonian creation myth, *Enuma Elish*. Chaos, order, and violence appear as ambivalent forces here that are distinct and yet entangled. Paul Ricœur points out that in the *Enuma Elish* both order and disorder emerge from a primordial chaos and violence is present in one form or another at various stages of the creation drama: "the Origin of things is so far on the other side of good and evil that it engenders at the same time the late principle of order—Marduk—and the belated representatives of the monstrous, and ... it must be destroyed, surmounted, as a blind origin."[23] Violence is both part of and emerges from the creative primordial chaos and becomes a means—or force—to establish order and defeat the primordial chaos that, "in time, is drained of its initial creative energy. Tiamat [one of the two primordial gods], in other words, stands for the dangerous principle of entropy, the negative, polluting force that seeks to dissolve all new life forms back into the silent slumber and amniotic inertia of death."[24] The primordial chaos encompasses both creative and destructive forces and is capable of bringing forth new life and of destroying it in a blind rage. The symbolism of the Babylonian creation myth expresses that violence can appear in and take on many forms. It can be destructive and destroy life, it can emerge from creative and life-giving forces, and it can bring forth order and justice. Ricœur's observation and analysis is important for approaching media violence. The world of narratives in general and media narratives in particular is a world rich in symbols. In fact, language itself is symbolic, expressing and mediating life experience, joy, guilt, or violence. Thus, the symbol speaks to us, engages us, and "gives rise to thought."[25] This world of symbols, however, is not a benign or unperilous one. Rather, it is an ambivalent, dynamic, fluctuating one in which old symbols fade, new symbols emerge, or symbols compete with each other.

Engaging with this rich world of symbols, we are never just neutral observers because a symbol or a narrative always prompts the reader/audience/observer for a reaction. As such, symbols want to engage us, and not only give rise to thought, but provoke, challenge, invite to self-reflection, and provide a moment of rupture in which something new can emerge.[26] The symbol, then, is a powerful expression of our *conditio humana*, an expression that provokes us to take a stance. With regard to on-screen violence, this means that the violent symbolic language can be a powerful way to throw us back to ourselves, to a starting point from which we can explore the question of what it means to be human anew. Violence, then, does not only serve entertainment purposes, but in many contexts, ranging from religious myths to national myths,[27] violence is being justified, serves a specific function, is the expression of power, and is often made plausible through narrative.[28] In many of these myths, however, the mythical narratives as well as the symbols employed are not unambiguous, they need to be interpreted to be understood, and they are open to more than just one interpretation. While national myths often try to provide some sort of (national) identity, through the interpretative openness of the narrative and the symbol, the myth can transform, further develop, criticize, and be criticized.

I am not trying to justify real life atrocities, encourage ultra-violence on-screen free from any restraints, nor do I want to embrace violence as founding myth, source of identity, or put the case for violence as a justified and valid course of action in conflict. Rather, my aim is to point out that we, as societies, as cultures, as embodied beings searching for meaning, are embedded in and immersed into stories of violence—for better or worse. We are told violent fairy tales when we are young, we expose ourselves to narrative violence (e.g. on-screen) as adolescents and adults, and we pass on stories of violence to our children. Different stories and formats serve, of course, different purposes and different social groups have their own interests and motivations for re-telling them, for example, economic ones. Yet, critics of media violence often tend to forget that narratives with and of violence do, in fact, serve a social and cultural function. Further, we need to be aware that a story or a narrative does not only consist of what is said, told, depicted, and visualized, but what is deliberately or undeliberately left out. A narrative, a story, an image, or a film is always only a kind of frame through which we look at the narrative or filmic world. This frame grants us access to this world, but what we see or hear is always only a fraction of the world behind the frame we look at. There is always also an "off," that which is outside the frame, invisible, inaudible, and yet makes up and contributes to the world we see. And even though we can only see or hear of a small part of the world, we cannot think of the narrative world without considering this "off."[29]

In the context of on-screen violence, the process of framing, i.e. determining what is on the screen and what is the "off," seems to be easy, at least at first sight: either re-frame the perspective so the violent action is not "on" the screen but happens in the "off" or prohibit this on/off dynamic altogether. What seems to be easy is, however, highly problematic, besides that this re-framing could also be called censorship. One problem of re-framing or censoring the narrative is related to a characteristic of the narrative itself. A narrative does not only consist of what is said, written, or shown on-screen, i.e. the letter, words, or (moving) images, but the narrative comes to life only in the interaction between the story-teller and the recipient. In other words, a narrative is always more than what is typed out, said, or captured and staged on-screen; it is both what is "out there" and what emerges and comes to life in our minds. The second problem is related to what happens in the "off": we experience (filmic) violence not only through what is shown, but also through the horror that is off-screen, invisible, unhearable, often only hinted at. While the motivation to move violence off-screen sometimes is a deliberate aesthetic and narrative means to deprive the recipient of the voluptuous gaze at the pain of the other (as is the aim of Austrian filmmaker Michael Haneke,[30] in his 1997 film *Funny Games* and in the 2007 English-language remake), it is true violence and horror nonetheless: violence off-screen, violence in our minds, and in some cases violence against and assault of the viewers themselves. What Twitchell contends regarding the fairy tale holds true for most narratives of/with on-screen violence: "What we censor, children replace. We tell these stories, unaware that their meanings are profound and socially important. We rarely realize we are playing out an ancient bardic role which human societies have established for growing children."[31] What the frame leaves out, our minds usually replace because our minds create the "off" according (or in addition) to the "on" on-screen.

Media violence as social ritual

Twitchell is not uncritical of violence in popular media and distinguishes between violence aimed at adolescents from violence aimed at adult viewers depending on the symbolism employed or the context of violent action. He proposes that male adolescents are probably the audience group most interested in on-screen violence and that portrayals of violence have served a social and ritual function throughout history.[32] In his argument, Twitchell draws on the anthropologist Victor Turner and suggests that watching horror films or torture porn (a term that emerged in the discussion of Eli Roth's horror flicks)[33] can be a transformative experience similar to the way that boys became men through rites of passages in tribal cultures.[34] While a rite of passage is, of course, a special and unique experience, a film can be re-watched providing both fun and entertainment and various differing experiences that can contribute to the processes of meaning making. While Twitchell focuses most of his argument on adolescents, I argue that the social function he attributes to media violence also applies to on-screen violence in general. "The question is not whether ... preposterous violence causes violent acts. That may be so. The question is instead to what degree sex and violence, if not repressed, will result in destructive forms. If a causality exists between fiction and fact, then it may be the reverse of what we expect—the real causes the pretend. Admittedly, when we look at modern mass media we may have second thoughts about how successful the deflection of violence has been, but when we look at the raves in modern history we may well prefer the vulgar ritual."[35]

   This does not imply that we need more on-screen media violence (or less, according to media critics) to have less "real-world" violence. Rather, on-screen violence can have a social and experimental function as well as relevance for our self-awareness, as

Gabrielle Murray argues: "intense violent action can bring us face to face with corporeality, the transient nature of our mortality."[36] On-screen violence—even in its most commodified form—offers a laboratory of meaning, a world in which we can experiment with action, values, and the adrenaline and excitement filmic action and violence can cause, and we can experience all that not only from a safe distance but without harming anyone else. While some argue that violence, in particular violence towards the other, should never be a safe experience, it can open up a space in which we experience ourselves in new ways and get to know dark or bright sides of ourselves that we would not be able to experience otherwise. This also allows us to live out fantasies of the past or future and creates an alternate universe in which the laws and rules of the "real" world are creatively undermined.

Tarantino's joy in the character's despair

Quentin Tarantino's cinema could be described with just a few words: it gives a lot of time to dialogues, it entertains aesthetics of blood and violence, and its characters often seek vengeance or are on a mission of revenge. Often, violence and revenge in Tarantino's films have a reason; whether they are an ethical endeavor, however, is a different question. All three elements—dialogue, aesthetics of violence, and revenge—are often intertwined and it is their unique combination that makes up not only the Tarantinian universe but the fun, the thrill, and the provocation of his films. An example of these three elements going hand in hand can be found in the beginning of *Pulp Fiction* when Jules Winnfield (Samuel L. Jackson) quotes from Ezekiel 25:17, culminating in a shooting sequence in what can be called a beautifully orchestrated scene. Other examples can be found in the *Kill Bill* films which almost endlessly elaborate in more or less philosophical ways the context of violence and why a violent rampage is not only justified but necessary to redeem the victim. The latest example is Tarantino's *Inglourious Basterds*, or what critics have called a "Jewish Revenge Porn" whose audience gets to enjoy "watching underdogs slaughter one of history's most sinister enemies. No mercy. No remorse. And all from the comfort of a cushy seat with a cup holder."[37]

The violence in Tarantino's films, in particular in *Inglourious Basterds*, might be justified from the filmic perspective as a *sine qua non* for the redemption of the victims, but this understanding provokes the question whether the "hyper-real ultra-violence" in *Inglourious Basterds* redeems the audience as well and provides for the catharsis the viewer needs and hopes to get from the average violence/action Hollywood blockbuster. Are the aesthetics of violence in *Inglourious Basterds* mere entertainment that caters to the audience's most brutish desires *panem et circenses*-style exploiting the depiction of sadistic violence against the other— even if this "other" is responsible for one of the darkest times of human history? In fact, critics have not only denounced the level of violence or the commodification of the Holocaust through *Inglourious Basterds* (and other films), but have criticized the very notion of Jewish violent revenge. As Dvir Abramovich argues, "Jews have taken revenge on the Nazis through the commemoration ... by saying 'Never Again' and by campaigning to ensure such genocide never re-occurs. Tarantino works against that aim— glorifying and deliriously celebrating humanity's most animalistic and darkest impulses which in a perverse way, identifies with Nazi, not Jewish, behavior."[38]

Abramovich is right when he points out that filmic symbols and filmic language can (and in fact do) become part of cultural visual traditions and narratives.[39] The question, however, remains if there is any meaning to the violence in *Inglourious Basterds* or if it really is nothing but entertainment. And if it really is mere entertainment, can we still say anything meaningful about it? To analyze the violent language of the film, two perspectives need to be considered: the *auteur*'s take on filmic violence and the symbolic language of the film.

Tarantino does not make a secret of his endeavor to break with norms, regulations, expectations, and social, cultural, and filmic conventions. In fact, the way he knits together bits and pieces to a storyline (or no story at all, as some critics argue) and stages his aesthetics of violence does not only break with filmic and narrative convention, but social and cultural ones as well. Don Thompson puts it quite bluntly in the context of *Kill Bill*:

Tarantino is really the provocateur of a the [sic!] new outlaw elite, the game boy intellectual who discards all the sham intellectuality and pretensions of enlightened, rational elitism and instead favors a populist Zen that states that God can be found anywhere, even in killing and violence—that God (or in the case of Uma Thurman, the Goddess) is as much lack of compassion as compassion, that the Goddess is as much a killer as a saint … Basically Tarantino hangs his hat on a thread of a story as an excuse for some kick-ass fight scenes like no other ever filmed—all in service to a young audience hungry to see Uma kick some butt.[40]

In creating his movies or drawing his characters, Tarantino points out that he tries to avoid imposing moral judgments. While a narrative can never be ethically neutral, as Ricœur points out,[41] Tarantino often tries to let his characters speak for themselves. That way, the film can become more than what is seen on-screen, it can become a shared experience enticing people to dig deeper into the film and creating a space for interpersonal communication. One way to do so (though not the only one) is using an aesthetic of violence. Yet, Tarantino openly admits to being an advocate of on-screen violence as entertainment and he certainly enjoys the power the staging of violence gives him over his audience and its emotions. He wants physical violence to be not only something that happens in the audience's mental movie, but something that happens *on*-screen in all its explicitness and graphicness. Despite the entertainment he aims for, all the blood he uses is his way of saying that being stabbed, shot, or having a swastika carved onto one's forehead is not something that "just" happens, but something that impacts the very substance of life. Blood has probably lost some of the symbolic power it once had, yet it still means something, does something, communicates something. According to Tarantino, violence makes for good cinematic entertainment, "[i]f a guy gets shot in the stomach and he's bleeding like a stuck pig then that's what I want to see—not a man with a stomach ache and a little red dot on his belly."[42] Further, Tarantino argues that through blood, the audience realizes that violence is something serious and life threatening; whenever people fight each other, lives are at stake.[43]

Compared to what the audience would expect of a war film (and made by Tarantino), there are only a few scenes that feature explicit violence in *Inglourious Basterds*. The most explicit ones are when the Bear Jew bludgeons the German soldier to death with his baseball bat, or when Lt. Aldo Raine carves the swastikas onto the foreheads of Pvt. Butz and Col. Hans Landa. There is blood spilled at the shooting in the village bar, when Shosanna and Pvt. Zoller kill each other in the projection room, and at the climactic "retribution" machine-gunning in the burning cinema, but much of the film is dedicated to dialogue.[44] Has Tarantino himself created what he criticizes about other films: a safer and cleaner war movie for adolescents? Has he given up controlling, or better playing with, the audience and their emotions?

Tarantino's violence-esque play with the audience

Many critics perceived Quentin Tarantino's *Inglourious Basterds* to be a violation of boundaries. What bothers these critics is not just "the" violence in the film or the re-writing of history, but the combination of violence, blood, dialogue, framing techniques, the filmic colors, and the narrative (or the re-writing of historical narrative) that adds up to what makes *Inglourious Basterds* the film it is. In contrast, the German film critic Georg Seeßlen argues that Tarantino's technique of showing some violence in the rare moments no one speaks, shows that language is, in fact, a weapon and images are far from being innocent, they can be treacherous, but also liberating.[45]

Tarantino's audacity allows him to trick the viewers into the cinema with the expectation of seeing another of Tarantino's violence-esque films only to find out that they, the viewers, and their expectations are being played with in Tarantino style. They hope for violence and catharsis only to find out that they do not get what they thought they paid for. In fact, Tarantino offers them a "poisoned present"[46] as Seeßlen puts it. In doing so, Tarantino makes obvious the audience's complicity with what happens on-screen; not with the Third Reich ideology (although the film can also be an opportunity to critically reflect on anti-Semitism, xenophobia and intolerance), but with the joy about the pain of the other and the entertainment we get out of it, the very reason we are watching Tarantino's film(s). Drawing on several key scenes, I will analyze how Tarantino tricks the audience and denies them the cathartic effect of on-screen violence.

Creating hope for a "happily ever after"

The first chapter of the film is called "Once upon a time ... in Nazi-occupied France".[47] Its title as well as its content is programmatic for the rest of the film. "Once upon a time" denotes the film we are about to watch as fairy tale, as something, that might have been passed on through generations, something that might or might not have happened, a story, in which historicity is not as important as the moral of the story. We know, we are about to watch a Tarantino film, and "Once upon a time" gives us the hope that all the violence we are about to see (or hope to see) will be resolved in the form of a "happily ever after."

Chapter One does not allow the audience to slowly immerse themselves into the film; rather, it starts playing with audience emotions and expectations right from the very beginning. With Christoph Waltz's award-winning acting, the first chapter is a masterpiece of violence aimed against the viewer to the point that audience gasps for air when Colonel Hans Landa sadistically enjoys his glass of milk or pseudo-rationally compares the Germans with hawks and Jews with rats. Both scenes show that violence can take on many forms and emerge in different contexts. There is no graphic violence or blood when Landa downs the glass of milk with one gulp and yet, the scene is torture of the audience. Two sounds dominate the scene which really gets under one's skin: Landa swallowing the milk and the sound of his leather coat. The fact that Landa prefers milk over wine aims to refer to the Jewish family LaPadite is hiding. In the Bible, the Promised Land has often been described as land flowing with milk and honey. Landa (and Tarantino) is playing with LaPadite as much as with the audience because he creates a tension of non-information, gives hints of what he knows but still leaves the option open that he does not know anything after all. Language, silence, and symbols are weapons which can be as powerful as, or in this case perhaps even more violent than, the traditional and expected images of cinematic physical violence.

The second important scene in Chapter One in which Tarantino plays with the audience and shows their complicity in allowing violence is Landa's lecture on the characteristics of the Jewish people. When he points out that the animosities towards the Jewish people are irrational, the viewers almost get a glimpse of hope that he might let the Jewish family hiding underneath the floor escape. That hope, however, fades away quite quickly as Landa shows his determination to catch the family. More so, he accuses LaPadite—and with LaPadite the audience that identifies with him or his "goodness"—of their complicity in the repressions of minorities and people with different ethnic backgrounds in general. The scene culminates in Landa pulling out his Sherlock Holmes-style pipe, underscoring the theatricality and artificiality of the scene. At the same time this scene ridicules the audience for relying all too easily on stereotypes when watching a film. On first sight, Landa seems to be one of the bad guys, but as it turns out he is not easy to categorize. He is one of the bad guys and at the same time he just does what he does best: be a detective who only cares about the hunt, the game, the fun.

The chapter ends with Landa saying "adieu" which is immediately followed by the soldiers opening fire to kill the family hiding under the floor. All the tensions and the expectations of seeing Nazis run amok so the spectator can be disgusted and condemn their bloody deed, however, remain unreleased and unfulfilled. We know the family is being murdered in that very moment but we do not see any blood or the murder itself. The spectator is forced to complete the scene mentally and feels cheated of the expected violence, even under the pretense that the crime might be better "witnessed" and condemned. The escape of Shosanna renews the hope that she will survive the war and that Landa will receive just punishment. After maintaining that hope for a few seconds, Landa shouts "au revoir, Shoshanna" and laughs. Once again, there is a feeling that the narrative seems to mock our expectant gaze.

Tarantino invites the audience to be open to narratives and interpretations beyond social stereotypes. He is by no means defending the perpetrator, rather he points out that whenever we reject violence or the violation of human dignity, more often than not we are in one way or another complicit in what is happening.

Bread and circuses, or the unfulfilled lust for violence

In Chapter One, Tarantino relies primarily on violence rooted in language to unmask the audience's complicity. When Tarantino stages physical violence, he uses it as a means to give the audience what it wants (blood) yet denies it at the same time. In two scenes, the teasing of the audience becomes particularly obvious: the appearance of the Bear Jew and the shooting of Hitler and his Nazi gang.

The second chapter introduces the audience to the Basterds whose mission it is to kill Nazis. Interrogating captured German soldiers, their commander, Aldo Raine, attempts to get information on German troops stationed nearby, but the German Sgt. Rachtman politely and even heroically refuses to give out any information. The refusal to cooperate with the Basterds leaves their leader but one choice, to call upon the Bear Jew who until now has been waiting in a cave to do what he also seems to do best: smash Nazi heads with his baseball bat. The atmosphere is electrifying, if not terrifying. Before the Bear Jew appears on-screen, we hear his bat beat against some metal rods inside the cave several times. The audience and the German soldiers know what that sound means and what it will bring. We see a close-up of two of the other captured German soldiers; one is terrified and in tears. The tension builds up and the screen goes black to introduce the monstrous Bear Jew, but all that happens is that Eli Roth emerges from the cave appearing rather ordinary. In his analysis of the scene, Seeßlen points out that refusing to follow the genre expectations of a horror film, Tarantino denies his audience the satisfaction of a climax. He resolves—and thus refuses—the climax by letting the Bear Jew fall very short of the audience's expectations of what a monstrous avenger is supposed to look like and thus exposes how much we rely on stereotypes when we engage with and perceive both the filmic world and "real" reality.[48] "When the Bear Jew clubs Rachtman, the audience finally gets to see some graphic violence, but it does not come without an aftertaste. Asked by the Bear Jew if he got his order of merit for killing Jews, Rachtman stoically replies: "bravery," and we can almost glimpse some respect for Rachtman in the Bear Jew's eyes (or a mix of respect colliding with the goal of revenge) right before he smashes his head. The scene, however, provides little emotional satisfaction for the audience and leaves them self-reflective: Rachtman heroically faces death, the German "bad guys" are not utterly evil but appear ambivalent, the avenger subverts genre stereotypes, and the good guys dare to admit enjoying hunting down and killing Nazis. "Watching Donny beat Nazis to death is the closest we ever get to going to the movies."[49] The audience, however, does watch a Tarantino film to see just that.

The second important scene with regard to Tarantino's approach to violence in *Inglourious Basterds* can be found in the fifth and final chapter, the "Revenge of the Giant Face." This chapter begins with the heroine Shosanna dressed in red on the night of the premiere of *Nation's Pride* in her movie theater and she is preparing herself for the event to the sounds of David Bowie's song "Cat People (Putting out Fire)." The symbolisms of red and fire literally point to the "justified" violence the audience has awaited the entire film, the well-deserved slaughtering of Hitler and the leading Nazi elite.

During the screening of *Nation's Pride*, we see Hitler sadistically laughing at the enemy's death, congratulating Goebbels for his masterpiece. The propaganda minister is clearly moved as the slaughtering on-screen continues. Hitler laughs at more enemies getting shot when the film cuts back to the screening of *Nation's Pride* showing a close-up of Zoller shouting "Who wants to send a message to Germany?" Shosanna suddenly appears on-screen and answers Zoller's question. The cuts from Hitler's face to Zoller's face to Shosanna's face to Goebbels' face and back yet again to Shosanna's face seem disturbing and natural at the same time. Disturbing, because with Hitler and Zoller, the entire Nazi audience is cheering about the kills Zoller "accomplished." Once Shosanna appears on-screen, the cheering halts and we as the *Inglourious Basterds* audience can literally feel the change of atmosphere in the fictional Parisian theater. As Goebbels watches, his film, his masterpiece, turns against him. At the same time, the dynamic appears natural because the three faces—Hitler, Zoller, and Shosanna, in particular the faces of Zoller and Shosanna—share similarities. Both Zoller and Shosanna are shot from a similar perspective; Shosanna is looking down onto the Nazi audience in the same way Zoller is looking down onto his enemies. While Hitler and Zoller sadistically laugh, Shosanna has a rather cold facial expression, but all three evoke determination and share in the responsibility of violence and other people's death. As the screening hall bursts into flames, two members of the Basterds who remained in the theater enter Hitler's loge and riddle Hitler, Goebbels, and his mistress with bullets while their bodies twitch, jerk, and flinch like fish out of water. After killing Hitler and Goebbels, the two Basterds begin shooting the locked-in audience climbing over one another to attempt escape. The bombs hidden in the theater explode. Tarantino directs it in the following way in his screenplay: "The effect this [the exploding bombs] has on the people in the room is very similar to that of the effect an M-80 blowing up in an ant hill would have on the ants. The auditorium is a literal red rain of legs, arms, heads, torsos, and asses."[50]

As the movie theater explodes, the audience finally gets what it wanted all along: a violent, bloody revenge Tarantino-style. But did the audience really get the catharsis they have been looking for? Or is the showdown just another of Tarantino's poisoned presents for an audience craving blood and violence?

Compared to most of the film, there is an abundance of physical violence in the theater scene. Yet the way Tarantino stages the violence, the aesthetic means he relies on and more importantly in what he shows and refuses to show, he denies the audience the satisfaction of Hitler's death. Instead of making the most out of Hitler's death by creating a dramatic spectacle, he does exactly the opposite. As Seeßlen argues, "[i]n fascistic aesthetics, the hero dies to become an eternal image, an image that is omnipresent."[51] Rather, Hitler's death is no less or more horrific or "monumental" than the violent deaths of the other characters in the film. In the short close-up we do see, Hitler can barely be recognized because his face is riddled with bullet holes.

In *Inglourious Basterds*, Hitler does not get the satisfaction of becoming an eternal image, of surviving in the image, of dying a melodramatic death. Similarly, the audience does not get the satisfaction of being allowed to indulge in Hitler's suffering, or in a dramatic demise. We see people panic, get shot, and the theater burst into flames, but that is not what we have been waiting for the entire film. We came to see Hitler, the epitome of evil, die, and to celebrate a "triumphant" victory of good over evil, but by denying our gaze to enjoy Hitler's death, Tarantino denies us the moment of catharsis. Instead, Tarantino achieves two things: first, seeing Hitler being perforated does not leave room for his return. While Tarantino's film is not and does not want to be historically accurate, he denies Hitler and his inner circle the memorability of fascistic narratives.[52] In doing so, Tarantino is not opposing the necessity to never forget the Nazi atrocities, but he consciously avoids a filmic aesthetic that might make Hitler's death appear heroic. Secondly, the cinema scene really is another of Tarantino's poisoned presents to his audience. The Nazis laugh about their enemies being slaughtered on-screen and applaud Zoller for his accomplishments. In particular, we experience Hitler's laughter to be quite repulsive and sadistic. Soon thereafter, the Nazis get slaughtered, and we might find ourselves laughing at the well-deserved revenge and punishment for Nazi atrocities. But, as Seeßlen points out, by laughing about people getting shot (even if they are murderers), do we not emulate Hitler?[53]

Happily *n*ever after ...

The final scene of the film in which Landa surrenders himself to Raine ties the film back to the beginning and—together with the opening chapter—forms a bracket around the entire work. *Inglourious Basterds* starts with Landa killing Shosanna's family but allowing her to escape. Shosanna does get her revenge—not on Landa himself but on the rest of the Nazi establishment—but still dies from Nazi, i.e. Zoller's, bullets. Landa, however, survives and may well make his way to a property purchased for him on Nantucket Island by American gratitude. To put it bluntly: the ending is unfair—to Shosanna, her partner Marcel, Landa, and to the audience.

But Landa's survival has its price, both for Landa and the audience. When Raine permanently marks him with a swastika, the audience gets to see the carving in all its bloodiness and the perpetrator is finally punished. Catharsis at last? Hardly. The blood we see and the pain we hear is not intended to meet the expectations of spectacle. Rather, Tarantino wants to point out the ambiguity that lies within language and signs. Raine's marking of Landa with the swastika expresses that Landa's non-ideological attitude does not make him less guilty, rather it shows that he was part of and played along with the social and symbolic structures the swastika stands for.

The mark of the swastika on Landa's forehead can also be compared with the biblical mark of Cain. Contrary to today's popular understanding of the mark of Cain as sign of sin and guilt, it was originally meant as a protective sign to safeguard both the perpetrator and society. The mark protects the perpetrator from further random acts of vengeance or violence and thus protects society from becoming like the perpetrator: "In antiquity, certain criminals were offered limited asylum when uncontrolled reprisals posed a greater social danger than the criminals themselves."[54] Raine surely did not mean the swastika to be a sign of protection for Landa. Yet, we can understand it as protective sign for society, for us: a reminder to oppose all forms of discrimination and oppression.

Conclusion

Inglourious Basterds has been criticized for altering history, for being too violent, and for blurring the roles between victims and perpetrators. Tarantino does indeed play with history, stereotypes, and roles. Above all, however, he uses violence as deliberate aesthetic means to shift the conventional relationships between the audience and cinema. As in his other films, he uses references to his own films (e.g. the recurring topic of feet) and those of other directors to unveil something new. Most importantly, the way he modifies the material he is drawing on adds additional subtexts and meanings, and offers a challenging perspective to watching and understanding his film(s) and his messages.

With his unique and often exaggerated aesthetic of violence, Tarantino's film(s) can be understood as modern ritual site and laboratory of meaning, emotions, hopes, dreams, and visions of life. In particular, *Inglourious Basterds* provides a space to play out and envision a "what if" scenario or alternative ending to WWII, which, as the July 20, 1944 attempt to assassinate Hitler shows, is not even so far fetched. This alternative the "kosher revenge porn"[55] offers, provides "a deep sexual satisfaction of wanting to beat Nazis to death"[56] as Eli Roth asserts, or can be understood as "a fucking Jewish wet dream"[57] as Lawrence Bender points out (both Roth and Bender have a Jewish background). This Jewish perspective to the film (which is not shared by everyone in the Jewish community as the film critiques show), can be applied in a similar way to the non-Jewish audience as well. The tensions in the film, the aesthetics, the struggle to survive, and the intensity caused by the blood, the violent outbursts, and the symbolic violence express a "carnal rage for life itself."[58] This struggle of life and death does not only have to be dealt with in serious art house productions. In fact, reading in between the lines, frames, and references, Tarantino's staging of violence as spectacle (and in some ways as anti-spectacle), in all its variations and intensities, is more than an exploitation of the suffering of the other. It suggests the fragility of life and allows for experiences otherwise not possible. *Inglourious Basterds* can thus be understood—and experienced—as a laboratory of meaning, values, emotions, and feelings, in which we can safely explore the transgression of boundaries and its consequences. This filmic laboratory not only shows that violence can take on many forms but that violence itself is a complex phenomenon which is tied to the very phenomenon of life itself. What Gabrielle Murray claims in her analysis of Sam Peckinpah's films can be applied to *Inglourious Basterds* as well: "We are projected out of our ordinary existence, and although we know it is not real, our experience has all the intensity of the 'present' ... Like ancient blood rituals ... sequences of violence grant form, meaning, and resonance to the tragedies and miseries of human brutality, violence, and death, while also offering insights into our transitory, yet corporeal being."[59]

Instead of censoring these images, then, we should understand them as an opportunity to explore existential questions of human existence, fear, and death. Above all, they offer an opportunity to reflect on how we as individuals and as society engage with and encounter the other. *Inglourious Basterds* points to the fact that we, as audience, with our gaze, are complicit in violence— on-screen and off-screen. It provides a safe laboratory in which we can experiment with violence and human values in a way neither possible nor desirable in real life.

Notes

1 Dvir Abramovich, "Hollywood Should Stop Exploiting the
   Holocaust," *The Age*, 3.11.2009, http://www.theage.com.au/opinion/
   society-and-culture/hollywood-should-stop-exploiting-the-holocaust-
   20091102-ht5a.html (accessed September 13, 2010).

2 Rafael Seligmann, "Juden sind keine besseren Menschen," *Stern*,
   19.08.2009, http://www.stern.de/kultur/film/rafael-seligmann-ueber-
   inglourious-basterds-juden-sind-keine-besseren-menschen-1504002.
   html (accessed September 14, 2010); Georg Seeßlen, *Quentin
   Tarantino gegen die Nazis. Alles über Inglourious Basterds.* (Berlin:
   Bertz u. Fischer, 2009).

3 As I have pointed out elsewhere, it is important to distinguish
   between "violence in media" and "media violence" even if a
   differentiation between those two terms is blurry. "Violence in
   media" refers to the portrayal of violence or violent action in media
   whereas "media violence" emphasizes the (intentional) emotional
   impact of media exposure/consumption on the audience. There
   are, of course, many shades, forms, and variations in between.
   See Alexander D. Ornella, "Cat and Mouse. Haneke's Joy in the
   Spectator's Distress," in *Fascinatingly Disturbing. Interdisciplinary
   Perspectives on Michael Haneke's Cinema*, eds. Alexander D.
   Ornella and Stefanie Knauss. (Eugene/OR: Pickwick Publications,
   2010), 147.

4 Margaret R. Miles, *Seeing and Believing. Religion and Values in the
   Movies*, 1st digital print ed. (Boston: Beacon Press, 2002), 66.

5 Miles, 182–93.

6 Miles, 183.

7 One problem for studies of media violence is the definition of
   violence. What consumers might not find violent content at all, e.g.
   cartoons, might be considered as highly violent action by research,
   because physical harm is done to a character. On the other hand,
   studies often fail to address non-physical forms of violence. Ornella,
   Cat and Mouse. Haneke's Joy in the Spectator's Distress, 147–9.

8 Christina Regenbogen, Manfred Herrmann and Thorsten Fehr, "The
   Neural Processing of Voluntary Completed, Real and Virtual Violent
   and Nonviolent Computer Game Scenarios Displaying Predefined
   Actions in Gamers and Nongamers," *Social Neuroscience*, 5, no. 2,
   (2010), 233f.

9 Regenbogen, 237.

10 Regenbogen, 222.

11 Cf. Ursula Ganz-Blättler, "Zu den blinden Flecken in der Medienwirkungsforschung. Anmerkungen zur Berliner Längsschnittstudie über Gewaltmedien," *Medienheft*, November 27, 2009. http://www.medienheft.ch/de/nc/14/date/0000/00/00/zu-den-blinden-flecken-in-der-medienwirkungsforschung-branmerkungen-zur-berliner-laengsschnittstudi/browse/1/select/gewalt-in-den-medien/article/8.html (accessed December 16, 2010). Cf. also Paul Hirsch, "On Not Learning from One's Own Mistakes: A Reanalysis of Gerbner et al's Findings on Cultivation Analysis II," *Communication Research* 8 (3), 1981, 3–37.

12 Paul M. Haridakis and Alan M. Rubin, "Motivation for Watching Television Violence and Viewer Aggression," *Mass Communication & Society*, 6, no. 1, (2003), 34.

13 Haridakis and Rubin, 41f.

14 Haridakis and Rubin, 45.

15 Haridakis and Rubin, 49.

16 Haridakis and Rubin, 50.

17 Haridakis and Rubin, 49.

18 "A great spectacle is the death of a human being brought about by another human being." Seneca Ep. Mor. 95, 33, quoted in: Burkhard Gladigow, "Gewalt in Gründungsmythen," in *Der Krieg in den Gründungsmythen europäischer Nationen und der USA*, eds. Nikolaus Buschmann and Dieter Langewiesche. (Frankfurt/Main: Campus Verlag, 2003), 36, translation is mine.

19 James B. Twitchell, *Preposterous Violence. Fables of Aggression in Modern Culture*. (New York: Oxford University Press, 1989), 4.

20 Twitchell, 23f. With "preposterous" (3), Twitchell means a staging of violence that is so exaggerated that it is obvious for the audience that what they see is staged and not real.

21 Gladigow, *Gewalt in Gründungsmythen*, 23–38; Stig Förster, "Mythenbildung und totaler Krieg. Ein Versuch," in *Der Krieg in den Gründungsmythen europäischer Nationen und der USA*, eds. Nikolaus Buschmann and Dieter Langewiesche. (Frankfurt/Main: Campus, 2003), 39–55.

22 Gladigow, *Gewalt in Gründungsmythen*, 24f.

23 Paul Ricœur, *The Symbolism of Evil* (Boston: Beacon Press, 1969), 178.

24 Norman J. Girardot, "Chaos," in *Encyclopedia of Religion*, ed. Lindsay Jones, 2nd ed., Vol. 3 (Detroit: Macmillan Reference, 2005), 1539.

25 Ricœur, *The Symbolism of Evil*, 348.

26 Paul Ricœur, *Time and Narrative*, Vol. I. (London: The University of Chicago Press, 1984), 59; Paul Ricœur, *Oneself as Another.* (Chicago: The Univ. of Chicago Press, 1994), 163–8; Richard Rorty, "Der Roman als Mittel zur Erlösung aus der Selbstbezogenheit," in *Dimensionen ästhetischer Erfahrung*, eds. Joachim Küpper and Christoph Menke. (Frankfurt/Main: Suhrkamp, 2003), 50f.

27 See the edited volume on founding myths in Europe and the USA: Nikolaus Buschmann and Dieter Langewiesche, eds., *Der Krieg in den Gründungsmythen europäischer Nationen und der USA.* (Frankfurt/Main: Campus, 2003).

28 Gladigow, *Gewalt in Gründungsmythen*, 23f.

29 Gilles Deleuze, *Das Bewegungs-Bild. Kino 1.* (Frankfurt/Main: Suhrkamp, 1997), 31f.

30 Ornella, *Cat and Mouse. Haneke's Joy in the Spectator's Distress.*

31 Twitchell, *Preposterous Violence. Fables of Aggression in Modern Culture*, 23.

32 Twitchell, 20f., 32f., 61, 236, 278, 285.

33 David Edelstein, "Now Playing at Your Local Multiplex: Torture Porn," *New York Magazine*, January 28, 2006: http://nymag.com/movies/features/15622/, (accessed January 21, 2011).

34 Twitchell, *Preposterous Violence. Fables of Aggression in Modern Culture*, 35.

35 Twitchell, 36.

36 Gabrielle Murray, "*Hostel II*: Representations of the Body in Pain and the Cinema Experience in Torture-Porn," *Jump Cut: A Review of Contemporary Media*, 50, (2008).

37 Karine Cohen-Dicker, "Jewish Revenge Porn. Once upon a Time, in a Tarantino Movie ... " *Forward*, June 12, 2009. http://www.forward.com/articles/107073/ (accessed January 31, 2011).

38 Abramovich, *Hollywood Should Stop Exploiting the Holocaust.*

39 Abramovich.

40 Don Thompson, "The Yin Yang of Kill Bill," http://webdelsol.com/SolPix/sp-yinyang.htm (accessed January 10, 2011).

41 Ricœur, *Oneself as Another*, 115.

42 "Quentin Tarantino: Violence is the Best Way to Control an Audience," The *Telegraph*, January 12, 2010. http://www.telegraph.co.uk/culture/film/film-news/6975563/Quentin-Tarantino-violence-is-the-best-way-to-control-an-audience.html (accessed December

13, 2010); see also Quentin Tarantino, "Interview with Quentin Tarantino by Charlie Rose," http://www.charlierose.com/view/interview/10567 (accessed December 15, 2010).

43 Quentin Tarantino, "'Am Ende kommt eine Pastetenfüllung heraus'—Ein Interview mit Quentin Tarantino über digitale Bilder, Entenpressen, Blutbäder und *Kill Bill*. Von Peter Körte," in *Quentin Tarantino*, eds. Robert Fischer, Peter Körte and Georg Seeßlen (Berlin: Bertz+Fischer, 2004), 7–10 (first published in: *Frankfurter Allgemeine Zeitung*, October 16, 2003); "I have seen many battle scenes recently, and they had surprisingly little blood, as if nothing matters. The two new *Star Wars* films (1999/2002; George Lucas) feature impressive battle scenes—but who is fighting? Robots! There is this big massacre, but it's a safe one, it's a massacre for kids/teenagers with their parents or legal guardians ... In my film [*Kill Bill*], bang, an arm gets chopped off, blood splashes. I think, even the most prudish audience realizes that something is at stake, as crazy as this may sound." All translations are mine unless otherwise noted.

44 The German film critic Georg Seeßlen argues that in *Inglourious Basterds* there is an almost endless struggle for words and images which is interrupted by only a few but intense violent scenes. Seeßlen, *Quentin Tarantino gegen die Nazis. Alles über Inglourious Basterds*, 139.

45 Seeßlen, 141, 143.

46 Seeßlen, 142.

47 Seeßlen points out the similarities between the opening scene of *Inglourious Basterds* and Western film, 38.

48 Seeßlen, 47.

49 Lt. Aldo Raine, film quote.

50 Quentin Tarantino, *Inglourious Basterds*. Screenplay (2009), 162. http://twcawards.com/assets/downloads/pdf/Inglourious_screenplay.pdf (accessed March 15, 2011).

51 Seeßlen, *Quentin Tarantino gegen die Nazis. Alles über Inglourious Basterds*, 139, translation is mine.

52 Seeßlen, 139f.

53 Seeßlen,142.

54 Wayne A. Meeks, ed., *The Harper Collins Study Bible*. Based on the New Revised Standard Version 1989, (New York: HarperCollins, 1993), 11, comment to Gen 4.13-16. See also Michael Fishbane, "Cain and Abel," in *Encyclopedia of Religion*, ed. Lindsay Jones, 2nd ed., Vol. 3, (Detroit: Macmillan Reference, 2005), 1344.

55   David Cox, "*Inglourious Basterds* is Cinema's Revenge on Life,"
     The *Guardian*, August 20, 2009. http://www.guardian.co.uk/film/
     filmblog/2009/aug/20/inglourious-basterds-tarantino-change-history
     (accessed September 3, 2010).

56   Jeffrey Goldberg, "Hollywood's Jewish Avenger," *The Atlantic*,
     (September 2009). http://www.theatlantic.com/magazine/
     archive/2009/09/hollywood-8217-s-jewish-avenger/7619/ (accessed
     February 13, 2011).

57   Goldberg.

58   Gabrielle Murray, "The *Auteur* as Star: Violence and Utopia
     in the Films of Sam Peckinpah," in *Stars in our Eyes: The Star
     Phenomenon in the Contemporary Era*, eds. Angela Ndalianis and
     Charlotte Henry. (London: Praeger, 2002), 139.

59   Gabrielle Murray, *This Wounded Cinema, this Wounded Life: Violence
     and Utopia in the Films of Sam Peckinpah*, (London: Praeger, 2004), 59.

Works cited

Abramovich, Dvir. "Hollywood Should Stop Exploiting the Holocaust."
     The Age, November 3, 2009. http://www.theage.com.au/opinion/
     society-and-culture/hollywood-should-stop-exploiting-the-holocaust-
     20091102-ht5a.html (accessed September 13, 2010).
Buschmann, Nikolaus and Dieter Langewiesche, eds. *Der Krieg in den
     Gründungsmythen europäischer Nationen und der USA*. Frankfurt/
     Main: Campus, 2003.
Cohen-Dicker, Karine. "Jewish Revenge Porn. Once upon a Time, in a
     Tarantino Movie … " *Forward*, June 12, 2009. http://www.forward.
     com/articles/107073/ (accessed January 31, 2011).
Cox, David. "*Inglourious Basterds* is Cinema's Revenge on Life."
     The *Guardian*, August 20, 2009. http://www.guardian.co.uk/film/
     filmblog/2009/aug/20/inglourious-basterds-tarantino-change-history
     (accessed September 3, 2010).
Deleuze, Gilles. *Das Bewegungs-Bild. Kino 1*. Frankfurt/Main:
     Suhrkamp, 1997.
Edelstein, David. "Now Playing at Your Local Multiplex: Torture Porn."
     New York Magazine, January 28, 2006. http://nymag.com/movies/
     features/15622/ (accessed January 21, 2011).
Fishbane, Michael. "Cain and Abel." In *Encyclopedia of Religion*, edited
     by Lindsay Jones. 2nd ed. Vol. 3. Detroit: Macmillan Reference, 2005,
     1344–5.

Förster, Stig. "Mythenbildung und totaler Krieg. Ein Versuch." In *Der Krieg in den Gründungsmythen europäischer Nationen und der USA*, edited by Nikolaus Buschmann and Dieter Langewiesche. Frankfurt/Main: Campus, 2003, 39–55.

Funny Games. Directed by Michael Haneke. Austria, 1997.

Funny Games. Directed by Michael Haneke. USA/UK/France/Austria, 2007.

Ganz-Blättler, Ursula. "Zu den blinden Flecken in der Medienwirkungsforschung. Anmerkungen zur Berliner Längsschnittstudie über Gewaltmedien." *Medienheft*, November 27, 2009. http://www.medienheft.ch/de/nc/14/date/0000/00/00/zu-den-blinden-flecken-in-der-medienwirkungsforschung-branmerkungen-zur-berliner-laengsschnittstudi/browse/1/select/gewalt-in-den-medien/article/8.html (accessed December 16, 2010).

Girardot, Norman J. "Chaos." In *Encyclopedia of Religion*, edited by Lindsay Jones. 2nd edn. Vol. 3. Detroit: Macmillan Reference, 2005, 1537–41.

Gladigow, Burkhard. "Gewalt in Gründungsmythen." In *Der Krieg in den Gründungsmythen europäischer Nationen und der USA*, edited by Nikolaus Buschmann and Dieter Langewiesche. Frankfurt/Main: Campus Verlag, 2003, 23–38.

Goldberg, Jeffrey. "Hollywood's Jewish Avenger." *The Atlantic*, September, 2009. http://www.theatlantic.com/magazine/archive/2009/09/hollywood-8217-s-jewish-avenger/7619/ (accessed February 13, 2011).

Haridakis, Paul M. and Alan M. Rubin. "Motivation for Watching Television Violence and Viewer Aggression." *Mass Communication & Society*, 6, no. 1 2003, 29–56.

Hirsch, Paul. "On Not Learning from One's Own Mistakes: A Reanalysis of Gerbner et al's Findings on Cultivation Analysis II," *Communication Research* 8 (3), 1981, 3–37.

Hostel. Directed by Eli Roth. USA, 2005.

Inglourious Basterds. Directed by Quentin Tarantino. USA/Germany, 2009.

Kill Bill: Vol 1. Directed by Quentin Tarantino. USA, 2003.

Kill Bill: Vol. 2. Directed by Quentin Tarantino. USA, 2004.

Meeks, Wayne A., ed. *The Harper Collins Study Bible*. Based on the New Revised Standard Version 1989. New York: HarperCollins, 1993.

Miles, Margaret R. *Seeing and Believing. Religion and Values in the Movies*. 1st digital print ed. Boston: Beacon Press, 2002.

Murray, Gabrielle. "The *Auteur* as Star: Violence and Utopia in the Films of Sam Peckinpah." In *Stars in our Eyes: The Star Phenomenon in the Contemporary Era*, edited by Angela Ndalianis and Charlotte Henry. London: Praeger, 2002, 129–47.

—"Hostel II: Representations of the Body in Pain and the Cinema Experience in Torture-Porn." *Jump Cut: A Review of Contemporary Media*, 50, 2008.

—*This Wounded Cinema, this Wounded Life: Violence and Utopia in the Films of Sam Peckinpah*. London: Praeger, 2004.

Ornella, Alexander D. "Cat and Mouse. Haneke's Joy in the Spectator's Distress." In *Fascinatingly Disturbing. Interdisciplinary Perspectives on Michael Haneke's Cinema*, edited by Alexander D. Ornella and Stefanie Knauss. Eugene/OR: Pickwick Publications, 2010.

The Passion of the Christ. Directed by Mel Gibson. USA, 2004.

Pulp Fiction. Directed by Quentin Tarantino. USA, 1994.

"Quentin Tarantino: Violence is the Best Way to Control an Audience." The *Telegraph*, January 12, 2010. http://www.telegraph.co.uk/culture/film/film-news/6975563/Quentin-Tarantino-violence-is-the-best-way-to-control-an-audience.html (accessed December 13, 2010).

Regenbogen, Christina, Manfred Herrmann, and Thorsten Fehr. "The Neural Processing of Voluntary Completed, Real and Virtual Violent and Nonviolent Computer Game Scenarios Displaying Predefined Actions in Gamers and Nongamers." *Social Neuroscience*, 5, no. 2, 2010, 221–40.

Ricœur, Paul. *Oneself as Another*. Chicago: University of Chicago Press, 1994.

—*The Symbolism of Evil*. Boston: Beacon Press, 1969.

—*Time and Narrative* Vol. I. London: University of Chicago Press, 1984.

Rorty, Richard. "Der Roman als Mittel zur Erlösung aus der Selbstbezogenheit." In *Dimensionen ästhetischer Erfahrung*, edited by Joachim Küpper and Christoph Menke. Frankfurt/Main: Suhrkamp, 2003, 49–66.

Saw. Directed by James Wan. USA/Australia, 2004.

Seeßlen, Georg. *Quentin Tarantino gegen die Nazis. Alles über Inglourious Basterds*. Berlin: Bertz u. Fischer, 2009.

Seligmann, Rafael. "Juden sind keine besseren Menschen." *Stern*, 19.08.2009. http://www.stern.de/kultur/film/rafael-seligmann-ueber-inglourious-basterds-juden-sind-keine-besseren-menschen-1504002.html (accessed September 14, 2010).

Tarantino, Quentin. "'Am Ende kommt eine Pastetenfüllung heraus'—Ein Interview mit Quentin Tarantino über digitale Bilder, Entenpressen, Blutbäder und *Kill Bill*. Von Peter Körte." In *Quentin Tarantino*, edited by Robert Fischer, Peter Körte and Georg Seeßlen. Berlin: Bertz+Fischer, 2004, 7–10 (first Published in: *Frankfurter Allgemeine Zeitung*, October 16, 2003).

—*Inglourious Basterds*. Screenplay, 2009. http://twcawards.com/assets/downloads/pdf/Inglourious_screenplay.pdf (accessed March 15, 2011).

— "Interview with Quentin Tarantino by Charlie Rose." http://www.
charlierose.com/view/interview/10567 (accessed December 15, 2010).
Thompson, Don. "The Yin Yang of *Kill Bill*." http://webdelsol.com/
SolPix/sp-yinyang.htm (accessed January 10, 2011).
Twitchell, James B. *Preposterous Violence. Fables of Aggression in
Modern Culture*. New York: Oxford University Press, 1989.

12

Counterfactuals, quantum physics, and cruel monsters in Quentin Tarantino's *Inglourious Basterds*

William Brown

Inglourious Basterds (2009) shows us history as it wasn't. The titular Basterds are a bunch of predominantly American Jews dropped into occupied France, where it is their business to kill Nazis. They discover that a Parisian cinema is hosting a screening of Joseph Goebbels' latest film, *Nation's Pride*, a propaganda piece recounting the exploits of German war hero Fredrick Zoller (Daniel Brühl). Attending the screening are all of the Nazi high command: Goebbels (Sylvester Groth), Hermann Goering, Martin Bormann and the Führer himself (Martin Wuttke). Also at the screening is cinema owner and Jewish refugee Shosanna Dreyfus (Mélanie Laurent), who, separate from the titular Basterds, has her own plot to assassinate Hitler—by burning down the cinema using her dead aunt's collection of 350 nitrate films as fuel. These plots to kill Hitler *work*: the *Führer* is assassinated at the hands of the Basterds, with Shosanna's plan to burn down the cinema also coming to destructive fruition. In complete *discordance* with what happened historically, then, we are led to believe that the war ends early (although this is not actually confirmed in the film), meaning that rather than a factual or even fact-inspired version of historical events, we have here a *counter*factual version of events.

In this essay, I shall use theories of counterfactual history and cinematic affect to argue that, while we often think of narrative cinema as being purely fictional, in some senses it might not be. I shall argue that cinema may function as something of a "counterfactual" machine that challenges the traditional boundary between reality and fiction, precisely because cinema can have real and *physical* effects on us. And, by looking closely at *Inglourious Basterds*, I shall argue that Tarantino's film is in many respects aware of the power of cinema in a physical and a cultural sense, and that the film deliberately explores how cinema can and does posit its own reality.

Counterfactuals, physics and philosophy

Ben Walters has written that the counterfactual WWII history of *Inglourious Basterds* is not unique to cinema: *Let George Do It!* (Marcel Varnel, UK, 1940) and *The Great Dictator* (Charles Chaplin, USA, 1940) are both examples of counterfactual films contemporary to the war itself.[1] However, where both of these wartime films involve fantasy resolutions depicting how the war *might have* ended, *Inglourious Basterds* is made some sixty-four years after the war and as such should "know better" about the course that events really took.

In his discussion of counterfactual history, historian Niall Ferguson says that "[w]e should consider as plausible or probable *only those alternatives which we can show on the basis of contemporary evidence that contemporaries actually considered.*"[2] That is to say, counterfactual history is useless if, even with humor, it descends into utterly improbable versions of events. Rather than proposing an "alternative" ending to the war based on the different outcome of a known set of circumstances (e.g. Germany defeated the Soviet Union[3]), *Inglourious Basterds* is based upon the insertion into history of a group of entirely fictional elements, including the Basterds themselves, Shosanna Dreyfus, and SS Colonel Hans Landa (Christoph Waltz). As such, contrary to Walters, the film would not qualify as counterfactual according to Ferguson's "reasonable" version of what counterfactuals are when applied to history.

However, while Ferguson might not see the history depicted in *Inglourious Basterds* as "relevantly" counterfactual, since the film is perhaps too improbable for his liking, there is scope to contest the "reasonable" version of counterfactual history that he puts forward. Ferguson himself outlines the changes, predominantly in physics, that helped to bring about the recognition of counterfactuals as potentially instructive. I shall discuss those changes here.

It was Werner Heisenberg who discovered that one cannot measure both the position and velocity of a particle, for the more accurately one measures its position, the less accurately one can measure its velocity—and vice versa.[4] As a result, the velocity and position of a particle can only be measured as a function of *probability*, not of certainty (hence the phrase "uncertainty principle"). Furthermore, all such efforts at precise knowledge must recognize the input of the observer, who in using at least one particle of light, or photon, to carry out her measurement, affects the position and velocity of the particle being measured and thus to a certain extent determines the outcome of the experiment. The insertion of uncertainty into calculations regarding where a particle will go or what it will do challenges classical physics: rather than a universe governed by a set of inviolable laws that, if understood correctly, should allow us to predict precisely what the particle will do and where it will be at a certain moment in time, Heisenberg and colleagues show that the best we can do is to provide a set of *likely* outcomes to this experiment. Never can we know how a particle will behave exactly, not least because in order to find this out, we will affect its behavior.

Given that we can only measure a set of probable outcomes when we try to predict the behavior of a particle, we know that whatever is the *actual* outcome to a *particular* experiment, it is only one of a set of possible outcomes that may have happened. "Common sense," however, would say the following: it does not matter that something else could have happened; this is what did happen and that is the only thing that is important. But while common sense might say this, the same experiment can be repeated with the same initial conditions and have a *different* outcome. In other words, it was not a matter of inevitability that the experiment ended as it did, but a matter of *chance*. As a matter of chance, those other possible outcomes were not only equally valid until the "one" outcome did happen, but they can also be considered equally *real*. It is not, therefore, that we discover at the last which of the possible outcomes to the experiment was the real one all along, but that all of the possible outcomes are real until, as per Heisenberg's uncertainty principle, the observer helps to determine which of those real and co-existing outcomes becomes the *actual* outcome (which is most "real" to us).

If we write large this world of quanta, which after all are the unpredictable matter from which we and the rest of the universe are made, then the outcome of history is not necessarily inevitable, but is also an outcome of *chance*. Not only might history turn out differently were it to run again, but the knock-on effect of one particle acting in a different manner might lead to other particles acting in a different manner, which in turn has a knock-on effect that, on the grand scale of events that humans know, might lead to an outcome that is so distinct from the reality that surrounds us that it would be unrecognizable. As per the analogy from chaos theory concerning the butterfly flapping its wings in Brazil, which leads to the tornado in Texas, the slightest change in conditions can lead to the greatest difference in outcome.[5]

Given that Niall Ferguson adopts a "reasonable" approach to the alternative possible outcomes of historical events, we might conclude that he does not take seriously the possible *reality status* of these alternative/counterfactual versions of reality. Indeed, Ferguson argues that from the historian's perspective, there is little point in taking seriously the notions of possible worlds put forward by the likes of physicist Michio Kaku.[6]

However, physicists such as Kaku and Paul Davies have written about how we might take seriously the idea that the "alternative" outcomes of particle measurements *are* equally real, and that on the grandest scale our universe is only one of many co-existing and parallel universes, or possible worlds.[7] This style of reasoning is influenced by physicist Hugh Everett III, whose "many-universes interpretation of quantum theory" is "far removed from the commonsense one."[8] Everett argued that all possible outcomes to an experiment are real within what he terms *superspace*. The single, or actual, reality that we humans perceive is merely a fragment of superspace, and if for each experiment there is an infinity of possible outcomes, then absolute reality, or superspace, is likewise infinite.[9]

In the realm of philosophy, David Lewis has not only argued in favor of counterfactuals, but also, in the face of criticism along the lines of Niall Ferguson's "reasonable" version of counterfactuals outlined above, he has argued in favor of *modal realism*.[10] For Lewis, modal realism means that possible worlds share an equal ontological status to our world, but we do not have access to them. This we can compare to conceptualism, which argues that possible worlds are constructs of language and mind, but that they do not have the same ontological status as the actual world.[11]

Although this foray from physics into philosophy is so brief that it runs the risk of oversimplifying the work of its authors, it is useful because it can lead us towards the notion of cinematic affect that I wish to outline in this essay, which is tied to the notion of counterfactuals, and which in turn is relevant for our consideration of *Inglourious Basterds*. It is not that films are alternative possible realities that show us how events might have turned out had things happened differently, but films are (interchangeably) alternative, parallel, possible, and counterfactual realities or worlds. *Inglourious Basterds* is not a realistic portrayal of an alternative outcome to WWII, but I shall argue that it *does* constitute its own reality or world, which *does* co-exist alongside our real world, and that while the film presents an improbably counterfactual history, it *does* self-consciously explore the way in which the "fictional" cannot be divorced from reality, particularly with regard to cinema. For contrary to David Lewis' modal realism, which argues that possible worlds have an equal ontological status to our own, but that we cannot gain access to them, we can certainly gain access to the world of a film—precisely by watching it. However, unlike conceptualism, which argues that possible worlds are constructs of language and mind, we know that films are not simply mind-dependent, but that they have an existence "out there," and they are materially *real*, not least because they affect us physically. As such, films are somewhere between modal realism and conceptualism, and it is the concept of counterfactuals, or possible worlds, that can help us to understand them.

In order to bring the notion of cinematic affect into the argument, let us consider possible shortcomings in Rescher's version of conceptualism. In saying that possible worlds are mind-dependent, he overlooks how the mind is an embodied phenomenon. As per the work of, *inter alia*, neuroscientists Antonio Damasio and Francisco J. Varela, our "higher order" functions such as thought and mind do not stand in opposition to our bodies, but in fact grow out of them.[12] If we did not have a body, we would not have rational thought; our viscera inform our sentiments, which inform our emotions, which inform our thoughts—and what triggers off this process is not only having a body, but having a body that exists in the world. And if films can—and do—affect us physically and mentally (or *phenomenologically*, as discussed most prominently by Vivian Sobchack, Laura U. Marks, and Jennifer M. Barker[13]), then it is not because films are false and illusory, but because films have a perceptible effect/affect on viewers, lending to them at least a partially equal ontological status to the world around us. In other words, cinematic affect, in conjunction with counterfactuals and possible worlds, serves as a means to explain the paradoxical status of films as simultaneously real and fictional. As I shall now explain, *Inglourious Basterds* is a film that self-consciously explores these issues.

The White Hell of Pitz Palu

German Minister of Propaganda Dr. Joseph Goebbels is well known for believing that cinema can function as a tool for propaganda, that is, as a tool for ideological education/indoctrination, because cinema has an effect in and on the real world.[14] *Inglourious Basterds* explicitly makes reference to how the German Reich understood the powerful affective nature of cinema. In a short scene inserted into a longer scene featuring an injured Bridget von Hammersmark (Diane Kruger) telling the Basterds about Hitler's impending presence at the screening of *Nation's Pride*, we see the *Führer* himself saying that his attendance will be "meaningful" in the face of an imminent American invasion into occupied France. That is, Hitler is shown here as believing that *Nation's Pride* might help to turn around the ailing fortunes of the German war effort.[15]

Not only does *Inglourious Basterds* consciously reference the way in which the Germans saw film as an integral part of the war effort on account of its affective capabilities, however, but the film itself also seems to share this position—that cinema can erupt into and have a real and literal effect on the actual world.

The film opens in 1941 with SS Colonel Hans Landa paying a visit to dairy farmer Perrier LaPadite (Denis Menochet) in the French countryside. As Landa approaches the LaPadite homestead in a car, one of Perrier's daughters puts up a white sheet that obscures the car from our view. As the online bloggers from Mstrmnd have explained, the sheet can be understood as a second cinema screen, and it is from behind this screen that Landa's car emerges to approach the farmhouse—an early sign that that which is supposedly on or behind the screen can come into and have an effect on reality.[16]

After our introduction to the Basterds in the second of the film's five "chapters," we then move in the third chapter to Paris in 1944. Shosanna, who has escaped the opening assassination of the rest of her family at the hands of Landa's soldiers, is running the Gamaar cinema. Screening at the Gamaar is G. W. Pabst and Arnold Fanck's 1929 German film, *Die weiße Hölle vom Piz Palü/The White Hell of Pitz Palu*, which starred Leni Riefenstahl as a mountain climber, Maria, who gets stuck on the titular Piz Palü together with her husband, Hans (Ernst Petersen), and an obsessed second climber, Dr. Krafft (Gustav Diessl). Krafft has for years been wandering the mountain in search of his dead wife (Mizzi Götzel), and he in turn now dies from exposure having given his coat to Hans to keep him warm. Hans and Maria are rescued by their friend and ace pilot Ernst Udet, who was a real life pilot playing himself.

Showing a 1929 German film in a Parisian cinema in 1944 is not implausible, but it is perhaps also unlikely, even in a city whose cinemas are as conscious of film history as those in Paris. The choice of film, then, is no mere coincidence. First, by featuring Ernst Udet as a real life "hero" in his own film, the real *Piz Palü* mirrors the fictional *Nation's Pride* which shortly thereafter will show at the Gamaar, and which will feature ace German sniper Fredrick Zoller who, like Udet, plays himself. Secondly, the film functions as a reminder of the work of Leni Riefenstahl, in *Piz Palü* an actress, but perhaps most famous as the director of pro-Nazi propaganda documentaries *Triumph des Willens/Triumph of the Will* (Germany, 1935), which is about the Nuremberg rally of 1934, and *Olympia* (Germany, 1938), about the 1936 Berlin Olympic Games. Thirdly, *Piz Palü* was re-edited by the Nazi Party in the 1930s: the original name of the Ernst Petersen character, Karl Stern, was thought to sound too Jewish and so was changed to Hans Brandt in 1933, with scenes featuring Jewish actor Kurt Gerron also being cut from the film, Gerron himself being killed in Auschwitz in 1944.[17] Fourthly, it is important that when we see that the Gamaar is showing this film, Shosanna, now known as Emmanuelle Mimieux so as to hide her Jewish identity, is up a ladder. This is important and it is related to *Piz Palü* because there is a consistent parallel between Shosanna and heights in this film, as if she now were the intrepid mountaineer who, an inversion of what the Nazi Party did to the original *Piz Palü*, will re-cut *Nation's Pride*—but this time in order to insert her own, Jewish presence into the film. And it is also important because Shosanna's inserted film will accompany the destruction of the Gamaar and the death of the Nazi high command thanks to the ignition of her inherited 350-title film collection. In this way, and again perhaps as an inversion of, or more problematically a complement to, the Goebbels and Riefenstahl-led desire to use cinema to change/affect the world, Shosanna's inserted film will itself literally burst forth from the screen and wreak destruction/revenge in the real world.

America and Germany: parallel histories

Simultaneous to Shosanna's plot is Operation Kino, which is launched in the film's fourth chapter, when Archie Hicox (Michael Fassbender), an English film critic who has written two books on 1920s German cinema, is sent to join the Basterds in France. Hicox and two German-speaking Basterds, Hugo Stiglitz (Til Schweiger) and Wilhelm Wicki (Gedeon Burkhard), rendezvous in an underground tavern with Bridget von Hammersmark, a German actress who, we learn later from a poster in the Gamaar, is the star of a film that features the word *Doktor* in the title.

I will return to the importance of this poster below, but presently I shall analyze the tavern scene, in which Hicox and the Basterds discover that the tavern is being patronized by a group of German soldiers celebrating the birth of one of their number's son. For this scene, too, reflects directly upon the power of cinema to affect or influence the real world—and how not just Germany, but the USA as well, has a history of exploiting this power of the medium.

The soldiers are playing a game in which players must ask questions to discover the identity of the person whose name is written on a card stuck to their forehead—a game that is then repeated by von Hammersmark, Hicox, Stiglitz and Wicki when they are joined by Gestapo officer Dieter Hellstrom (August Diehl). Among the famous people and characters that feature across the two games are pro-German spy and exotic dancer Mata Hari, Beethoven, Genghis Khan, and Marco Polo, as well as movie actresses Pola Negri, Brigitte Helm, Brigitte Horney, director G. W. Pabst, *King Kong* writer Edgar Wallace (in the first game) and (in the second game) King Kong himself.

Not only do these names function as meaningful pointers to the time in which the film is set—as period details—but they bring to mind the *ideological* nature of 1920s and 1930s cinema. Negri and Horney both left Germany/the German film industry for the USA (Negri before the war; Horney afterwards) and Helm moved to Switzerland in 1935. Pabst similarly travelled between the USA and Germany in the 1930s, returning to Germany in 1938 and making films under Goebbels during the war. The reason that these names remind us of the ideological nature of 1920s and 1930s cinema, then, is because 1930s and war-time cinema was considered on both sides as part of the war effort: where you made films functioned not as an indicator simply of artistic ambition, but also of political alignment—as is made clear at a separate point in *Inglourious Basterds* when Goebbels refuses to hear talk of Lilian Harvey, a polyglot actress who made English-, French- and German-language films in the 1930s, but who fled Nazi Germany to France and then the USA. The trans-Atlantic journeys of European talent also help to show the *links* between Germany and the USA, as we shall see presently.

In guessing that he has been given King Kong, Hellstrom recasts the story as being an allegory of slavery in the USA. Carried across the ocean in chains, where white Americans use the "savage" King Kong for profit, Hellstrom's reading of *King Kong* as allegorical of the slave experience in the USA also reminds us of the ideological nature of cinema: cinema does not just tell us entertaining stories, but these stories also have "hidden" meanings that, in the case of *King Kong*, reveal the capitalist and racist ideology of the United States. At this point, we have already heard Goebbels bemoan the fact that "it's only the offspring of slaves that allows America to be competitive athletically ... American Olympic gold can be measured in negro sweat," a comment that would superficially suggest that the USA has abandoned its formerly racist ideologies in allowing athletes like Jesse Owens to be so prominent at the Berlin Olympics. However, the racism of the Germans, which can also be seen when Landa refuses to let Shosanna/Emmanuelle's black projectionist and seeming lover, Marcel (Jacky Ido), work or be seen during the screening of *Nation's Pride*, in fact would seem to *mirror* that of the USA.

The links are complex but they can be seen quite clearly in various places. First, when Shosanna flees Landa in the opening scene, he steps from Perrier LaPadite's house in a shot entirely reminiscent of John Ford's *The Searchers* (1956)—as a silhouette framed in an open doorway that shows the countryside beyond. In that film, John Wayne plays Ethan Edwards, a man who hates Comanche Indians because of the violent atrocities that they commit. By having Landa step through the LaPadite door as Edwards does at the end of *The Searchers*, a link is made between Nazi racism and American racism. Furthermore, since we see Shosanna running away in this same shot, she is implicitly linked to Debbie Edwards (Natalie Wood), the girl who is kidnapped and raised by the Comanches in Ford's film. But where Debbie is rescued from miscegenation with the Comanches in *The Searchers*, Shosanna is forced outwards by Landa, equating the Nazi treatment of Jews with the settlers' treatment of Native Americans.

Chief Basterd Aldo Raine (Brad Pitt) is also known as the Apache—claiming that he has Apache blood in him (as well as being a direct descendant of mythomaniac frontiersman Jim Bridger). One of two non-Jews among the Basterds (with Stiglitz), Aldo's pro-violent attitude toward the Nazis can be read, like

Shosanna's and the Jewish Basterds', as a personal mission of vengeance against racism. Aldo bears a neck scar reminiscent of a rope-burn that might have been caused by a lynching typical of the American south—and the association between vengeful Native Americans and vengeful Jews only serves to reinforce the links between those who historically have persecuted them, respectively European settlers in the USA and Nazis. The link is made clearer still when, in the build-up to the destruction of the Gamaar, Shosanna uses make-up to paint "war stripes" on her face: like Aldo, she considers herself an Apache gaining vengeance against those who have killed her family.

Given that the racism of American settlers against Native Americans is mirrored with the racism of Germans against Jews, Hellstrom's interpretation of the King Kong character functions not to make the USA seem a counterpoint to Germany, but to point out what they have in common: an imperialist racist tendency (which perhaps is also implicit in the guessing game's use of Winnetou, an Apache character of German novelist Karl May, whose Westerns were immensely popular in the late nineteenth and early twentieth centuries). Through the reference to King Kong, one of cinema's most enduring characters, we can see how *Inglourious Basterds* makes implicit reference to the ways in which both Germany and the USA have historically used cinema for ideological purposes.

Herr Doktor

Before arguing how the use of space in *Inglourious Basterds* furthers but also complicates the blurring of the boundary between American and German racism and violence, I shall return to the aforementioned poster of the film that features the word *Doktor* in its title. The poster is important because when we see it, it is in frame with Shosanna, who has just put on her make-up/war paint. This could link Shosanna to von Hammersmark, the film's star and whose motivation for being a pro-Allies spy is never made clear. But it is the word *Doktor* alongside Shosanna that is more telling. First, *Herr Doktor* is one of the real-life nicknames of Joseph Goebbels—and in a film that takes nicknames like the "Jew Hunter," the "Bear Jew" and the "Apache" seriously, this surely is intentionally meant to link Goebbels not only to the film industry but also to Shosanna, in that he is one of the objects of her revenge plot. Furthermore, as has been suggested, the word might also be a reference to Sylvia Plath's poem, "Lady Lazarus," in which a woman who is trying to die is kept alive by oppressive figures referred to as "Herr Doktor" and "Herr Professor."[18]

This might seem a tenuous link, but Plath's poem (and others in *Ariel*, the collection to which it belongs[19]) is often referred to as one of her "Holocaust poems," in that it is considered an attempt by Plath to equate oppression with Nazi Germany. Secondly, "Lady Lazarus" ends with the speaker deciding to eat her oppressors so that next time she dies they will not be able to resurrect her—having been resurrected by them in the form of a phoenix, the mythical beast which rises from its own ashes, thereby surviving death. This is particularly resonant with *Inglourious Basterds*, because not only does Shosanna "rise from the dead" in the film, since her image appears on the screen featuring *Nation's Pride* after she has been shot dead by her admirer Zoller, but this "ghost" also appears to consume (in flames if not literally) those who have oppressed her, including *Herr Doktor* Goebbels himself. In this way, Shosanna's revenge plot does not go wrong in that she dies, but rather it is perfectly realized, in that her risen and phoenix-like form consumes her evil oppressors—hopefully in such a way that now she will be laid to rest.

Perhaps to be expected from a filmmaker as "postmodern" and "intertextual" as Quentin Tarantino, *Inglourious Basterds* is full of references to other films.[20] However, as discussed, many of these references point to the history of cinema as a tool for propaganda (i.e. as a tool for affecting the way people think and feel) both in the USA and in Germany. They also relate to how the film itself tells a story in which cinema—from Landa's car emerging from behind the sheet/screen, to Shosanna's image arising from the flames and consuming the Germans in the Gamaar—can erupt into the real world.[21]

Monster movies

The grip of Nazism on Germans and others during the 1930s onwards is implicitly signaled in *Inglourious Basterds* as being constructed upon a film industry spearheaded by Goebbels, Riefenstahl, Pabst, and others. If the contents of films are not real, but do have an effect on reality, then we must consider how and why this medium has the effect that it does. To do this, we shall return to the notion of cinematic affect, before linking it back to counterfactuals.

Jean-Luc Nancy has written about how cruelty derives from the Latin word *cruor*, or the spilling of blood, which he differentiates from *sanguis*, which is blood circulating inside a body.[22] The act of spilling blood, of cruelty, is related to sacrifice, which literally means to make sacred or to make other. Nancy also says that monsters are other, or sacred, and that images are *monstrances*. That is, "the creation of images is the creation of the other, it is a making sacred, or sacrifice. Being sacred, the image is outside of or exceeds the world; it is outside of language and outside of meaning. The image is *evidence of the invisible*."[23] As "evidence of the invisible," an image is not that which it represents, nor is it a signifier representing a signified. Rather, an image makes visible not the objects that are its content, but the *force* that these objects possess, a force that enables change/affect. The image makes this force visible, meaning that this force is proper to the image and is otherwise invisible. When force is put to work, the result is violence, or change, and violence, by dint of its power to change, by dint of its *force*, is irrational or "stupid." Violence obliterates established order and in this sense it is violence that is, or which makes, truth. For truth, like violence, overthrows the established order, and truth, like violence, is revealed through monstration: "violence is exposed as a form without form, a monstration, a showing (*ostension*) of that which has no face."[24] Elsewhere, Nancy continues in his description of truth as a monster: "The truth is a singular monster, like all truths: it is at once true of the most tender kiss, as well as of the most horrendous slaughter; it is tenderness and cruelty combined in a fearsome chimera, exchanging their roles, almost like tender flesh (fresh raw meat) and the splendor of blood (*cruor*, blood spurting forth, versus *sanguis*, blood flowing in the organs)."[25]

Linking images, violence, truth and cruelty, then, is monstrosity. In terms of cinema, cinema is monstration, in that cinema *shows*. It is not so much the contents of the images that are important as the fact of images: their otherness, their sacred nature, their distinction, is excessive, violent, truthful and cruel, showing us raw (*cru* in French) images that we must then work hard to understand or of which we must make sense. Between filmmakers and viewers, we must create narratives (tellings) to cope with the otherwise incomprehensible experience of senseless presence, the violent *showings* that always exceed the meaning of signs.[26] Cinema's images are capable of affect, an affect that is not always intellectual, but which can also take place on a plane *before* intellection and sense-making (images are pre-sense/"present"), and which is, as various studies of cinema have tried recently to make clear, haptic (or visceral or immersive).[27] Cinema *touches* us. Cinema, in Nancy's terms, has skin: cinema is an exposed or "ex-peau-sed" (*peau* is skin in French) little skin (*pellicule*, the French for a strip of film).[28] Cinema has a presence, a pre-sense, which we see, but which we also *feel*: sensation before sense.

Inglourious Basterds is, after Nancy, cruelly violent: it is full of, among other things, scalpings, baseball bat beatings, shootings, fingers being stuck into bullet wounds, swastikas being carved on to foreheads, and faces being disfigured by repeated and point blank-range machine gunfire. These are affective images that can make spectators flinch, squirm, feel nauseous, and even cause moral outrage. During the shootout that follows the guessing game in the basement tavern, blood even spatters on to the camera in one shot, suggesting (once again) that what is on the screen can erupt into and have an effect on the real world.

These are images with what Nancy terms *force*. Cinema does not so much show us real things or people as capture their *force* or, as Janet Harbord might argue, their *energy*.[29] To think about Nancy's theoretical argument from the physical point of view, light, which consists of elementary particles/photons, is imprinted on to film—and then when a film is projected light similarly passes from the projector through a film, on to a screen, and out into the audience. The intensity of that light hits the audience in a similarly *physical* and therefore affective manner: there is a transfer of energy across time from the moment of filming to the moment of viewing as, metaphorically speaking, photons also physically travel from the moment of filming to the moment of viewing.

Cinema as a whole touches us, then, with greater or lesser degrees of intensity. Since it touches us, or affects us with its force, it does violence to us and can show us the truth. Not the truth of that which it represents, but the truth of the invisible forces/ energies that surround us. However, if *all* cinema is in this way monstrous, cruel, and sacred, *Inglourious Basterds* is *knowingly* monstrous, because it shows us violent images, the intensity of which is heightened because of their cruel and bloody nature. These images overthrow the established order, particularly (and playfully) the "order" of history, which dictates that what we see in this film did not take place. The film does not re-represent to us a history that it did not capture; rather it *presents* to us an autonomous reality, a counterfactual world not just in terms of being a false history of WWII, but a real and alternative world, a parallel universe, which is pre-sense in that its *meaning* is hard to tell, but which is sensed by our bodies before our intellects can and do make sense of it. *Inglourious Basterds* is a raw (*cru*) film; it is a realization (the French call the director of a film the *réalisateur*) and a monstrous monstration of a possible world, which touches us and has an effect/affect on our world.

Basements are boomin'

This essay has discussed the ways in which cinema as a whole, and *Inglourious Basterds* in particular, can and does affect us physically, an argument that builds upon and, via the notion of the embodied mind mentioned earlier, is closely tied to the way in which cinema can also influence us intellectually/ideologically, something upon which *Inglourious Basterds* in particular seems self-consciously to reflect. By way of a conclusion, then, this section will look at how space is constructed in *Inglourious Basterds*, for the use of space in this film reflects those who are in a position of power. Furthermore, those characters that emerge the most powerful in *Inglourious Basterds* are those who specifically resist, seem immune to, or manage to avoid the power of images.

The aforementioned scene involving the guessing game takes place in a basement tavern, the setting of which is described at length as problematic by Aldo before Hicox, Stiglitz and Wicki enter to meet von Hammersmark. Inevitably, the scene turns into a bloodbath, but it is the film's WWII context that makes of the basement a meaningful setting. For, the violence in this scene, like much of the violence of *Inglourious Basterds*, takes place underground or in enclosed spaces.

The scene in which we first meet the Basterds involves Donny "The Bear Jew" Donowitz (Eli Roth) emerging from a dark tunnel to beat German officer Werner (Richard Sammel) to death with a baseball bat. German soldiers lie scalped (another token of Apache/ Jewish revenge) in this brick landscape that seems to have been reclaimed in part by nature; the space is reminiscent of the similarly reclaimed extermination camps that were documented in films such as *Nuit et brouillard/Night and Fog* (1955).

The Gamaar functions in a similar fashion: Marcel, the only black character in the film and thus, given the references to negroes elsewhere, also a signifier not just of Nazi oppression but of American slavery, locks and bars the doors to the cinema, thereby preventing anyone from escaping the inferno. The fact of locking all of the victims in is, like the other enclosed spaces of combat in *Inglourious Basterds*, reminiscent of the extermination camps, here the gas chambers in particular.

Inglourious Basterds, then, does not show the landing beaches or the rural and urban conflicts that mark so many other WWII films, but, as the Mstrmnd blog suggests, the invisible and similarly enclosed extermination camps that are redolent of the war's most atrocious violence.[30] The effect of using such spaces transfers the film from being a "simple" war film, to sharing features with the Holocaust film.

That it is the Basterds wreaking havoc in these spaces, as opposed to Nazis, problematizes the "good guys/bad guys" dichotomy that the film might on first appearances seem to uphold. While racist America and racist Germany might, as discussed, be linked through the film's intertextual references, the violence committed by the Basterds, and by Shosanna and Marcel, seems not so much to be "justified" (although we might be forgiven for thinking that way), but rather implicitly to be linked to the very genocidal policies against which it is aimed. Returning to the scene in which Werner is beaten to death, then, it is no surprise in this tale of revenge that the Bear Jew emerges from a black hole/the invisible bowels of the extermination camps to exact his revenge in a way that suggests that the violence of cinema and the cinema of violence cannot be separated from their roots in the Holocaust and Hitler.

If the Gamaar cinema becomes an extermination camp, this again suggests the importance of cinema in the war, be it for better or, as seems possible, for worse. Parallels have been made between the architecture of the Gamaar and temples, especially the shot of Shosanna against the circular window through which we can see the poster of the *Doktor* film starring von Hammersmark.[31] It is not that the film attacks religion per se, but this shot might suggest that cinema functions as a religion: belief in cinema, like belief in religion, can lead to atrocious violence.

Shosanna emerges, then, as high priestess in this temple of film, an association made all the clearer by her links to Leni Riefenstahl and her appearance on the ladder in the scene featuring the reference to *The White Hell of Pitz Palu*. Heights are an important aspect of space in *Inglourious Basterds*, since all of the main characters are associated somehow with high places.

Not only is Shosanna on the ladder in two scenes (when she meets Zoller and when Hellstrom forces her to lunch with Zoller, Goebbels, and his translator Francesca Mondino, played by Julie Dreyfus), but she also comes to occupy elevated positions such as the balcony and the projection room in the cinema. Only in the opening sequence, during which Shosanna is depicted (fittingly, as persecuted Jew) underground and enclosed beneath the LaPadite household, is she depicted as lower down than her enemies. During that scene, as Landa has Shosanna's family killed, the camera gives us an aerial view of Landa walking through the LaPadite household. This is an aerial view that is mirrored later on in the Gamaar as Shosanna steps through the cinema to enact her revenge.[32] Not only might this link Shosanna to Landa (and suggest that she can, like Landa, think both like a "rat" and like a "hawk"), but it also illustrates how Landa, too, has access to high places. At the premiere of *Nation's Pride*, Landa, like Shosanna, occupies the balcony, descending from it to expose von Hammersmark and Aldo Raine, who has come dressed as an Italian after the demise of Stiglitz and Wicki in the basement tavern. Raine himself is a man from the Tennessee Mountains—and he is acutely aware of the tactical advantage provided by high places when he refuses to enter the basement and when he gets Werner and then Butz (Sönke Möhring), a German whom the Basterds allow to survive, to explain where snipers might be hiding in the baseball bat sequence.

Hicox, meanwhile, claims to be from the mountains when he tells Hellstrom that he is from Piz Palü, but this is exposed as a lie and he dies as a result. Landa laughs uncontrollably when von

Hammersmark tells him that the cast on her recently injured leg is due to a climbing accident: not only are there no mountains in Paris for this story to be plausible, but it seems also that Landa considers von Hammersmark as unworthy of an elevated position. Similarly, Zoller might know that high places like clock towers provide tactical advantages (as documented in *Nation's Pride*), but he is always looking up at Shosanna and, importantly, is an avowed cinephile.

As a cinephile, Zoller is, like many characters, including Basterd Omar (Omar Doom), who seems momentarily incapable of dragging himself away from *Nation's Pride* as Donny tries to initiate an improvised version of Operation Kino, always looking up at the pictures on the screen that looms above him, and not down on them from the projectionist's booth like Shosanna.

Cinephilia here takes its place in the film's layers of meaning: implicitly those that believe in/worship in the temple of cinema are fools who, seemingly, desire the violence of images and who, through Shosanna, are mercilessly given it. Shosanna herself never comes forth as a cinephile: she says that she is not a fan of *Piz Palü*, and she dodges Zoller's questions about cinema, except to say that the French respect directors. Furthermore, neither she nor Landa nor Raine watches *Nation's Pride*—or if Shosanna does watch the film, it is not as a film to enjoy, unlike most of the Germans (and Omar). In fact, rather than consume pictures, Shosanna creates and subverts pictures, re-cutting *Nation's Pride* and adding her own ending. Though this does not save her life (perhaps, as per "Lady Lazarus," she does not want it to be saved), it is enough to allow her to consume the image-eaters, rather than to worship images.

Without wishing to overlook some of the ambiguities surrounding Zoller (he is a cinephile, but he seems to dislike *Nation's Pride*; he knows that elevated positions enable survival, but looks up at/ worships Shosanna), it seems that it is the trio of Raine, Landa and Shosanna who refuse to be taken in by (the ideology of) images. In fact, it is because none of them believes in anything other than themselves that they succeed in their mission (Shosanna) and/or survive (Raine and Landa, albeit problematically for the latter, given that the former engraves a swastika into his forehead). This is reflected in their business-like demeanor: Shosanna cares only for her revenge; Landa is happy to betray the *Führer* for his own profit; Aldo views killing Nazis as business ("and, cousin, business is a-*boomin'*"). In other words, all three are "immune" to images, particularly as perpetuated through cinema, and each is motivated only by personal suffering (Shosanna's family is murdered; Aldo has the neck scar; Landa will have the swastika scar).

For a "cinephile" filmmaker like Quentin Tarantino, this may seem an unusual message. And yet for all that Tarantino is versed in many periods of world cinema history, he relentlessly recycles images and themes not for the sake of pure homage, but for his own purposes, as the intertexts in *Inglourious Basterds* suggest. In other words, he is not a "mere" consumer of images, but, like Shosanna, is a maker of images, someone who does violence to "official" cinema—and history—by making "monstrous" and violent films. As a "counterfactual" film, *Inglourious Basterds* may for someone like Niall Ferguson be irrelevant, shedding no light on what really happened in WWII and how things might realistically have turned out differently. However, if cinema in general is a machine for showing us counterfactual realities that, after Nancy, have a real effect in the real world, then *Inglourious Basterds* is not simply fiction.

Inglourious Basterds is a film that explores in great depth the reality of images, paradoxically doing so through a film that presents to us a counterfactual history that most definitely was not. It is a film that no doubt affects audiences in diverse ways and with differing levels of intensity, but it is a film that deliberately sets out to affect its audience through its emphasis on violence. These cruel images make visible, or at the very least felt, the invisible energies that affect us, bringing to mind the fact that the "real" version of the very history that *Inglourious Basterds* so overtly subverts, had at its root the affective and motivating powers of cinema itself. Cinema may be false but, to invoke Gilles Deleuze, many of whose ideas are bubbling somewhere under this essay, the "powers of the false" are profound and tangible in the real world.[33] Those who succeed in this film are those who do not worship at the temple of cinema (Raine, Landa, Shosanna), but they surely do understand the power that images have over people. For cinema is not just illusion and trickery; it is its own reality, its own potentiality that is *realized* by each and every film that is made. Every film is a counterfactual reality that touches and influences us, and not just a fiction divorced from us; by deliberately embracing this aspect of cinema, Quentin Tarantino, after Aldo Raine and the film's last lines, "might just have made his masterpiece."

Notes

1   Ben Walters, "Debating *Inglourious Basterds*," *Film Quarterly*, 63:2, (Winter 2009), 21.

2   Niall Ferguson, "Introduction: Virtual History: Towards a 'chaotic' theory of the past," in *Virtual History: Alternatives and Counterfactuals*, (edited by Niall Ferguson, London: Papermac, 1998), 86 (original italics).

3   See Michael Burleigh, "Nazi Europe: What if Nazi Germany had defeated the Soviet Union?" in *Virtual History: Alternatives and Counterfactuals*, (edited by Niall Ferguson, London: Papermac, 1998), 321–47.

4   See Werner Heisenberg, *Physics and Philosophy*, (London: Penguin, 2000 [1958]), especially 14–25.

5   See James Gleick, *Chaos: The Amazing Science of the Unpredictable*, (London: Vintage, 1998), 9–31. In addition, I should mention how *Inglourious Basterds* is in fact a self-consciously "complex" film. Bereft of the space to explain this in detail, we can conceive of it thus: if any of the film's scenes ended differently (had Shosanna not escaped; had Hicox survived the basement slaughter; had the Gamaar not been chosen as the location for the screening of *Nation's Pride*; had the Führer not decided to attend the screening; had Landa exposed Shosanna in the restaurant when he had the seeming chance, a chance made clear by the thematic use of milk/dairy products that also feature in the opening scene), then the film would have ended in a vastly different manner. For more on the milk (as well as the film's use of Leslie Charteris' *The Saint in New York*), see David Bordwell, "(50) Days of summer movies (part 2)," *Observations on Film Art* by David Bordwell and Kristin Thompson, *http://www.davidbordwell. net/blog/?p=5446 (accessed November 19, 2010)*.

6   Ferguson, 74.

7   See Michio Kaku, *Parallel Worlds: The Science of Alternative Universes and our Future in the Cosmos*, (London: Penguin, 2005); and Paul Davies, *Other Worlds: Space, Superspace and the Quantum Universe*, (London: Penguin, 1988).

8   Davies, 136.

9   See Davies, 136–7.

10 See David Lewis, *Counterfactuals*, (Cambridge, MA: Harvard University Press, 1973); and *On the Plurality of Worlds*, (Oxford: Blackwell, 1986).

11 For more, see Nicholas Rescher, "The Ontology of the Possible," in
    Logic and Ontology (edited by Milton K. Munitz, New York: New
    York University Press, 1973), 213–28.

12 See Antonio Damasio, *Descartes' Error: Emotion, Reason and
    the Human Brain*, (London: Putnam, 1994); *The Feeling of What
    Happens: Body and Emotion in the Making of Consciousness*,
    (London: Vintage, 2000); and Francisco J. Varela, Evan Thompson,
    and Eleanor Rosch, *The Embodied Mind: Cognitive Science and
    Human Experience*, (Cambridge, MA: MIT Press, 1991).

13 See Vivian Sobchack, *The Address of the Eye: A Phenomenology
    of Film Experience*, (Princeton: Princeton University Press, 1992);
    Laura U. Marks, *The Skin of the Film: Intercultural Cinema,
    Embodiment and the Senses*, (Durham, NC: Duke University Press,
    2000); and Jennifer M. Barker, *The Tactile Eye: Touch and the
    Cinematic Experience*, (Berkeley: University of California Press,
    2009).

14 See Paul Virilio, *War and Cinema: The Logistics of Perception*,
    (translated by Patrick Camiller, London: Verso, 1989), 8.

15 Paul Virilio mentions that Goebbels and Hitler were desperate to
    make the "greatest film of all time," even though defeat was staring
    them in the face. In this respect *Nation's Pride* loosely translates into
    Kolberg (Veit Harlan, Germany, 1945). The two films have parallel
    stories: Zoller defends a besieged clock tower from attacking G.I.s,
    while Harlan's film sees a small German town hold out against
    Napoleon and his armies. That said, if, as Virilio implies, Goebbels
    insisted that Agfacolor be developed to rival American Technicolor
    as part of the war effort, *Nation's Pride* should really be a color
    instead of a black-and-white film. See Virilio, 8–9.

16 Mstrmnd. "The Mirror of Leni Riefenstahl: Secrets of *Inglourious
    Basterds*," http://www.mstrmnd.com/log/1394 (accessed November
    19, 2010).

17 See StummFilm MusikTage, "*Die weiße Hölle von Piz Palü* (D.
    1929)," *StummFilm MusikTage*, not dated.

18 Mstrmnd.

19 See Sylvia Plath, *Ariel*. (London: Faber & Faber, 1968).

20 On how Tarantino is "postmodern," see Cristina Degli-Esposti,
    "Postmodernism(s)," in *Postmodernism and Cinema*, (edited by
    Cristina Degli-Esposti, London: Berghahn), 9; and Paul A. Woods,
    Quentin Tarantino: The Film Geek Files, (London: Plexus, 2000),
    124. On how Tarantino is "intertextual," see Chris Pallant,
    "Tarantino the Cartoonist," *animation: an interdisciplinary journal*,

2:2, (2007), 171–86; and Glyn White, "Quentin Tarantino," in *Fifty Contemporary Filmmakers*, (edited by Yvonne Tasker. London: Routledge, 2002), 343.

21 In its casting, *Inglourious Basterds* also shows intertextual self-awareness regarding the counterfactual history that it presents. Mélanie Laurent is in *Ne t'en fais pas, je vais bien/Don't Worry I'm Fine* (Philippe Lioret, France, 2006), which involves parents creating a counterfactual world for their daughter (played by Laurent) so that she does not learn about the death of her brother. Similarly, Daniel Brühl stars in *Goodbye Lenin!* (Wolfgang Becker, Germany, 2003), in which he creates a counterfactual history in order to hide from his mother the fact that the Berlin Wall has fallen while she was in a coma.

22 See Jean-Luc Nancy, *Au fond des images*, (Paris: Galilée, 2003).

23 Nancy 2003, 30 (my translation).

24 Nancy 2003, 38 (my translation).

25 Jean-Luc Nancy, "Claire Denis: Icon of Ferocity," in *Cinematic Thinking: Philosophical Approaches to the New Cinema*, (edited by James Phillips. Stanford: Stanford University Press, 2008), 163.

26 Nancy 2003, 55.

27 There have been many scholars who have of late turned towards the haptic with regard to film studies, although I shall limit myself to mentioning the three scholars named earlier in relation to film and phenomenology: Sobchack, Marks, and Barker.

28 Nancy, 2008, 163.

29 See Janet Harbord, *The Evolution of Film: Rethinking Film Studies*. (Cambridge: Polity, 2007).

30 See the Mstrmnd blog.

31 Again, see Mstrmnd.

32 Again, see Mstrmnd.

33 See Gilles Deleuze, *Cinema 2: The Time Image*, (translated by Hugh Tomlinson and Robert Galeta, London: Continuum, 2005).

Works cited

Barker, Jennifer M. *The Tactile Eye: Touch and the Cinematic Experience*. Berkeley: University of California Press, 2009.

Bordwell, David. "(50) Days of summer movies (part 2)." *Observations on Film Art*, by David Bordwell and Kristin Thompson *http://www. davidbordwell.net/blog/?p=5446 (accessed November 19, 2010)*.

Burleigh, Michael. "Nazi Europe: What if Nazi Germany had defeated the Soviet Union?" In *Virtual History: Alternatives and Counterfactuals*, (edited by Niall Ferguson. London: Papermac, 1998), 321–47.

Damasio, Antonio. *Descartes' Error: Emotion, Reason and the Human Brain*. London: Putnam, 1994.

—*The Feeling of What Happens: Body and Emotion in the Making of Consciousness*. London: Vintage, 2000.

Davies, Paul. *Other Worlds: Space, Superspace and the Quantum Universe*. London: Penguin, 1988.

Degli-Esposti, Cristina. "Postmodernism(s)." In *Postmodernism and Cinema*, edited by Cristina Degli-Esposti. London: Berghahn, 1998, 3–18.

Deleuze, Gilles. *Cinema 2: The Time Image*. Translated by Hugh Tomlinson and Robert Galeta. London: Continuum, 2005.

Die weiße Hölle vom Piz Palü/The White Hell of Pitz Palu. Directed by G. W. Pabst and Arnold Fanck. Germany, 1929.

Ferguson, Niall. "Introduction: Virtual History: Towards a 'chaotic' theory of the past." In *Virtual History: Alternatives and Counterfactuals*, edited by Niall Ferguson. London: Papermac, 1998, 1–90.

Gleick, James. *Chaos: The Amazing Science of the Unpredictable*. London: Vintage, 1998.

Goodbye Lenin! Directed by Wolfgang Becker. Germany, 2003.

The Great Dictator. Directed by Charles Chaplin. USA, 1940.

Harbord, Janet. *The Evolution of Film: Rethinking Film Studies*. Cambridge: Polity, 2007.

Heisenberg, Werner [1958]. *Physics and Philosophy*. London: Penguin, 2000.

Inglourious Basterds. Directed by Quentin Tarantino. USA/Germany, 2009.

Kaku, Michio. *Parallel Worlds: The Science of Alternative Universes and our Future in the Cosmos*. London: Penguin, 2005.

Kolberg. Directed by Veit Harlan. Germany, 1945.

Let George Do It! Directed by Marcel Varnel. UK, 1940.

Lewis, David. *Counterfactuals*. Cambridge, MA: Harvard University Press, 1973.

—*On the Plurality of Worlds*. Oxford: Blackwell, 1986.

Marks, Laura U. *The Skin of the Film: Intercultural Cinema, Embodiment and the Senses*. Durham, NC: Duke University Press, 2000.

Mstrmnd. "The Mirror of Leni Riefenstahl: Secrets of *Inglourious Basterds*," http://www.mstrmnd.com/log/1394 (accessed November 19, 2010).

Nancy, Jean-Luc. *Au fond des images*. Paris: Galilée, 2003.

—"Claire Denis: Icon of Ferocity." In *Cinematic Thinking: Philosophical Approaches to the New Cinema*, edited by James Phillips. Stanford: Stanford University Press, 2008, 160–8.

Ne t'en fais pas, je vais bien/Don't Worry I'm Fine. Directed by Philippe Lioret. France, 2006.

Nuit et Brouillard/Night and Fog. Directed by Alain Resnais. France, 1955.

Olympia. Directed by Leni Riefenstahl. Germany, 1938.

Pallant, Chris. "Tarantino the Cartoonist." *animation: an interdisciplinary journal*, 2:2, 2007, 171–86.

Plath, Sylvia. *Ariel*. London: Faber & Faber, 1968.

Rescher, Nicholas. "The Ontology of the Possible." In *Logic and Ontology*, edited by Milton K. Munitz. New York: New York University Press, 1973, 213–28.

The Searchers. Directed by John Ford. USA, 1956.

Sobchack, Vivian. *The Address of the Eye: A Phenomenology of Film Experience*. Princeton: Princeton University Press, 1992.

StummFilm MusikTage. "*Die weiße Hölle von Piz Palü* (D. 1929)." *StummFilm MusikTage* (accessed November 19, 2010). http://www.stummfilmmusiktage.de/de/archive/movies/weisse_hoelle.php.

Triumph des Willens/Triumph of the Will. Directed by Leni Riefenstahl. Germany, 1935.

Varela, Francisco J., Evan Thompson and Eleanor Rosch. *The Embodied Mind: Cognitive Science and Human Experience*. Cambridge, MA: MIT Press, 1991.

Virilio, Paul. *War and Cinema: The Logistics of Perception*. Translated by Patrick Camiller. London: Verso, 1989.

Walters, Ben. "Debating *Inglourious Basterds*." *Film Quarterly*, 63:2, Winter 2009, 21–2.

White, Glyn. "Quentin Tarantino." In *Fifty Contemporary Filmmakers*, edited by Yvonne Tasker. London: Routledge, 2002, 338–45.

Woods, Paul A. *Quentin Tarantino: The Film Geek Files*. London: Plexus, 2000.

13

"What shall the history books read?" The debate over *Inglourious Basterds* and the limits of representation

Todd Herzog

In the early 1990s, Mike Godwin formulated a theory of internet behavior that has since become known as Godwin's Law of Nazi Analogies: "As an online discussion grows longer, the probability of a comparison involving Nazis or Hitler approaches one."[1] I would like to propose a corollary to Godwin's Law: Any discussion of counterfactual history—scholarly or popular, pro or contra—will eventually turn to Hitler or Nazi Germany as an example.[2] This might be attributable at least in part to the fact that these texts are often in conversation with one other, so they will naturally cite similar examples to make their points. I think, however, that there is a more fundamental reason for the prevalence of references to Hitler and National Socialism in texts that seek to explore the relationship between history and fiction: the Holocaust (which, even when not mentioned directly, is the ultimate reason for the Hitler and Nazi references) is perhaps the only remaining event where the stakes of delineating the space between fact and fiction still seem high enough to provoke controversy and criticism.

Almost four decades have elapsed since Daniel Bell identified a "new sensibility" that "breaks down all genres and denies that there is any distinction between art and life."[3] This no-longer new sensibility has come to be referred to as postmodernism and has become an established concept in both popular and academic culture. Mash-ups that are one part history and two parts fantasy abound to the point where a book that reimagines the sixteenth President of the United States as a vampire hunter and the Civil War as being as much about vampirism as slavery can unproblematically make it to the *New York Times* bestseller list.[4] But any text that questions or plays with the borders between fact and fiction in relation to the Holocaust comes in for sharp and pointed debate.[5] This is especially true of cinematic texts, which, because of their ability to reach a wide public, are quite frequently at the center of the most heated debates. It is worth noting that nearly all Holocaust films are based directly on actual historical figures and events and take great pains to announce their being based on a true story and convey that story as historically accurately as possible.

When Holocaust-themed films do depart from a somber and historically painstaking narrative, they inevitably attract great controversy. Roberto Benigni's award-winning 1997 film, *Life is Beautiful*, for example, sparked a fierce debate over the question of whether the Holocaust can be the stuff of comedy.[6] The debate over whether the Holocaust can be sexy has an even longer history, going back to the mid-1970s, when Susan Sontag published her classic essay "Fascinating Fascism" in the *New York Review* of Books and Don Edmonds' cult classic Nazisploitation film *Ilsa, She Wolf of the SS* first appeared on screens.[7] More recently, and perhaps even more startlingly, the Holocaust has been used as the backdrop before which to tell stories of romantic love—such as in Max Färberböck's 1999 German film *Aimee & Jaguar*.

Quentin Tarantino's *Inglourious Basterds* is not, strictly speaking, a Holocaust film. It does not take place in a concentration camp. It does not focus primarily on Jews in hiding. It does not explore the decision-making process leading to the implementation of the Final Solution. On the contrary, Tarantino has repeatedly referred to it as a WWII film. But the fact that the film's central characters are a French Jew who escapes death and plots revenge against those who murdered her family, a group of mostly Jewish-American soldiers who seek revenge on the Nazis, and a German officer nicknamed "The Jew Hunter" necessitates that the film be seen in the context of the Holocaust. Had Tarantino wished to concentrate on the military aspects of the film, he could have set it among the French Resistance and not emphasized the ethnicity of the main characters. Instead, Tarantino opens his film with a tense, tour-de-force scene of Jews being discovered hiding in a French country house and murdered on the spot.

Inglourious Basterds is not really a work of counterfactual history—neither of the scholarly variety nor as an intellectual parlor game. Although he evokes and dramatizes the famous counterfactual event of Hitler's assassination, Tarantino is not interested in pursuing the question of what would have happened if history had taken this course. Would the war have ended early? Would another person have assumed the position of *Führer*? Would lives have been spared? Tarantino doesn't really address these questions in the film. And he certainly is not interested in exploring such issues as the relationship between history and memory or the role of human agency in bringing about historical change. Had Tarantino kept the bullets and blood and cinematic in-jokes, but set his violent revenge film in a different time and place, it would have garnered a very different reception. I don't recall anybody criticizing the *Kill Bill* films for their historically inaccurate portrayal of wedding rehearsals. But by evoking the Holocaust and playing fast and loose with history, *Inglourious Basterds* provoked interesting—and often surprising—reactions that pose a question more pointed than those raised by previous controversial Holocaust films: Can the Holocaust be the stuff of fiction?

This chapter revisits the debate over the film by exploring its contentious critical reception. This reception was particularly heated in the United States, where Tarantino was sharply criticized for mixing fact and fantasy in his film, and particularly surprising in Germany, where critics and audiences welcomed the film as a refreshing new approach to Germany's twentieth century history. I then turn to a phenomenon that has outlived the critics' debates and examine the ways in which this film has sparked the imaginations of fans who continue to create elaborate fanfictions that draw on Tarantino's story and reimagine it.

Made in movieland: the American reception of *Inglourious Basterds*

Inglourious Basterds was both a critical and box-office success in its initial American release. It boasts an impressive 88% "fresh" rating among critics and 87% "fresh" rating among audience members on *Rotten Tomatoes*, the well-known website that consolidates both professional and amateur movie reviews.[8] With over $120 million in domestic box office revenues, it ranked 25th among all films (and second only to *The Hangover* among R-rated films) released in the United States in 2009, making it the most financially successful film of Tarantino's career to date.[9] Although the film's detractors were a minority, they were vigorous in their criticism and represent some of the most prominent film critics working today.

Daniel Mendelsohn launched the first attack on the film in a column for *Newsweek* that appeared a week before its official opening in U.S. theaters. Evoking the traditional view of Tarantino's filmmaking style as a postmodern pastiche that draws its content from, and plays off, other movies, Mendelsohn argues that "[t]he problem is the movies aren't real life, and this is where Tarantino, with his video-store version of the world, gets into trouble."[10] Mendelsohn predicts that the discussion surrounding the film "will focus on the appropriateness (or inappropriateness) of using the Holocaust, even tangentially, as a vehicle for a playful, postmodern movie that so feverishly celebrates little more than film itself."[11] This debate is, of course, completely in line with the tradition of fictional and counterhistorical narratives about the Holocaust that I mentioned previously, so it is not surprising that it played out just as Mendelsohn predicted.

Manohla Dargis pronounced the film's representation of National Socialism and invocation of the Holocaust "repellent" and "vulgar in the extreme."[12] "Mr. Tarantino is only serious about films," she writes, "not history."[13] Jonathan Rosenbaum notes "the blindness to history that leaks out of every pore in this production" and deems the film "morally akin to Holocaust denial."[14] As the film reaches its climax, Michael Wood writes, "[w]e are now in the realm not only of the fictional but of the deeply counter-factual."[15] J. Hoberman's review in *The Village Voice* proclaims ironically that "*Inglourious Basterds* makes Holocaust revisionism fun" and views it as "a form of science fiction. Everything unfolds in and maps an alternative universe: The Movies."[16] Tarantino's retreat from history into a world consisting purely of cinema is a frequent refrain among critics. Like Hoberman, Kim Newman sees Tarantino as "flirting with science fiction" and writes that the film takes place in "movieland rather than history."[17] Proclaiming the film "an extravagant jest about the Second World War," David Denby puts Tarantino's retreat from history into movieland in colorful terms:

> In brief, Tarantino has gone past his usual practice of decorating his movies with homages to others. This time, he has pulled the film-archive door shut behind him—there's hardly a flash of light indicating that the world exists outside the cinema except as the basis of a nutbrain fable.[18]

Or, as Mendelsohn writes, "in this new movie, the movies aren't just a subtle (or not so subtle) element in an allusive esthetic game; they are, at last, front and center."[19]

Even the positive reviews of the film—which, as I mentioned above, greatly outnumbered the negative reviews—agree that *Inglourious Basterds* lives in movieland rather than history. "For Tarantino," writes Scott Foundas in an appreciative article in *Film Comment*, "cinema has always been a perfectly valid parallel reality ... But in *Inglourious Basterds*, the world of cinema is, for the first time, the primary reality of the film as well as its primary subtext."[20] Peter Travers concludes his review of the film in *Rolling Stone* by predicting, as Mendelsohn had, that this film will be the topic of heated debate: "Tarantino rewrites history with the only authority he has: his sovereignty as a filmmaker. Will *Basterds* polarize audiences? That's a given. But for anyone professing true movie love, there's no resisting it."[21]

The dividing line in the debate over *Inglourious Basterds* is thus clearly and strongly drawn between those who praise the film and those who criticize it, but there is actually little disagreement between the two camps as to what Tarantino is doing in the film: he is making cinema, not history. His sources are other movies, not historical events. The difference lies only in how one evaluates this approach. Tarantino's detractors have long criticized his trademark use of graphic "violence that is presented without any apparent moral comment" to the delight of an audience "whose moral response to violence, it is feared, has been alarmingly dulled by too much popular entertainment," as Mendelsohn wrote in his negative review of *Kill Bill: Vol. 1*, published in December 2003, anticipating the reaction that he would have to *Inglourious Basterds* six years later.[22] "[T]he most troubling thing about Tarantino and his work, of which *Kill Bill* may well be the best representative," he continues, is "not the violence but the emptiness, the passivity, the sense that you're in the presence not of a creator but of a member of the audience—one who's incapable of saying anything about real life because everything he knows comes from the movies."[23] The result of Tarantino's and his films' living entirely in a world of movies, Mendelsohn argues, is "the ultimately vacant quality of so much of his work."[24] Denby refers to it as "an eerie blankness ... too shallow to be called nihilism."[25] This absence of feeling is rendered all the more acute in *Inglourious Basterds*, because, as Mendelsohn points out, "these bad guys were real, this history was real, and the feelings we have about them and what they did are real and have real-world consequences and implications."[26]

Mendelsohn has an explicit suggestion for how to fill this allegedly vacant space in Tarantino's film:

> An alternative, and morally superior, form of "revenge" for Jews would be to do precisely what Jews have been doing since World War II ended: that is, to preserve and perpetuate the memory of the destruction that was visited upon them ... [27]

This brings us to the crux of the difference not only between Mendelsohn and Tarantino, but between *Inglourious Basterds* and its critics—both those who praise the film and those who criticize it. Mendelsohn, Dargis, Hoberman, and other critics of the film insist that it is deeply unethical to be (in Denby's words) "mucking about with a tragic moment of history"[28] and that (in Mendelsohn's words) to indulge fantasies "at the expense of the truth of history would be the most inglorious bastardization of all."[29] Hoberman calls it "a consummate Hollywood entertainment—rich in fantasy and blithely amoral."[30] Dargis suggests that the only thing that matters to Tarantino "is the filmmaking."[31] Mick LaSalle, on the other hand, who praises it as "Tarantino's best movie ... the first movie of his artistic maturity, the film his talent has been promising for more than 15 years," suggests that "*Inglourious Basterds* celebrates cinema—its power and dangerous allure" and never loses sight of "what it can't do and what war does do"—the difference between cinema and "real life."[32] In this film, writes Foundas, "it is cinema itself that reigns victorious."[33]

The assumption running through all of these criticisms is that by letting the story play out in "movieland" rather than "history," Tarantino exhibits a little concern for the catastrophe of the Holocaust and its victims and elevates cinema itself to a position of heroism. "The cinema, it seems, is both innocent and heroic," writes Denby, "it creates great art, and it will end the war."[34] Even Tarantino takes this approach to his film, at least in his public comments: "The power of cinema is going to bring down the Third Reich—I get a kick out of that!" he exclaimed at a press conference in Cannes.[35]

But I would argue that the critics of this film—and Tarantino himself—misunderstand the role that cinema plays in *Inglourious Basterds*. It is indeed a film made more in movieland than in any reality—and it reminds the viewer of this fact in nearly every frame of this 156-minute-long film. The first scene packs in direct references to at least three Spaghetti Westerns—*Navajo Joe, Once Upon a Time in the West,* and *The Good, the Bad, and the Ugly,* backed up by an immediately recognizable Ennio Moriccone soundtrack, just in case we miss the visual references—and ends with an homage to the iconic shot through doorway from *The Searchers.*[36] These references—many of which even a casual film buff would catch—work to keep the viewer from being immersed in what is otherwise an exceptionally tense scene. And that's just the first scene of the film, which will pile up more references and incorporate cinema more directly as it goes on.

Although Tarantino's lush and overpacked *mise-en-scène* might initially seem to be precisely the opposite of Hans-Jürgen Syberberg's 1977 film *Hitler: a Film from Germany*, which takes place on a clearly-artificial soundstage, both films actually work to accomplish the same type of distantiation from their subject matter. What Anton Kaes writes of Syberberg's film is equally applicable to Tarantino's:

> His radically contrived and artificial mode of presentation also attacks those allegedly authentic, in actual fact hopelessly platitudinous reconstructions of the past in which images shot by the Nazis themselves are recycled. Syberberg's film destroys direct referential illusion. What reality, after all, should the film mirror? Past reality is absent and not repeatable; it cannot be visited like a foreign country. A deep gulf separates history as experience from its re-presentation. What is presented can never be identical with the presentation itself.[37]

Tarantino's pastiche not only reminds us constantly that we are watching a cinematic re-presentation, but goes a step further even than Syberberg, reminding us that—over sixty years after the end of WWII—very few people can access this moment in history through memory. Most of us have experienced it only through media, and especially through visual representations. Indeed, we access the past not only through mediated representations, but most of those representations are themselves based on other representations. Notice how many of the references in *Inglourious Basterds* are to films that are themselves derived from other films. The Spaghetti Westerns that Tarantino draws upon throughout *Inglourious Basterds* draw in turn upon classical American Westerns that are themselves fantasies recorded long after the historical moment that they represent. They are conscious recyclings of motifs from films that were themselves historical representations.

This conscious re-presentation of a representation is announced in the film's curious title, a misspelled version of the English-language title of a 1978 Italian WWII film, *The Inglorious Basterds*.[38] The poster for that film made its debts to an earlier American WWII film quite clear: "Whatever the Dirty Dozen did they do it dirtier."[39] Tarantino's film thus announces itself to be a derivative of a derivative in its very title—misspelled, at that, to drive home the point that accuracy is not going to be an issue here. Other such second- and third-order representations abound throughout the film. The final chapter, for example, starts with what is to all intents and purposes a music video set to the title song from Paul Schrader's 1982 remake of a WWII-era film, *Cat People*.[40] *Inglourious Basterds* doesn't just question whether a representation can ever be identical to the presentation itself, but whether it can ever be anything other than a re-presentation drawn from other representations.

Cinema is indeed everywhere in this film. But it hardly celebrates cinema, as commentators have repeatedly claimed. Rather, it problematizes it, insisting that we understand how it registers emotional effects, and how it is responsible for molding our understanding of history. In the climactic scene, the cinema is—literally—a death-trap and film itself (as Samuel L. Jackson informs us in a voiceover) is deadly. This scene takes place during the screening of a Nazi propaganda film, *Stolz der Nation* (Nation's Pride), which shows its hero, Fredrick Zoller, slaughtering American soldiers and carving swastikas into buildings to the delight of Hitler, who laughs uproariously at the violence and tells Goebbels that this is his "finest film yet."

Commentators on the film invariably report the uproarious laughter by those in the theater audience during the most violent scenes in *Inglourious Basterds*.[41] These shots of Hitler laughing at a hyper-violent WWII propaganda film are hardly subtle in their relationship to the theater audience watching Tarantino's hyper-violent WWII film. "[O]nly a thoughtless viewer will not see him or herself reflected in shots of Hitler cackling as he watches Americans being slaughtered," as Ben Walters has pointed out.[42] And only a thoughtless director would fail to see the connection between the film's final line—in which Lt. Aldo Raine announces: "I think this just might be my masterpiece" (referring to the swastika he has just carved into Colonel Hans Landa's forehead)—and Zoller's earlier statement that Goebbels "thinks this film [*Stolz der Nation*] will prove to be his masterpiece."[43]

Films (whether masterpieces or B-movies, whether overtly propagandistic or not, whether documentary or fictional) are tools—weapons, might be the more apt metaphor here—that can be deployed to register emotional effects and to represent historical events. Tarantino knows this. And he makes sure that his viewer knows this as well. In many movies there are moments that draw the viewer's attention to the artifice of the film and prompt reflection on a meta level about what the film is doing to represent its subject matter. In this film, every one of its 156 minutes is such a moment. We never leave the film archive to which the door has been pulled shut (to return to Denby's image), but we never forget that we are trapped in that archive and are unable to access any "history" or "reality" or "memory" that does not come to us mediated through the representations housed in that archive. That's where film gets both its power and its danger.

Once upon a time in twenty-first century Germany

If the reception of *Inglourious Basterds* in the United States was largely predictable on the basis of criticisms of previous Holocaust-themed films that had departed from historical re-enactments and the divisive effect of Tarantino's previous films, the German reception was much more unpredictable and ultimately surprising. In the wake of negative reviews and negative audience reactions to less audacious recent films about the Third Reich—such as Dani Levy's counterfactual farce *My Führer* and Bryan Singer's Hollywood heroic epic *Valkyrie*[44]—Tarantino's counterhistorical bloodbath seemed destined to anger German critics and turn away German audiences. "All the German historians and critics who were left gasping for air by Tom Cruise and his efforts to portray an accurate image of Stauffenberg," predicted the journalist Tobias Kniebe long before the film's premiere, "will be so shocked by 'Inglorious Bastards' [sic] that they will tear it apart it on the spot."[45]

When *Inglourious Basterds* was released in Germany on August 20, 2009, it opened on 439 screens and topped the box office for the weekend. It added screens in the coming weeks and grossed over $23 million for the year, making it the 12th highest-grossing film in Germany in 2009 and Tarantino's most successful German release by far.[46] German audiences were enthusiastic at screenings, cheering and laughing just as much as their American counterparts, much to the delight of the film's biggest star: "I'll tell you what was great," exclaimed Brad Pitt, who portrays Lt. Aldo Raine in the film, "was seeing this film with a German audience ... I think they enjoyed it more than any audience."[47]

This enthusiastic reception was surprising, not only in light of the negative treatment accorded to other recent films—German and Hollywood—that dared to take on the subject of Nazi Germany, but also in light of *Inglourious Basterds'* unnuanced depiction of Germans during the Third Reich. The film begins with the title card: "Once upon a Time in Nazi-Occupied France," a phrase that Tarantino has claimed is the film's unofficial subtitle.[48] Not "Occupied France" or "German-Occupied France," as Michael Wood points out, but "Nazi-Occupied France:" "the party is the country, the only Germans are Nazis."[49] As the Basterds go about collecting their famously allotted "100 scalps," they don't bother checking for party memberships or SS badges on the German soldiers they kill, nor on those that they let go with a swastika carved into their forehead. I don't think that either Tarantino or the Basterds are entering into the debate over how to characterize the role of the *Wehrmacht* in the Third Reich or parsing the difference between perpetrators and bystanders; they are simply not interested in making fine distinctions.

Interestingly, none of the German-language reviews I have come across was interested in the film's lack of interest in differentiating Germans and Nazis. Nor did I find the kind of handwringing about historical accuracy that was present in the negative American reviews of the film. The film's most audacious departures from reality and tradition were, in fact, celebrated, not condemned. Reviewing the film for the Austrian daily, *Die Presse*, Christoph Huber evoked the accusations made by Mendelsohn and other American critics, then promptly dismissed them: "*Inglourious Basterds* is less of a historical film than an alternative-reality science-fiction film; and in its cheerful insolence it is more rewarding than the countless recent 'respectable' films about the Holocaust, even in those places where it comes up short."[50] Tobias Kniebe, who had earlier predicted that German critics would tear the film apart, argues in a review that appeared in the Munich-based *Süddeutsche Zeitung* that Tarantino doesn't just cheerfully avoid the customs to which Holocaust films typically adhere, but rather drives a "battering ram against the gates of the Olympus of Cinema" and "throws gasoline into the fire of the Nazi film."[51] Kniebe continues:

Much more than the horrors, Tarantino fears the conventions that have long surrounded the Nazis and the Holocaust: the leaden, sepia-toned suggestion of authenticity that a feature film can never really live up to ... and the dead-end into which cinema has maneuvered itself.[52]

"A crazy idea," concludes Kniebe, "So crazy that it just might work."[53] The consensus among German and Austrian critics was that Tarantino's "crazy idea" did, in fact, work. In his review for Berlin's *Tagesspiegel*, Jan Schulz-Ojala pronounced the film "a politically-historically unbelievably liberating story."[54] In a later review, Schulz-Ojala elaborated on what he thinks makes *Inglourious Basterds* so liberating:

> This is not camp, this is not pulp—such categories miss the point with Tarantino. Rather, this is a vision that has never before been seen in the world of cinematic images. It took 65 years for a filmmaker to eschew bringing Germany's evil 20th-century history back to life in order for us to bow before it while shuddering, and instead simply to dream around it.[55]

The term *befreiend* (liberating) comes up frequently in German reviews of the film. When you exit the theater, Claudius Seidl wrote in a long and enthusiastic review in the *Frankfurter Allgemeine Zeitung*, "you notice a certain liberating feeling in your head, a clarity and a profound exhilaration that can't be dampened by the realization that you might have fallen for Tarantino's scheme."[56]

One might at first glance view this liberation as a release from the oppressive burden of having to live with the reality of Germany's history. This is what American critics such as Jonathan Rosenbaum accused Tarantino of when they compared *Inglourious Basterds* to Holocaust denial.[57] This interpretation would see Tarantino as swooping into Germany and settling the quarter-century old *Historikerstreit* (historian's debate) by making that troubling German "past that will not go away" finally go away after all.[58] But upon closer inspection, the German critics weren't praising Tarantino for liberating them from the oppressive past, but rather for liberating cinematic representations of the Holocaust from the oppressive mores that have constrained them for decades. Seidl referred to the film as "a singular attack on laws of aesthetic purity," that has the courage to stage its plot not as tragedy, but farce—"That's what happens with artistic freedom: wonderful."[59]

Georg Seeßlen takes the argument a step further. *Inglourious Basterds* not only liberates cinema from the political, historical, and aesthetic restraints under which Holocaust films have been placed. He traces these restraints back to National Socialism itself: "That this is one of the few films that doesn't more or less just continue to tell the story of German Fascism, that doesn't fall back on Nazi death kitsch ... is due not least of all to its narrative strategy."[60] Tarantino's great achievement in *Inglourious Basterds*, Seeßlen argues, is to resist constructing a coherent narrative that purports to tell a linear, accurate, and complete story:

> Someone tells something. On the one hand, in order to put the past behind him. On the other hand because he has interests. Sadism, narcissism and curiosity are always present. But in the end every story gives the impression of being complete and sincere. As soon as it appears, a story becomes a form of power. Tarantino belongs to those who oppose this narrative structure.[61]

Seeßlen evokes Saul Friedlander and the continuing debate over representing the Holocaust that I discussed earlier: "Can one represent the Holocaust as a soap opera? ... Can one laugh at Hitler? ... Can one send a couple of crude barbarians to finally let Hitler die once and for all?"[62] Any film that tells such a story will, as we have seen, "drag behind it a comet tail of journalistic, academic, and pedagogical discourse" marked by a profound sense of discomfort. With *Inglourious Basterds* Tarantino "puts an end to this discomfort" and resists a deadly serious and totalizing narrative that brings the Nazis back to life yet again as fascinating demons that oppress their weak and hopeless victims—"next to 'final victory,'" argues Seeßlen, "that would be the Nazis' second favorite fantasy."[63] By refusing to follow the well-established and strictly enforced rules of the Holocaust film, Tarantino not only liberates Holocaust cinema from the laws of aesthetic purity, he liberates it from the grip of the Nazis themselves.

It is noteworthy that the German and Austrian critical reception of *Inglourious Basterds*—like the American reception—viewed the film within the context of Holocaust cinema. Tarantino may not have set out to make a Holocaust film, but that is how it has entered into public discourse. Instead of criticizing its excesses like some of the most outspoken American critics of the film, German critics praised these same excesses. They too pinpointed the central theme of *Inglourious Basterds* as cinema itself, not history. They too recognized that the film primarily addressed other films. But rather than criticize a retreat from history into "movieland," they extolled the liberating effect of freeing Holocaust cinema from the strict rules under which the genre has long operated. In retrospect, the problem with films such as *Schindler's List* or *Valkyrie* was not that they took too many liberties with the truth, but that they took too few.

To be continued ... the Basterds and their fans

Considering that *Inglourious Basterds* inspired passionate responses from even the most sober film critics, it should come as no surprise that it has attracted its share of extremely devoted fans. The most engaged fans of the film are not content with only the already leisurely 2½-hour-long narrative and are not about to wait for the prequel that Tarantino is rumored to be working on.[64] They have taken matters into their own hands and re-imagined and extended the world of *Inglourious Basterds* by creating numerous mash-ups that are published by and for fans in several online communities devoted to the film. These stories and images adhere to a genre known broadly as fanfiction, which takes pre-existing characters (sometimes fictional, sometimes historical) and places them into new narratives. Fanfiction (often abbreviated as "fanfic" or simply "fic") is an example of what Henry Jenkins has referred to as "convergence culture," in which the production and the consumption of content becomes increasingly blurred.[65] Tarantino's films—especially *Inglourious Basterds*—are not only tailor-made for this convergence culture, they are themselves examples of it.

It is, therefore, not surprising that *Inglourious Basterds* has attracted numerous communities devoted to producing fanfiction based on its characters. Communities such as "Operation Kino" (currently with 999 members and 733 journal entries), "100 Scalps" (740 members and 591 journal entries), "Basterds" (531 members and 247 journal entries) and "Un Amico" (132 members and 127 journal entries) are four of the more active interest groups devoted to sharing fanfiction based on *Inglourious Basterds*.[66] What is perhaps most remarkable about the *Basterds*' fanfictions is how much they resemble fanfictions based on other popular franchises, from *Harry Potter* to *Kill Bill*.[67] The stories are almost always interested in what is called "shipping"—pairing characters in romantic and sexual relationships not depicted in the film. As with other fanfictions, erotic fiction is the standard genre and pansexuality is prevalent. A quick look at a couple of representative stories will illustrate the general tendencies.

One long serial fic takes its title from the first line of the David Bowie song that opens Chapter Five of *Inglourious Basterds*: "These Eyes So Green." The author spent almost fourteen months developing this twenty chapter narrative, which centers around the character of Hans Landa, who is put through a dizzying series of sexual adventures with other characters from the film and newly invented characters, most prominently Desiree Mendelsohn, a French Resistance fighter, who (spoiler alert!) escapes to the United States at the end of the story, pregnant with her and Landa's child.[68] What is noteworthy about this series is that the twenty chapters that make up the story and which were posted every couple of weeks over the course of more than a year are interspersed with posts detailing what can only be described as the author's obsession with the Austrian actor Christoph Waltz, who portrays Landa in the film, as well as confessions that the Jewish-American author is obsessed with the Holocaust, Nazi uniforms, and Austrian and German men.[69] I will forego any attempts at psychoanalysis; what is noteworthy here is the intermingling of reality (tracking the activities of Christoph Waltz), psychology (the author's) and fantasy (inspired by Tarantino's characters) in a manner as free flowing as the sexuality in the story itself. The result is an elaborate mash-up of fantasy and reality that further blurs the lines already blurred in the film.

Another serial focuses on a romantic relationship between Shosanna Dreyfus and Fredrick Zoller.[70] Titled "King for a Day," this story imagines an alternative ending to Tarantino's already alternative history. The author includes characters from the film, unfilmed information gleaned from Tarantino's script, and additional characters and details provided by the author and the community of readers that meet on the "LiveJournal" community to imagine the relationship that might have developed between these two fictional characters had they not ended up killing each other as they did in the film. It begins with the scene in the film where Shosanna is in the projection room preparing her revenge, and imagines it playing out differently than it does in the film. Shosanna realizes that she is in love with Fredrick and, instead of their shooting each other to death, Shosanna and Fredrick escape together while the theater burns and begin a romantic relationship. As is customary in the fanfiction genre, this story is broken up into chapters that are posted over an extended period of time. In between these chapters, the author posts pictures and thoughts on the characters, the story, and the actors who portray the characters. This author also intersperses other posts detailing his ongoing interest in bringing these two fictional characters into a romantic relationship that is not accorded them in the film—such as the numerous photoshopped images made to look like the two actors/characters posed for a formal portrait together and an album of compiled songs dedicated to the characters.[71] Like the author of "These Eyes So Green," the author of "King for a Day" frequently conflates the characters (Dreyfus and Zoller) with the actors who portray them (Mélanie Laurent and Daniel Brühl).[72] But this author is less interested in self-psychoanalysis and more interested in film analysis to provide evidence for his notion of a romantic bond between Dreyfus and Zoller. In one post, for example, he painstakingly examines an extended version of the lunch scene where the two characters meet for the first time to illustrate the potential for a romantic bond between the two.[73]

But perhaps the most striking aspect of these fanfictions is what is absent: any interest in mashing-up fictional characters with historical figures or even historical events. Hitler appears in these tales exceedingly infrequently—and when he does, it is in a farcical way, such as the imagined three-way with Donny Donowitz and Santa Claus in "The Best Christmas Day Ever."[74] The characters and events that inspire these stories could just as easily have come from the Harry Potter books or the Star Wars films. The Holocaust and even WWII play little or no role here except as a backdrop to the romances. Taken with the critical reaction to the film that I outlined previously, I think these fanfictions point to an ongoing normalization of the Holocaust. These are not a return to the debates of the 1980s about comparative genocides. Rather, this points to a normalization of Holocaust aesthetics—breaking out of the perceived limits of representation. To return to the question posed at the opening of this chapter: Can the Holocaust be the stuff of fiction? Clearly it can. It is always dangerous to point to the present as a historical turning point, but it seems reasonable to suggest that *Inglourious Basterds*, as an audacious work of art and a contentious cultural phenomenon, might someday be viewed as the point at which the "limits of representation" of the Holocaust were breached. As Landa asks Raine in the film's final chapter: "What shall the history books read?"

Notes

1 Mike Godwin, "Meme, Counter-meme," *Wired,* (October 1994). http://www.wired.com/wired/archive/2.10/godwin.if_pr.html

2 See, for example: Johannes Bulhof, "What If? Modality and History," *History and Theory* 38:2, (May 1999), 146; Martin Bunzl, "Counterfactual History: A User's Guide," *The American Historical Review* 109:3, (June 2004), 847; E. H. Carr, *What is History?* (New York: Vintage, 1967), 45; Randall Collins, "Turning Points, Bottlenecks, and the Fallacies of Counterfactual History," *Sociological Forum* 22:3, (September 2007), 247; and Simon T. Kaye, "Challenging Certainty: The Utility and History of Counterfactualism," *History and Theory* 49:1, (February, 2010), 41. Gavriel D. Rosenfeld has devoted an entire book to a discussion of WWII counterfactualism: *The World Hitler Never Made: Alternate History and the Memory of Nazism.* (Cambridge: Cambridge University Press, 2005).

3 Daniel Bell, *The Coming of Post-Industrial Society: A Venture in Social Forecasting.* (New York: Basic Books, 1973), 478.

4 Seth Grahame-Smith, *Abraham Lincoln, Vampire Hunter.* (New York: Grand Central Publishing, 2010). The book debuted at #4 on the "NY Times Bestseller List" and received mixed critical reviews, but not the outrage that Quentin Tarantino's less-supernatural, but similar (cinematic) mash-up of fiction and history, *Inglourious Basterds* first garnered. It may be, however, that the film version of Grahame-Smith's book scheduled for release in summer 2012 will attract more controversy. See: Michael Cieply, "Aside from

Vampires, Lincoln Film Seeks Accuracy," *New York Times*, May 9, 2011, http://www.nytimes.com/2011/05/10/movies/abraham-lincoln-vampire-hunter-rewrites-history.html?_r=1

5   See, for example, the discussion in Saul Friedlander's seminal collection of articles on the subject, *Probing the Limits of Representation*, (Cambridge, MA: Harvard University Press, 1992). The literature on the topic is vast and, since the present study focuses on popular reception rather than academic historiography, will not be discussed in any detail in this chapter. See, for example: Robert Eaglestone, *The Holocaust and the Postmodern*, (Oxford: Oxford University Press, 2004); Deborah E. Lipstadt, *Denying the Holocaust: The Growing Assault on Truth and Memory*, (New York: Plume, 1994); and James E. Young, "Toward a Received History of the Holocaust," *History and Theory* 36:4, (December 1997), 21–43.

6   Maurizio Viano details the controversy and defends the film in "*Life is Beautiful*: Reception, Allegory, and Holocaust Laughter," *Jewish Social Studies* 5.3, (1999), 47–66. The debate, incidentally, goes back at least to Mel Brooks' 1968 comedy, *The Producers*. That film, is however, even more tangential to the Holocaust than Tarantino's.

7   Susan Sontag, "Fascinating Fascism," *The New York Review of Books*, February 6, 1975. http://www.nybooks.com/articles/archives/1975/feb/06/fascinating-fascism/?pagination=false. *Ilsa, She Wolf of the SS* (dir. Don Edmonds, USA, 1974). On Nazisploitation films in general see Daniel H. Magilow, Elizabeth Bridges, and Kristin T. Vander Lugt, eds. *Nazisploitation! The Nazi Image in Low-Brow Cinema and Culture*. (London and New York: Continuum, 2011).

8   See http://www.rottentomatoes.com/m/inglourious_basterds/

9   "*Inglourious Basterds*," *Box Office Mojo*, http://boxofficemojo.com/movies/?id=inglouriousbasterds.htm

10 Daniel Mendelsohn, "*Inglourious Basterds*: When Jews Attack," *Newsweek*, August 14, 2009, http://www.thedailybeast.com/newsweek/2009/08/13/inglourious-basterds-when-jews-attack.html

11 Mendelsohn, "*Inglourious Basterds*: When Jews Attack."

12 Manohla Dargis, "Tarantino Avengers in Nazi Movieland," *New York Times*, August 21, 2009, http://movies.nytimes.com/2009/08/21/movies/21inglourious.html?partner= Rotten%20 Tomatoes&ei=5083

13 Dargis.

14 Jonathan Rosenbaum, "Recommended Reading: Daniel Mendelsohn on the New Tarantino," JonathanRosenbaum.com

15 Michael Wood, "At the Movies," *London Review of Books* 31:17 (September 10, 2009). http://www.lrb.co.uk/v31/n17/michael-wood/at-the-movies

16 J. Hoberman, "Quentin Tarantino's *Inglourious Basterds* Makes Holocaust Revisionism Fun," *The Village Voice*, August 18, 2009, http://www.villagevoice.com/2009-08-18/film/quentin-tarantino-s-inglourious-basterds-makes-holocaust-revisionism-fun/

17 Kim Newman, "*Inglourious Basterds*," *Sight & Sound* 19:9, (September 2009), 73.

18 David Denby, "Americans in Paris," *The New Yorker*, August 24, 2009, http://www.newyorker.com/arts/critics/cinema/2009/08/24/090824crci_cinema_denby?currentPage=all

19 Mendelsohn, "*Inglourious Basterds*: When Jews Attack."

20 Scott Foundas, "Kino über alles," *Film Comment* 45:4 (July–August, 2009), 32.

21 Peter Travers, "*Inglourious Basterds*," *Rolling Stone*, August 20, 2009, http://www.rollingstone.com/movies/reviews/inglourious-basterds-20090820

22 Daniel Mendelsohn, "It's Only a Movie," in *How Beautiful it is and How Easily it Can be Broken*. (New York, Harper Collins Publishers), 2008, 152.

23 Mendelsohn, "It's Only a Movie," 160.

24 Mendelsohn, "It's Only a Movie," 160.

25 Denby.

26 Mendelsohn, "*Inglourious Basterds*: When Jews Attack."

27 Mendelsohn, "*Inglourious Basterds*: When Jews Attack."

28 Denby.

29 Mendelsohn, "*Inglourious Basterds*: When Jews Attack."

30 Hoberman.

31 Dargis.

32 Mick LaSalle, "Review: *Inglourious Basterds*," *San Francisco Chronicle*, August 21, 2009, http://articles.sfgate.com/2009-08-21/movies/17177293_1_inglourious-basterds-nazi-movie-star

33 Foundas.

34 Denby.

35   Quoted in Foundas.

36   See *Navajo Joe* (dir. Sergio Corbucci, Italy, 1966); *Once Upon a Time in the West* (dir. Sergio Leone, Italy, 1968); *The Good, the Bad, and the Ugly* (dir. Sergio Leone, Italy, 1968) and *The Searchers* (dir. John Ford, USA, 1956). "The Filmspotting Forum" contains an in-progress list of film references on *Inglourious Basterds*. (http://www.filmspotting.net/forum/index.php?topic=6410.0)

37   Anton Kaes, "Holocaust and the End of History: Postmodern Historiography in Cinema," *Probing the Limits of Representation*, 210.

38   *Quel maledetto treno blindato* (*The Inglorious Bastards*, dir. Enzo G. Castellari, Italy, 1978).

39   The film being referenced here is *The Dirty Dozen* (dir. Robert Aldrich, USA, 1967). The poster for *The Inglorious Bastards* can be viewed at: http://3.bp.blogspot.com/-8orkL6IVXwI/TWj2uhrNmUI/AAAAAAAAANE/L_z8XPQtMF4/s1600/Inglorious_bastards.jpg

40   *Cat People* (dir. Paul Schrader, USA, 1982); *Cat People* (dir. Jacques Tourneur, 1942). Tarantino might be "careless" about his history, but he is extremely careful about his cinematic references. He uses the original Bowie recording of "Cat People (Putting Out Fire)" from the film, not the remake recorded on the album *Let's Dance* and released in 1983. Although using the remake of a song from a movie that is a remake would have been a nice touch.

41   See, for example, Wood, "At the Movies."

42   Ben Walters, "Debating *Inglourious Basterds*," *Film Quarterly* 63:2, Winter 2009/2010, 22.

43   Walters, 21.

44   See, for example, David Crossland, "Germany Not Amused By Hitler Comedy," *Der Spiegel Online*, January 8, 2007, http://www.spiegel.de/international/0,1518,458387,00.html; Henryk M. Broder, "Dani Levy's Failed Hitler Comedy," *Der Spiegel Online*, January 9, 2007, http://www.spiegel.de/international/spiegel/0,1518,458499,00.html; and Hanns-Georg Rodek, "Schüchtern—So ist Tom Cruise in 'Walküre,'" *Die Welt Online*, December 16, 2008, http://www.welt.de/kultur/article2882336/Schuechtern-So-ist-Tom-Cruise-in-Walkuere.html

45   Qtd. in Gina Serpe, "Tarantinos neuester Film erzeugt bereits Kontroverse," *E-Online*, September 8, 2008, http://www.eonline.com/news/Tarantinos_neuester_Film_erzeugt_bereits_Kontroverse_/27650

46 See *Box Office Mojo*, accessed September 14, 2011. *Inglourious Basterds* finished one place ahead of the American production of Bernhard Schlink's Holocaust novel *The Reader* and well ahead of *Valkyrie*. In comparison, *Kill Bill: Vol. 2* (the second highest-grossing Tarantino film in Germany) made just $7.4 million at German box office (see *Box Office Mojo*, http://www.boxofficemojo.com/movies/? page=intl&country=DE&id=killbill2.htm). *Inglourious Basterds* was even more successful in Austria, due no doubt in part to Austrian actor Christoph Waltz's Oscar-winning performance as Colonel Hans Landa (see *Box Office Mojo*, http://www.boxofficemojo.com/intl/austria/yearly/?yr=2009&p=.htm).

47 See Larry Carroll, "*Inglourious Basterds* Exclusive: Quentin Tarantino Lets Germans Laugh," *MTV Movie News*, August 20, 2009, http://www.mtv.com/news/articles/1619154/quentin-tarantino-lets-germans-laugh-at-basterds.jhtml

48 See Assaf Uni, "The Holocaust, Tarantino-style: Jews scalping Nazis," *Haaretz*, October 7, 2008, http://www.haaretz.com/jewish-world/news/the-holocaust-tarantino-style-jews-scalping-nazis-1.255095

49 Wood.

50 Christoph Huber, "'Inglorious [sic] Basterds': Tarantino, Trash & Triumph, *Die Presse*, August 19, 2009, http://diepresse.com/home/kultur/film/filmkritik/502952/Inglorious-Basterds_Tarantino-Trash-Triumph

51 Tobias Kniebe, "Die guten, brutalen Jungs," *Süddeutsche Zeitung*, August 19, 2009, http://www.sueddeutsche.de/kultur/kino-inglourious-basterds-die-guten-brutalen-jungs-1.173385

52 Kniebe.

53 Kniebe.

54 Jan Schulz-Ojala, "Das schönste Attentat der Welt," *Der Tagesspiegel*, May 20, 2009, http://www.tagesspiegel.de/kultur/kino/das-schoenste-attentat-der-welt/1517694.html

55 Jan Schulz-Ojala, "*Inglourious Basterds*: Bring mir den Skalp von Adolf Hitler!" *Der Tagesspiegel*, August 16, 2009, http://www.tagesspiegel.de/kultur/kino/bring-mir-den-skalp-von-adolf-hitler/1580866.html

56 Claudius Seidl, "Lasst uns Nazis skalpieren!," *Frankfurter Allgemeine Zeitung*, August 19, 2009, http://www.faz.net/artikel/S31176/video-filmkritik-inglourious-basterds-lasst-uns-nazis-skalpieren-30074896.html

57 See Rosenbaum.

58 Ernst Nolte's article, published on June 6, 1986 in the *Frankfurter Allgemeine Zeitung*, which kicked off what became known as the *Historikerstreit*, was titled "Die Vergangenheit, die nicht vergehen will."

59 Seidl, "Lasst uns Nazis skalpieren!"

60 Georg Seeßlen, "Mr. Tarantinos Kriegserklärung (*Inglourious Basterds*)," *GETIDAN*, http://www.getidan.de/kolumne/georg_seesslen/3561/mr-tarantinos-kriegserklarung-„inglourious-basterds

61 Seeßlen.

62 Seeßlen.

63 Seeßlen.

64 See Russ Fischer, "An *Inglourious Basterds* Prequel is More Likely Than We Thought," */Film*, June 25, 2009, http://www.slashfilm.com/an-inglourious-basterds-prequel-is-more-likely-than-we-thought/

65 Henry Jenkins, *Convergence Culture: Where Old and New Media Collide*. (New York: NYU Press, 2006).

66 All are hosted by LiveJournal.com, one of the largest online diary sites featuring fanfictions. See: "Operation Kino" (http://operation-kino.livejournal.com/), "100 Scalps" (http://100-scalps.livejournal.com/), "Basterds" (http://basterds.livejournal.com/), and "Un Amico" (http://un-amico.livejournal.com/), the last of which focuses on just two of the film's characters, Shosanna Dreyfus and Fredrick Zoller.

67 For *Kill Bill* fanfiction see FanFiction.net (http://www.fanfiction.net/movie/Kill_Bill/). For *Harry Potter* fanfiction see, the communities on LiveJournal such as "hp-fanfiction" (http://hp-fanfiction.livejournal.com/). There's at least one big difference between *Inglourious Basterds* fanfiction communities and *Harry Potter* fanfiction communities—the size. One large site (HarryPotterFanfiction.com) has approximately 75,000 members (http://www.harrypotterfanfiction.com/).

68 Links to the chapters at: http://deborahkla.livejournal.com/54488.html

69 "On Studying the Holocaust," http://deborahkla.livejournal.com/4712.html

70 "King for a Day," http://suspiriorum.livejournal.com/112701.html#cutid1

71   See "Fanmix: So that Tonight I Might See," http://suspiriorum.
     livejournal.com/114142.html#cutid1
72   See, for example, "Even More Stuff," December 30, 2009, http://
     suspiriorum.livejournal.com/86143.html
73   See "Shosanna/Fredrick Picspam," December 22, 2009, http://
     suspiriorum.livejournal.com/85020.html
74   "The Best Christmas Day Ever," http://100-scalps.livejournal.
     com/138416.html

Works cited

Aimee & Jaguar. Directed by Max Färberböck. Germany, 1999.

Bell, Daniel. *The Coming of Post-Industrial Society: A Venture in Social Forecasting*. New York: Basic Books, 1973.

Broder, Henryk M. "Dani Levy's Failed Hitler Comedy." *Der Spiegel Online*, January 9, 2007. http://www.spiegel.de/international/spiegel/0,1518,458499,00.html (accessed September 14, 2011).

Bulhof, Johannes. "What If? Modality and History." *History and Theory*, 38:2, May 1999.

Bunzl, Martin. "Counterfactual History: A User's Guide." *The American Historical Review*, 109:3, June 2004.

Carr, E. H. *What is History?* New York: Vintage, 1967.

Carroll, Larry. "'*Inglourious Basterds*' Exclusive: Quentin Tarantino Lets Germans Laugh." *MTV Movie News*, August 20, 2009. http://www.mtv.com/news/articles/1619154/quentin-tarantino-lets-germans-laugh-at-basterds.jhtml (accessed September 14, 2011).

Cat People. Directed by Jacques Tourneur. USA, 1942.

Cat People. Directed by Paul Schrader. USA, 1982.

Cieply, Michael. "Aside from Vampires, Lincoln Film Seeks Accuracy." *New York Times*. May 9, 2011. http://www.nytimes.com/2011/05/10/movies/abraham-lincoln-vampire-hunter-rewrites-history.html?_r=1 (accessed September 5, 2011).

Collins, Randall. "Turning Points, Bottlenecks, and the Fallacies of Counterfactual History." *Sociological Forum*, 22, September 3, 2007.

Crossland, David. "Germany Not Amused By Hitler Comedy." *Der Spiegel Online*, January 8, 2007. http://www.spiegel.de/international/0,1518,458387,00.html (accessed September 14, 2011).

Dargis, Manohla. "Tarantino Avengers in Nazi Movieland." *New York Times*, August 21, 2009. http://movies.nytimes.com/2009/08/21/

movies/21inglourious.html?partner=Rotten%20Tomatoes&ei=5083 (accessed September 9, 2011).

Deborahkla. "These Eyes So Green." http://deborahkla.livejournal. com/54488.html (accessed September 16, 2011).

Denby, David. "Americans in Paris." *The New Yorker*, August 24, 2009. http://www.newyorker.com/arts/critics/cinema/2009/08/24/090824crci_ cinema_denby?currentPage=all (accessed September 9, 2011).

The Dirty Dozen. Directed by Robert Aldrich. USA, 1967.

Eaglestone, Robert. *The Holocaust and the Postmodern*. Oxford: Oxford University Press, 2004.

Fischer, Russ. "An *Inglourious Basterds* Prequel is More Likely Than We Thought." */Film* (June 25, 2009). http://www.slashfilm.com/ an-inglourious-basterds-prequel-is-more-likely-than-we-thought/ (accessed September 17, 2011).

Foundas, Scott. "Kino über alles." *Film Comment*, 45:4, July–August 2009.

Friedlander, Saul, ed. *Probing the Limits of Representation*. Cambridge, MA: Harvard University Press, 1992.

Godwin, Mike. "Meme, Counter-meme," *Wired*, October, 1994. http:// www.wired.com/wired/archive/2.10/godwin.if_pr.html (accessed September 5, 2011).

The Good, the Bad, and the Ugly. Directed by Sergio Leone. Italy, 1968.

Grahame-Smith, Seth. *Abraham Lincoln, Vampire Hunter*. New York: Grand Central Publishing, 2010.

Hitler – ein Film aus Deutschland/Hitler: A Film from Germany. Directed by Hans-Jürgen Syberberg. West Germany/France/UK, 1977.

Hoberman, J. "Quentin Tarantino's *Inglourious Basterds* Makes Holocaust Revisionism Fun." *The Village Voice* (August 18, 2009). http://www.villagevoice.com/2009-08-18/film/quentin-tarantino-s- inglourious-basterds-makes-holocaust-revisionism-fun/ (accessed September 9, 2011).

Huber, Christoph. "'Inglorious [sic] Basterds': Tarantino, Trash & Triumph." *Die Presse* (August 19, 2009). http://diepresse.com/home/ kultur/film/filmkritik/502952/Inglorious-Basterds_Tarantino-Trash- Triumph (accessed September 15, 2011).

Ilsa, She Wolf of the SS. Directed by Don Edmonds. USA, 1974.

Inglourious Basterds. Directed by Quentin Tarantino. USA/Germany, 2009.

Jenkins, Henry. *Convergence Culture: Where Old and New Media Collide*. New York: NYU Press, 2006.

Kaes, Anton. "Holocaust and the End of History: Postmodern Historiography in Cinema." In *Probing the Limits of Representation*, edited by Saul Friedlander. Cambridge, MA: Harvard University Press, 1992.

Kaye, Simon T. "Challenging Certainty: The Utility and History of Counterfactualism." *History and Theory*, 49:1, February 2010.

Kill Bill: Vol. 1. Directed by Quentin Tarantino. USA, 2003.

Kill Bill: Vol. 2. Directed by Quentin Tarantino. USA, 2004.

Kniebe, Tobias. "Die guten, brutalen Jungs." *Süddeutsche Zeitung*, August 19, 2009. http://www.sueddeutsche.de/kultur/kino-inglourious-basterds-die-guten-brutalen-jungs-1.173385(accessed September 15, 2011).

La vita è bella/*Life is Beautiful*. Directed by Roberto Benigni. Italy, 1997.

LaSalle, Mick. "Review: '*Inglourious Basterds*.'" *San Francisco Chronicle*, August 21, 2009. http://articles.sfgate.com/2009-08-21/movies/17177293_1_inglourious-basterds-nazi-movie-star (accessed September 9, 2011).

Lipstadt, Deborah E. *Denying the Holocaust: The Growing Assault on Truth and Memory*. New York: Plume, 1994.

Magilow, Daniel H., Elizabeth Bridges, and Kristin T. Vander Lugt, eds. *Nazisploitation! The Nazi Image in Low-Brow Cinema and Culture*. London and New York: Continuum, 2011.

Mein Führer – Die wirklich wahrste Wahrheit über Adolf Hitler/*My Führer*. Directed by Dani Levy. Germany, 2007.

Mendelsohn, Daniel. "*Inglourious Basterds*: When Jews Attack." *Newsweek*, August 14, 2009. http://www.thedailybeast.com/newsweek/2009/08/13/inglourious-basterds-when-jews-attack.html (accessed September 5, 2011).

—"It's Only a Movie" in *How Beautiful it is: and How Easily it Can be Broken*. New York: Harper Collins Publishers, 2008.

Navajo Joe. Directed by Sergio Corbucci. Italy, 1966.

Newman, Kim. "*Inglourious Basterds*." *Sight & Sound*, 19:9, September 2009.

Once Upon a Time in the West. Directed by Sergio Leone. Italy, 1968.

The Producers. Directed by Mel Brooks. USA, 1968.

Quel maledetto treno blindato (*The Inglorious Bastards*). Directed by Enzo G. Castellari. Italy, 1978.

Rodek, Hanns-Georg. "Schüchtern—So ist Tom Cruise in 'Walküre.'" *Die Welt Online*, December 16, 2008. http://www.welt.de/kultur/article2882336/Schuechtern-So-ist-Tom-Cruise-in-Walkuere.html (accessed September 14, 2011).

Rosenbaum, Jonathan. "Recommended Reading: Daniel Mendelsohn on the New Tarantino." http://www.jonathanrosenbaum.com (accessed September 9, 2011).

Rosenfeld, Gavriel D. *The World Hitler Never Made: Alternate History and the Memory of Nazism*. Cambridge: Cambridge University Press, 2005.

Schindler's List. Directed by Steven Spielberg. USA, 1993.

Schulz-Ojala, Jan. "'*Inglourious Basterds*: Bring mir den Skalp von Adolf Hitler!" *Der Tagesspiegel*, August 16, 2009. http://www.tagesspiegel. de/kultur/kino/bring-mir-den-skalp-von-adolf-hitler/1580866.html (accessed September 15, 2011).

—"Das schönste Attentat der Welt." *Der Tagesspiegel*, May 20, 2009. http://www.tagesspiegel.de/kultur/kino/das-schoenste-attentat-der-welt/1517694.html (accessed September 15, 2011).

The Searchers. Directed by John Ford. USA, 1956.

Seeßlen, Georg. "Mr. Tarantinos Kriegserklärung (*Inglourious Basterds*)." *GETIDAN*. http://www.getidan.de/kolumne/georg_seesslen/3561/mr-tarantinos-kriegserklarung-„inglourious-basterds" (accessed September 15, 2011).

Seidl, Claudius. "Lasst uns Nazis skalpieren!," *Frankfurter Allgemeine Zeitung*, August 19, 2009. http://www.faz.net/artikel/S31176/video-filmkritik-inglourious-basterds-lasst-uns-nazis-skalpieren-30074896. html (accessed September 15, 2011).

Serpe, Gina. "Tarantinos neuester Film erzeugt bereits Kontroverse." *E-Online*, September 8, 2008. http://www.eonline.com/news/ Tarantinos_neuester_Film_erzeugt_bereits_Kontroverse_/27650 (accessed September 14, 2011).

Sontag, Susan. "Fascinating Fascism." *The New York Review of Books*, February 6, 1975. http://www.nybooks.com/articles/archives/1975/ feb/06/fascinating-fascism/(accessed September 5, 2011).

Suspiriorum. "King for a Day." http://suspiriorum.livejournal. com/112701.html#cutid1 (accessed September 17, 2011).

Travers, Peter. "*Inglourious Basterds*." *Rolling Stone*, August 20, 2009. http://www.rollingstone.com/movies/reviews/inglourious-basterds-20090820 (accessed September 9, 2011).

Uni, Assaf. "The Holocaust, Tarantino-style: Jews scalping Nazis." *Haaretz*, October 7, 2008. http://www.haaretz.com/jewish-world/ news/the-holocaust-tarantino-style-jews-scalping-nazis-1.255095 (accessed September 14, 2011).

Valkyrie. Directed by Bryan Singer. USA/Germany, 2008.

Viano, Maurizio. "*Life is Beautiful*: Reception, Allegory, and Holocaust Laughter." *Jewish Social Studies* 5.3, 1999, 47–66.

Walters, Ben. "Debating *Inglourious Basterds*." *Film Quarterly* 63:2, Winter, 2009/2010.

Wood, Michael. "At the Movies." *London Review of Books* 31:17, September 10, 2009. http://www.lrb.co.uk/v31/n17/michael-wood/ at-the-movies (accessed September 9, 2011).

Young, James E. "Toward a Received History of the Holocaust," *History and Theory*, 36:4, December 1997.

NOTES ON
CONTRIBUTORS

William Brown is a Lecturer in Film at the University of Roehampton, London. He is the author of *Supercinema: Film Theory in the Digital Age* (Berghahn, forthcoming) and, with Dina Iordanova and Leshu Torchin, of *Moving People, Moving Images: Cinema and Trafficking in the New Europe* (St. Andrews Film Studies, 2010). He is the co-editor with David Martin-Jones of *Deleuze and Film* (Edinburgh University Press, 2012) and has published articles in, among others, *Deleuze Studies*, *animation: an interdisciplinary journal*, *New Review of Film and Television Studies*, *Studies in European Cinema*, *Studies in French Cinema*, *Third Text* and *Projections: The Journal for Movies and Mind*. Brown has also directed two films, *En Attendant Godard* (2009) and *Afterimages* (2010). His third feature *Common Ground* is due for completion in 2012.

Lisa Coulthard is Associate Professor of Film Studies at the University of British Columbia in Vancouver, Canada. Her research focuses on film sound and film violence and she has published widely on contemporary European and American cinemas. She is currently completing a book on sound and music in the films of Quentin Tarantino entitled *The Super Sounds of Quentin Tarantino*.

Robert von Dassanowsky is Professor of German and Film Studies at the University of Colorado, Colorado Springs. He is co-founder of the International Alexander Lernet-Holenia Society and contributing editor of *The Gale Encyclopedia of Multicultural America*, 2nd Ed. His most recent books are *Austrian Cinema:*

A History (McFarland, 2005), *New Austrian Film* (co-editor with Oliver C. Speck) (Berghahn, 2011), and *The Nameable and the Unnameable: Hugo von Hofmannsthal's 'Der Schwierige' Revisited* (co-editor with Martin Liebscher and Christophe Fricker) (Iudicium, 2011). His edited anthology on *World Film Locations: Vienna* will be published by Intellect in 2012. He is also active as an independent film producer.

Chris Fujiwara is a film critic and the Artistic Director of the Edinburgh International Film Festival. His books include *Jerry Lewis* (University of Illinois Press); *The World and Its Double: The Life and Work of Otto Preminger* (Faber & Faber); and *Jacques Tourneur: The Cinema of Nightfall* (Johns Hopkins University Press). He has written on film for numerous periodicals and anthologies and is the editor of *Undercurrent* (www.fipresci.org/undercurrent), an online film-criticism magazine.

Todd Herzog is Associate Professor of German Studies at the University of Cincinnati. He is co-editor of the *Journal of Austrian Studies* (formerly *Modern Austrian Literature*) and author of *Crime Stories: Criminalistic Fantasy and the Culture of Crisis in Weimar Germany* (Berghahn, 2009). He has co-edited *A New Germany in a New Europe* (Routledge, 2001) and *Rebirth of a Culture* (Berghahn, 2008). He is currently working on a filmography of German cinema to 1945 and a book on surveillance and art in the twenty-first century.

Eric Kligerman is an associate professor of German and Jewish studies at the University of Florida. In addition to his *Sites of the Uncanny: Paul Celan, Specularity and the Visual Arts* (2007), he has published on representations of the Red Army Faction in New German Cinema and the paintings of Gerhard Richter. His current research examines post-colonial ruins in Southeast Asia alongside Walter Benjamin's *Arcades Project*.

Imke Meyer is Helen Herrmann Professor and Chair of the Department of German at Bryn Mawr College. She has published widely on authors and filmmakers such as Ludwig Tieck, Arthur Schnitzler, Hugo von Hofmannsthal, Franz Kafka, Ingeborg Bachmann, Elfriede Jelinek, Barbara Albert, and Michael Haneke.

Her new book, *Männlichkeit und Melodram: Arthur Schnitzlers erzählende Schriften* (Masculinity and Melodrama: Arthur Schnitzler's Narrative Writings) appeared in 2010.

Alexander D. Ornella is Lecturer in Religion at the University of Hull, UK. He has received his doctorate in theology from the University of Graz, Austria. As member and project coordinator of the international and interdisciplinary research project "Commun(icat)ing Bodies" which is based at the University of Graz and funded by the Austrian Science Fund (FWF), he is studying the relationships between the body, religion, media, and communication technology. Together with Stefanie Knauss he is the co-editor of *Fascinatingly Disturbing: Interdisciplinary Perspectives on Michael Haneke's Cinema* (Pickwick, 2010).

Michael D. Richardson is Associate Professor of German Studies and Chair of the Department of Modern Languages and Literatures at Ithaca College. His research interests encompass twentieth and twenty-first century literature, theater, and film, from the Weimar Republic to contemporary Germany. His current research focuses on two areas: constructions of history in recent German cinema, and the image of Hitler in American and German popular culture. He is the author of *Revolutionary Theater and the Classical Heritage: Inheritance and Appropriation from Weimar to the GDR* (Peter Lang, 2007), a co-editor of *Visualizing the Holocaust: Aesthetics, Documents, History* (Camden House, 2008) and co-editor of the forthcoming volume, *A New History of German Cinema* (Camden House, 2012). He is also a contributing editor of *New German Critique*.

Heidi Schlipphacke is Associate Professor of German and European Studies at Old Dominion University. She has published widely on the European Enlightenment and on post-war German and Austrian literature and film in journals such as *Screen, Camera Obscura, The German Quarterly, Journal of English and German Philology*, and *Modern Austrian Literature*, among others. Her book, *Nostalgia After Nazism: History, Home and Affect in German and Austrian Literature and Film* (Bucknell UP), appeared in 2010.

Oliver C. Speck is Associate Professor of Film Studies at Virginia Commonwealth University's School of World Studies. His areas of expertise are French and German cinema. Dr. Speck's book, *Funny Frames: The Filmic Concepts of Michael Haneke* (Continuum, 2010), explores how a political thinking manifests itself in the oeuvre of the Austrian director. He is also co-editor (with Robert von Dassanowsky) of *New Austrian Film* (Berghahn, 2011).

Srikanth Srinivasan is a cinephile living in Bangalore, India and is an electronics engineer by education and profession. He has written for film magazines based in India such as *Indian Auteur*, *Dear Cinema*, *Culturazzi*, *The Hindu Cinema Plus* and *Projectorhead*. His blog "The Seventh Art" was selected as one of the 43 top film criticism sites by *Film Comment* in 2010.

Justin Vicari is an award-winning poet, critic and translator. He is the author of *The Professional Weepers* (Pavement Saw Press, 2011), *Male Bisexuality in Current Cinema: Images of Growth, Rebellion and Survival* (McFarland, 2011) and *Mad Muses and the Early Surrealists* (McFarland, 2011). He is a contributor to the anthology *New Austrian Film* (Berghahn, 2011) and has also translated François Emmanuel's *Invitation to a Voyage* (Dalkey Archive Press, 2011). His next book will be about the films of Gus Van Sant.

Sharon Willis is Professor of Art History and Visual and Cultural Studies and Director of the Film and Media Studies Program at the University of Rochester. A Co-editor of *Camera Obscura*, she is author of *Marguerite Duras: Writing on the Body*, and *High Contrast: Race and Gender in Contemporary Hollywood Film*, and editor, with Constance Penley, of *Male Trouble*. She is completing a book project on representations of the civil rights movement in popular cinema.

INDEX